A SPY AMONGST US

A SPY AMONGST US

Daniel Defoe's Secret Service and the Plot to End Scottish Independence

MARC MIEROWSKY

YALE UNIVERSITY PRESS
NEW HAVEN AND LONDON

For information about this and other Yale University Press publications, please contact:
U.S. Office: sales.press@yale.edu yalebooks.com
Europe Office: sales@yaleup.co.uk yalebooks.co.uk

Set in Minion Pro by IDSUK (DataConnection) Ltd

Printed and bound in the UK using 100% renewable electricity at CPI Group (UK) Ltd

Library of Congress Control Number: 2025947244
A catalogue record for this book is available from the British Library.
Authorized Representative in the EU: Easy Access System Europe, Mustamäe tee 50, 10621 Tallinn, Estonia, gpsr.requests@easproject.com

ISBN 978-0-300-26016-8

10 9 8 7 6 5 4 3 2 1

> I need not narrate here what was done in this Parliament, there being a very exact History published by one Daniel Defoe, who was sent to Scotland by the prime minister of England, the Earl of Godolphin, on purpose to give a faithful account to him from time to time how every-thing past here. He was therefor a Spy amongst us, but not known to be such, otherways the Mob of Edinburgh had pulled him to pieces.
>
> John Clerk of Penicuik, *Memoirs, 1676–1755*

In the margins, next to this mention of Defoe, Clerk added the following comment:

> This History of the Union deserves to be read . . . There is not one fact in it which I can challenge.

CONTENTS

ILLUSTRATIONS AND MAPS

ILLUSTRATIONS

MAPS

A NOTE ON THE TEXT

By the time Defoe began working as Harley's agent, most European nations had adopted the Gregorian calendar. This involved dropping ten days from the Julian calendar and marking the start of the year on 1 January as opposed to 25 March. England would not do the same until 1752. The result is that for all of Defoe's life, the English calendar was roughly ten days behind calendars in use on the Continent. Complicating matters further is that in 1600 Scotland opted to record the year beginning from 1 January, but without dropping the ten days to bring their calendar in line with the Gregorian model. To streamline things, I have opted to give dates in the Old Style but have assumed that the year begins on 1 January and not 25 March.

I have chosen to modify quotes from Defoe and his contemporaries selectively. I have altered punctuation for legibility and expanded the abbreviations. In most cases I have preserved the original spelling, except where it would alter the sense for modern readers. I have preserved most of the capitalisations and italics of eighteenth-century print and selectively preserved the cyphers and codes used by early modern spies.

To avoid confusion, I have opted to refer to people using the title they held for the majority of the period considered here. For example, Harley was created first Earl of Oxford in 1711; I refer to him as Harley throughout.

All calculations of present-day value were carried out with the currency converter supplied by the National Archives.

CAST OF CHARACTERS

Archibald Campbell, 1st Duke of **Argyll** (1658–1703): politician and nobleman, Queensberry's ally against the Act of Security, patron of Beaufort.

John Campbell, 2nd Duke of **Argyll** (1680–1743): army officer and politician, son of the 1st Duke, Lord High Commissioner 1705.

John Murray, 1st Earl of Tullibardine and 1st Duke of **Atholl** (1660–1724): army officer and politician, brother-in-law to the 4th Duke of Hamilton. Lord Privy Seal 1703–5, from 1704 opponent of Union. Chosen as Representative peer for Scotland in 1710.

Simon Fraser of **Beaufort** (1667/8–1747): instigator of the Scotch plot, Jacobite conspirator, fugitive. Restored as 11th Lord Lovat in 1716.

John Hamilton, 2nd Lord **Belhaven** (1656–1708): politician, director of the Company of Scotland, speechmaker, sometime poet, and opponent of Union.

William **Carstares** (1649–1715): Kirk minister and political advisor. Chaplain to William III when he was Prince of Orange, Royal Chaplain for Scotland during his reign. Principal of Edinburgh University 1703–15, Moderator of the General Assembly of the Church of Scotland 1705, 1708, 1711 and 1715.

Major James **Cunningham of Aiket**: army officer, councillor on the first Darien expedition, Queensberry's agent.

Daniel **Defoe** (1660?–1731): businessman, writer, polemicist, spy; Harley's agent 1704–8, 1710–14, Godolphin's agent 1708–10.

Mary **Defoe**, née Tuffley (1659–1732): married Daniel Defoe in 1683, ran his businesses during his many absences.

Anne Hay, Countess of **Erroll** (1656–1719): Jacobite agent, member of the Juncto, runner of spies and supplies in Scotland, and sister to Perth.

Charles Hay, 13th Earl of **Erroll** (1677–1717): nobleman, son of Anne Hay, Lord High Constable of Scotland 1704–17.

David **Fearne:** advocate, Harley's agent in Scotland from 1706.

Andrew **Fletcher of Saltoun** (1653?–1716): politician, political theorist, writer and fierce Scottish patriot.

Frances **Fox**: agent for the Earl of Melfort and Earl of Middleton.

Sidney, 1st Earl of **Godolphin** (1645–1712): politician and statesman, Lord Treasurer 1700–1, 1702–10. Member with Marlborough of the duumvirate. With Marlborough and Harley, member of the triumvirate.

William **Gregg** (bap. 1673, d. 1708): traitor, conspirator, Harley's agent in Scotland 1705, appointed junior clerk in Harley's office in 1706.

Charles Montagu, Baron **Halifax** (1661–1715): statesman and politician, member of the Whig Junto, created 1st Earl of Halifax in 1714.

Anne, suo jure Duchess of **Hamilton** (1632–1716): head of a magnate family, leading figure in the extra-parliamentary opposition to Union.

James, 4th Duke of **Hamilton** (1658–1712): politician and soldier, son of Anne Hamilton, sometime figurehead of the Scottish opposition to Union.

Robert **Harley** (1661–1724): politician and spymaster, Speaker of the House of Commons 1701–5, Secretary of State for the northern department (including Scotland) 1704–8, Chancellor of the Exchequer 1710–11, Lord Treasurer 1711–14. Created 1st Earl of Oxford and Earl Mortimer in 1711.

Sir Charles **Hedges** (bap. 1650–1714): lawyer and politician, Secretary of State for the northern department 1700–1, 1702–4, Secretary of State for the southern department 1704–6.

Nathaniel **Hooke** (1664–1738): Jacobite spy, advisor, agent in the French secret service, and politician.

John **Ker of Kersland** (1673–1726): spy and memoirist, reported to Queensberry and Godolphin.

David Melville, 3rd Earl of **Leven** (1660–1728): army officer and politician. Commander-in-chief of the army in Scotland 1706, Representative peer 1707–10.

George **Lockhart of Carnwath** (1681?–1731): Jacobite politician, memoirist, and historian.

John Erskine, 22nd or 6th Earl of **Mar** (bap. 1675, d. 1732): army officer and politician, Secretary of State in Scotland 1705–7, Secretary of State for Scotland 1707–9, Representative peer 1707–15, leader of the Jacobite rising of 1715.

John Churchill, 1st Duke of **Marlborough** (1650–1722): politician and army officer. Appointed Ambassador-Extraordinary and Commander of the English forces by William III, Captain-General and commander-in-chief of Queen Anne's armies, husband to Sarah Churchill (née Jenyns).

Sarah Churchill, Duchess of **Marlborough** (1660–1744): courtier and politician, friend and favourite to Queen Anne, created Mistress of the Robes, Groom of the Stool, Keeper of the Privy Purse and Ranger of Windsor Great Park in 1702, dismissed from these offices by the Queen in 1711.

Charles, 2nd Earl of **Middleton** (1649/50–1719): soldier, politician, Secretary of State to James II in exile 1693–1701, and courtier at St Germain.

Sir David **Nairne**: undersecretary to Mar.

Daniel Finch, 2nd Earl of **Nottingham** (1647–1730): politician. Secretary of State for the southern department 1689–93, 1702–4.

Captain John **Ogilvie**: soldier in the army of James II, Harley's agent from 1704, Jacobite double agent (loyal to Harley) from around 1705.

William **Paterson** (1658–1719): projector, director of the Company of Scotland trading to Africa and the Indies, agent of the English government from 1704.

James Drummond, 4th Earl of Perth and Jacobite 1st Duke of **Perth** (1648–1716): nobleman, courtier at St Germain, chief agent for James II in Scotland until 1688.

John **Pierce**: Defoe's agent in the southwest of Scotland in 1706.

James Douglas, 2nd Duke of **Queensberry** (1662–1711): politician, Lord High Commissioner of Scotland 1700–4, 1706–7, Secretary of State for Scotland 1709–11.

James Ogilvy, 4th Earl of Findlater and 1st Earl of **Seafield** (1663–1730): politician. Lord High Commissioner to the General Assembly of the Church of Scotland 1700–4, Lord Chancellor of Scotland 1702–4, 1705–8, Keeper of the Great Seal of Scotland 1713–14.

John **Shute** (1678–1734): Dissenting theologian, politician, Whig agent in Scotland during the Union debates.

John Somers, 1st Baron **Somers** (1651–1716): jurist and politician, Lord President of the Council 1708–10, member of the Whig Junto.

John Dalrymple, 1st Earl of **Stair** (1648–1707): jurist and politician, Secretary of State in Scotland 1691–5, key pro-Union negotiator.

James Francis Edward **Stuart** (1688–1766): son of James II and Mary of Modena, exiled Prince of Wales, the Pretender (later Old Pretender), and putative James III and VIII.

Charles Spencer, 3rd Earl of **Sunderland** (1675–1722): politician, member of the Whig Junto, Secretary of State for the southern department 1706–10.

Jean Baptiste Colbert, Marquis de **Torcy** (1665–1746): French diplomat and foreign minister.

John Hay, 2nd Marquess of **Tweeddale** (1645–1713): Lord High Commissioner of Scotland 1704, Lord Chancellor 1704–5, leader of the New Party and later Squadrone Volante.

Thomas Wharton, 5th Baron **Wharton** (1648–1715): politician, member of the Whig Junto, created Marquess of Wharton and of Malmesbury in 1715.

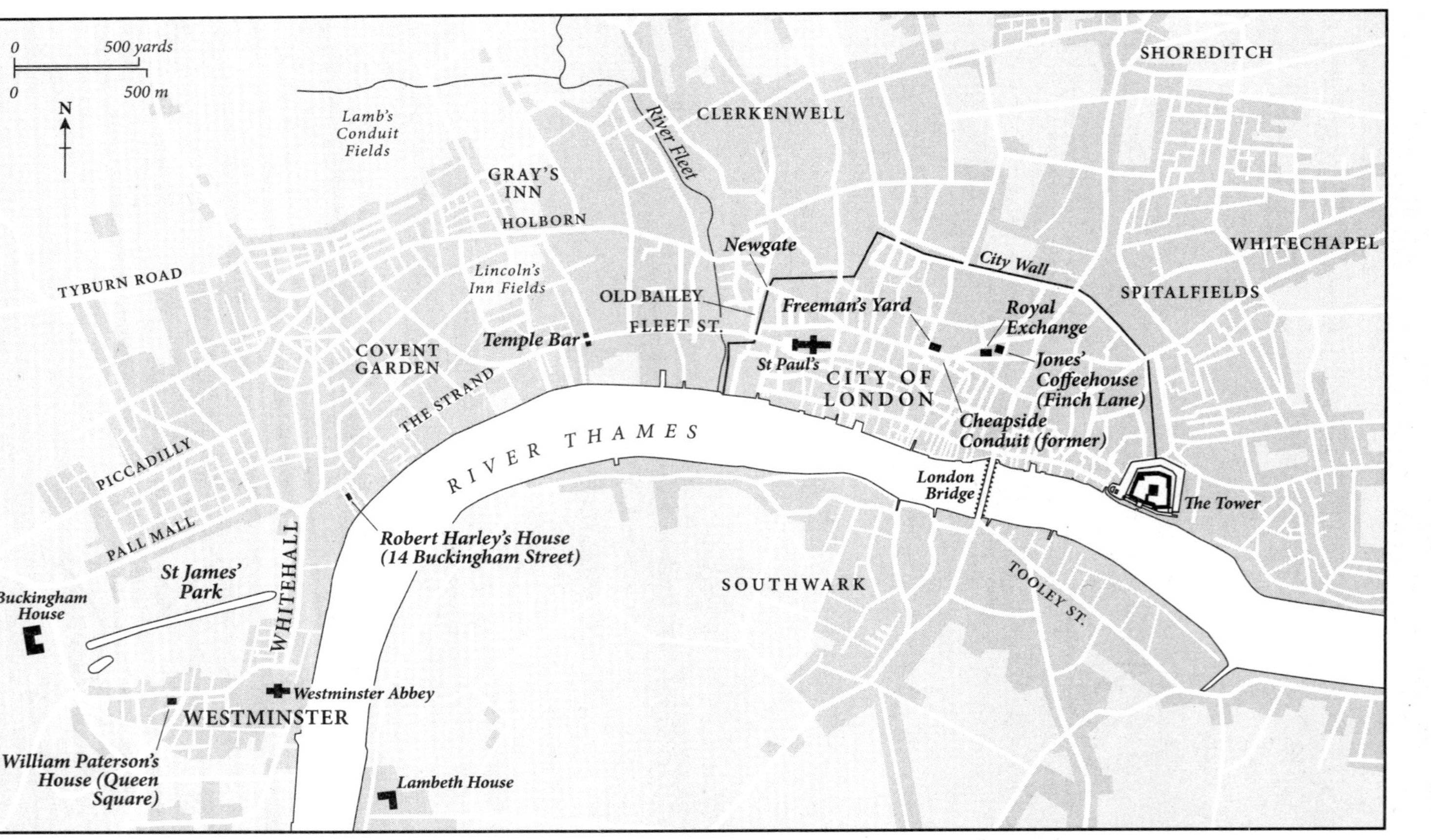

1. London, 1703–10.

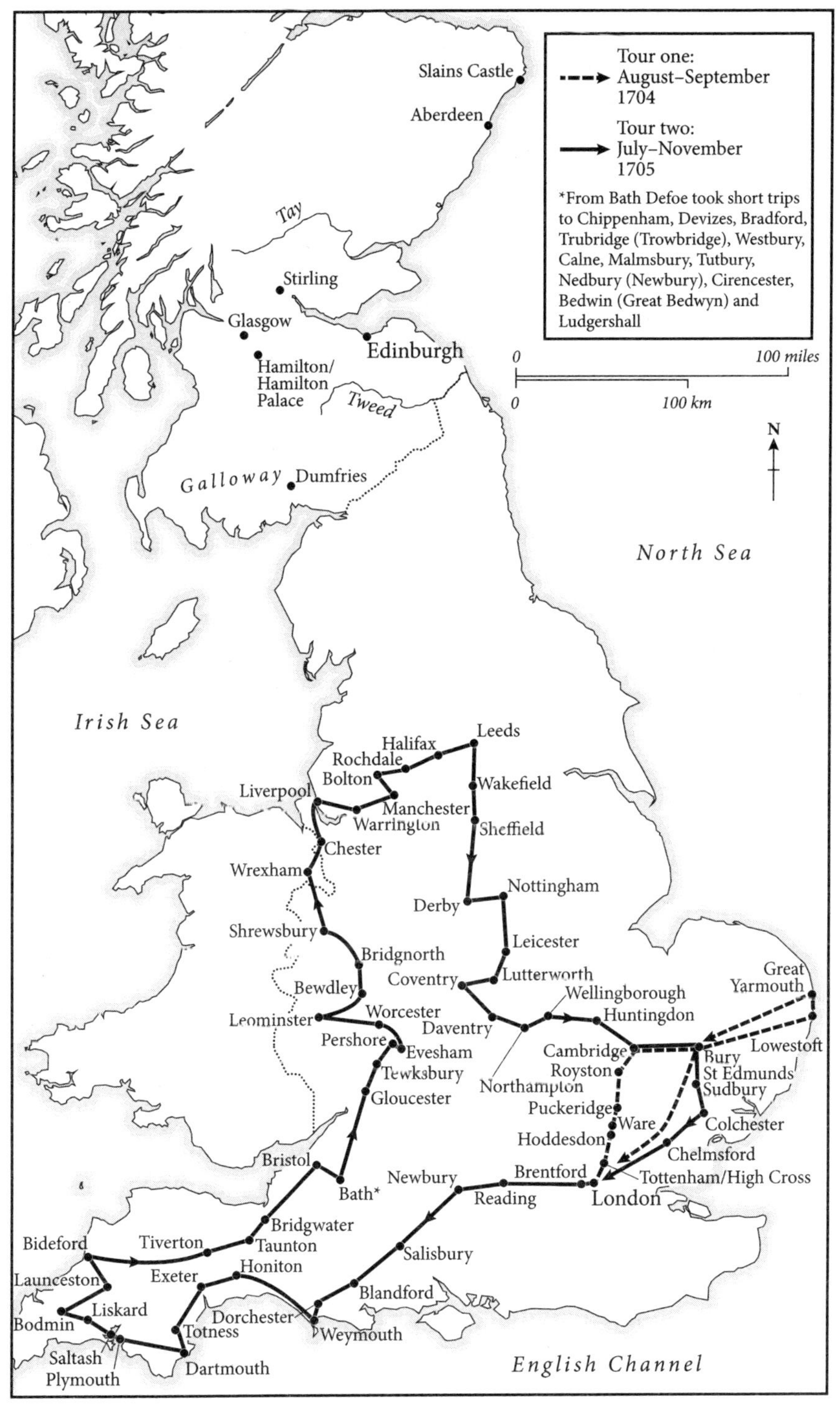

2. England and Scotland, 1704–11, showing Defoe's tours.

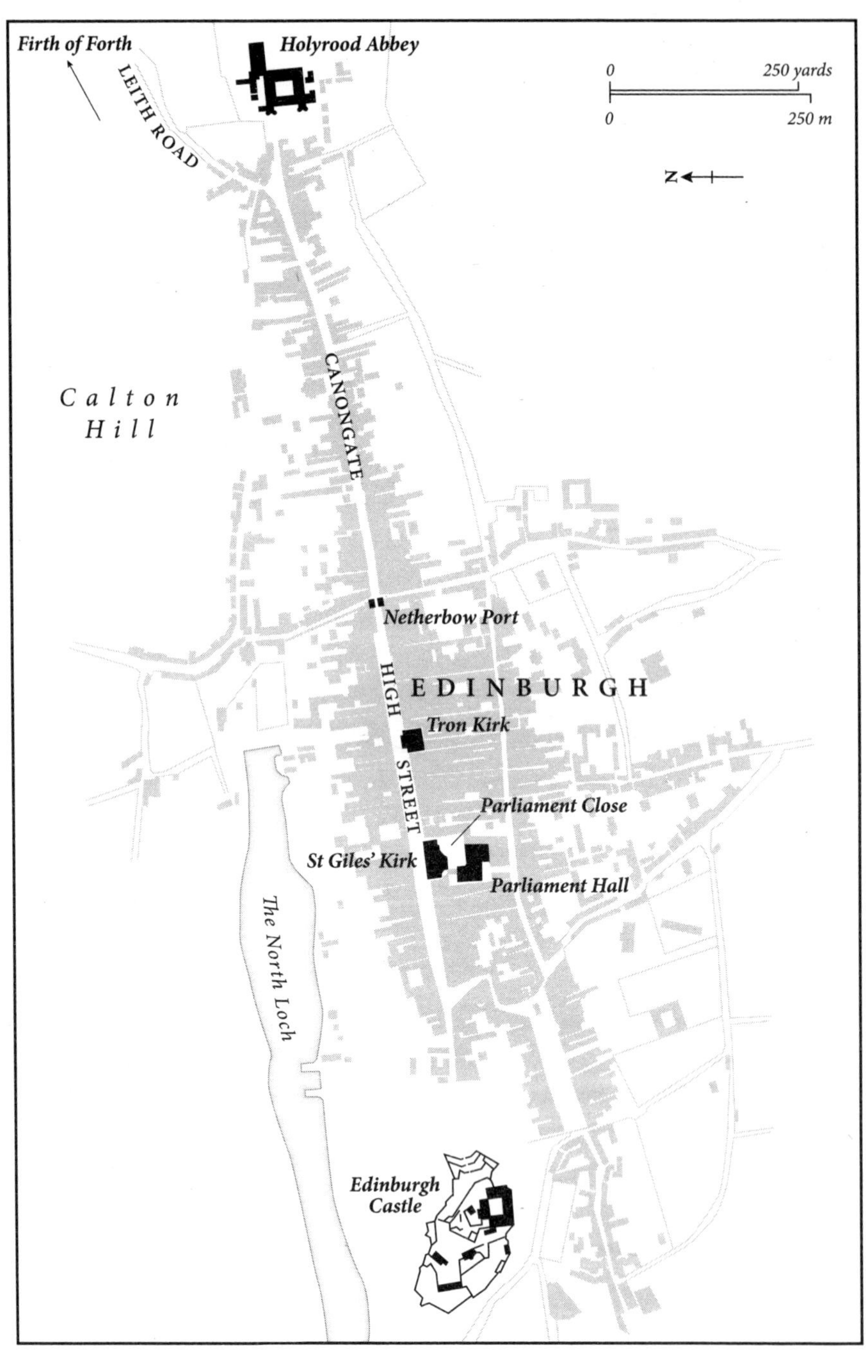

3. Edinburgh, 1705–10.

Part One

ENGLAND

INTRODUCTION

HAMPSTEAD PONDS

27 April 1703

Beneath the southernmost pond at Hampstead, below the point where its grassy edge tucks loosely under the moss-dark water, there is a network of pipes made from the bored-out trunks of elm trees. One set runs south through the Heath then east to the Parish of St Pancras, branching off at each point into a cluster of lead-quilled capillaries, which carry the pond's water to street level – to houses in Hampstead Village and across Kentish Town. The other takes a more direct route south, covering close to four miles before tacking east to surface in Marylebone, and dispersing south and east again to Mayfair and Soho.[1] The water drawn into the ponds and out through the elms comes from the same source as the River Fleet. Moving down through London, the two arterial pipes shadow the river's passage. The water that courses through them fast overtakes this natural guide, though it is hardly a fair competition. Choked with the dung, guts and blood of the Smithfield meat market, the Fleet sputters along – in parts above ground and below – before its path broadens midway between Gray's Inn and the Old Bailey. From that point, until it reaches the Thames at Blackfriars, the Fleet is an open ditch, cleaving the city in two. On the west bank are the aristocratic suburbs supplied by the Hampstead Water Company. On the east, Clerkenwell, a hub for gangs and pickpockets, and Grub Street, where hack writers and publishers congregate. To enter London's underworld, one had to cross the Fleet. Its decline from river to brook to foetid ditch was thought to chart the fall of those who ended up there.[2]

William Paterson did not have to walk far from his lodgings in Westminster to feel the low gastric rumble of the network.[3] On wet days the shaking puddles that gathered in the stoned corners of the streets marked its course. One such day was 27 April 1703. It had rained for most of the month and Paterson grew increasingly restless: his usual refuge, St James' Park, a short walk from his house on Queen Square, was too sodden to pace.[4]

Paterson liked to walk when he thought – a habit that had once imparted seriousness but at forty-five, and with a series of public failures weighing against him, was now beginning to attract derision. 'If a man had a fancy to be reputed wise,' went one quip, 'the first step he was to make, was to mimic *Paterson's* phiz': his apparently natural look of calculation – his eyes down, his mouth moving but emitting no sound.[5]

Turning away from the park and onto the street, Paterson would have fixed his mind on the same set of ideas that had kept him going these last three years, since he had returned from New York in what he did not yet know would be his final transatlantic crossing. Paterson was a man of many plans. He had a plan to increase England's credit; a plan to pay down the national debt; a plan to streamline England's bookkeeping; and a plan to seize the principal ports of the West Indies for the Crown. His attention to this last scheme was intensified by his regret for Darien – the abortive Scottish colony he had promoted in Panama – and by his desire to return to the Caribbean – the place where he had lost everything but where nonetheless a man like him, with no title or family backing, might talk his way back to prominence.

Brisk, silent, determined, he moved through Westminster in the direction of Mayfair, weaving through a crowd of people who walked faster than their forbears: members of the gentry who had taken to the commercial life of the city just as the West End was being gentrified to meet them. Paterson did not keep pace with the powdered men of the suburbs, but with the lines of his own thought. His daily walks gave him the chance to follow each idea to the point where it converged with his wider view of the world. In step, his plans to pay off the national debt became a way to fund a war with Bourbon

France, England's greatest geopolitical foe. His plans to seize the ports of the West Indies a way to draw French troops away from that war. His plans to enter a constitutional union with Scotland a way to prevent internal disunity, creating a Britain strong enough to dominate Europe and extend the hand of empire across the Americas. Even his plan to create a library filled only with books on economics took on a grander function as an educational centre for a new class of technocrats, who would oversee the empire and, importantly for his purposes, open its borders to free trade.

His stride was as dogged as it had ever been. Yet bouts of light headedness – the remnants of a delirium suffered on an expedition to Central America – meant that he had to stop more frequently. Looming over him as he gathered himself, its orange façade almost shining in the bright wet April afternoon, was Kensington Palace: once the city residence of William III and Queen Mary and now a beacon to their memory. Under its glare, Paterson could not help but be reminded of his former influence and the compromises he was now willing to make to get it back.

Two years earlier, he had taken this same set of ideas to King William. For the rest of his life Paterson would boast of the sway he had over the King at that meeting. Though no doubt with some exaggeration, the talkative Paterson told listeners how he found the King 'in much perplexity and concern about the state of his affairs'.[6] Casting himself as the world-weary advisor, Paterson put the case to the monarch that his 'misfortunes did not . . . proceed from the variable tempers and humours of his people', but because he had 'trusted his business' to men who lacked either 'capacity' or 'experience': counsellors who had made their way to the halls of power solely on their status and personal connections. It is unlikely that Paterson was so direct in his criticism. Yet the way he represents the advisors who encircled the King reveals much. Paterson could barely hide his contempt for the fact that William had never truly fulfilled the promise on which he had come to the throne, as a new kind of monarch authorised by parliament and imbued with the mercantile pragmatism that Paterson associated with the Dutch.

William of Orange was the King Paterson had wanted; the King whom he had spent hours plotting to install as England's monarch, conspiring with fellow exiles in the coffeehouses of Amsterdam a decade earlier. It was the reign of William and Mary that opened the marketplace to men of ideas, giving Paterson room to put forward the scheme for which he remained proudest: a plan to found a central national bank – the intellectual structure that in 1694 led to the establishment of the Bank of England.

Warm though it appeared, the palace had an unmistakably austere aspect. And whatever nostalgia it evoked tended to blend with recrimination. It was William III who had hindered Paterson's imperial ambitions, who had refused to come to the aid of the Scottish settlers when the colony of Caledonia at Darien, founded on Paterson's plan, collapsed around them, its supplies exhausted, its farms abandoned, its four hundred graves too few for the nine hundred men, women and children who died on shore.

As with so much in Paterson's life, his meeting with the King was almost comically ill timed. A few months after Paterson had tendered his final proposals, William fell from his horse and broke his collar bone. Laid up, he could not go to parliament; could not throw the weight of his majesty behind a scheme to send colonists to the West Indies or to press for negotiations with Scotland. Instead, the King sent a message conveying these intents. Paterson clung to this message. To him it showed how much of his advice William had taken 'to heart'.

Paterson was one of many voices the King heard. The tendency of advisors is to see their work in anything adopted by the principal that aligns with their general view. Paterson believed that he had moved the King, 'convincing him that nothing could tend more to his glory, and to render this Island great and considerable', than a union with Scotland. He was likewise pleased that the King seemed to embrace his argument on the need to take the principal ports of the Spanish West Indies – Cartagena, Havana and Darien – a move which Paterson thought would not only hamper European foes but fund the ongoing war against France by opening and securing 'a direct trade, forever, between those rich and vast continents of Mexico and Peru' and William's kingdom.

King William never recovered. During his convalescence he caught pneumonia and died. Paterson was bereft. As he told it, the King's death put 'such a damp' upon his 'spirits' that he 'lost all hopes of being further useful'. Paterson had lost the most direct means to put any plan into action. The succession of William's sister-in-law and cousin Anne unnerved him. The new Queen's first speech to parliament raised the prospect of a union, but the Presbyterian Scot bristled at its nationalistic undertones. Anne's emphatic defence of her own Englishness and the Englishness of her Church worried him. And so, in the months after King William's death, Paterson began to do something he never thought he would. In search for a patron, and in exchange for an audience, he began to pass small bits of intelligence to two of the most powerful politicians of Queen Anne's reign: Sidney Godolphin, the Lord High Treasurer, and Robert Harley, then serving as Speaker of the House of Commons. He had previously sent each his schemes for trade, but never before had he enclosed secret dispatches from the Continent.[7]

⸸

At the start of Anne's reign, Robert Harley was very much the junior partner in a compact built on mutual respect for efficiency. His two allies, Godolphin and John Churchill, 1st Duke of Marlborough, the commander of the English and Dutch forces in the War of the Spanish Succession, had a longstanding friendship. Godolphin was a small man, dark in complexion and stern in demeanour. He had an accountant's love for accuracy and order. His widely respected expertise in finance had kept him close to the engines of power for more than thirty years. He first served Charles II, who cracked that Godolphin was 'never in the way, never out of the way', always present but rarely an obstruction: a good pose to assume in an era when so much depended on the monarch's whim.[8] Though Godolphin was a pioneer in bringing modern financial methods to government, he was not always the most agile thinker in other areas. His aversion to anything that deviated from his systematic ideal meant that he was often flustered in a crisis. Harley, on the other hand, was an instinctive politician – energetic, sociable and calm under pressure. Like Godolphin, he sought a mode of independent ministerial government that could rise above the partisan fray of parliament. Harley was said to have spent a significant amount of money on first entering the Commons, paying clerks to copy all the papers the House received; papers he then studied diligently.

His studies meant he had an arsenal of procedural arcana at the fore of his mind, and he used it to stall, delay, push votes and sway legislation without in many cases dirtying himself by direct argument. According to contemporary journalist Abel Boyer, Harley's 'unwearied application' to House of Commons affairs brought him much attention early in his career. Unlike Godolphin, the self-sufficiency of his expertise did not render him aloof. Harley was 'plain' and 'familiar' in Boyer's telling. He was also deeply flexible and dextrous in how he managed people, charming and disarming them.[9]

Yet for all this appearance of openness, Harley was careful not to disclose his thinking. He had been raised in a prominent family of religious Dissenters, deeply pious and austere in their morality. From an early age, Harley's natural affability chafed against his family's expectations. He had few options but to hide large parts of himself from those around him. The intensity of parental surveillance shaped Harley into a politician who wore elusiveness as a second skin. He did not have to think in order to remain non-committal; he could appear an ally to all. Few who spoke with him left able to fix him to a particular position. The downside to this posture spilled onto the pages of Harley's correspondence, where he had to work hard against a tendency towards qualification, his clauses stacked to guard against umbrage. In front of large crowds too, when cornered to take a position that could be corroborated, he was apt to devolve so that his speech became a 'circumgyration of incoherent words'. Marlborough's wife Sarah scoffed that he had 'long accustomed himself to much dissemble his real intentions & to use the ambiguous & obtuse way of speaking that he could hardly even be understood when he really designed it'.[10] The Duchess' assessment relishes its cruelty. In truth, when face to face or in small committees, Harley displayed considerable tact. On paper, and before a big audience, he was unable to gauge his interlocutors' reactions, unable to key his approach to their moods, or turn their counter-arguments to his cause.

Aware of this deficiency, he respected clarity in others. Experience taught him that good words could bring the world to his view, and that he could shape the content of this prose by overseeing the efforts of propagandists in his employ. To this end, Harley lobbied Godolphin from 1702. He wanted the Treasurer to be on the lookout for 'a discreet writer of the government's side', one who could 'state facts right'. Harley believed that the populace 'err for want to knowledge', and because they are 'imposed upon by the stories raised by ill designing men'.[11] He realised before most the growing influence public opinion had over the exercise of power. He appreciated its force in bringing a nation together or rending it apart. He wanted a writer who could shape opinion in his favour, who could make the government's case, and disabuse readers of the rumours spread by opponents in the press and on the street. Paterson fitted the brief.

Harley gave Paterson the impression that he trusted him as an advisor on economic matters. If nothing else, Harley appreciated his ingenuity and admired him as a promoter and spin doctor from the early days of the Darien affair, during which Paterson had been able to persuade large parts of Scotland's nobles and merchants to risk the country's future and fortune on the uncertain promise of empire. Godolphin thought him a 'useful man', but was left confused by what Paterson proposed, how he saw his role or how Harley meant to employ him.[12]

The idea of a government press organ did not fit with Godolphin's preconceived notions of bureaucratic order. He did not think that Paterson should be employed as a government propagandist. And he was sceptical of the counsel that a man in Paterson's state could offer. In a letter to Harley, Godolphin made it clear that 'the most use that could be made' of Paterson 'will be by his correspondence and the intelligence he may give'.[13] In the early eighteenth century, gathering and passing on intelligence from a vantage in London was neither respected nor glamourous. In Jonathan Swift's haughty estimation, spies were 'the most accursed, and prostitute, and abandoned race, that God ever permitted to plague mankind'.[14] Military scouts, who tracked the enemy's movements in the field, provided perhaps one instance of morally acceptable intelligence. Agents who traded in letters – who listened in at ports and eavesdropped at coffeehouses – were seen as inherently untrustworthy, liable to sell their wares to the highest bidder. This was probably why Godolphin regarded Paterson's position as a minor intelligencer as terminal, and why he was so quick to dismiss the man's schemes as mere 'notions', not really worth his true consideration.

Paterson had sent the two politicians a flurry of letters. When allowed to see Godolphin in person no amount of gentle nudging could push him off track. He filled the Treasurer's rooms with schemes, foreign and domestic. His face tended to get redder as he spoke, more so when he tried to vent all his ideas in meetings hastened by Godolphin's impatience. Godolphin and Harley savvied that Paterson saw the intelligence he provided as a means to an end, a way to prompt them into lending the support and cachet he needed to revive his career. He had relocated to Westminster for this very purpose. He admitted this much to Harley, letting slip that he wanted a residence in St James' Street because its location promised 'easy access to persons and places'.[15] From Queen Square, where he eventually settled, it was a short walk to Whitehall. Turn upriver and Paterson could reach the York Buildings that abutted the Strand, where Harley lived. In sheer physical proximity he was as close to the backrooms as he had been since meeting the late King. But, as he fast realised, physical closeness and 'easy access' are two very different things.

⸸

Regaining his balance and pushing beyond the eye of the palace in the early hours that afternoon, Paterson was confident that he had finally found a way in; a way to gain, at last, the ready access to the Treasurer he was promised when he first began to act as an agent. That morning, before he set out on his walk, he sent his largest ever dispatch to Godolphin: a report from a crucial asset in Amsterdam that detailed the movement of French troops and the state of the ordnance on both sides. The report, which Paterson translated himself, laid out the tactics that England and her Dutch allies would have to employ to make progress in the War of the Spanish Succession, the pan-European conflict sparked by the death of Charles II of Spain in 1700. King Charles had left no children. His closest heirs were members of the Austrian Habsburgs and French Bourbons. The English and their allies fought to install a Habsburg. Louis XIV of France fought to place his grandson Phillip on the Spanish throne. As with so many defenders of English liberty, Paterson feared that

Phillip's accession would allow the Bourbons to secure a universal monarchy, radically altering the balance of power in Europe and giving the French control over the expansive Spanish Empire. If this came to pass, he believed that the French would monopolise international trade and impose Catholicism and arbitrary rule across the globe. By Paterson's reckoning, the time to strike was now – both in Europe and the new world. With the Spanish monarchy in crisis, England could make a play for the Caribbean. He was certain that money from this venture would reverse the financial advantage of the French, bringing the war in Europe to a swift end. In his mind he had evidence enough to set in motion the chain of ideas he had spent two years binding ever tighter.

⸸

Paterson was a traveller by nature. Years spent at sea allowed him to see the lines of the map in the ground before him. Heading towards Mayfair with the intent of stopping at one of the coffeehouses on the way – Elliot's or perhaps Old White's – he could trace the path of the plumbing system underfoot. He knew the households the Hampstead Water Company connected and the fees each one paid. The company was his design. It had had its start a decade earlier in the small drawing room of his former residence on Denmark Street, near the Church of St Giles-in-the-Fields.

He considered the system to be part of his London. To a man seeking access to the secret workings of the state, the implications of an underground network designed by him and at his service must have seemed irresistible. The problem was that metaphor was no longer grounded to reality. Paterson's plans to extend the waterworks to Piccadilly and Southwark remained on paper. He had been forced to sell his stock in the company soon after he made his final crossing from New York: the last leg in the journey from Central America that had left him with nothing. In the new world he had lost his fortune and his family. He had buried his first wife Elizabeth Turner, the widow of a New England Puritan, years before in Boston, where the two had met: she a respectable widow; he a pious but promising merchant.

His second wife Hannah Kemp was of a different cast. A coffeehouse keeper from Birchin Lane, Kemp was the likely proprietor of the

Mariner, a favourite haunt for traders and merchants returned from the Americas. The thrill of the new world pulsed through her London, following her as she served coffee, tea and hot chocolate and listened in to the lectures on geometry, navigation and philosophy that brought men to the coffeehouse – her eye trained to the debates that arose as patrons sat, drank, talked, picked up and passed around the newspapers scattered across the Mariner's communal tables. Paterson had persuaded her to go with him to Darien. There she remained, buried in the thick red Panamanian soil, along with their only child, a son.

The rumour that Paterson had lost his mind in Darien spread through London almost as soon as he returned: so quickly that Godolphin seemed 'surprised' by how well the man appeared when the two were reacquainted. He looked better, the Treasurer thought, than he had ten years earlier. Though offhand, Godolphin's remark – which Paterson made a point of repeating to Harley – had the same effect on him as a walk to Mayfair or Soho, or a day trip to the Heath. Paterson was brought back to the 1690s, to the Denmark Street days, to the room where he planned the waterworks and devised the initial plans for a Scottish colony at Darien, the place where he plotted and promoted his plan for establishing the Bank of England.

The air of self-possession that jarred Godolphin is clearer in this light. Through boon and loss Paterson kept faith to the projector's dictum that people do not invest with a man who looks as if he needs their money. The problem with this approach is that it can undo itself. Confidence in the face of losses such as Paterson had suffered can quickly shade in the minds of onlookers from optimism to pathos.

Judging from a surviving portrait, Paterson had a long forehead and serious, deep-set eyes, one slightly smaller and higher than the other – the imbalance inviting an air of kindness otherwise absent. Like all portraits, this one is biased in its own particular ways, both consciously and unconsciously.[16] Serving as the frontispiece to a manuscript edition of Paterson's letters, it casts an image of the author as he wanted to be seen. In the drawing Paterson's bewigged bust sits atop a pedestal. At the foot is the inscription '*sic vis non vobis*' ('You work but not for yourselves'). This is what Virgil is said to have uttered in response to the poetaster Bathyllus after the latter took credit for a verse celebrating Rome that Virgil had written and circulated anonymously. The image Virgil invoked was of bees making honey. The idea that his labour benefited others – that it contributed to the national good – was central to Paterson's self-justification. Like Virgil, Paterson thought his work was often ascribed to others. His better ideas were often assumed to be those of his social superiors. In some cases, this was due to the ineluctable hierarchy of English society; in others, because Paterson was often better at formulating a plan than following it through. In his mind, he is the magnanimous bee toiling for the benefit of the greater good. But the portrait betrays him. If he was so comfortable working in secret for the greater good, then why draw attention to it? The portrait asks for a recognition that Paterson knew had to be denied to the kind of work he did.

1. Portrait of William Paterson.

Drawn towards the end of Paterson's time as an agent, the portrait prompts us to ask why he felt overlooked. What did he do for his native Scotland, for England or for Britain that he wanted to insinuate into the historical record? These questions are important. But they cannot be answered in isolation. If he is but one bee, who else populated the hive? The portrait may ask for singular recognition, yet the motto brings to mind an interconnected series of workers, hidden from view. In this way it accurately, if unwittingly, captures the fact that Paterson's most significant mission was closely bound to the work of others.

Returning home that afternoon, brushing the wet from his overcoat and setting himself by the fire – the day's exertions taking the edge off his whirring mind – Paterson began to wait. Two days passed without response from Godolphin. On the third, when the post came, Paterson was sure it would bring the Treasurer's considered answer to his schemes. Or at least an offer to meet in person. Instead, Paterson was handed a letter that would entangle him in the life of its writer. Unsettlingly sharp in its reading of Paterson's situation, the writer knew too much and his ask carried significant risks. The writer was on the run from the government. There was a bounty on his head. And he needed Paterson's help.

⸸

The letter came from Daniel Defoe. There is not enough evidence to trace its origin. It is marked 'in Covert' and Defoe signed it 'your Exil'd Friend', giving credence to the rumour that he was in the Netherlands – long a refuge for English radicals. If Paterson had been following Defoe's progress, he might have come across a pamphlet published that January, in which the writer recounted his thrilling escape from a bounty hunter in Hackney fields. In this account, designed to scare off anyone who might want to turn him in, Defoe 'drew upon' the bounty hunter, frightening him 'out of his wits' before forcing him down on his knees and making him 'swear that if he ever met him again' he 'should shut his eyes' until Defoe was at least half a mile away.[17]

At the end of his life, the story Defoe told was that he had been sheltered in Barnet, on the edge of Hertfordshire, by his brother-in-law

Robert Davis. His intention was to flee to Scotland, but he was drawn back to London in order to sign documents that would prevent his property from being seized (a common provision levelled against fugitives). Like Robinson Crusoe, Defoe ignored a prophetic dream that came to him the night before he was due to set out. In the dream, Defoe was back 'in his old lodgings in London' when two men came to the door. They said they were messengers. But as soon as they had identified him, they seized him, arresting him on charges of sedition. Defoe woke Davis, who assured his nervous brother-in-law that 'he should give no heed to' the dream. Davis settled Defoe, bid him 'compose himself' and helped him back into bed. The dream came again, and again Defoe woke Davis, who again wearily comforted the writer. As the night wore on, Defoe fell back to sleep – out of sheer exhaustion rather than any ease of feeling. When he woke the next day, he could not slough off the sense of foreboding. Defoe believed that some dreams were the result of angelic ministration. Already watchful, he took further steps to heed the message from above, disguising himself, and opting to travel by foot so that he could take the more secluded path over Enfield Chase through Southgate, Hornsey and on to Islington. As he made his way down to the capital, Defoe's mind remained 'heavy and oppressed'. He grew tired and wanted to stop. But when he recognised someone at Hornsey, he knew he would not be able to spend the night there. Scared he would be discovered, he had to catch a bit of rest wherever he could, stepping off the path. Nearly thirty years after he had made the journey, Defoe claimed that he went to London resigned to his fate.[18] The care he took suggests otherwise.

None of these stories can be confirmed. It is difficult to separate the truth from the many fictions Defoe deployed to throw his pursuers off course or to make his biography at different times, and for different purposes, more respectable or more exciting.

Defoe was on the run because of something he had written. The English parliament was dominated that session by a High Church faction. In 1702 it looked as if they would roll back the measure of toleration William III had afforded Dissenters – those whose Protestantism fell outside the bounds of Anglican communion. Like

Paterson, Defoe was a Presbyterian. In response to the threat he and his fellow Dissenters faced, Defoe wrote *The Shortest Way with the Dissenters* (1702), a satiric pamphlet in which he mimicked the rhetoric of a High Church preacher and appealed for a quick, easy and brutal solution to the question of religious nonconformity. Whipping himself and his congregated readers to mania, Defoe's preacher calls for Dissenters to 'be rooted out of this nation',[19] purged by execution and exile from the English body politic. The pamphlet was unnervingly persuasive. When it was revealed that the author was himself a Dissenter, the hoax was exposed and those lured to the logical – if exaggerated – endpoint of their prejudices were forced to respond. *The Shortest Way* was too widely read and the scandal it caused too dangerous to the cohesion of Church and state to let pass. Defoe admitted to Paterson that the satire had reached further than he had intended, hitting members of the ministry who stood behind the Anglican clergy Defoe targeted. Though it escaped his control, *The Shortest Way* was an object lesson in the credulity of the reading public, one that Defoe would not soon forget.

The letters Defoe sent during his time on the run emphasise at every possible point his remorse for the effects of the pamphlet. Yet they also give voice to a man impressed with his power over readers. Trapped, Defoe saw that the only way out was the way he had come in. His ability to move the reading public would have to save him. He would offer his services as a writer to the Queen, or to any MP who could help win him a pardon.[20]

The question of why Defoe approached Paterson is intriguing. Defoe had written to more powerful men, like Daniel Finch, 2nd Earl of Nottingham, who was tasked by Harley and Godolphin to hunt down the writer of *The Shortest Way*. He also wrote to William Penn, whose close connections to the ministry placed him in a far better position to help than Paterson. Defoe above all things was able to 'read Mankind', as one friend put it. It was this quality that made him a novelist. Alive to the smallest of details, with an uncanny ability to read in them the flaws and needs of character, he gently reminded Paterson of a time when Paterson had promised to introduce him to Harley. The assumption that underlies this reminder is that Paterson – his fortune gone and his followers lost – would seek his return to public life through Harley.

In the letter Defoe thanks Paterson for the concern he had shown for his 'Suffering'. Apparently, the 'Few Friends' who helped Defoe evade prosecution kept in contact with Paterson. It was through them that Paterson had passed on his regards. There is a tantalising but unsubstantiated link between this murky group of 'Friends' and the clandestine networks of Dissenters active in London.

Whatever his reasons, Defoe correctly supposed that Paterson was in contact with Harley. And he put himself between the two in a way that manages to be at once opaque and insistent:

> If you should Find Room for my name in your conversation with the gentleman I Mentioned [i.e. Harley], I Suppose I Need Not Name him, If you Find him Enclin'd to have Compassion for One who Offended him Onely because he Did Not kno' him, Venture in My name in the Humblest Terms to Ask his Pardon, and whether Ever I am Restor'd to my Native Country Or Not, I Shall Never Name him but with Some Epithite Suited to Express his Merit; Let him kno' that I Sollicit you with More Earnestness To Convince him of my Sence of his Resentment, and my Earnest Desire to be set Right in his Thoughts, Than I Do for the Obtaining a Recall from This Banishment Forasmuch as I Vallue the Esteem of One Wise man above abundance of blessings.

Amidst this apology, drawn out to flatter and supplicate in equal measure, is Defoe's promise to 'Never Name' Harley 'but with Some Epithite [epithet] Suited to Express his Merit'. Here we have a vow from one of the age's most gifted satirists that he will only write about Harley – one of England's canniest political operators – in the most positive of terms. A small promise to be sure, yet one Defoe clearly thought enough to win him some favour.

The context of the apology is significant in this regard. On its own the paragraph rings slightly hollow: it is the very least the writer could do to warrant Harley's intervention. A positive mention here or there in exchange for a pardon and Defoe's return from 'Banishment' is paltry at best. But viewed within the letter as a whole, Defoe's offer to promote Harley's merits becomes something far more interesting: the founding premise for a contract designed so that writers and thinkers of Defoe's and Paterson's talents might serve a political patron.

Defoe is uncharacteristically cautious as he proceeds – wary, it seems, not simply of the power of his words but of their potential to imperil him further. The letter is vague, with Defoe requiring a lot of cloak and dagger work of his sentences. He opens, 'I Can Not but with Regrett Look back on the Former Discourses we have had Concerning Things Done before Now'.[21] It is not immediately clear what Defoe regrets, nor what he and Paterson had talked about, nor, indeed, what things had been done. The two had known each other since the 1690s. Both had spent their early careers peppering the late King and his ministers with projects, though Paterson had far more success than Defoe. Both offered schemes to expand the empire. But where Paterson ventured to the Americas, Defoe remained in London. There was a grudging admiration between the two. Defoe included some of Paterson's ideas for social welfare in his *Essay on Projects* (1697) and Paterson sought to include several of Defoe's books in his proposed library of trade. This was not enough to suppress their rivalry. The two were very similar. On the make, neither had the luxury of time that money affords and so their much-vaunted industry often tipped to rashness, each man ceaselessly lured by the promise of the next new thing. When your flaws are reflected in another, it either generates empathy or makes you, as it did with Paterson and Defoe, taste twice your own shortcomings.

The firmest evidence of discord between the two comes to us indirectly, via a bundle of letters deposited in Oxford's Bodleian Library in 1955 by Defoe's last surviving relative.[22] Two of the letters are copies: the originals addressed directly to King William III and dated November and December 1701, a few months before the King's death.

The letters offer the King advice. Their main concern is a scheme to manage the levying of taxes from subjects. The author is confident that if done efficiently and without current levels of graft and corruption, the government will be able to discharge all public debts within ten years and have the requisite funds to wage a successful war with France. The letter writer connects his concerns with French power to affairs in the West Indies, putting forth a second plan to seize Darien, Cartagena or Havana. The third point he makes is on a union with Scotland. There has to be a unity within the British Isles, the writer argues, before Britain can exert dominance in Europe and the Americas. The writer must be Paterson. The individual plans and the logical chains connecting them are unmistakable.

We do not know why Defoe had a copy of these plans, nor when they came into his possession. That he had them at all is suspicious. The letters are respectful but authoritative in tone. The views they present are synthesised and explained for the King's advantage. They adopt the pose of an advisor, a man who could speak on matters of finance, conquest, war and peace. A man who realised the power of the people and sought to increase the popularity of the ruler, not simply with hollow gestures but with public works and targeted welfare. The writer was not an aristocrat. He was elevated by the strength of his ideas alone. In this, the letters go a long way to explaining why, on the run and in need of a pardon, Defoe began to tout the idea that he was King William's agent. A long-time admirer of the former King, Defoe had published a series works in defence of William. By claiming the King as his employer after the fact, he could make these works count as service. Defoe would hold to this story from then on. It was central to his sense of worth, to the idea that he wrote for the state and not simply for bread. Half-truths were moulded into certaintics and thc story repeated so often that it settled into one of the anecdotes that made up his life.

Was the apology Defoe offered Paterson in part an acknowledgement that he had exploited elements of Paterson's biography for his own advantage? There is not enough evidence to do more than speculate. But in seeking Paterson out, Defoe implied an affinity between them. He conveyed to Paterson and, through him, Harley, the notion he might provide a similar service to the one he assumed Paterson was then providing. Defoe had attempted to contact Harley before, when he was imprisoned for debt. But nothing had come of it.[23] Pegging his hopes to Paterson, Defoe overestimated the Scottish projector, believing that he was on his way to regaining the kind of influence he had once had. Paterson must have recognised his own plight in the hope of Defoe's idea. Here was a fuller conception of service, one built on a man's skill with a pen, the strength of his mind, and not simply the intelligence he could gather. And yet Paterson was reticent. Defoe's schemes were better on paper than in action. Associating with an outlaw had its own dangers. The plan could backfire and, instead of bringing Paterson to greater notice, disclosing his contact with the writer could by dint of his connection with the underworld downgrade Paterson's status from intelligence agent to mere informer. It was with this risk in mind that Paterson carried Defoe's letter for close to a month, waiting until Defoe was captured and in Newgate Prison before he delivered it to Harley.[24]

†

Our story begins with this fugitive letter, not because its writer or recipient felt its significance in the moment but because the connections it forged between Paterson, Defoe, Harley and Godolphin formed over the course of the next decade an important node in a growing intelligence network that developed to meet the needs of the modern state. Paterson could have destroyed the letter, yet he passed it on, realising the ingenuity of its writer and willing, it seems, to risk the association if it could help him extend the terms of his own service to the ministry. Alive to politics, sharp and endlessly productive, Defoe was able to rouse the sleeping giant of public opinion. If he served as an agent, he had the requisite skills to do more than gather intelligence and offer the odd bit of advice. He could act as propagandist and intermediary, promoting the interests of the ministry in public and behind the scenes. He could fold himself into the apparatus of government, taking Paterson along with him.

Dependent, insecure, yoked by self-interest to their vision for a new state, by the spring of 1703 Defoe and Paterson began to carve the outline of a creature unknown in their day but recognisable to ours: the professional political operative. How they did so, the influence they gained and the effects this new kind of actor had on the emergence of the British state are the focus of this book.

Like the pipes of the Hampstead Water Company, the paths that Defoe and Paterson would soon employ to gather and dispatch intelligence can be followed, the connections and divergences mapped as each spy travelled between London and the Highlands, extending in the process Westminster's reach across the British Isles. Tracking them as they travel the length of the country brings to the surface an intricate web of underground networks formed by Dissenting communities, French infiltrators and Jacobite spies; networks Defoe and Paterson made use of in the most significant campaign of their career – the campaign to unify Scotland and England – and those that stood in opposition to this mission.

My aim in seeking the spies out is to catch their work at the high point of its influence. As tasks go, this can sometimes feel like trying to catch water in your hands. Influence is a slippery thing, and the influence of those who wish to remain undetected in public but known to power is more slippery still. The history that follows is staked on the belief that whatever we grasp brings us that much closer to the truth of how Scotland lost its parliamentary independence and how the united government of Great Britain emerged in its wake.

Since it focuses on only one set of players, this history is partial. The following chapters do not offer a comprehensive portrait of the Union and its making. Nor do they provide complete biographies of Defoe, Paterson, Godolphin or Harley – or close study of Harley's mastery of the press.[25] What they do, in setting the lives of these players around a campaign that changed the careers of each of them, is draw out the personal relationships between the principals themselves and between the principals and their agents – the relationships through which power and influence are channelled; the relationships that connect design to endeavour, plan to action. In the making and breaking of these personal and professional connections we find the compromises, clashes of belief and personality, and competing impulses of ideology and pragmatism that constitute the everyday life of political work. That this work cleared the way to the Act of Union puts lie to the belief that a parliamentary union between England and Scotland was a fait accompli.

But nor was the making of the Union simply a 'political job', carried out through well-placed bribes and the manipulation of patronage. Robert Burns' line that Scottish sovereignty was 'bought and sold for English gold' by a 'Parcel of Rogues' has been repeated so often that in certain quarters it is accepted as fact. It certainly allows a point of blame: parliamentarians betrayed the people whose patriotism would never have allowed their independence to be sold so cheaply. New research on the anti-Union campaign shows that this line sells opposition forces short as well. The Scottish campaign against the Union ran on more than the spontaneous expression of patriotism. It was centralised and coordinated to bring public opinion to bear on the decisions of the Scottish parliament. Such insight demands a fresh look at the other side. The 'political job' orchestrated in Whitehall and carried out on the ground by Defoe and his fellow agents was more sophisticated than Burns could know. The agents opened up vital lines of communication and dissemination. They gathered and deployed intelligence in order to shape thought and action, popular belief and governmental policy. In doing so, they pioneered new ways to sample, understand and thereby influence the opinions and behaviour of the people and their leaders – in Scotland and in England.[26] The story of their work is now as relevant as ever, as the campaigns for the future of the Union and Scottish independence continue to seek the kind of public mandate and parliamentary power that can redefine a nation's constitution – and, with it, that nation's sense of its self and place in the world.

CHAPTER 1

NEWGATE PRISON

On 21 May 1703, five months after he set *The Shortest Way* into the world, and a month after he wrote to Paterson, Daniel Defoe was captured in the Spitalfields home of Nathaniel Sammen, a French Huguenot weaver.[1] In Defoe's coat, folded between drafts of his satires and 'libels', was a set of papers in a disguised hand – a technique designed to conceal the writer's identity.[2] This was enough to condemn him in the eyes of his pursuer, Daniel Finch, 2nd Earl of Nottingham. The arrest warrant that Nottingham signed had that January called for the writer to be seized 'along with his papers'. Unusually, it had also asked that he be delivered for interrogation by Nottingham himself.[3]

As Secretary of State for the southern department, Nottingham was responsible for overseeing the prosecutions of writers who were accused of sedition. By the time of Defoe's arrest, he had been on the trail of the author of *The Shortest Way* for close to six months. Soon after the pamphlet's publication, Godolphin relayed to Nottingham a conversation he had had with Harley. In Godolphin's telling, Harley 'has had a mind to speak with you about a book lately come out called *The Shortest Way with the Dissenters.* He seemed to think it absolutely necessary to the service of the government that your lordship should endeavour to discover who was the author of it'.[4] Barely a week later, Defoe was publicly outed in *The Observator* as the pamphlet's author.[5] Nottingham remained on the case. He and Harley were long-time rivals and while they agreed that it was important to find the writer, they had very different motivations. Attuned before his time to the impact of propaganda, Harley wanted to neutralise those who wrote against the government. Nottingham, on the other hand, hunted shadows. He suspected that an underground network of plotters connected to the parliamentary Whigs had put Defoe up to writing *The Shortest Way*, and he was determined to root them out.

Nottingham was a large man, and he carried himself so that others noticed it. Defoe described him as 'a huge tall man' and by 'appearance a man of grandeur'.[6] In portraits his face is stiff and formal, his arching forehead broken only by a set of thick serious eyebrows, which must have been of great use in examining witnesses. A slight shift or dubious raise would have pierced the silence just enough to bait a nervous target into speaking.

By the time Defoe was seized, Nottingham had built a case against him with characteristic method. On the same day that *The Observator* divulged Defoe's identity, Nottingham sent an arrest warrant to Henry Allen, one of the Queen's messengers. The warrant called for the seizure of Edward Bellamy, a Whig propaganda agent who was suspected of delivering *The Shortest Way* to the printer. The warrant mobilised all 'mayors, Sheriffs, Justices of the Peace, Constables . . . Officers Civil and Military', along with all Queen Anne's 'Loving Subjects', to seize the agent for 'high Crimes and Misdemeanours'.[7]

Nottingham knew that Bellamy worked for the Whigs in Holland as well as England.[8] Bellamy's ability to move between the two countries spurred the Secretary's belief that he was on the track of an extensive, coordinated opposition network, funded by exiles and fomented by the Junto, the five Whig lords who directed the party for much of Anne's reign. Intelligence that the pamphlet had been printed and distributed in Holland suggested a coordinated effort by Whigs who 'pretend to patronize the Dissenters', in order 'to raise all the Jealouses' and 'Frighten & Terrifie them into some Desperate Fooleries'.[9]

Bellamy did not last long. The Secretary maintained a patrician silence between questions, giving him too much time to consider his fate. The threat of gaol; the public reaction against the pamphlet; the fact that Nottingham could pin responsibility for its seditious content on him: all proved too much. Bellamy confessed that he had taken the manuscript to the printer, George Croome, and that Defoe was indeed the work's author. Alerted to this betrayal, Defoe remarked that Bellamy – a one-time ally – was little better than an 'informer'.[10] After he had arrested Croome, who corroborated Bellamy's account, Nottingham had what he needed. He struck a bargain with the two men, arranging their release on the condition that they 'personally appear . . . and give evidence against Daniel Defoe for having written a Scandalous Pamphlet'.[11] All he needed now was the writer himself.

The warrant issued for Defoe's arrest and the seizure of his writings was followed by an advertisement in *The London Gazette* the following week. With this, Nottingham made the hunt public, offering £50 to anyone who could report the whereabouts of one 'Daniel de Foe, *alias* de Fooe'. It was a large reward for its day; enough for a frugal person to live on for a year. The advertisement also contained the first public description of the writer:

> *He is a middle sized spare man, about 40 years old, of a brown complexion, and dark brown coloured hair, but wears a wig, a hooked nose, a sharp chin, grey eyes, and a large mole near his mouth, was born in* London, *and for many years was a hose factor in Freeman's-yard, in Cornhill, and is now owner of the brick and pantile works near* Tilbury-Fort *in Essex.*[12]

The image is of a thoroughly average merchant; a former hosier, now producer of bricks and rooftiles. The pointed chin, hooked nose, grey eyes and the mole near his mouth give form to a man struggling to hide his rat-sharp nature beneath an all-too-affected dress. There is some pathos to his attempt. Defoe dressed like he thought a gentleman should. His wig was too long for its day: not the short shoulder wig worn by those comfortable brushing up against each other at levees and balls, but a longer piece, dragged from the last century and liable to drop into someone else's drink at a coffeehouse. He was fond of ruffles and had been seen flashing a pinkie ring.[13] His foppishness was notable, and a target for satire. In marking his dress this way, the advertisement issues an image of a man audacious enough to strive beyond his station. Why was the son of a tallow-chandler, a man of respectable merchant class upbringing, dressing like a rake of last century's Court? Why, for that matter, did he stick his hooked nose into affairs of state?

The advertisement in the *Gazette* deflated Defoe. He was hurt by what he felt an unseemly fixation on his appearance.[14] And yet, at the same time, the reward that accompanied it conveyed just how dangerous Nottingham considered him. This was the dynamic that would define their exchange. To Nottingham, Defoe was at once laughable and sinister. The reports that he had jumped out of a window to evade Nottingham's men; the stories of his escapades in London; the rumours that he was in Holland: all fed Nottingham's anger during Defoe's five months on the run. That a man so far beneath him could resist his authority galled the Secretary. If Nottingham was keen to depict Defoe as an impostor, a man of pretensions, uneasy in society, he might well have been projecting his own niggling unease. The threat Defoe posed was that he was a different kind of man, one who drew his authority from the public value of his talent, not his preordained social place. Defoe was a writer who wanted to be treated as a gentleman by virtue of his skill and the reach of his words. Nottingham was a statesman who refused to concede anything but birth as the means of entrance to the ruling class.

⸸

In the end it took two men – a messenger and a constable – to capture Defoe.[15] They were tipped off by one of the small circle of friends and associates privy to the writer's whereabouts. The informant collected the £50 reward but did so through an intermediary.[16] Defoe did not know who betrayed him – and nor do we. The London newspaper *The Post Man* reported that Defoe was questioned for three days straight, before being taken under guard to Newgate. Few records of the interrogation exist. In one account, favourable to Nottingham, the Secretary put his case to the writer 'strictly', examining the pamphlet before its writer, counting the ways he had incurred 'her Majesty's displeasure by so malicious and factious a paper'. To Nottingham, the proof of malice was self-evident. Defoe had obviously intended to do the country 'ill'. One only had to look at the outrage *The Shortest Way* caused to see that. According to this all too brief report, Defoe's response was unsatisfactory. He prevaricated and dodged. He offered extenuating circumstances but at no point was he able to defend his writings outright.[17]

Defoe's account of the interrogation comes to us via a thinly veiled allegory that he composed seven years later, the sting of his treatment by the imperious Nottingham sharp as ever. The allegory transposes the events of London to the moon, where writers are depicted as tailors; their writings as coats. It works from the premise that representation is a form of dress – of putting something on. The idea is that if the coat fits, it adequately represents the wearer. By the same token, if the reader sees themselves in the satire, then that reader is its target.

The scene opens with the figure of Nottingham attacking the man who bears the coat – most likely Croome, the printer:

> *What Dog's that?* Says he [Nottingham] — *A Villain* — *A Rogue* — *Why that Coat's made for me*; and up he runs to the poor Man [Croome], and began to bluster. *Pray, my Lord, Good my Lord*, says the Man, *It is not made for your Highness*, it was made for my Neighbour *Such-a one* — You lie you Villain, *says my Lord*, it was made for me, and I'll have you hang'd, *if there were no more Taylors in all the Moon* — *Indeed my Lord*, says the Man again, *it could not be made for you, for it will not fit your Lordship* — *I'll try that*, says his Lordship, *you Dog, and if it does, I'll have you hang'd immediately.* Upon which my Lord put the Coat on — But the poor Man was confounded, when he saw, that with but the least Stretching it *fitted his Lordship* to a Hair —

Offenders were not typically hanged for seditious libel. Some faced the pillory, which was in itself a dangerous prospect. The greater risk was that the financial penalties were severe. Those who could not pay were remanded to prison indefinitely. Croome's fear is well justified and gives some sense of what Defoe must have felt when he was subject to Nottingham's interrogation. In the allegory Defoe projects this fear outwards, revelling in how far the satire reached. *The Shortest Way* might have been a particularly tailored coat but, in the anger Nottingham expresses, it is made to fit a whole swathe of the political establishment. As the Lord of Defoe's allegory raves through the 'Assembly' more and more politicians identify themselves as targets. In the end 'no less than 114 of them challeng'd the poor Man for bringing this Coat out to expose them in particular'.

The assembly Defoe writes of is clearly parliament. Croome was not, however, brought before the Commons and nor, for that matter, was Defoe. The allegory conflates the interrogation of the printer with another event that took place soon thereafter: the formal complaint Nottingham lodged against the author in absentia. On 25 February 1703, Nottingham took Defoe's satire to the Commons in much the same way as the coat was paraded before the assembly, its contents examined and debated for their reflection on the parliament's members. In the allegory, the 114 politicians who thought that the coat fitted them particularly and exactly are the 114 Tory members. In fact, the events were less partisan. The Commons resolved that Defoe's pamphlet contained 'scandalous reflections on this Parliament', that it promoted 'sedition' and as such that it was to be 'burnt by the common hangman' the following day in 'New-Palace Yard'.[18] As Defoe's satire burned, its smoke adding to the haze that settled over the city, the Queen herself entered the House to deliver to the Commons and Lords a speech that one contemporary called 'remarkable'. Before both Houses, Anne defended the established Church, praised the parliament for ensuring the 'quiet satisfaction' of her subjects and moved in pursuit of both ends to argue for 'some further laws for restraining the great license which is assumed, of publishing and spreading scandalous pamphlets and libels'.[19] There was no mistaking that the Queen had Defoe in her sights. From that point on, she took a personal interest in his prosecution.

While the allegory casts the assembly as a figure of fun, its collective weight still crushes the poor man, forcing him to give up the tailor:

> The Man was in great Distress, and had no Way at last to bring him self out of this Broil, but by telling, them the Name of the

Taylor, who made the Coat — Which having done, he made his Escape, and the poor *Taylor* was sent for.

Defoe confessed that he felt a great deal of guilt for those who suffered as a result of his pamphlet, some of which he tried to expiate in this lunar fiction.[20] Here the pressures of the assembly give Croome an excuse for faltering. They also offer an opportunity for Defoe to demonstrate his own steadfastness.

Enter Defoe as the self-aggrandising 'Poor Taylor', 'bold Fellow' who 'fear'd no Colours', to be examined by the assembly's clerk:

Clerk. Did you make this Coat, Sir?
Taylor. Yes, I did.
C. Did you make it for a *Representer*, or Character-Coat?
T. *Yes* Sir.
C. Who was it to Represent?
T. It was made to represent him that it represents, Sir.
C. But who is that, Sir?
T. Why I tell you, Sir, *Says the Taylor Briskly, him that it represents.*
C. Well, but here are a great many Gentlemen who say it represents them.
T. What all of them?
C. Yes, all of them.
T. It's strange, Men should be all K—s [kinds] of like Dimensions.
C. But how say you, *was it made to represent them?*
T. If it represents them, *it must be made* to represent them.
C. But did you design to represent them?
T. What do you tell me of Designs, my Design was to make the *Coat.*
C. But here is my Lord A—, he says, the Coat represents him —
T. Has he try'd it on, and *does it fit him?*
C. Exactly.
T. 'Tis impossible — Pray look on the Coat; the Coat is a *Fools Coat*, and his Lordship is too much something else to be a Fool.
. . .
C. But it may fit my Lord *C*—.

> *T.* No it can't neither; for *turn it again*, and then 'tis a *States-man's Coat*, and it is well known, my Lord is no more a States-man than he is a Conjurer.
> *C.* Well, but *they may think it fits them*.
> *T.* Their own Guilt may do much, but 'tis not good Manners in me to think so.
> *C.* Well, but what say you to the rest of the Gentlemen that challenge it? Pray, give them Satisfaction.
> *T.* Why truly, as to 114 Gentlemen belonging to the Great Hall [House of Commons], if it fits them all I cannot help it, they may take it among them, and then every one will have his Share — 'Tis a strange thing, a Man cannot dress up a Monkey, but every Man calls him Cousin.
> And with this he threw the *Coat* down in the Middle of the Hall.[21]

The tailor is too clever by half. He cannot be pinned down on whether the coat represents a particular person or indicates a character type. As each lord tries it on, this question ceases to matter. Those it fits become tokens of the wider type. They *are* the character: the intolerant High Church Anglican willing to end religious Dissent with violence. Each politician's willingness to assume such a position renders him a fool. The tailor is left with no choice but to conclude that the exercise of trying on the coat is analogous to dressing up a monkey. Where that reveals the monkey's similarity to man, this exposes the apish inhumanity of the Tory MPs.

Nottingham did attempt to get Defoe to confess to particular targets. His greater concern, though, was that Defoe wrote on behalf of a collection of radical Whigs and Dissenters. He had received a piece of intelligence in January that *The Shortest Way* 'was certainly contrived and hatched by stronger heads than the pretended author Danl. Fooe'.[22] If Defoe was merely the patsy, then this arrest did not halt the destabilising forces that had put him to the task. Nottingham's fear was that Defoe worked for the same Whig lords who had stymied his own efforts to criminalise Dissent. Two years earlier the Whig Junto had quashed Nottingham's pet bill to penalise occasional conformity, the practice whereby Dissenters would attend Anglican services occasionally and in doing so pass the sacramental test required of all office holders. Nottingham was convinced that Defoe was privy to their schemes when, in truth, he was not. Nottingham's haughtiness seems to have led him to underestimate the writer. He pored over Defoe's papers looking for a point of connection to men whom he considered more worthy of his rivalry.

From such heights, Nottingham missed some crucial details. His complete unwillingness to compromise led Defoe to burn the most incriminating of his papers before the arrest in fear of 'Lord Nottinghams fury'.[23] And because of his lack of tact as a reader, Nottingham missed the significance of what he did eventually lay his hands on. The 'over-vigilant minister',[24] as Defoe put it, passed over some of Defoe's works thinking that they were personal papers.

Defoe was proud that he withstood Nottingham's three-day long interrogation. But there is no way that he was as brazen as the tailor. This much can be established by the circumstances leading to his arrest. Defoe did not come before parliament. He evaded it with skill. He slipped the grasp of Henry Allen, the Queen's messenger, for as long as he did because he knew London intimately. Defoe remembered when the lanes of Spitalfields were 'deep, dirty and unfrequented' and the crowded Spitalfields market was 'a field of grass with cows feeding on it'. The area had changed fast. Gridded streets replaced the open fields; the area was now 'close-built and inhabited with an infinite number of people'. 'Numberless ranges of building[s]' stretched, as Defoe described it, 'from Spittle-yard, at Northern Fallgate, and from Artillery Lane in Bishopsgate street ... to Brick Lane, and the end of Hare street, on the way to Bethnal Green'.[25] The inhabitants of this newly developed suburb were mostly French Huguenots, Protestants who fled religious persecution in France as refugees. Defoe was a long-time defender of their rights and found much sympathy in the community. Relatively prosperous, densely populated and increasingly suspicious of government, Spitalfields was one of the few places in the city where Defoe could make his way undetected.[26]

It was on the busy but well-paved streets of the artisan East End that Defoe mounted his defence. In London, he published a pamphlet explaining that *The Shortest Way* was 'an Irony . . . free from any seditious design.'[27] This is a world away from the bravado of the tailor, who ensured that the satire fitted or applied to every Tory. On the run, Defoe spent considerable time trying to take back the offence he had caused. Far from paralysing him, the fear of pursuit spurred a nervous burst of activity designed to keep him from prison.

Defoe wrote public defences along with letters to powerful men he hoped might take up his cause. His concern was not simply for himself but for his family. There is evidence that he kept in contact with them during this time. If he ventured to see them in person, he would have done so with extreme caution. Even if he did not, Spitalfields was not far from the house and warehouse in Freeman's Yard where his wife Mary and their six children lived. Their proximity and his powerlessness in the face of their suffering weighed on him. His family had to endure the ignominy of having a fugitive for a father and husband – something he could justify by his belief in the nobility of his cause. He could not reason away the fact that their financial situation grew ever more strained the longer he remained at large. Defoe knew that they suffered because of his absence. And he knew the financial penalties incurred by a charge of seditious libel were likely to make their situation worse. In a moment of throat-knotting desperation, Defoe sent Mary to plead his case with Nottingham.

⸸

Mary Tuffley was the daughter of a wealthy cooper, a man who had made good through trade; who had risen along the usual path artisans took from his apprenticeship to become an improver, a journeyman and then a master, acquiring land and property enough in the process to endow his daughter with a £3,700 dowry when she married Defoe in 1684. Daniel and Mary's marriage was not typical of its day. Defoe believed that marriage was a partnership in which husband and wife were bound by a duty to love; a duty that obliged them to moderate their tempers, to work, without subjugating one another, towards steering the household and educating their children. What Defoe advocated was very much a bourgeois ideal: in his mind, this partnership extended to the husband's business, which he believed wives should have the requisite skill to manage. Defoe's high-minded notion of marriage relied on an equally lofty idea of the perfect wife. Well bred and well educated, she was a 'creature without comparison; her society ... the emblem of sublime enjoyments; her person is angelic, and her conversation heavenly; she is all softness and sweetness, peace, love, wit and delight'.[28] (Faced with such a paragon, the husband must not have had to moderate his temper much.) The idea that husbands would not trample over wives reveals an uncharacteristic naivety in Defoe's idealism. In this period, a woman's property devolved to the man she married. Wives had no legal personhood and little recourse. Domestic violence was both common and widely accepted. With these strictures in place, the best Defoe's model wife could do was make her way from 'upper servant' to 'junior partner'.[29]

Defoe's views on marriage reflect the respect he had for Mary's mind. During their courtship he worked hard to win her over in writing, presenting her with a collection of histories, anecdotes and stories. On the page he revealed his seriousness, his agile, wide-reaching mind, his constant endeavour to draw moral purpose from the past and its narratives. Their life together was filled with conversation, with schemes and with business. Ever resourceful, Mary had managed the family affairs when Defoe could not – during his bankruptcies and now that he was on the run. As much as he admired how able Mary was in his absence, Defoe was guilt-stricken each time he left. When she ventured to Whitehall to meet Nottingham, Mary had six children – four daughters and two sons – and was solely responsible for running her husband's brickworks.

Whitehall Palace wore its history on the outside. Sewn together were buildings from various reigns. Some showed damage from the fire of 1698. The newer set were unmarked by the black stains of the flames. Inside it was both topsy and intimidating, its labyrinthine passageways too obvious a nod to the furtive workings of state. Entering through the cloister court, its stone passages arching over her, Mary was taken to the Cockpit, formerly the grounds of a theatre, but now the offices and lodgings for the ministry. As comfortable as Mary was in the world of business, coming to beg for her fugitive husband and 'Ruin'd Family' at the seat of power cowed her.[30]

Nottingham did little to put her at ease. The Secretary was proud and dismissive. He remained unmoved by her plight and that of her children. Each time she professed that her husband meant none of the offence, that his intent was not seditious, the Secretary responded: 'Let him surrender.'[31] Defoe felt guilty about subjecting his wife to the unbending Nottingham for much of his life. It pained him to think that he had sent this 'Vertuous and Excellent Mother . . . a woman whose fortunes I have Ruin'd' to Lord Nottingham who 'first Insulted her, Then Tempted her'. There is no external corroboration for the accusation that Nottingham attempted to seduce Mary after rebuffing her pleas for her husband. It is not, however, the kind of thing that the generally prudish Defoe would have made up.

His bitterness, though, had to be put aside. Nottingham was still on his trail and still held the power to stay his prosecution. To have to face the man who made advances to his wife – to beg *his* forgiveness and mercy – split Defoe in two. In a letter to Nottingham, Defoe prostrated himself, lying down at the feet of the Queen and making the plangent offer to serve her with 'my hand, my Pen, or my head' – to fight in her army or to write for her ministers. In an attempt to disabuse Nottingham of the idea that he was merely the figurehead of a conspiracy, Defoe implored him to write down 'any Questions you Think Fitt . . . and [have them] Sent to, or left at my house'. He would answer them as soon as he could, on pain of 'Death from your Resentments'.

Such offers meant little to a man convinced of his own powers of interrogation. Suspecting as much, Defoe attempted to justify why he remained at large. He impressed upon Nottingham that he had a 'Body Unfitt to bear the hardships of a Prison, and a Mind Impatient of Confinement'. He had experienced the Queen's Bench Prison and, as a debtor, he had been left to linger in the Fleet Prison twice in the past ten years. Memories of these experiences brought on a biting claustrophobia. The idea of 'Prisons, Pillorys, and Such like', he confessed, was 'worse to me Than Death'.[32] The intensity to which Defoe had worked himself while on the run – his focus set to the future and the world around him – found release as a centrifugal force. He feared what might happen if he were trapped, if his fast-paced mind were turned inwards by confinement, its probing power set loose upon itself.

When the messenger and the constable pushed through Sammen's door in Spitalfields, Defoe knew his journey would end in prison. His world shrank in the moment he was loaded into a carriage and taken under guard from Nottingham's rooms at Whitehall to Newgate.

⸸

Newgate was a clustered assault on the senses. The only question was which one it hit first. The prison was visually imposing. Approached from the east the traveller's eye was drawn up across the height of the walls to three statues: of justice, fortitude and prudence. The first represented Newgate's value to society; the second two the values that supposedly kept people from ending up inside. Men and women were sent to Newgate for misdemeanours and debts, not just felonies. Poverty was more likely than anything else to land one in prison. As any of London's poor could have told you, money makes it easier to practise prudence and show fortitude. The statues were just one way the grandeur of the building was out of step with the social ills it was meant to reform. Its location in an elegant part of town was another. One Justice of the Sessions referred to Newgate as the 'castle of misery'. A contemporary account of public buildings was just as damning, noting that the 'cost and beauty of the structure' were far more than necessary, 'because the sumptuousness of the outside' was meant to aggravate 'the misery of the wretches within'.[33]

On a warm day it was probably the smell of the place that struck first. Even before the high walls and arched entrance came into view, there was a distinct shift in the quality of the air, from the poor-but-tolerable smell of a city whose inhabitants considered bathing too often to be dangerous, to the foul thick air of a place where bodies were confined with little to no sanitation.[34] An early prison reformer described how after a visit to Newgate his clothes reeked so much that he could not close the windows of his carriage on the ride home. Eventually the smell became so bad that he gave up on the carriage and travelled to and from Newgate on horseback. The notebook in which he recorded the experience of prisoners was left yellowed and 'tainted' by the air. After his visits it could not be used 'till spreading it an hour or two before the fire'.[35]

Newgate was a chaotic place. Unlike modern gaols, it was not built to confine prisoners long term, but to house people before their trials, before corporal or capital punishment was meted out, or before they were transported to one of England's penal colonies. Visitors came in and out of Newgate with relative ease. The state did not pay the keeper, who collected fees from prisoners and their relatives for room and board, for food and for the large quantities of alcohol consumed within its walls. The role he played lay somewhere between an extortionate publican and oppressive colonial governor. The gaol itself was hot and loud with activity. Relatives bringing food and money were joined by the occasional crowd that came to gawk at famous rogues and highwaymen before they were executed. The constant activity was intimidating from the first encounter, a den of 'horror and confusion'.[36]

Defoe cast his first impressions of Newgate in fiction nearly twenty years after he had set foot in the place, in the voice of Moll Flanders:

> 'tis impossible to describe the terror of my mind, when I was first brought in, and when I look'd round upon all the horrors of that dismal Place: I looked on myself as lost and that I had nothing to think of, but of going out of the World, and that with the utmost Infamy: the hellish Noise, the Roaring, Swearing and Clamour, the Stench and Nastiness, and all the dreadful croud of Afflicting things that I saw there; joyn'd together to make the Place seem an Emblem of Hell itself, and a kind of Entrance into it.[37]

Newgate had no reception ward. When Defoe entered this earthly hell, he did so through the lodge at the southern end of the building. It was here, or in the rooms directly abutting it, that prisoners were placed in iron fetters. Keepers had wide discretion over the use of restraints, the weight of them, and whether handcuffs would be needed as well. A political prisoner describes the way turnkeys would jangle the various manacles in a macabre dance designed to extort the newly arrived into buying them and the wardsmen – prisoners who assisted the staff – the wine, beer, brandy and tobacco on offer in the prison taphouse, a makeshift bar where crooks and warders, felons, debtors, murderers and petty thieves mingled. In this account the prisoner is met at the lodge by a 'parcel of ill looking fellows', who eyed him 'as if they would look me through, and examined every part of me from head to toe, not as tailors to take measure of me but as footpads [highwaymen who rob on foot] that survey the goodness of the clothes first, before they grow intimate with the linings'.[38]

The fleecing began as soon as one entered Newgate. Two and sixpence had to be paid on arrival. Those who could not pay were placed in the condemned hold, the rank dungeon just below the gates, where men and women sentenced to death awaited execution. To Colonel John Turner, who was executed in 1662, the hold was worse than death. The condemned had nowhere to rest. Without bench, bed or stool they 'lie like swine upon the ground, one upon another, howling and roaring'.[39] For those, like Defoe, who could afford it, the entrance fee was merely the deposit for a costly incarceration.

Defoe managed to find lodging in the Press Yard, the most comfortable and thus most expensive area of the prison. He paid twenty guineas for the pleasure. His rent was a further twelve shillings a week. The yard was paved in Purbeck stone and, though dank and cramped, it was more open than the rest of the gaol.[40] There was room for two or three people to walk side by side through the yard. Sleeping quarters were considerably tighter. Some chambers had three or four beds and when at capacity each bed homed two or three prisoners. The beds themselves were made of boards with hardly enough feathers or stuffing to warrant the name.[41] Defoe had to pay for access to the bed and for the harsh sheets thrown over it. The Press Yard was not overpopulated during his imprisonment. There were only three other men in his room: a murderer, a felon whose crime was not recorded, and a French spy.[42]

To keep his mind in line Defoe continued to write, working on his epic poem *Jure Divino*, in which he tore down the divine right of kings and defended the original sovereignty and constitutional force of the people. When he turned his gaze away from his work he would have seen a dirty stone chamber, with scraps of scripture daubed all over the walls. The passage from the Book of Job that begins 'Man is born to trouble as the sparks fly upwards' was a predictably popular choice. Defoe had committed much of the Bible to memory. He copied out the Pentateuch in shorthand during the panic of the Popish Plot, fearing that a return to Catholicism might lead to the confiscation of personal bibles. He did not need the patchwork piety of the walls. When he looked up, he could see beyond them to the dappled light that cast through the uneven windows of his cell, its stream broken and warped by bars that one inmate described as 'thick as a man's wrist'.[43]

In Newgate, Defoe was subject to a more concerted surveillance than most other inmates. Nottingham tasked the keeper with monitoring all of Defoe's visitors. Back at Whitehall, he continued to examine the papers he had seized from the writer. In the end, though, the Secretary relented and Defoe was released on the punitively high bail of £1,500. He paid a third himself. His brother-in-law Robert Davis arranged for the rest. Defoe was released on 5 June 1703, a fortnight after his capture, on the proviso that he return to stand trial at the Old Bailey, that sat just off the southern door of the prison.

†

Out on bail, Defoe found little relief. The danger that lay before him was in his view 'as terrifying as possible'. Those he asked for advice counselled him to save himself. Even some of the friends who had helped pay his bail advised him to run, knowing full well that they would lose their money as a result. As Defoe tells it, the good character of his friends and his own reputation 'outvoted fear ... and obliged me to bear the utmost indignities, rather than quit the cause I had undertaken'.[44] Defoe had good reason to fear. The charge against him was brutal in its wording. It alleged that he was 'a seditious man' with 'a disordered mind', 'a person of bad name, reputation and conversation', who had, 'by a disgraceful felony perfidiously, mischievously and seditiously', contrived to cause 'discord between ... the Queen' and her 'subjects'. The piled-on adverbs sound clumsy to modern ears. These words did, however, serve a legal purpose in that they conveyed his intent in the most strenuous of possible terms. The charge was that Defoe knowingly set out to sow dissension in an attempt to sever the bond between sovereign and subjects. Recorded at the Old Bailey, Defoe was also accused of turning subjects against each other by causing fear amongst religious Dissenters and inciting the greater part of the population – who belonged to the Anglican Church – to attack their Dissenting brethren. It is only if you ignore the ironies of *The Shortest Way* that these charges have any merit. So too the final allegation that Defoe attempted to 'prevent the union of the ... Kingdoms of England and Scotland' – a cause he in fact supported wholeheartedly.[45] The inflated charges reveal more about the contemporary anxiety surrounding England's religious settlement and relationship with Presbyterian Scotland than they do the documented effects of Defoe's writing.

But this is what Defoe was up against. In the early eighteenth century, the law of evidence was lax. The adversarial court system was more combative as a result. Trials were not so much a contest between two theories of the case as a direct confrontation during which the prosecution came at the defendant with an accusation and battered them with whatever evidence came to hand. The court was open to members of the public, who paid a shilling on entrance. Barristers shouted over the crowd. The defence had to fend off accusations amidst the fray and before a judge and jury whose attention was at once compressed – to a proceeding that lasted thirty minutes on average – and stretched, because judges and juries heard a batch of up to six cases a sitting.

William Colepepper volunteered to defend Defoe pro bono. Colepepper was a capable advocate but symbolically a bad choice. He had been one of the Kentish men who petitioned parliament two years earlier. Representing Kent, the county closest to France, and fearing that they would suffer the brunt of any French invasion, the petitioners implored the Speaker – Robert Harley – to allow the King to assemble and maintain a standing army in peace time. Legally, this right was restricted to parliament. To the parliament sitting in 1701, the petition was not simply monarchical overreach but a direct challenge to the constitutional mechanics that kept both the King and the people in check. The petition embarrassed Harley. For Defoe, it was a cause célèbre. When the Kentish men were arrested for sedition, Defoe became their most prominent champion. Surrounded by sixteen citizens, he presented Harley with *Legion's Memorial*, a pamphlet that demanded the release of the Kentish men, promoted the sovereignty of the people and defended their right to intervene in public affairs. 'Our name is Legion and We are Many': in repurposing a verse from the Gospel of Mark, the final line made clear the reach of public opinion and the writer's ability to wield it.[46]

The fact that Colepepper now defended him gave Defoe a pleasing sense of symmetry. Defoe had helped Colepepper escape the charge of sedition in the public mind, and he hoped that Colepepper could return the favour in court. Colepepper was more of a realist. He understood the difference in circumstances between the two events. The affair of the Kentish Petition aroused public support and had the added benefit of speaking to the values of the Whigs in parliament. Defoe had no such allies. There was no party thumbing the scales of justice on his behalf. Working with Colepepper might have given Defoe the gust of earlier victories. The trade-off, though, was that his choice of advocate could not help but confirm his public image as a rabble-rouser. Aware of Defoe's reputation and of what this might do at trial, and assured by the prosecution that they would look favourably if Defoe plead guilty, Colepepper persuaded the writer not to contest the charges. In cases of seditious libel all the jury had to do to determine guilt was prove authorship. Nottingham had already established this in Defoe's case thanks to the testimony of Croome and Bellamy, the printer and propaganda agent. Colepepper's counsel was sound, albeit overly trusting of the prosecution: Defoe's safest course of action was to show remorse and hope for mercy from the six judges who sat that session.

The penalties for seditious libel ranged so widely that the discretion of the judges had the potential to change the course of Defoe's life. Some offenders got away with a small fine. Though rare, there was technically nothing to stop the judges from sentencing a writer to public execution. Nor was there a clear guide as to how they might rule.

Whatever bravery or defiance was left in Defoe, whatever hope for clemency, was sapped when on 7 July he entered Justice Hall in the Old Bailey and faced the bench. The recorder that session – who managed the trial and issued the sentence – was Sir Salathiel Lovell. He was eighty-four when Defoe came before him. He would act as a judge for another ten years, clinging to life, as one historian put it, 'to sentence a man to death'.[47] Lovell was harsh and erratic. He forgot things. He meandered. His breathy sentences, as Defoe noted, could 'kill or save', and he tended to favour the former. Lovell was no fan of Defoe's, either. In a sweeping satiric poem published the previous year, Defoe accused the judge of serving those who 'pay him well'. In Defoe's characterisation, Lovell 'never hangs the Rich, nor saves the Poor'. Defoe made it known that Lovell profited from sin, protecting the more organised and sophisticated criminal enterprises as a means of income and condemning men and women who robbed for subsistence.[48] In more ways than one, then, Defoe was hit at trial by a ricochet from his own writing. He had tried to reform the system by pointing out the faults of its players. Now he was in their hands, forced to beg the mercy of men whom he did not respect, and to publicly disavow the intent of the piece of writing while he kept his private faith in the reforming impulse behind its composition.

Defoe's future and the survival of his growing family were at stake, and yet he could not entirely suppress the sharpness of his wit. To modern readers he looks like a man who thrilled to danger, who thought short-term and was unwilling to let a good line go, even if it put his freedom at risk. In reality, Defoe thought that his skill was bestowed by God: the speed at which ideas came to him; the truth which he felt lay behind his lines of attack confirmed in him a divine gift. As in the Parable of the Talents, he had to put that gift to good use, to invest it well for the good of society. To bury it would have been a sin.

Defoe fared little better with the other judges. Sir John Fleet and Sir Edward Ward had been governors of the Old East India Company, which Defoe had attacked loudly and publicly for the corrupting effects its massive wealth had on government. The writer had criticised Sir Thomas Abney, a fellow Dissenter, for his occasional conformity. Perhaps even greater than the animus from the bench was that which Defoe and Colepepper found in the opposing counsel. Sir Simon Harcourt, the Solicitor-General, chose to prosecute the case personally. Defoe had earlier depicted him as a ruthless bigot, a man whose core evil came because he rejected the divinity of Christ. By Defoe's reckoning, Harcourt was a conniving bully who relied less on his talent as an orator than on his ruthlessness. He won his convictions by badgering the accused. Harcourt was no doubt offended by these ad hominem attacks. The prosecutor also viewed *Legion's Memorial* as a personal slight against his politics and, as a result, took lip-smacking relish in the chance to punish its author. His contempt for Defoe seeped through his forensic examination of *The Shortest Way*, which he delighted in taking apart piece by piece, highlighting each moment Defoe's writing posed a danger to the government, each rhetorical flourish that, he argued, showed the author unabashed in his sedition.

It is no surprise then that Defoe's sentence was harsh. The short trial ended with him condemned to stand in the pillory three times. In addition, he had to pay a fine of 200 marks (about £133 in Defoe's day; just over £14,000 today), and he was to remain in custody until such time as he could find sureties that would guarantee his good behaviour for seven years. As the court adjourned, Defoe faced not only the prospect of repeated public humiliation, but the purgatory of an indefinite stay in Newgate.

†

Defoe's faith was providentialist. Setbacks showed the hidden hand of God. The task of the faithful was to find reason for why one was tested, and a way to overcome it. Defoe's time in the pillory was set to begin on 19 July. He had just under two weeks to avoid this fate. The pillory was an instrument of state censure: a writer's head and hands were secured between two wooden beams, which physically held the offender up, displaying them alongside the seditious work, which was nailed above its author's head. While the pillory held the writer in back-bending display, its ritual form of justice was usually left to the crowd below, who pelted dirt, rotten produce and, depending on their caprice and the nature of the offence, rocks and stones. There were reports of pilloried men being beaten. In other cases, the pilloried collapsed under the weight of hurled debris. Men fell from the stool on which they were forced to stand. Bones were shattered and skulls fractured.[49] The mob did not just take an eye for an eye but at a whim could take the legs, heads, torso and dignity of the writer. The reputational damage alone was enough to make Defoe abhor the prospect.

With the pillory looming, Defoe set to writing, taking his mind off the cold stone comforts of his cell by turning it to poems and pamphlets written in self-defence and to letters sent out to Dissenting ministers and advocates for religious nonconformity: people he thought could reconcile him with his community and potentially help his case. In concert with Colepepper, Defoe sketched out his legal strategy. The first step was to approach Nottingham with a petition for the Queen. It was a last ditch move and unlikely to work, given the Queen's hostility to the writer and support for harsher licensing and censorship laws. As it turned out, winning the monarch's favour was a moot point. Waiting at Windsor, Colepepper encountered a party of naval officers. He asked one of them about the controversial admiral Sir George Rooke, which the officers took as a slight. A fight broke out between Colepepper and Sir Jacob Banks, a staunchly Tory officer. Banks beat Colepepper, a man he viewed as an upstart Whig. Colepepper was ejected from the palace. The 'Accident', as Colepepper sheepishly referred to it, further soured Nottingham against Defoe. From that point on, the Secretary did not show the writer or his attorney the barest modicum of 'civility' or 'good-will'.[50]

Defoe wrote to William Penn, the founder of the Pennsylvania colony, in the hope of finding support. He offered his thanks in terms that reveal his desperation. Before Penn had agreed to intervene, Defoe calls him his 'saviour' and praises him for being 'a friend' to a virtual 'stranger', an 'unknown captive', as Defoe styles himself. While the two men did not know each other personally, Defoe's was the kind of case Penn took up: at stake in Defoe's punishment were Penn's own deeply held commitments to liberty of conscience and freedom of the press. The letter suggests that Penn interacted with Defoe through his eldest son William Penn Jnr. It was not unusual for Penn and his son to visit prisons and minister to inmates. As a Quaker and as one who had been imprisoned for his beliefs, Penn Sen. was a committed advocate of penal reform. Invoking Penn as a 'friend' in the same idiom with which he referred to his own Presbyterian brethren, and the term by which Quakers addressed one another, Defoe implies an affinity in their confessional affiliation. He hitches his case to Penn's activist cause. Penn was a useful ally to have. He was on good terms with the Queen, Godolphin, Harley and Nottingham; there is some evidence to suggest that Godolphin made use of Penn's charitable openness to society's underbelly by deploying him as a go-between, 'carrying messages to people' the Treasurer 'did not think proper to converse with himself'.[51]

Defoe repeated what he had told Nottingham and what he had told the Privy Council who examined him before and after his trial: that he had no accomplices and no backers, no information that might discredit the Whig ministers, nor about their diplomatic work during the last King's reign. In short, he remained unwilling to disclose anything that might confirm Nottingham's belief that his political opponents were behind the pamphlet and had deployed a global infrastructure of publishing and distribution to ensure it did maximum damage. Penn was keen to find a way to lessen Defoe's punishment and willing to 'beg' that his 'disgrace be deferred if not pardoned' entirely.[52] In this pursuit Penn presented Defoe as more willing to compromise than he was in fact. On 16 July, three days before Defoe was due to stand in the pillory, Penn met with Godolphin. In Godolphin's account of the meeting, which he sent to Nottingham, Penn made it known that 'Defoe was ready to make an oath to your Lordship [Nottingham] of all that he knew, and to give an account of all his accomplices in whatsoever he has been concerned'. His only proviso was that 'he may [be] excused from the punishment of the pillory' and not called as evidence against any of his alleged conspirators.[53] Defoe's desire to avoid the pillory informed Penn's sympathetic presentation of his case, which, in turn, shaped Godolphin's notion that Defoe was finally willing to confess. When this broken line of communication reached Nottingham, the Secretary thought his persistence had at last paid off. He deferred Defoe's sentence and arranged for the writer to be taken to Windsor for what he hoped would be a final interrogation. His confidence in the result can be discerned from the fact that he invited Godolphin and the Queen to attend. This added a further administrative burden, for he had to secure a writ of habeas corpus to bring Defoe to Windsor. Removing the prisoner from London would otherwise have voided his sentence.[54]

Both the prisoner and his interrogator entered Windsor Castle confident in their powers of persuasion. Defoe thought he could in some way convince all assembled that he had meant no offence; that he was simply a man who let a parody run too far and too free. Defoe placed ultimate trust in his ability to talk his way out of the pillory. Nottingham, on the other hand, came to the examination firm in his belief that the weight of the impending punishment, freighted on Defoe's consciousness by the majesty of the surroundings, would push him to a full confession. Both men left the interview disappointed. The Queen thought that what Defoe did disclose amounted to 'nothing'.[55]

Embarrassed by his failure and driven now more than ever by a desire to recoup the efforts he had expended in chasing the wily satirist, Nottingham took one final run. On the morning of 23 July, a few hours before Defoe was due to be escorted to the Royal Exchange in Cornhill for the first of three days of public shame, Nottingham asked the Keeper of Newgate to keep the prisoner back. He and John Sheffield, Duke of Buckingham and Lord Privy Seal, would do what was close to unthinkable for men of their status and position. They would venture to Newgate itself. With 'promises of reward', the two courtiers proceeded to coax Defoe into a confession. By venturing to Newgate, they only confirmed Defoe's sense of his own exceptionalism. As he would later recount, the two 'took such a low step as to go to . . . the dungeon where they had put him, to see if they could tempt him to betray his friends'. The writer would not reproach the late King or his Whig ministers. What he knew of their diplomacy, of the radical underground, of the secret veins of satire and propaganda that coursed through the city he kept to himself. Two years later, he boasted that what they sought 'remains a secret to this day'.[56] The back and forth was finally over. Nottingham gave up and Defoe's sentence had to be executed.

⸸

That summer it rained. When Defoe was led on 29 July, shortly after noon, up to the wooden platform, he was damp – his sweat reaching outwards as the rain came in. The pillory stood at the Royal Exchange in Cornhill, London's financial centre, not far from Defoe's house in Freeman's Yard. This was his neighbourhood. It was where he had grown up and where he and Mary had settled nineteen years earlier, the place they had raised their children. The choice of location was designed to shame. Amidst the crowd below, some of whom had gathered for hours in anticipation of the spectacle, were people who knew him: people he had lived amongst and worked with for two decades.

Defoe stood on a stool while his hands and neck were enclosed in a rigid wooden frame that pulled his shoulders outwards. He had to remain still for fear of falling. If the stool slipped, he would be left dangling. The position defied his natural reflexes. He could not raise his hands to shield his face against the dirt that flew from the crowd. He could not wipe the sweat or brush the rain from his eyes. He had to stand vulnerable for an hour and take whatever came.

For a great number of people who were pilloried, the experience remained the defining feature of their lives. Defoe knew this. When it was clear that he would not be spared, he set about completing *A Hymn to the Pillory*, a poem that he hoped might stave off the damage to his reputation. Published on his first day in the pillory, it was distributed to the gathering crowd at the Royal Exchange, just as it was the following two days when the pillory was moved to the Cheapside Conduit and Temple Bar. The poem is catchy. It was composed quickly. The author steels himself, assuring all that the pillory will not mark him. Speaking to the lifeless wooden frame, he takes strength from his belief that 'Men that are men, in thee can feel no Pain'. Staring down 'The undistinguish'd Fury of the Street', he must have gone over the lines in his head, mouthing them in mantric repetition as he waited, exposed. As the couplets move and shift, first to accommodate and then offset his fear, he turns away from the threat of physical pain to the stark symbolism of this cold machine of law. It is no crime to be pilloried. Many are led there unjustly and so, the poet cries, the pillory should not stain the man who stands within it. Stretching from couplet to triplet, he makes his case:

> Thou art no shame to Truth and Honesty,
> Nor is the Character of such defac'd by thee,
> Who Suffer by Oppressive Injury

The man who faces the fury of the crowd is no criminal. He is there only because 'he was not understood'. It cannot harm his character, and yet that is precisely what the pillory intends to do. With his fear sublimated to the righteousness of his cause, the poet turns to the wooden frame and attacks it once more in an attempt to blunt its significance. The 'terrors' of the pillory's '*Grisly Face*' force men to turn 'Rogues to shun Disgrace'. Far from punishing crime and upholding honesty, the pillory creates crime and punishes honesty. Freed from shame, the poet can at last plead his case: he was 'too bold', 'And told those Truths, which shou'd not ha' been told'.[57] The image Defoe projected was that throughout his ordeal he stood silent, stoic, unwilling to let the effects of the punishment register. Through his hymn he preached, asking those who stood reading below to repeat the words that ran through his head, to speak the truth that this man was punished because he refused to give up his friends. When Defoe was taken down in the early hours of the afternoon, the feeling coming back to his neck and arms, he knew the poem had worked. He had not suffered any of the physical injuries he feared. The crowd, it turned out, had been largely sympathetic.

The location for Defoe's second day in the pillory was the Cheapside Conduit. Formerly a water source, it was now one of London's widest thoroughfares. Well paved, with neat rows of well-apportioned shops on each side, it was a place for the well-to-do. Its grand concourse was part of the parade ground that brought each new Mayor of London to his offices in Westminster. Like the Royal Exchange, the Conduit was chosen for maximal exposure. And like Defoe's experiences in the pillory the day before, the crowd was largely kept in check by the murmured hymn, passed from person to person, the literate reading for those who could not. Again, Defoe was taken off the wooden scaffold with few injuries. The story that became part of Defoe's legend sometime during the nineteenth century is that the crowd that day threw flowers instead of dirt. While

2. Defoe in the pillory, from a set of playing cards. Earliest known image of the writer.

there is nothing to substantiate it, the currency this story gained indicates the successful publicity campaign that Defoe waged in an effort to lessen the physical and social damage of the pillory.

As July ended, Defoe ascended the pillory's raised platform a third and final time. The location this time was Temple Bar, the historic entrance point for the city of London on the western side of Fleet Street, home to the heaving engine of the city's printers. Rising behind the platform were statues of Queen Elizabeth and her successor, King

James I, son of Mary, Queen of Scots and the first King of both England and Scotland. Again, the people crowded below were not violent. They may have been held back by the plaintive *Hymn*. Or perhaps groups of city Whigs and Dissenters pressured them into submission, as some of Defoe's detractors maintained. If this was the case, then these so-called allies must have gotten over the hurt of *The Shortest Way* more quickly than most assume.[58]

Things had gone far better than expected. The movement of the pillory was intended to cast the arc of Defoe's disgrace across the city. And yet he managed to draw sympathy from Londoners of all walks. Still, on that final day, Defoe was exhausted. The sheer exertion of standing as a prop, the cycles of adrenaline and relief, that had invigorated then drained him, had all taken their toll.

If the rain had broken as he was led down the platform, he would have glimpsed Whitehall, where Nottingham busily turned to other matters, washing his hands of the whole affair as he tried to save his career from the embarrassment it had caused. Wherever Defoe's mind might have wandered when on high, it was brought back down as the carriage took him to Newgate. There was now no clear sign of how or when he would be released.

CHAPTER 2

THE SOUTH

When in London, Robert Harley lived and worked at 14 Buckingham Street. His residence, a smart four storeys set above a basement, was part of the York Buildings. This series of mansion houses stood between the Thames and the Strand: the main way from the city to the Palace of Westminster. As previous occupant Samuel Pepys had found it, number fourteen proved ideally situated as a hub of administration and sociability – a place for Harley to keep his papers and to meet the people who sustained him and gave his politics its personal edge.

Harley was accustomed to the westward arc of the Strand. But from his house in the opposite direction to Westminster, only a mile or so down the road, was Temple Bar, where Defoe had spent his third and final day in the pillory. Even if Harley had not witnessed the event himself, news certainly reached him of how the writer managed to command the respect of the mob. Harley had kept watch over Defoe from the time he was discovered as the author of *The Shortest Way.* He was present in the Commons when the pamphlet was condemned and would have seen the smoke from New Palace Yard when it was burned the following day.[1] It was Harley who set in play the events leading to Defoe's arrest. Apprised of the interrogation at each stage, he was impressed by Defoe's capacity to withstand Nottingham's onslaught. The writer proved far more discreet than he initially assumed.

3. Mezzotint of Robert Harley, after Sir Godfrey Kneller (1714).

In Harley's rooms, amidst the reams of paper – the letters coming in and going out that his secretaries passed to him for oversight – was the letter Defoe sent via Paterson. The letter in which Defoe promised to serve the Queen with his capable pen. Like Paterson before him, Harley kept its contents to himself, waiting, it seems, for a politic moment to respond.

⸸

Harley's most frequent visitor was Godolphin. The two would meet as often as twice a week, in Harley's house, Godolphin's, or in the rooms towards the rear of the Cockpit set aside for the Treasury. The second of these visits was usually on a Sunday, either before or just after the formal cabinet meetings.[2] During these visits the presence of Marlborough – the other member of the triumvirate – was felt through his frequent letters. As diligent as Marlborough was, his direct line was interrupted by the accepted frustrations of correspondence across the Channel. A 'contrary' wind could hold back letters to Godolphin so that, after days with none, three might arrive at once. Even if the weather was fine, Marlborough still worried about privateers taking the letter-carrying boats. There were any number of more mundane ways a letter could be lost as it passed between the hands that carried and delivered it. Waiting, one could never be entirely sure if the silence was logistical or if something else stopped the exchange – a shift in temperament, an offence felt, a change in the terms of an alliance. Despite this unease, what writing gave him, especially in letters to Sarah and Godolphin, was an imperfect connection to the kind of society denied him at foreign courts and as the head of a command. His letters to them have a rare sense of emotional ease as a result. There is no shame when Marlborough tells his friend, 'I long extremely to be with you'; no reticence when with the same openness he tells his wife, 'I doe love and estime [esteem] you with all my hart and soull.'

The General was probably more at ease during the winters he spent with Godolphin, when the two would chart England's course. As a French spy assessed, Marlborough was more open and affable than Godolphin but would not act without first taking his friend's advice.[3] The two started including Harley in this work from around 1700, soliciting his opinion on diplomacy and public finance, as well as seeking and deploying his expertise on the management of parliament.[4] Harley was the new man. His talent and mind were of use to the duumvirs, but that did not shake his sense that he could never be fully embraced by an alliance formed more by deep personal ties than political sympathy. Godolphin's friendship with Marlborough had weathered the death of Godolphin's wife Margaret in childbirth. It continued even as the two took opposing sides during the Revolution of 1688 and after, when, in another reversal, Godolphin served William III on the Treasury commission and Marlborough was dismissed as head of the King's army. Like Godolphin, Marlborough had married for love, not status. This gave them a shared outlook on family that became shared in a more complete sense with the birth of Willgo, beloved son of Godolphin's only child Francis and his wife Henrietta, the Marlboroughs' eldest daughter.

Godolphin and Marlborough measured themselves in friendship, with each man gauging a sense of his purpose and virtue by its reflection in the purpose and virtue of the other. Godolphin never remarried. Both he and Marlborough had lodgings at Whitehall; and because Godolphin spent significant time with Sarah when Marlborough was on campaign, there were rumours that the two were having an affair. The truth was considerably more complex. As Sarah put it soon after Godolphin's funeral, 'hee was certainly the truest friend to me & all my family that ever was'.[5] Sarah's love for Godolphin was in part an extension of her love for Marlborough. The independent friendship she pursued with Godolphin became a way to direct her marriage towards the equal level she felt was its truest form – when Sarah, an ardent Whig, far more radical in her politics than her husband or his friend, was treated by both as a confidant and strategist. Behind this ideal was her wish (often fulfilled) that the two men would respect her clear-cut political mind for its own sake and not limit her value to her relationship with the Queen. It was Sarah's longstanding friendship with Queen Anne that had brought Marlborough and Godolphin into the closest circles at Court in the first place.

The Duchess and Duke turned to Godolphin, to each other and to the Queen in 1703, when their only surviving son John contracted smallpox. Sarah journeyed to Cambridge, where the seventeen-year-old was studying. Godolphin arranged for the Queen's personal physician to attend. Marlborough himself remained away at first, but reports from the doctor and his wife left him with a sense of 'uneasynesse' so difficult to bear that the thought of John's illness continuing made him question his own ability to 'live' through it. He arrived at the university town just in time to be with Sarah and to watch their son die. The loss for both parents was immense. Withdrawing from view of the city and the Court to mourn, they returned to Holywell House, their summer residence on the outskirts of St Albans. Marlborough's mourning period was cut short, though, by a duty his wife hoped he had put behind him. He embarked to the Continent for the next

4. Engraving of Sidney, Earl of Godolphin, after Sir Godfrey Kneller (1738–42).

campaign a few short weeks after John's death. Abroad, he took the only comfort he could from the 'dear letters' of his wife. After reading two that arrived together, he returned: 'you are dearer to mee ten thousand tims then ever you were. I am so intierly yours, that if I might have all the world given mee, I could not be happy but by your love.' Behind this effusiveness is his guilt for having left her for the world so soon after John's death. His declaration of love countenances the disfiguring effects of grief: he draws himself to Sarah in the hope that their shared loss would bind them closer and not rend them apart.

Godolphin lent emotional as well as practical support throughout, telling Sarah, 'The best use, of one's best friends, is to assist and support one another under the most grievous afflictions.'[6] He knew of what he spoke. After his wife Margaret died, Godolphin suppressed his grief, worried it would paralyse him. Margaret had encouraged him to leave his position at Court in order to seek a more religious life. After her death, his work was all that kept him. Even Margaret's closest friend, the diarist John Evelyn, conceded that Godolphin needed public business, without which he worried Godolphin might 'intirely resigne himselfe to Thoughts which will certainly consume him'.[7] Like Marlborough's return to the Continent, despite Sarah's desire for him to retire, Godolphin's return to Court was conflicted. The work maintained him, yet the guilt gnawed. For both men, their alliance in the pursuit of government had a psychic, even a sacred, dimension – at once animated by, but in excess of, their personal ambitions.

Harley could not retrospectively create the kind of history that sustained the connections of his senior allies – not that he didn't try. In an unusually vulnerable letter, he chooses his words carefully, blackening out those that do not quite fit and rearranging things to show Godolphin that the letter opens his very 'soul'. He confesses that his debts to Marlborough are not simply those that all England owed for the General's 'valour', but included 'private favours' held in such esteem that Harley would pass them as an 'heirloom' to his children. Godolphin's friendship, he tells the Treasurer, 'united my very soul to you that I cannot allow a thought disagreeable to you'.[8] The prose is cloying. Its writer is all too aware of his status at the edge of the alliance, all too conscious that his favour with the Queen derived from the regard Godolphin and Marlborough showed him.

The advantage to Harley's distance was that it gave him the means to understand how the alliance was perceived from without. Unlike Marlborough, who tried to shield himself from public criticism, and Godolphin, whose engagement with the wider public was limited to his Thursday levee, where attendees came specifically to gain his support, from the time he first assumed the Speakership, Harley received intelligence on how the public viewed him.[9]

Authority flowed from the Queen through her chief ministers. To many, the balance of power in Europe seemed to lie firmly in Marlborough's hands. Ambassadors and foreign agents correctly perceived, though, that the day-to-day management of foreign policy lay as much with Godolphin and Harley as it did the General. In non-military matters, even more so. With this perception came tranches of correspondence. In the first years of Anne's reign the question of Scotland took up much of it.

†

There had been many attempts to unite England and Scotland over the centuries: Edward I of England tried it by force; Henry VIII offered a treaty and a marriage between his son (the eventual Edward VI) and Mary, Queen of Scots – though neither came to pass. The prevailing spirit, in Defoe's words, had no precedent or comparison: 'Never' were there 'two Nations that had so much Affinity in Circumstances', that 'have had such Inveteracy and Aversion to one another in their Blood'. If only they had united, England would not have suffered defeat at Bannockburn, Scotland would have been spared the bloodshed of Flodden and Pinkie. Defoe's speculation glosses over the very real outrages that marked these battles. He could not help wondering how history might have unfolded if Scotland's 'Treasure of men', who fought for foreign princes as mercenaries, had combined with England's naval power. One key instance suggests all: if the Scottish soldiers who fought for the Dauphin when he faced Henry VI's forces had instead fought for England, England would possess Lancastrian France.[10]

The aversion between the nations continued even as England and Scotland came to share a monarch in 1603, when the Scottish King James VI, son of Mary, Queen of Scots, acceded to the throne after the death of his cousin Elizabeth I. Far from elevating Scotland, the union of the crowns had the effect of subordinating the Scottish parliament. As Defoe put it, they were now under the 'Manageement of the *English* Court' in the 'Political Sense', though not the legal one. From that point on, the Scottish parliament had to seek royal assent from the monarch in London. Overseas diplomacy was determined in London; and Scotland's place in the world was now controlled by their powerful neighbour to the south. It was by Defoe's assessment a state of 'Subjection without the Advantages'.[11]

James VI of Scotland, now James I of England, envisioned a united parliament but never achieved one. The binding force of the union during his reign and after was primarily dynastic. In 1638, with James' son Charles I on the throne, an agreement signed by the people of Scotland came to public notice. Designed to resist Charles' imposition of an Anglican liturgy and prayer book, the Covenant made obedience to the monarch dependent on his upholding the true religion, which in Scotland meant Presbyterianism. Charles responded with military force. These were the Bishops' Wars, so called because their underlying cause was a deep-seated division in Church government between those who favoured presbyters elected by Church ministers and those who favoured Episcopacy, a government by bishops, who were typically appointed by the monarch. The Presbyterian Covenanters triumphed, confirming their definition of polity, liturgy and government. The Scottish Covenanters successfully rebuffed the will of the monarch. The Bishops' Wars thus set off the Civil Wars, the series of conflicts that saw the execution of Charles I and the emergence of the Commonwealth.

Under Cromwell, the Scottish parliament was dissolved, and though a select few Scottish members did decamp to Westminster, their power was limited. For the most part, Scotland was governed by English commissioners. Power shifted once again with the restoration of Charles II in 1660. While the Scottish parliament was restored, its members took an oath of allegiance that upheld royal supremacy, effectively disavowing the tenets of the Covenant, once again subordinating the position of Scotland's parliament and national Church to the monarch in England. During Charles II's reign, negotiators attempted to work out a union treaty. Their efforts ended without profit in 1670.

The nature of the regnal union shifted decisively with the Revolution of 1688–9. The justifications for removing the Catholic James II and replacing him with his Protestant daughter Mary and her husband William of Orange differed in the two kingdoms. The English Declaration of Right gave the impression that James had abdicated; the Scottish Claim of Right made it seem that his incursions upon the rights of his subjects meant that he essentially 'forefaulted' the Crown.[12] Scots generally supported the arrival of Mary and William. Paterson called it the 'happy accession'.[13] But for those who did not, the more fundamental assault on the hereditary monarchy contained in the Claim only fed a nostalgic yearning for the Stuarts, the line of Scottish kings that issued in James II, now in exile in France.

After the Revolution, England's ministers frequently interfered in Scottish affairs. The majority of Scots had little love for the English parliament, a body that suppressed Scotland's access to trade and impeded its colonial ambitions. In the face of such public disapproval, the regnal union proved too loose a compact to settle the state with any degree of comfort. The accession of the new monarchs papered over divisions within the Scottish Kirk. It also displaced the connection to the Scottish kings of old by one crucial degree. Across Scotland, and particularly in the Highland clans, there remained a sizeable body of those who stayed loyal to the King in exile and took the epithet Jacobite from his Latin name. In the end the union of crowns could no longer counteract the entrenched belligerence that had worn in its groove by centuries of English armies marching north and Scottish armies south.

William III was driven less by an innate desire to unite Britain than the earlier Stuarts had been. He did not visit Scotland during his reign, a reflection of his tendency to push Scottish matters aside. By 1701, he was forced out of this passivity by the campaign to secure compensation for the loss of Darien, and by Tory attempts to stoke opposition in Scotland as a way of hampering his Whig allies in England. The remedy the King proposed by way of proclamation was a 'firm and entire union' with a single, united parliament. Paterson took personal encouragement from the proclamation, believing, falsely, that he had swayed the King's opinion. Because the proclamation turned out to be William's last, it ended up as a bequest, giving verbal form to the situation that Anne and her ministers inherited. The desire for union it expressed showed just how much England's security and the maintenance of a Protestant line of succession rested on making Scotland more governable.

To Godolphin and Harley, finding a way to exert tighter control over Scottish politics from Westminster was both an immediate concern and one that required a longer-term solution. With an eye to the latter, the English and Scottish parliaments agreed to appoint commissioners to negotiate the terms of a potential parliamentary union. On the Scottish side the commissioners included nobles Argyll, Seafield, Tarbat and Stair, as well as the merchant and parliamentarian Sir Patrick Johnston. For England, the Archbishop of York, Earl of Carlisle, Earl of Scarborough, the Chief Justice Sir John Cook and Godolphin.[14] Harley was appointed too, but was largely uninvolved in the meetings.[15]

The Scottish commissioners were due to arrive at the Cockpit that November. In the meantime, though, the more urgent question was whether or not the Queen should dissolve the Scottish parliament and call for new elections. On this, Harley and Godolphin were divided. Godolphin was consistently more optimistic about Scotland than Harley. He was aware that the Whigs in parliament had stirred the anger of certain Scottish nobles for their own political gain. But, as he put it, he was 'not without hope that things will end quietly there'. Legally speaking, Scotland was due a general election. According to statute, the Scottish parliament had to meet twenty days after the King's death, and once convened should sit for no more than six months.

The parliament sitting when William died was the Convention first elected in 1689. They did not resume sitting till 9 June 1702, three months after his death. The Convention parliament was dominated by two main parties, looser in affiliation and discipline than their modern equivalents. The Court party that for the most part gave its support to the government was at this point led by James Douglas, 2nd Duke of Queensberry. The main opposition Country party was led by the rakish and impulsive James, 4th Duke of Hamilton. News quickly reached Godolphin that on the first day of the session Hamilton and seventy-four of his supporters resigned to protest the legality of the Convention.[16] The gesture was designed to bring about a new election. Queensberry resisted. As Lord High Commissioner, Queensberry was the Queen's personal representative. The Convention had voted through enough supply to maintain the armed forces and civil list in Scotland till 1704, and so in his view there was no immediate need to go to the polls. His abiding unease about the kind of parliament a general election might deliver outweighed any sense of legal obligation.

In public, Harley maintained that he had little interest in Scotland. So little, he would swear to the Commons, that 'he knew no more of Scottish business than of Jappan, and that he avoided even the conversation of those of that Country'. Few in Scotland believed this. There was already a sense amongst Scottish agents in London that Harley and his 'emissaries' were deeply 'imbroile[d]' in Scotland's affairs.[17] Harley held back because Godolphin took the lead on Scotland. Marlborough's interest was global. Unrest in Scotland had the potential to distract from his military goals, diverting funds and soldiers from his campaign in Europe. Without the security of a parliamentary union, Scotland also posed a threat as a possible landing point for a French invasion from the north.[18] Harley did not want to give the appearance that he was forcing himself into Godolphin's domain. Nor did he want to be publicly associated with the vexed issue of Scotland. Yet when he found a procedural answer to the question of the election, he had to present it.

Writing to Godolphin, Harley emphasised what the Treasurer undoubtedly knew: that he had informants in Scotland. Harley corresponded with William Carstares, former chaplain to King William III. Harley no doubt appreciated Carstares' evenness of temper and moderate views. Harley was not satisfied with only soliciting information that might confirm his beliefs. Amongst his letters to and from Scottish nobles, the Earls of Mar and Leven, are letters from Hamilton. When events in Scotland started to worry him, he began to solicit information about the situation on the street. By presenting his advice as drawn from across the political spectrum and authenticated by those on the ground, Harley managed to secure enough latitude to intervene or, at the very least, to have his opinion taken seriously.

The Scots, Harley assured Godolphin, welcomed the dissolution of the current parliament. But that did not mean that a new parliament should be called. Harley had the backing of precedent: 'it hath been usual in Scotland to dissolve Parliament and not appoint the meeting of another', he wrote. With the supply settled, there was no reason to rush. Wearing his knowledge of Scottish electoral procedure lightly, Harley laid out some temporising measures. Scottish election law required the election of county or shire representatives at Michaelmas, on 29 September. However, the burgh representatives need only be elected once the parliament had actually been called. The new assembly could come together in its three constitutive parts (nobility, shires and burghs), allowing Queensberry and Godolphin room to manoeuvre. As Harley put it, by proceeding in parts 'her Majestie will have an opportunity to see what Elections the countys make & so have it in her power either to call a Parliament if she like their choice, or defer it to another year when they must make another election'. Advancing slowly would, Harley argued, have the added benefit of assuring 'Her Majestie time to calme the minds of her subjects there'.[19] The fear of his Scottish emissaries, indistinguishable from Harley's own, was that Nottingham would persuade Queensberry and Godolphin that the election had to proceed immediately and all at once.

There were grounds for this fear. Nottingham remained convinced that a new election would deliver a Scottish parliament more sympathetic to his cause. His sources in Edinburgh sent troubling, though exaggerated, reports of how Presbyterian government threatened the very nature of monarchic rule.[20] He assumed that an election might return more Episcopalian members who could counter this threat. What tantalised him was the prospect that he might be able to establish an alliance between these members and the High Church Tories in England. In his mind, a new election was the first step towards a union of both Church and state. Godolphin was less persuaded by Nottingham's scheme than by the secession of Hamilton and his supporters. Without the Country party, the legality of the attenuated Scottish parliament was up for dispute. The Acts it had passed came under suspicion. Godolphin could not truck any challenge to supply, to the Act appointing the Union commissioners, nor to the Act that ratified the Queen's title and authority.[21]

The Scottish parliament was dissolved on 8 August 1702. The localised electoral process concluded in November. The new parliament that sat for the first time on 6 May 1703 upended the plans of both Nottingham and Godolphin, but not in a way that Harley could have predicted. The Country party lost ground. The Court did not really gain any. Instead, a third party emerged: the Cavaliers, whose base of support included Jacobites and the once dominant Episcopalians, who had lost power and postings with the re-establishment of Presbyterianism in the 1690s. At first, Queensberry was able to work with the Cavaliers to ratify the Queen's title. But the alliance crumbled when his ministry failed to enact legal toleration for Episcopalians. The Cavaliers moved towards the Country opposition, with Hamilton acting within this patchwork alliance to thwart Queensberry when whim, principle or external pressure moved him. This was the dynamic Queensberry would face for the next three years, as he tried to corral a parliament flush with new members, dispersed of customary lines of allegiance and without firm basis for broader consensus.[22]

At stake was the future of the regnal union. Queensberry needed the Scottish parliament to recognise the Act of Settlement (1701), which mandated that the Crown pass from Anne, whose last surviving child had died in 1700, to the heirs of Sophia, Electress of Hanover, the granddaughter of King James VI and I. Sophia was fifty-eighth in line to the British throne, but was shot up the order because she was a Protestant. The Act had passed the English parliament without the consultation of their Scottish counterpart.

Though recognition for the Act of Settlement was Queensberry's most pressing parliamentary need, it was not his only one. He needed statutory recognition that the supply passed for the civil list and army by the previous parliament was legal. He also needed to gain more funds for Marlborough's war against France. The failure of the negotiations in London meant that a constitutional union could no longer be counted on to satisfy these needs. The Scottish and English commissioners could not reach an agreement on taxes. The Scots, who had just emerged from a decade of famine, could not afford to impose the extensive English tax system. Nor could the commissioners come to any compromise on a religious settlement. The Scottish representatives did not want to see a return of Episcopal government at the expense of the Presbyterian Kirk. The future of Darien, crucial to Scotland's economic prospects and national confidence, and thus a central driver of the Scots to union, left the commission hopelessly deadlocked. They adjourned on 3 February 1703.

They were meant to resume that October, but never did. To one contemporary, the question of union represented 'one of the most problematical points in state affairs ever we had or almost could possibly have had under our consideration'.[23]

The impasse in London gave encouragement to the Country–Cavalier alliance in Edinburgh. Many Cavaliers held out hope for a second Stuart restoration and so resisted the Hanoverian succession. Members of the Country party turned the discussion of supply – of what they perceived as Scottish money for an English-aligned ministry – to Darien. In the hands of the alliance the failed colony and the settling of the succession became flash points for a wide-reaching debate on Scottish sovereignty. Access to trade, control over diplomacy and foreign policy, the legitimacy of the monarch: the concerns that Darien and the Hanoverian succession raised all reverted to the same fundamental question of Scotland's legislative and governmental independence.

⸸

By July Harley was eager to leave London. The opening session of Queen Anne's first parliament had drawn to a close on 27 February, soon after the collapse of the union negotiations. The summer weather was 'uncertain', Harley told his sister Abigail, settling on a word that reflected how clammy and closed in the city felt. The same unpredictable rain that had clogged the grass of St James' Park near Paterson's residence caused the Thames to spill into the 'rich meadows' by its banks as Harley's second wife Sarah prepared to decamp to the family estate at Brampton Bryan in Herefordshire. She would take Harley's three children: Abigail, Edward and Elizabeth, named for her mother, who died in 1691. Harley wanted to follow them as soon as possible. There was still business in London, though. He was agitated, he told his sister, by the state of affairs in Scotland, where 'they quarrel with one another, yet not one of them will venture to cure their wound'. The cure as Harley saw it lay in accepting the Act of Settlement. The Scottish MPs 'agree together against a protestant successor till he comes to buy it himself, but since they are for selling themselves I pray God they do it not for good and all'.[24] Their refusal was not in Harley's mind a principled stand but a cynical ploy, a negotiating position that revealed that some members could be bought. What worried Harley was that he and Godolphin might not be the only interested buyers.

Godolphin cultivated his own sources in Scotland. They tended to be people in power rather than their agents or clients. He wrote to Queensberry as a matter of course, but did so with a reserve coloured by his knowledge that the Queen never fully trusted the Scottish peer. Queensberry was a useful conduit to other Scottish politicians. When it appeared during this session of 1703 that Queensberry's grip on the Scottish parliament was loosening, Godolphin used their association to enter into a correspondence with James Ogilvy, Earl of Seafield. A Scottish Secretary of State and one of the Union commissioners, Seafield possessed the ingenuity of a second son born to a father deeply in debt. Having trained as an advocate he rose through the Scottish parliament by force of skill and capacity for compromise. He had opposed the removal of James II but served his replacement William III loyally. According to the reports of a Hanoverian spy, Seafield was 'very beautiful', 'graceful' in both his movements and behaviour. He was always 'smiling'. He spoke 'with a soft tongue' that gave the impression of 'Plainness and familiarity' belying, the spy thought, that he was not at all 'sincere'. Seafield's worth to Godolphin was that he understood 'perfectly well how to manage the *Scots Parliament*, to the advantage of the Court'.[25] He managed better than most to navigate the incestuous conflicts that arose between the powerful magnate families who controlled Scotland.

Godolphin's access to the Queen, the purse strings and the Lords meant that the Scottish nobility sought him out. From the start, Seafield acted as a broker, reporting to Godolphin and running the triumvirate's tactical plays in Edinburgh. In 1703, he drew Godolphin into contact with John Murray, Earl of Tullibardine, Privy Councillor and Lord Privy Seal. A 'proud fiery' man according to that same spy, when he spoke Murray tended to get choked with emotion – more so now, as he had just lost his father.[26] Seafield assured Godolphin that Murray would serve 'Her Majestie verie faithfullie' but urged the Treasurer to wait until Murray had buried his father before approaching him. When they did begin their correspondence, Murray was concerned that his patent of nobility, which would confirm him as the Duke of Atholl, not be delayed.[27] Queensberry had Godolphin's and the Queen's sanction to hold off granting patents as a way to bring difficult parliamentarians in line.[28] It was a fairly high-handed tactic, and one that would be used again in later negotiations. In this case, though, it only succeeded in embittering Murray towards Queensberry.

The soft power of personal favour was considerable and the soon to be Duke of Atholl sought advantage in the Treasurer's connections, not just to the Queen but to the Duke and Duchess of Marlborough. Atholl was proud of his military service. He had fought for King William where others in his family defended James II. He was proud too that his son was in camp with Marlborough, and in the letters he is less than subtle in trying to get Godolphin to see if the marriage of Mary, Marlborough's thirteen-year-old daughter, had been arranged. After the death of his son and before leaving for the Continent, Marlborough had drawn up a new will leaving £20,000 to Mary, provided she married with her mother's consent.[29] Atholl thought rather audaciously that his son would be a good match and sought Godolphin's 'assistance' as he did in 'my greatest concerns'.

The session of the Scottish parliament began with Atholl 'afraide our factions will not decrease'. Seafield feared the same. Ever the strategist, Harley thought there might be a way to draw the weakest faction out, convincing them that settling the succession would affirm their place and power.[30] The brokers in London and their allies in Edinburgh were reluctant to give the Scottish parliamentarians any more legislative time than was absolutely necessary. Godolphin made it known that he was even willing to compromise on settling the succession immediately, so long as 'an expedient might be fallen upon' that would exclude the Prince of Wales, the Catholic son of the late James II and VII, from the throne.[31]

Hopes in England for a quick, productive session of the Scottish parliament were quashed when Atholl sent news that efforts to preserve the gains of the Revolution of 1688 would be voted on 'terms' that 'may prove extremely inconvenient to [the] Queen'.[32] The Cavalier and Country opposition, rather than splitting as Harley hoped, united to put forth two acts, each expressing anger at incursions against

Scotland's independence. The first, An Act anent Peace and War, mandated that the monarch could not make peace or war without the consent of the Scottish parliament. It was hard to see the Act as anything but a rebuke against England for dragging Scotland into war with France. Godolphin's response was swift. He was at his house in Windsor when news of the Act reached him. After speaking with the Queen, he dispatched a letter to Seafield: the Queen would never allow Queensberry as Lord High Commissioner to consent to the Act. 'England is now in warr with France. If Scotland were in peace and consequently at liberty to trade with France, would not that immediately necessitate a warr betwixt England and Scotland also.'[33]

The second bill was more complex. Framed as an Act of Security, it claimed Scotland's right to determine the successor to the Scottish throne. Few observers in England missed the reactionary nature of the legislation. The Scottish opposition, angered that the Hanoverian succession was conferred without consulting Scotland, clawed back their right. The bill generated intense debate, requiring nineteen separate sittings, during which Atholl and some of the Queen's supporters attempted without success to vote down some of its more anti-English clauses.[34] The most dangerous of these was the one proposed on 16 July, specifying that Anne's successor in Scotland would not be the same as her successor in England unless Scotland was guaranteed certain rights – not least the independence of its Crown, the freedom of its parliament, the preservation of its religion and the liberty of its trade from English intrusion. A second clause stressed the economic point by asserting that there could be no shared monarch until Scotland was given unfettered access to English colonial trade.[35] Hamilton helped orchestrate these two acts in order to reduce the interference of the English ministry in Scottish affairs. But even the Court party, despite its ties with English ministry, pursued an economic agenda that set Scotland's finances against England's global interest. That session the Court supported the passage of the Wine Act, which legalised a trade in wine with France despite the English embargo. Scotland needed to reinvigorate trade and to generate customs revenue and was willing to defy the economic blockade England imposed as part of its strategy to win the war.

Godolphin was all too aware of the geopolitical ramifications of the 1703 acts, writing to Seafield:

> At another time, what should be done of this kind would perhaps concern Scotland itself alone. But wee are now in so criticall a conjuncture with respect to other nations, that all Europe must in some measure bee affected by the good or ill ending of the Parliament of Scotland.

He had hoped that England's power and global reach might convince the Scottish parliamentarians of 'the necessity of A speedy union between the two nations'. That this notion 'has soe little prevalency in the present Parliament of Scotland' worried him.[36] Each action Scotland took to disengage from England was not simply a problem in and of itself but a threat to England's force in Europe. The most decisive break came on 5 August when the Scottish parliament voted in favour of the Act of Security by a majority of fifty-nine.

⸸

Godolphin's fear that events in Scotland might change the course of the war in Europe sparked his first clandestine action soon after news of the Act's passage reached him. On 17 August, he recommended that Harley engage the secret services of Robert Cunningham, enclosing in a letter to the Speaker a bank bill of £100 'With which you may please to encourage him to apply his pains either to Scotland or to France, as you think it may be most probably for him to make any discoveries to the advantage of the Queen's service'.[37] Little is known about Robert Cunningham or where he was eventually sent.

It was common for English cabinet ministers and members of parliament to employ agents. Most had a few trustworthy people they relied on to monitor the press; men who could act as go-betweens or in some cases plenipotentiaries: who could report on the goings on at taverns and coffeehouses, or should the need arise infiltrate clubs and groups in London or in local electorates. Even Joseph Addison, who deplored political secrecy and warned those in power not to rely too heavily on any man 'who is capable of so infamous a Calling as that of Spy', conceded that spies and voluntary informers were 'absolutely necessary', giving

'The Eyes of a watchful Minister' the reach to 'run through the whole People'.[38] What is unusual in Harley's case is that with his growing but ad hoc networks in France and Scotland he began to amass significant responsibility for gathering foreign intelligence, a role that typically fell under the mandate of the two Secretaries of State.

Harley had obvious talent as spymaster. He had a capacious memory and relished in his mastery of detail. He possessed the kind of social fluency that warmed people to him in private, yet he was guarded in public, able simultaneously to seem open and to protect what he knew and thought.[39] Godolphin's trust in him was clear to all. Not long after Harley began to cultivate sources in Scotland, he received a note from Godolphin: the Lord Treasurer and the Queen had high hopes for 'The thread of intelligence' he was 'following'. The message he took was to continue assembling a network.

†

In prison, Defoe increasingly feared that he would become an 'Unknown Captive', adrift from his friends and allies, unable to help or take comfort from his family.[40] His brick and tile factory – the central means of support for Mary and their six children – teetered close to failure. And Mary was now pregnant with their seventh child. For Defoe, providing for his family was a moral imperative. He reserved a special kind of scorn for those unable to fulfil their paternal duties. In his final novel, *The Fortunate Mistress* (1724), the heroine marries a brewer, who squanders his inheritance and ruins his business, abandoning his young wife and their five children. It is hard not to read the bitter tinge of self-recrimination in Defoe's depiction of the man as a dangerous fool.

Defoe had clear cause for despair, but he was unwilling to abandon himself or his family to it. He would have sought to control his emotions using the techniques of Stoicism. In his later writings he was able to find clear links between this ancient philosophy and his Presbyterianism. He found in both a form of disciplined attention: a way of examining the workings of the mind and orienting the inner life according to the divine government of the world. This habit of thought promised a sense of control and composure. If Defoe accepted a higher order and sought to control not the external circumstances or impediments but his reaction to them, he could find peace even in prison. Or so was the Stoic ideal, laid out by Epictetus, who took Socrates' calm during his own imprisonment as one of the purest expressions of Stoic thought.[41] The frenetic pace of Defoe's life outside prison put him at odds with the studied compliance of the Stoics. In prison, his impatience with confinement left him restless; his schemes and dodges, his plans for recovery and service shaking him with the frustration of thwarted ambition.

Harley also considered himself a Stoic. His was perhaps an easier practice given the relative level of control he had over the world in which he moved. Defoe may have been one of his age's most acute observers of the motivations of political life. Still, the sensitivity and control of his response was limited by the necessary quickness of his pen and the information he could access. Even though Newgate was relatively porous, Defoe's incarceration robbed him of his vantage on politics. More pressingly, he did not know if his pleas for intercession had worked. Harley on the other hand had the sense of command that comes from direct access to the arcana of government. From his perspective, prison had neutralised the threat of Defoe's pen: a necessary precondition, he thought, to drawing him into government service.

Within a fortnight of Defoe's final day in the pillory, Harley approached Godolphin. He had a captive writer. His instinct was that Defoe might be able to help quell unease in Scotland. His suggestion was forceful enough to efface the traces of ambiguity and hedging that politeness sometimes leaves. Godolphin took the hint and thanked him for it, replying:

> I thank you for your hints about Scotland. Defoe would be the properest person in the world for that transaction, but I doubt the rigor of his punishment the other day will have made it scarce practicable to engage him. If you have any means of sounding him I wish you would try it.

Unlike Harley, who thought the pillory and the prospect of a lengthy stay in Newgate would leave Defoe with no option but to compromise his principles, Godolphin worried that the harshness of the punishment might forever turn him against the ministers who had instigated it. Looking for another option in case Defoe refused or proved unsuitable, he asked Harley, 'Could Mr. paterson bee of no use in Scotland?'[42]

Harley sounded out Defoe's state from James Stancliffe, the writer's friend. By the time he was ready to brief Godolphin, news of the Scottish parliament had reached the coffeehouses of London. *The Daily Courant* reported that Queensberry was ready to touch and thereby give royal assent to all acts except the Act of Security. The paper also noted that the Scottish parliament had debated the 'royal prerogative', brazenly discussing the rights and privileges of the Queen.[43] *The London Gazette* reported that a packet of letters had reached Whitehall, bringing an account that the 'Lord High Commissioner' had indeed already 'touched with the Scepter all the Acts that were voted excepting ... *An Act for the Security of the Kingdom*'.[44] Though no doubt mixed in with discussion of the war, of ships leaving to and arriving from North America, the wits of the coffeehouses and taverns knew that something was afoot up north that might bring the Scottish parliament into conflict with England's own.

Harley had better intelligence of the events in Scotland than the publishers of these newspapers. At the same time, he appreciated the reach and effect the newspaper had in England. Still, when it came to Defoe, he proceeded with care. 'I find Foe is much oppressed in his mind with his usage,' he told Godolphin. Defoe's ability to control his reactions faltered in the face of Newgate, a far more degradingly corporeal experience than Socrates' prison of the mind. For Defoe, this sense of oppression was deeply personal. He directed his anger to Nottingham and Buckingham, the lords who had served as his interrogators. According to Harley's assessment, Defoe remained 'willing to serve the Queen'. He recorded the 'private attempt' amongst Defoe's friends 'to raise the 200 Marks for his fine'. Given the amount, this attempt was unlikely to succeed.

Though Harley left the ultimate decision to Godolphin, he emphasised Defoe's capacity and outlined a way for the Queen to intercede in the writer's case that would bind him by an obligation greater than any financial reward:

> He is a very capable man, and if his fine be satisfied without any other knowledge but that he can alone be acquainted with it that it is the Queen's bounty to him and Grace, he may do service, and this may perhaps engage him better than any other rewards, and keep him more under the power of an obligation.

As to other potential agents: Harley informed Godolphin that Paterson 'would be glad to be owned in the service of her Majesty. His circumstances require it, and I fancy it would spur him to more activity both in this town and abroad where he hath many that believe in him.'[45] Paterson's use and currency lay in his ability to inspire belief, as he had proved in Scotland. His dire financial straits, by Harley's reckoning, would both motivate him and keep him in check.

Godolphin was won over. In the same week as he received Harley's report, he met with the Queen and read parts of it aloud to her. The Queen gave her sanction and Godolphin wrote back with haste: 'What you propose about Defoe may be done when you will and how you will.'

⸸

By the time the Queen agreed to employ Defoe, Harley was safely at Brampton Bryan Hall. The estate, close enough to the northern border of Herefordshire that it is almost in Shropshire, had been in his family since the fourteenth century.

The business of government was inevitably slowed when ministers retired to their estates. They could not meet, as they did in London or at Windsor, and relied on their correspondence. Godolphin had left Windsor for Bath, hoping the waters there would help with his 'stomach and head'. A 'violent cold' stymied their effects and Godolphin was left 'disordered', struggling to concentrate for much of the month.[46] In London, William Paterson eagerly awaited the Treasurer's arrival. By October, he began to worry. It is unclear if he was approached by someone working for Harley or Godolphin or engaged more formally as an agent some other way. In any case, soon after they had discussed possibly employing him, Paterson began to write and act as if on a new mission. He awaited Godolphin's return, he told Harley, so that he and the Treasurer could settle 'the necessary preliminaries of this new work I am about to begin'. Paterson thought the particulars of the assignment too sensitive to commit to writing.

What he was tasked with can be discerned in the first subsequent piece of intelligence he received. It most likely came from his contact Franco, Adam Francke, who had served as Resident in London of the East and West India Companies of Holland and had a clerkship in the English post office. It was in England where Harley first engaged him as an agent. There is evidence that he continued to pay him £50 a year for the intelligence he provided directly and through Paterson.[47] In this letter from Hanover, the seat of the new heirs to the thrones of England, Scotland, Wales and Ireland, Franco reveals an intense interest in what was happening in Scotland:

> Pray let me know what you think may be the consequences of the Queen's refusing her consent to the Act of Security, as also what are thought to be Her Majesty's chief reasons for doing, since I fancy her compliance in that matter might have contributed very much to the quiet of her own reign in the ancient kingdom. And I am afraid there are but few who think that her care of those who are named to succeed her hath been a strong motive on the other side.

After pressing Paterson for information, Franco reveals little in turn about 'the pinions here concerning the proceedings in Scotland', other than to note that George, the Elector of Hanover, and his ministers remained 'reserved on that head'.[48] The fear in England was that Jacobite agents had infiltrated Hanover, poisoning opinion there against the Act that would see the Elector succeed Anne as monarch of Britain. Their task was made easier by events in Scotland. Clauses in the Act of Security, as Franco pointed out, seemed directly aimed at the Elector. The most obvious: the proviso to exclude Lutherans from holding the Scottish Crown. The reasons why Anne refused to consent to the Act of Security were doubted by those who were ostensibly protected by such refusals. In Franco's assessment, people in Hanover thought giving consent to the Act would quell the trouble in Scotland; the reason for withholding it was seen by Hanoverians less as a defence of the succession than an expression of Anne's desire to assert her prerogative. The feeling, correct on the face of it, was that the Queen's ministers were far more invested in settling the succession on the Hanoverians than she was.

The careful trade of intelligence captures the work of the two agents well. Paterson and Franco aimed to reveal as little as they could to each other in exchange for as much as they could extract. Their care was necessary. Harley encouraged Paterson to exert control, having been disturbed by earlier reports of the 'lyes & Storyes' from English pens that reached Franco.[49] In the final months of 1703 Scotland became the focus of agents across England and Europe. Godolphin's apprehension – that the most 'fatal thing' to happen to Anne would be if the first session of the Scottish parliament ended without a resolution – looked increasingly likely.[50] Queensberry had been forced to touch and confer royal assent on one act seeking Scotland's independence (the Act anent Peace and War) while the second (the Act of Security) lay on his desk. He had lost control over his own ministry. His alliance with the Cavaliers had all but collapsed. As his power diminished, a vacuum opened, and his opponents in the Scottish parliament moved to withhold funds for the War of the Spanish Succession. Their gamble: they would continue to fund the war only if Queensberry consented to the Act of Security and asserted the right of the Scottish parliament to choose Scotland's next monarch. The union of the crowns faced a clear threat. More than ever before the way forward could take one of two paths: some form of political union or war between England and Scotland.

⚘

Years later, suffering from what he called 'the Infirmities of a Life of Sorrow and Fatigue', and fearing that his death was imminent, Defoe felt called to account for his public service – to offer some justification to posterity for a body of work he believed was misread in its own time. He never finished the work. While writing it he fell into 'a violet Fit of an Apoplexy' that weakened him for six weeks. Death did not come for another fifteen years. Defoe's publisher did not wait, clearly believing the writer would not recover. The unfinished account was launched into the world. In it, Defoe relates how he came to be released from Newgate. As he tells it, he was abandoned in prison 'without Hope of Deliverance', when a messenger came on Harley's behalf with a question carried by word of mouth from the statesman: 'Pray ask that Gentleman, what I can do for him?' Harley's message compelled Defoe to sit down in his cell and write the story of the blind beggar of Jericho who was asked that same question by Jesus. The beggar's answer that he wished for his sight to be restored (in the Gospels of Luke and Mark) is austere for its direct display of faith and reward. In the Gospel of Defoe there's a note of incredulity. What else could he ask for but freedom?

Though Defoe 'lay Four months in Prison' after this request, it was by Harley's hand that he was eventually freed. Defoe looked back on Harley's actions as 'the Foundation on which I built my first Sense of Duty to Her Majesty's Person and the indelible Bond of Gratitude to my first Benefactor'.[51]

In reality, circumstances did not conform quite so neatly to this parable of salvation and eternal, indelible gratitude. Harley convinced both Godolphin and the Queen that Defoe would serve them well, for on 4 November 1703, the Treasurer wrote to say, 'I have taken care in the matter of de Foe.' He was referring to a meeting the previous day in the Cockpit with the Attorney General and William Lowndes, Secretary to the Treasury and MP for Seaford, where it was resolved that Defoe's fine and the expenses he accrued in Newgate would be paid from the fund set aside for secret service. Lowndes, who kept exacting records of secret service money, noted that the Treasurer instructed that £150 was to be paid to James Stancliffe, Defoe's friend. The same records show that Stancliffe collected the money on 9 November.[52] Defoe had already appeared before Justice Thomas Lane on 3 November. His brother-in-law Robert Davis and three other men who accompanied him agreed before the court to provide sureties that Defoe would keep the peace. The men signed a bond for each £100 and Defoe signed one for £200. Defoe could not be released, however, until Stancliffe came forth and paid the fine and expenses. Stancliffe was a stand-in, a way for Harley and Godolphin to obscure the fact that the same government that had prosecuted Defoe now engineered his release. The cover was effective, for though many suspected Stancliffe acted on someone else's behalf, the general view was that the Whigs had come to Defoe's aid. One Tory writer went so far as to lament: 'Everyone is not a Daniel De Foe that has a Party to pay a Fine for him . . . It's no ungainful thing to be a Whig, let me tell you.'[53]

Released, Defoe wrote two letters. In the first to Stancliffe he carefully enclosed a second to Harley. The process of enfolding one letter into another shielded Defoe's communication with Harley from view. It also gave Defoe the opportunity to implore Stancliffe to make up for moments where Defoe felt his own words failed him. If he followed Defoe's instructions when delivering the letter to Harley, Stancliffe would have spoken 'Every thing you can Immagin a Man Overcome with Kindness Ought to Say'.[54] The letter to Harley is overwrought. Defoe plays the role of 'Grateful wretch'. Again, he takes his bearings from scripture. He is the tenth leper from Luke (17:11–19); the only one cured by Jesus who returned to thank him. The tropes of cure and saving, of divine intervention on behalf of the sick and blind, reveal a man desperate to find meaning in his suffering.[55] The belief that Harley had been moved to act by Providence, that his actions restored Defoe's health and sight, allowing the writer both to move in the world and perceive his place within it, gave life to Defoe's idea of service as an ideal fulfilment of the talent endowed in him by god. Thus resolved, he declared himself: 'A Man Ready to Dedicate my Life and all Possible Powers to The Intrest of So Generous and So Bountifull Benefactors.'[56]

Even as he lay prostrate before Harley, Defoe began gauging the Speaker's limits, establishing a pattern that would prevail for the rest of their correspondence. Defoe wanted Harley to disclose more about the other benefactors who had helped secure his freedom. He wanted a better sense of the people to whom he had just pledged his life-long service. He was not ungrateful. The measure against his joy came because the charge and the limits of the sureties still hung over him. Offend the wrong person and he would be back in Newgate. To escape that threat Defoe needed a pardon from the Queen herself.

EXCURSUS

The Scotch Plot

In the summer of 1703, the leader of a Highland clan landed in Scotland with the promise to remake his country's political destiny. He soon did. But not as he had hoped. His adventures created an intelligence breach that radically changed Scotland's relationship to England – and with it, the course of Defoe's life. In his own time this man would fast become 'the Talk of Coffeehouses' and 'the Subject of Pamphlets'. Worse, to his mind, he would also be 'exhibited as a Monster in Pictures': artists and writers would put his 'Treachery' on full display, exposing his 'Unsteadiness in Principles' and a dedication to 'Self-interest' so intense that it bordered on addiction.[1] The most famous of these pictures is the one sketched by William Hogarth years later, when the tall, thin man had gained more than a lifetime's worth of weight. In the drawing, the man's face is pinched as if caught mid-scheme. His arms, which strain to reach around his torso, barely allow his hands to meet as he counts his fate on his fingers. Hogarth's signal is unmistakable: Simon Fraser of Beaufort was a man both profligate and canny – lacking control but cunning enough to get his way.

Beaufort had been away from Scotland for just under a year. The story he told was that before he departed he travelled the length of his country, 'engaging the chiefs of the clans and those noblemen of the lowlands' who 'were ready to take up arms and hazard their lives and fortunes' for the Jacobite cause.[2] With this tale as his passport, he would gain access to the inner circles of Catholic power in Europe.

5. Portrait of Simon Fraser of Beaufort, copied from William Hogarth's portrait (1746).

What he neglected to mention was that he was driven out of Scotland by debt, squabbles over his estate and title, and a criminal prosecution.

⸸

Scotland was never far from Beaufort's mind. During the months he spent in France he was singularly preoccupied with finding a way to return home. He no sooner arrived in Paris than he sent for his cousin Sir John Maclean. A clan leader in his own right, Maclean had gone into exile with the deposed James II a decade prior and had spent the better part of his life since at James' makeshift Court in St Germain, sixteen kilometres west of Paris. Like any closed community, royal courts are governed by complex and shifting relationships of favour and alliance – as binding to those within the system as they are alluringly opaque to those outside of it. Cut off from its own subjects and dependent on French largesse, the significance of these relationships was magnified in inverse proportion to the exiled Court's direct influence over England. Maclean's knowledge was vital in this regard. He knew the players and the rules of the game. Though he had serious doubts about Beaufort's plan to return to Scotland at the head of a rebellion, he could nonetheless advise him that the best way to gain the Court's backing for such a scheme was to approach James Drummond, Jacobite 1st Duke of Perth.

The advice was prudent on the face of it. Of all the courtiers, Perth was the most likely to greet the news Beaufort carried favourably. Throughout his exile, Perth maintained an extensive set of connections with Jacobites in Scotland, as did most of the serious movers at the Court of St Germain. The problem they faced was that communication between the two countries was disjointed. Exiled Jacobites could send agents or messengers. They could also write, but because letters took between two and three weeks, the exchange was not quick enough to shape events directly.[3] Those in St Germain had to trust their people on the ground in Scotland.

This was a particular problem for Perth, who believed that the main line of the Stuarts could only be restored through force. To him and his faction, the way to restore the 'true' King lay in fomenting an armed uprising in Scotland as a prelude to a French-backed invasion. Connected to the main by intermittent dribs of information, Perth took any bit of intelligence that suggested the conditions in Scotland were primed for insurrection a bit too eagerly. He fell into what had already become a pattern at St Germain. The Jacobite courtiers tended to perceive events in Scotland in a naively hopeful way, yearning for a home that did not exist as they remembered it – if it ever had. This lack of clear-minded intelligence contributed to James II's military defeats in the 1690s and left Louis XIV wary of lending money or men to any further adventures.

Perth's chief rival at Court was Charles, 2nd Earl of Middleton. A more experienced and compromising politician, and a Protestant, Middleton believed that serious concessions would have to be made on the part of James II and his heirs if they were ever to return to the throne. After James died and attention turned to his fourteen-year-old son, James Francis Edward Stuart, Middleton remained convinced that negotiation would bear the fruit of rule. It seems that he was one of the Jacobites deceived by Godolphin and Marlborough into believing that Queen Anne secretly favoured her younger half-brother and would work to bring him back as her successor. This airy promise was often floated alongside the equally wispy notion that the exiled prince could convert to Protestantism and thus ensure both a Protestant succession and the return of the divine Stuart line.

Having met and advised Beaufort, Maclean left him in Paris for two days while he travelled to St Germain to arrange a meeting with Perth. He returned to the city to escort his cousin personally. Their journey was not difficult. A day's ride and the two would have spotted the grounds of the Court in exile. The final approach was steep, rising in an intimidating slope from the banks of the Seine to the plateau where the Château-Vieux de St Germain perched. The path they took upwards passed the royal stables, kennels, and a jeu de paume (indoor tennis) court. St Germain was famed for its gardens and terraces, ordered in a precise geometry designed to bend nature to royal will. But nature can only be kept back so far. Beaufort would have noticed that the southern front grew wilder as the avenue that branched from the château stretched to the forest beyond. Just west of the plateau stood the town that supplied the royals and their principal courtiers, and where the wider community of English and Scottish exiles lived.

The Château-Vieux de St Germain – given to James II and his wife Mary of Modena by the French King – had since been replaced as Louis' residence of choice by a new palace to its south at Versailles.[4] The French King's reasons were practical as well as acquisitive. Though grand, the château was not particularly well set out. Arranged around a central courtyard, the main building was narrow, and to get from one apartment to another, servants, courtiers and even the royals themselves often had to go outside to find the requisite entrance or staircase. Maclean knew his way, and guided Beaufort directly to Perth's rooms. Their meeting, by Beaufort's account, was wholly positive. Perth was 'charmed' by the steps the errant laird had taken to encourage an uprising: all the more so because Beaufort claimed that he had been commissioned in his task by the leaders of Scotland's clans. Convinced, Perth set out to introduce him to Mary of Modena.

†

Mary's rooms occupied what had once been the Grand Appartement du Roi. To enter them, Beaufort, Maclean and Perth had to take the Queen's staircase to the second floor of the château's east wing. There Mary kept a series of what appeared to be bedchambers. Her actual bed chamber was hidden from public view. Unaware of this, Beaufort assumed that he met the Queen in the place she slept, giving him an unusual sense of intimacy to power. With the death of her husband James II, Mary's importance had only increased. Her influence over her son gave her sway as a point of connection between the exiled Court, the French King and the Pope.

The reports of their meeting differ markedly. According to Beaufort, Perth and Maclean assured him that all true friends of the cause considered Middleton a 'faithless traitor'. They suspected that the English parliament paid the Earl for 'intelligence of all that passes at the court of St. Germains'.[5] Maclean disputed this, insisting that it was Beaufort who first asked Mary to keep the plan from her other ministers.[6] Safely encased within the tapestried walls of Mary's chambers, Beaufort told the former Queen 'That he was Commisionated from the greater part of the Chieftains of the Highland Clans, that they would rise in Arms with 10,000 Men if they were assisted from *France* with Money, Arms and Troops'. Maclean had serious misgivings about the number of clan leaders Beaufort claimed as backers. Though no one present was willing to admit that they were the one to swear the exiled Queen to secrecy, it was the right approach.

St Germain had serious difficulties in securing intelligence. The Court was so leaky that the Duke of Hamilton, a potential leader of the Jacobites, 'was cautious of speaking with any that came from *St. Germains*, where the factions were so great, that nothing was secret'.[7] The Church had its own network of agents with well-established ties and channels to the Scots Catholic Mission. Scottish Jacobite agents such as Captain Henry Straton came to St Germain frequently and so offered a more direct and secure line of communication than any Beaufort promised.

It was an open secret that Middleton ran spies. Prominent amongst them was the aptly named Mrs Frances Fox. Fox started her career as an agent for the Earl of Melfort, Middleton's predecessor. By the time she came to serve Middleton, she was a shrewd operator, acting as a crucial messenger between Middleton and Whitehall. She was one of many women spies in Early Modern Europe, whose activities historians are only just beginning to uncover.[8] Like other 'she-intelligencers', it is likely that Fox exploited contemporary prejudices that assumed women did not possess the mind, courage or capacity for moral compromise required of spies. With underestimation as her cover, Fox moved easily in society. She maintained a friendship with Lady Middleton, all the while meeting clandestinely with the Earl and his other spies in a room within a Benedictine convent in Paris. Beaufort knew of Fox and tried to seek her out as a potential ally, unaware that Middleton had tasked her with tracking him.

Beaufort's meeting with Mary had its desired effect. Within days, the former Queen introduced him to Jean-Baptiste Colbert, Marquis de Torcy, the French foreign minister, who in turn introduced him to Nathaniel Hooke, the young Irish agent who served as Torcy's adviser on Scotland. Urged by Torcy to offer something firmer, Beaufort agreed to draw up a list of the clan leaders who had commissioned him. With this, Torcy arranged for a meeting between Beaufort and Filippo Antonio Gualterio, the Pope's nuncio (ambassador) to France. Beaufort was now in the sights of two central brokers to the two most powerful Catholic interests in Europe. Intrigued though they were, neither was willing to embark on what would be a monumental foreign policy decision based solely on the self-interested promise of a leader with no clan behind him. Nor was Beaufort's plan as original as he presented. Around the same time, Hooke was busy preparing a more considered version.

Tipped off by Fox or another of his agents, Middleton soon became aware of Beaufort's invasion plan. If it was adopted, it would mean the end of Middleton's attempts at a diplomatic restoration. Sensing a shift in favour, Middleton questioned the levels of Scottish support and pressed his case to Mary that while an invasion might serve French interests it would not necessarily place her son on the English throne. Having aspersed the plan to little effect, Middleton took what many believed to be a cynical move. To demonstrate his complete loyalty, he retired to a monastery in Paris, where he converted to Catholicism.

Middleton was adept at combining the performance of Court politics with its mechanics. Leaving little to chance, he sent one of his spies, James Murray, to Scotland. Murray's brief was to speak with Hamilton and the other nobles in Beaufort's sights – to gauge their support for action and to warn them against Beaufort.[9] When Beaufort heard about Murray's mission he was sure that Murray had convinced potential militants in Scotland that France would not come to an uprising's aid, thereby snuffing out any embers of action before he had the chance to fan them. And fanning them was to be the upper limit of his task. Beaufort was deluded if he thought that Torcy and the French King would have adopted his plan in full and sent him back to Scotland at the head of an invasion. To them, Beaufort's use was as a spy. Torcy desired 'essential Assurances from the Chieftains of the Clans' that they would raise their troops. The evidence had to be unimpeachable and so Torcy and the Jacobite Court insisted that Beaufort be accompanied by at least one 'Scotsman in the French service'. Their choice was another Murray, Captain John Murray, whose task was to spy on the spy – to follow Beaufort into Scotland and hold him to the limits of his mission.[10]

†

Travelling between France and England when the two nations were at war was difficult. Beaufort and Murray spent a month moving between port cities on the French coast, looking for a way to cross the Channel unnoticed. This was made more difficult because they were accompanied by a couple of French servants and two other agents, Colonel Peter Graham and Major George Fraser, Beaufort's distant relation. Maclean was not part of the original set, though Torcy promised Beaufort that he would be sent later with updated orders. Noticing that packet boats exchanging prisoners of war passed between the warring nations with relative ease, Beaufort managed to bribe one of the captains. Disguised as captured English soldiers, the group sailed to Dover, before making their way on to London.

Arriving in a hostile territory always carries risks. For most of the group, however, these risks greatly decreased thanks to a proclamation issued by Queen Anne the previous spring that indemnified Scots who had committed crimes against the Crown in the period since the Revolution of 1688–9. Intended to draw rebels against King William to her side, the proclamation allowed the return of Scottish exiles. The fear of some in the English ministry was that in welcoming such people, the Queen was importing a set of sleeping assets, who could be roused in the event of an invasion.

For Beaufort, the indemnity offered scant protection. In Scotland he was a wanted man. He had letters of fire and sword drawn up against him, authorising the sheriff to use either fire or sword to apprehend him. The reason for his prosecution was a protracted dispute between Beaufort and his father on the one side and Lord James Murray, now Duke of Atholl, on the other. At stake was the claim of Beaufort's line to the lands and leadership of clan Fraser of Lovat.

The dispute had come to a head six years earlier when, after fighting openly with Atholl in the streets of Edinburgh, Beaufort took the impetuous action that was to mark him for the rest of his life: he rode to Castle Dounie, west of Inverness, to meet Amelia Fraser, Lady Lovat, Atholl's sister and widow to the previous Lord Lovat. Beaufort's plan was to arrange his marriage to Amelia's daughter. Finding the daughter absent, he corralled an Episcopalian priest and forced Amelia into a hasty wedlock instead. The travesty was accompanied by a piper, the high thrum of the music rendering Amelia's desperate protest inaudible. Beaufort later recognised the criminal stupidity of his actions, attempting to slough the marriage off as invalid – a prank. This did not diminish the rightful outrage nor lessen Atholl's seething enmity. In the eyes of the law, Beaufort had raped Amelia, Lady Lovat, to further his claims to the clan.

✝

Beaufort and his ring rode north from London, taking backways where possible. The first shadow of trouble set in when they came to Northallerton, the North Yorkshire town best known as the site of an

1138 battle between the English and Scots. There, Beaufort and the other agents took rooms in a local post house. Their French valets went downstairs to the public kitchen for a drink – or many. In a fit of drunken bravado one of them boasted 'that his master was just come from France, and that he was a partisan of King James the third'. Unfortunately for the valet, a local Justice of the Peace was in earshot. The Justice assembled the constables at speed, leaving Beaufort and Murray trapped in their apartment.

Beaufort's report of the episode is suspicious. He is the hero of the tale, standing with pistols cocked and a blunderbuss ready at the table beside him, willing to die rather than be captured. Murray, a naturalised French citizen and a prudent coward, hides to avoid an international incident. In the end the two avoid arrest by Beaufort's wit alone. As the Justice of the Peace bursts in, Beaufort embraces him as an old friend, introducing himself as the Duke of Argyll's brother:

> 'My dear sir, how happy I am to see you. It is almost two years since I had that pleasure with the duke of Argyle, at the races near this town.'
>
> The justice was struck with these words, and replied with a faltering voice,
>
> 'My lord, I ask your lordship a thousand pardons for having broke thus abruptly into your apartment. But my business was to beg your lordship's permission to treat you with a bottle of wine in this town, where I am a man of some consequence.'[11]

It was a good cover. The 1st Duke of Argyll was a patron of Beaufort's and Beaufort could ape the role of his brother. The story of how he overcame the local magistrate rests on Beaufort's innate sense of his own nobility and the prejudices of an age that believed a superior genealogical line could be traced in a person's bearing. Whether ashamed or charmed or both, the Justice did send for a bottle of Spanish wine. Beaufort promptly drank him into a stupor. When the official was carried home by the same constables he had summoned to arrest the suspected Jacobites, Beaufort and his party made their escape, slipping out unnoticed and setting off for Durham. It was

1 a.m., and while the darkness covered their tracks, it could not cloak Murray's rage. The man was ready to stab the French valet who had exposed them. Again, the self-styled hero steps in: Beaufort by his own account stood between Murray and the valet, overcoming the anger of one and the shame of the other by bringing each back to the overarching justice of their cause.

In Durham the group split up. They were close enough to the Scottish border that Beaufort could send Colonel Graham and Major Fraser north to discern the situation in Edinburgh. In the meantime, he would begin his mission in earnest, riding across Northumberland to seek out Jacobite families in the area. He carried a portrait of James Edward Francis Stuart, giving many English Jacobites their first glimpse of 'their King'. The form most of these visits took was not encouraging. Beaufort needed paper evidence that the Northumberland Jacobites were willing to rise in rebellion. Most of the families he visited refused, holding to the line that they would only commit to what was in effect treason once the armies of St Germain and France had landed on their coasts. They had reached an impasse: France would not back an invasion without clear support in the north of England and Scotland; Jacobites in England and Scotland would not offer their support until a French-backed invasion arrived.

The difficulties Beaufort experienced do not signal that his plan was unworkable, but rather that he was an imperfect vessel. (Nathaniel Hooke's comparable plan was the basis for the Jacobite uprisings of 1708 and 1715.) One could never truly separate the scope of Beaufort's campaigns from his unrelenting pursuit of personal benefit. It was this pursuit that encouraged him to find a path to Scotland even after Graham and Fraser returned with the dispiriting news that James Murray had beaten them to Edinburgh. Middleton's agent had polluted Hamilton's opinion – or so they presumed. What's more, Atholl knew Beaufort's arrival was imminent and had ensured that the Privy Council reissued the warrant against him on charges of rape, forced marriage and rebellion.

✝

Beaufort continued north, making a brief incursion into the Lowlands to meet with heads of families. His intent, in defiance of his orders, was to initiate the rebellion then and there, in the hope that his Highland allies would march south and that France would be compelled by the reality of military action to send troops. His rashness found no supporters, aside from the Countess of Erroll, Perth's sister, whom he described as possessing a 'masculine and superior genius',[12] his epithet of choice for women who happened to share his opinion. The Countess was a key member of the Jacobite underground, a leading agent in the Lowland cell, who sourced, passed on and carried intelligence, and arranged safe houses throughout the country for agents from the Continent. While her ring had a fair amount of autonomy, they could not initiate a military mission without broader support. The option of immediate hostility closed to him, Beaufort changed course. Once more, he relied on his old patron Argyll to get him out of trouble, riding south back across the border to meet his man at a house outside Newcastle.

At this point Argyll was a member of Queensberry's party. The two worked together to defeat the Act of Security and to push through the bill of supply. Their failure on both counts unsettled Queen Anne. For her, the Act of Security presented an insuperable problem. She could not assent to a law that would allow the Scots to choose their own candidate to succeed her. The prospect had shades of the Declaration of Arbroath (1320), which linked the independence of Scotland to the notion of contractual monarchy – the idea being that Scots could legitimately remove a king who no longer governed in their independent interest. The Queen blamed Queensberry for the failure. In an attempt to save face, Queensberry sent a series of defensive letters to Windsor blaming Atholl for thwarting him.

And so, when Argyll approached Queensberry with news that he had at his house a man lately arrived from France who was willing to share intelligence from the Court in exile, Queensberry did not hesitate to arrange a pass for this man to come to his residence at Holyrood. The mysterious stranger (who was of course Beaufort) insisted that his name be kept secret until he was granted a pardon and was safely in the employ of the Scottish government. A pardon and a pension offered a far less risky and more realistic means to secure a return to Scotland and the possibility, once there, to claim his land. This is not to say that Beaufort had given up on an uprising. While awaiting his appointment with Queensberry he made the long ride to the west of Scotland, sounding out support from the folk hero Rob Roy MacGregor and the Jacobite families of Argyllshire.

There are two accounts of the 'long Conference' between Queensberry and Beaufort. One comes to us via Queensberry's report to the Queen; the other from Beaufort's *Memoirs*. Although they differ wildly, there are enough common points to make out the shape of the exchange. Beset by the Queen's growing distrust, Queensberry's report is direct. He works hard to appear objective, offering himself up as the conduit for intelligence, not its author. He tells the Queen of letters 'from a Gentleman come from France in which he spooke with some assurance of overturning the Government here'. Sketching the plot for a French-backed Jacobite invasion, he added, 'God Knowes whether the Story be true or false; but my Author is a man of that quality and integrity, that I dare assure your Majesty, ther is neither Mistake nor trick on his part'. His faith in Beaufort would haunt him.

Queensberry misjudged Beaufort because his intelligence appeared to confirm what the Duke already suspected. Queensberry had reports from a military source of plans for a 'highland hunting', an assembly of 'six hundred of the best of the Laird of Grants men' to be attended by Hamilton and Atholl: all armed and, to the suspicious eye, in training for an attack.[13] He had also seen dispatches from the English Envoy to the Hague detailing a set of mysterious payments from Paris and Lisle to Scottish nobles, Hamilton chief amongst them.[14] Furthermore, Queensberry had been given a set of letters from St Germain to David Lindsay in Scotland, one of the men who had taken advantage of the Queen's proclamation and had returned home. The letters were intercepted by Nottingham's office. The agents who first encountered them did not recognise their language. The assumption was that they were encoded. The parts that Nottingham's office did eventually manage to decipher seemed to show that 'de Torcy' agreed that 'not only [should] Men and Arms be sent' to Scotland 'but also the Sums of *Money* they [Scottish Jacobites] demanded'.[15]

Jacobite operatives did avail themselves of codes. The more typical technique was to use 'cant code'. Writers would pose as everyday correspondents, disguising their political message as something mundane.[16] If need be, they could use invisible ink made from lemon juice or whitened lead to add further information between the lines. Using a completely false language or substituting certain words for numbers was risky. If intercepted, such correspondence would be immediately suspect, as these letters were. The translation presented a view of Torcy and France as far more supportive than they were in fact. France had a history of using agents and communiqués to destabilise England. Without knowing the source of the letters, it is hard to discern their intent. They did, however, lend credence to Beaufort that his reputation in any other circumstance would have denied him.

Over a couple of days at Holyrood, Beaufort told Queensberry that Hamilton's efforts to bring the Scottish parliament to a close were the first steps towards open rebellion; that the plotters intended to quash resistance by removing Queensberry as Lord High Commissioner; that the French had already sent money and would in the next few seasons prepare a fleet and troops; that there was an extensive correspondence between Perth and nobles in Scotland; and, most damning of all, that Mary of Modena herself had written to Hamilton, who was commissioned by France as their Scottish commander.[17] Beaufort then made the offer to turn double agent, provided he could get a pass to come to London incognito to give a full account there, as well as some sort of protection under which to travel to France to become Queensberry's spy at St Germain.

At first Queensberry was cautious. He could not grasp why Beaufort would reveal so much and offer to undertake such a risky mission. Still, Queensberry recommended that the Queen employ the man. As he put it, the man's circumstances were such that 'it can hardly be expected that he will forefault what he may expect from France without getting some termes from your Majesty'.[18] Throughout his correspondence, Queensberry kept Beaufort's identity hidden.

In Beaufort's telling, Queensberry was far less open-minded. At their first meeting, the Duke made it known that he already had significant intelligence of an insurrection and homed directly in on the role that Hamilton and Atholl were to play. Coaxing Beaufort, Queensberry reminded him that 'Lord Athol and the duke of

Hamilton were two Persons, who had for a long time endeavoured to deprive him of estate, reputation and life'. Queensberry wanted a way in turn to deprive 'these two lords of the power of counteracting and opposing his administration'. He was not the only one. Harley's ally William Carstares mused that 'it would be of great advantage if it could be made appear that some of those that have deluded some honest men by a pretended zeal for the liberty and independence of their country were discovered to have been compromised by St Germain'.[19] Beaufort spied an opportunity. Atholl's power was the greatest impediment to Beaufort's liberty. He gave Queensberry what he wanted: intelligence showing the deep connection between St Germain and his rivals, not least a letter from Mary of Modena to L.J.M, Lord John Murray (Atholl), an address likely forged by Beaufort himself.

Beaufort's retrospective account has to be approached with caution. By his own profession he was indeed a double agent but one whose loyalties remained with the Jacobites. He had fooled Queensberry with 'chimerical' intelligence in order to return to France to continue his mission.[20] The little evidence there is suggests that Beaufort was still playing both sides. It is hard to hit precisely at what occurred between him and Queensberry. The truth is probably slightly closer to Queensberry's account than Beaufort's. But the salient detail remains: Beaufort managed to extract a pass from Queensberry to travel to London, and was confident enough in their relationship to use Queensberry as his cover to escape England.

Unfortunately for Queensberry, news of the plot was not enough to shift the Queen from her course of action. Just two weeks after he had first reported the existence of the stranger from France, Anne instructed her Lord High Commissioner to prorogue parliament. The rationale was that if the Scottish parliament no longer sat, it could do no further damage to the unravelling bonds of the regnal union.

Prorogation was a temporising measure at best, and the clearest indication yet that the management of Scotland had slipped Queensberry's grip. At the conclusion of the session the Commissioner was recalled to London 'with all Convenient speed' to receive further instructions from the Queen.[21] Beaufort followed soon after, stopping first to buy new horses for the journey for fear that he would be recognised on a public coach. Closer to the capital he enlisted Colin Campbell, a London Jacobite, to help him enter and move through the city without notice.[22]

⸸

To stay hidden in London, Beaufort tapped into the Jacobite underground there – a loose collection of sympathisers embedded in the city. He moved between Campbell's residence, next door to the Hampshire-Hog in Charles Street Westminster, and the Marine Coffeehouse in Piccadilly, where he rendezvoused with William Keith, who was to be his main guide and contact. For the most part, though, he kept himself hidden in a house in Watling Street, not far from St Paul's, owned by Thomas Clarke, an apothecary. At Clarke's house, Beaufort met with Robert Ferguson, an Aberdeenshire man whose politics had shifted across the decade. The once radical Whig was now considered a Jacobite, though his past left him suspect in the eyes of true adherents.[23]

In an age marked by plots and intrigue, Ferguson distinguished himself to such a degree that he was given the epithet 'Plotter' Ferguson. An adept propagandist, his dark arts fanned the frenzy of plots across the spectrum of his ever-changing loyalties. The event that most defined his reputation was, however, the 1685 rebellion against James II led by the Duke of Monmouth, the illegitimate son of Charles II. It was Ferguson who penned the document that justified an open rebellion against the King in the name of Protestantism and English liberty. Ferguson was with Monmouth when he invaded the west country. In concert with a Scottish invasion led by the 9th Earl of Argyll, father of Beaufort's patron, the aim was to overthrow the King. The rebellion was decisively put down by Royal forces, largely because Monmouth failed to obtain even the most basic of miliary intelligence. Monmouth was caught on the battlefield not knowing the depth of the stream that cut across it. His troops could not cross the water. They were stuck, found, hunted down and killed.[24] Defoe himself witnessed the disaster as a member of Monmouth's cavalry, and would never forget this lesson in the necessity of good intelligence.

Monmouth's rebellion gave Ferguson his reputation as an instigator; a man 'always unquiet, and setting people to mischief'.[25] Aphra Behn, the writer and spy, depicted him as a master of the 'Black Art', who had used all of his sinister charm to push Monmouth into action.[26] Beaufort believed that Ferguson was an agent of St Germain. The risk was that the crafty agent might be on Queen Anne's payroll too.[27] That Beaufort sought out Ferguson is suspicious; to those around him, it certainly looked like he wanted Plotter Ferguson as a co-conspirator, the kind who could move a plot from the backroom to the field of battle.

✝

Beaufort quickly realised that leaving England would be impossible without documentation. Not only did war restrict international movement, but talk of a Jacobite plot filtered through London. Beaufort turned again to Queensberry. With Keith waiting in a carriage outside Queensberry's London house, Beaufort hurried inside. The Scottish Duke had arranged a passport, signed by Nottingham himself, giving Beaufort permission to sail to Rotterdam under an assumed identity: John Campbell.[28] As the boat departed, Beaufort settled himself into a kind of melancholic relief. A fellow traveller, noticing his broad Scots accent, turned the topic to Scotland. Before the traveller could say much, Beaufort 'began to talk of the Union' and, though resigned in tone, was firm in his belief that Scotland could 'never be happy if United with England'.[29]

✝

Arriving in Rotterdam, Beaufort shed the Campbell alias in favour of a new identity: John Smeaton. He had directed his compatriots in England to write to him as such. But when the first letter to Smeaton arrived in Holland, the news it carried was most unwelcome. Beaufort's cousin and confidant Maclean had sailed to England, been intercepted at Folkestone, had surrendered himself and was now in custody in the Tower of London.

Maclean returned to England and Scotland on Perth's orders – to try and find proof of Beaufort's success. It appears, though, that Maclean had other intentions from the start. He was increasingly miserable in France and wanted to defect: to make use of Queen Anne's indemnity and return home. Along with his wife and two children, he spent eleven days in a fishing boat on the open waters. Frances Fox accompanied the family, disguised as Lady Maclean's sister. Beaufort's reaction to this news veered between sadness and panic. He could not understand why Maclean would 'throw' himself 'in an open Boat' and give himself up so easily 'to the Government'. In a faintly disguised letter to his dear 'Cus' in the Tower, Beaufort urged Maclean to keep faith to 'your Master's Intrest'. To give up details of the plot would 'so ruin your Reputation, that tho' I love you intirely, I had rather see you buried than that you should be guilty of it'. The last line rang as a threat. But Beaufort was an ocean away and any intimidation he attempted paled against the full punitive weight of the English state that was now sealed around Maclean.

With Maclean in custody, the House of Lords finally had a witness who could help them uncover what lay behind the rumours, the chatter, the snippets of intelligence that all suggested an invasion from Scotland might be imminent.

⸸

Beaufort was wrong to trust Ferguson. The Plotter was indeed playing both sides. And Beaufort had told him just enough of his intentions that he was able to reveal to Atholl that Beaufort 'was not only gone to St. Germains with ill designs against' the Queen but, as Atholl reported to Queen Anne herself, that Queensberry intended to use Beaufort's revelations of a plot to ruin the 'Reputations, Lives and Fortunes' of Atholl and Hamilton.[30] Not trusting Ferguson's story alone, Atholl corroborated parts of it by going over Nottingham's passbook and finding that the Secretary had in fact signed a pass for someone matching Beaufort's description and had done so on Queensberry's direct request.

Atholl's report to the Queen, Maclean's confession and the intercepted letters pushed the House of Lords to investigate. Their initial findings were such that, on 17 December, Queen Anne addressed parliament on the 'Conspiracy in Scotland', informing the assembled that:

> I have had unquestionable Informations, of very ill Practices and Designs carried on in Scotland by Emissaries from France, which

> might have proved extremely dangerous to the Peace of these Kingdoms'.[31]

The problem that the investigators came up against was that the events described by Maclean validated suspicions without ever truly confirming them. Marlborough had reports that Hamilton was in correspondence with Jacobite agents.[32] Hamilton was considered enough of a threat that English agents routinely intercepted his letters. But Ferguson's testimony that parts of the plot had been concocted to impugn Hamilton and Atholl complicated matters. Was this all a sham driven by Queensberry in a moment of desperation? Was Beaufort a double agent? And if so, where did his loyalties lie?

The Whig lords who drove the initial investigation and the series of secret committees that followed considered the plot credible. It posed a threat to peace in the kingdom, as the Queen herself asserted. But these lords were not exactly honest arbiters. The plot gave them a much-needed line of attack against Nottingham and they were not going to let a lack of evidence stand in their way. Behind the scenes, Harley was determined to get to the truth, but he ran into the same impasse that the Whig lords had simply glossed over. The one person who could answer these questions, Simon Fraser of Beaufort – a notorious Jacobite, no less – had escaped, aided by Queensberry and Nottingham.

✝

The effects of the plot were far-reaching, just not in the way Beaufort ever intended. Incensed that Queensberry had 'trumped up the plot upon him', Atholl turned. According to a Jacobite informant, had it not been for the plot, Atholl would have continued to move between the Court and the Cavaliers, voting as interest served him. Queensberry's move against him pushed Atholl into opposition, drawing him into a competitive quasi-alliance with his brother-in-law, the Duke of Hamilton.[33] As his sympathy for Jacobites grew, he began to style himself as a Cavalier leader, seeking a position at 'the head' of the confederated opposition to 'outrival the Duke of Hamilton'.[34] Atholl's move into opposition was the last in a series caused by serious miscalculations on Queensberry's part. Not only was Queensberry's failure to manage the Scottish parliament dire enough that the succession hung in the balance, but in an attempt to save himself he had become an unwitting pawn in the plot of an enemy agent. His position as Lord High Commissioner was no longer tenable. He was forced from office in March 1704.

This left Nottingham. The Lords condemned him in their report on the plot, prompting the Tory-dominated Commons to defend him. The question of how Nottingham let Beaufort escape and failed to prosecute other potential conspirators provided the basis for a conflict between the Whig Lords and the Tory Commons that ended in a constitutional rift. Nottingham was prescient enough to see that the plot might be used to remove him. In an attempt to parry this attack, he asked the Queen to dismiss two of the Whig lords who led the charge. Her refusal may as well have been written on the wall. Nottingham resigned as Secretary of State.

On a wider plane, the plot made public what Whitehall and Windsor knew but preferred not to admit: that England's global position depended on settling the succession, which in turn showed just how necessary it was to reach some kind of parliamentary union with Scotland. Defoe satirised the debacle as a 'a deep *Livonian* plot', drawing a parallel to the teetering federation of Poland-Lithuania; a comparison that suggested England and Scotland needed stronger bonds.[35] The failure to address networks of spies running between St Germain and the British Isles exposed a dire failure of intelligence on the parts of Queensberry and Nottingham, only serving to confirm the view of the man who would ultimately replace Nottingham as Secretary of State: that England needed a more systematic approach to Scotland, and to domestic intelligence – and that the two were intimately linked.

CHAPTER 3

THE EASTERN COUNTIES

When talk began to circulate that Harley would be appointed Secretary of State, he made it known that this was not a role he campaigned for – or even desired. Godolphin and Marlborough were the ones who pressed it upon him. They had wanted to replace Nottingham for some time. Strident and uncompromising, Nottingham had become increasingly difficult to work with. He had also grown to dislike the position. His dissatisfaction with the direction of the ministry played out in ways that only served to alienate his colleagues further. He interfered with Marlborough's war plans and, despite the rift it caused in parliament and beyond, he refused to give up his attempt to penalise occasional conformity, going so far as to threaten to attach or 'tack' his bill against the practice to a public money bill to ensure its passage through the Lords. Anyone who allowed Dissenters to take Anglican communion on occasion – so that they could hold office – was accused by Nottingham of weakening the Church's bind on civic morality.

Cries of 'the Church in danger' stoked divisions within a city already crowded with discontent. The abrupt nature of Nottingham's departure did little to calm things; quite the opposite. So, while Godolphin and Marlborough could finally install an ally, their sense of relief was dampened by the intense pressure to find someone who would not exacerbate partisan tension, and fast. Harley was not their first choice. He had not served as a diplomat and had little experience as an administrator. But he had a diplomatic temperament. Godolphin, for one, took solace in Harley's steadiness. He was comforted by Harley's talk 'of calming people' and in the past had pledged to walk beside him in taking the steps 'towards making men a little more moderate'.[1] When entanglements of conflict ruled out other possible secretaries, Harley began to appear fated to the role.

At first Harley refused Godolphin's offer. He was reluctant to leave the Commons. He was uncertain out of parliament and feared that becoming Secretary would jeopardise the source of his power within it: his carefully managed reputation as an arbiter of national interest. Godolphin and Marlborough wanted Harley because he appeared above the fray. Harley demurred because he worried that accepting the position would place him amidst it in ways he could not control.

No doubt Harley registered the subtle transit of power that came with his refusal. The longer he took, the more Godolphin and Marlborough appeared to need him. On campaign Marlborough wrote to Godolphin begging him to 'take noe excuse from 46 but that he must emediatly come in' (46 was their numerical code for Harley).[2] In the end, Harley managed to hold out for three weeks before finally coming into the Secretaryship. When friends congratulated him, he struggled to accept their good wishes, knowing the responsibility that now bore down upon him. He told one that he expected condolences, 'because you know the weight of the work and my weakness'.[3] The weakness he felt and that he feared others saw in him was his relative lack of experience in foreign policy.

The weight of the work was immense. The two Secretaries of State were equally responsible for domestic affairs and split their coverage of foreign affairs latitudinally. The Northern Secretary was responsible for what was then considered northern Europe, including the Dutch Provinces, Austria, Scandinavia, the German States and Scotland. The Southern Secretary was responsible for France, Spain, Portugal, Switzerland, the Italian States, Greece and the Ottoman Empire. Custom dictated that the Secretary of State for the southern department was the senior position. Instead of directly replacing Nottingham in this role, Harley opted to take charge of the north, with Charles Hedges, the former Northern Secretary, who had covered both roles after Nottingham's resignation, taking the south.

It was clear, though, that Harley would be the premier Secretary and that the obliging Hedges would continue to 'receive instructions' from him.[4] This was not the only change to tradition. Harley would also remain as Speaker. In allowing Harley this unprecedented concentration of power, Godolphin signalled a clear break from his previous pattern of relying on Tories as allies in government. Opting for the moderate, calming middle ground that Harley represented was itself a partisan action – for to move beyond party is by implication a party move, requiring one to form new coalitions and cater to new constituencies. Harley's roles as Speaker and Secretary of State, and his admission following this latter appointment to the Privy Council, were built on the perception that he was temperamentally inclined to seek unity at home and peace abroad. The contemporary historian John Oldmixon thought that one reason that Harley had been appointed was a hope that his talents as a peacemaker might help break the impasse with Scotland.[5]

⸸

While Harley was negotiating his new place in the capital, Defoe was struggling to return to his old one. The reprieve he felt after his release from Newgate was cruelly short-lived. His time in prison concentrated his thoughts on freedom so that when it finally came he was left disoriented. Despite the incursion of the outside world into Newgate, Defoe was still apart. When he re-entered society he remained a step out of time with the world and his family. Mary was pregnant with their seventh child. His creditors were calling in debts. Running the numbers over in his mind, he worried that 'Not less than a Thousand Pounds will Entirely Free me'.[6] Compounding his problems as it did his debts was the fact that, post-release, Defoe had few ways to make money. His conviction prevented him from securing a new line of credit. The sureties placed on his good behaviour made writing an even riskier venture than it had been before.

The event he blamed for the final wreckage of his finances was the great storm that lashed London soon after his release. The storm was 'a Calamity so Dreadful and Astonishing', according to Queen Anne, that it had no precedent in collective memory.[7] Travelling down from the North Atlantic, the storm laid waste to England's fleet. When it made landfall its violent winds plucked trees from their roots as if they were weeds, pockmarking the countryside and battering Bristol and London into new and terrifying shape. In all, the storm killed close to ten thousand people. For Defoe, the events seemed to bring the violent ruptures in his life outwards, painting them across the downed buildings and debris-strewn streets of his city.

As a justification for his ruined business, the storm gave Defoe a way to paper over some of his own failings. As a manifest sign of God's judgement, it moved him to reflect on the wider social ills that had invoked divine wrath. Just as others picked up the pieces of their houses, Defoe began collecting eyewitness accounts: he pieced them together as *The Storm* (1704), an innovative work designed to seek out the causes – both meteorological and providential – and commit to posterity the effects wrought by this extraordinary weather event. Defoe included letters and stories from across the country without altering their style, a choice he justified to readers, whom he trusted to discern the biases of each letter and see in their particular 'Garb' the character of their authors.[8] Readers would come to a varied but comprehensive picture of the country. And yet for all this apparent freedom, the ultimate significance of what they saw lay in Defoe's overarching scheme. The power to know and shape a collective response to the disaster was held in the hands of the man who not only gathered but analysed testimony and intelligence. *The Storm* gave Defoe a way to understand the nation in parts and as a whole. Its success confirmed that writerly industry had the alchemical force to transmute disaster into public benefit – and personal gain.

There is no doubt that financial need motivated Defoe's writing. Yet his almost continuous production cannot be explained by need alone. Writing gave Defoe purpose. The power and fluency of his talent instilled in him a private confidence that could never be adequately matched by public recognition. The gulf between the two is on display in the writer's early letters to Harley, which are too laden with need to waste time on subtlety. It is clear that Defoe wanted a stipend, not a sinecure: a steady line of income that would both ease his financial woes and acknowledge his usefulness to the government. When Joseph Addison was commissioned to write a poem commemorating Marlborough's victory at the Battle of Blenheim – the event that turned the War of the Spanish Succession to England and its allies – Defoe took it as a personal insult. Defoe wrote his own poem commemorating the victory, but that was beside the point. Addison's was the kind of commission he sought: one that offered a clear brief and fulsome praise from readers at Whitehall and Jones' Coffeehouse alike.

Jones' in Finch Lane, near the Royal Exchange, was where Defoe went to read the news and hear the talk of the town. At Jones' he awaited Harley's instructions – carefully. Defoe had the unnerving sense that he was being watched. He took care not to expose the reputation of his new patron to the damage it would incur if he openly met with a 'Man Lately Made Despicable'. Such secrecy imbued the fleeting meetings with a danger that only increased their importance. Defoe fretted on days when he arrived at the coffeehouse too late, finding Harley's notice requesting a meeting after the appointed time had passed.[9] The anxiety was one-sided. Harley preferred to keep Defoe at a remove. His reserve, like Defoe's abject desire for the security of contact, discloses something the writer was not yet willing to admit. Perhaps he was not like Addison. Perhaps the events of his life had so tainted his reputation that, no matter his God-given talent, he might not find such grand, public acclaim.

Still, Defoe had other ways of being useful. In early 1704, months before victory at Blenheim revived public support for the war, Defoe began his *Review*. Its full title suggests the periodical's initial purpose and catches in (not so) brief its first engagement with readers. 'A Review of the Affairs of France: And of All Europe, As Influenc'd by that Nation: Being, Historical Observations, on the Publick Transactions of the World; Purg'd from the Errors and Partiality of *News-Writers*, and *Petty-Statesmen* of all Sides'. The *Review* extolled the administrative and military success of France with the intent of shaking English readers from their complacency. Any perceived lag in support for military action was met with a precise rendering of the threat France posed to England – and its place in Europe.

For much of its first year the paper's focus was on the influence that 'French *Grandeur*' had over 'the *Affairs* of Poland, Sweden, *and Hungary*': all within Harley's new domain.[10] Mr Review, as Defoe styled himself, drew a lot of criticism for being too enamoured with the enemy. This risk was inherent to Defoe's strategic placement of the *Review* above the domestic partisanship of the 'Street-Scriblers'. In formal terms this strategy was made manifest in the paper's essayistic style and appeals to moderation. In early issues Mr Review laid out a warning to those '*News-Writers* and *Petty-Statesmen*' who 'Impose Absurdities' on the unsuspecting populace. His self-styled task was to correct them and, in doing so, disabuse readers who 'are posest with wrong Notions of Things'.[11] The wording bears too close a resemblance to Harley's search for a writer to 'state facts right' and correct the public when they are 'imposed upon by the stories raised by ill designing men' to be a coincidence.[12] If the aims of the *Review* were not directly guided by Harley, then they show a clear tact on Defoe's part for sounding out what his powerful patron wanted.

Traditionally the Secretaries of State were responsible for the management of 'the intelligence': a category whose tasks included the collection and dissemination of open-source news at home and abroad, monitoring the press, as well as obtaining and utilising secret sources.[13] In a set of pamphlets written after his release, Defoe grapples with press freedom and its limits. Defoe was against a system that would require works to be licensed before publication. This was Harley's view too. Not so much because the incoming Secretary championed a free press, but because he realised that there were better, more subtle, ways to exert control. By surveilling writers and prosecuting those whose works were deemed threatening, he could act as censor. The treat of punishment was also designed to impose a rigorous regime of self-censorship, one that in many cases was far more inhibiting than anything the state could muster.[14]

During the early months of his compact with Harley, Defoe wrote with more freedom than would be expected from someone who had been so recently prosecuted. One of Harley's informers was shocked by Defoe's audacity. The informer had infiltrated a meeting of Dissenters and found clear proof that Defoe had written a new anti-Tory satire that violated the terms of his release.[15] Knowing that he had a secret protector gave Defoe some latitude – but not quite as much as he took. From the start he kept some of what he wrote from Harley, maintaining an ability to critique the government. He was testing the boundaries, finding ways he could justify writing for the state while staying true to the steely core of his principles. There was secrecy on Harley's part, too. Though Godolphin knew Harley had employed Defoe, he remained unaware that Defoe was the author of the *Review*. Midway through the first year of its run, he wrote to Harley to complain that the paper's 'magnifying of France is a thing so odious in England, that I can't think any jury would acquit this man if discovered'.

Gradually, though not universally, the *Review* began to toe the Harleyite line. It broadened its focus from France and in soliciting and responding to readers' letters (even those Defoe might have written himself) it found a novel way to know and influence its audience. On 31 July 1704, Defoe was given a full pardon from the Queen. And with it, Harley was given royal sanction. The Queen let her new Secretary of State know that she approved 'entirely of what you … promised' the writer and would 'make it good'.[16] Defoe was now officially Harley's agent.

With the looming threat gone, Defoe's attention turned to the more immediate problem of his debts. Dogged by creditors across London, he wanted an assignment that would take him out of the city. His hope was that this would give him room to plot a way out of the financial mire. This need and the lack of any stable assignment from Harley prompted Defoe to try and define his own position. In this pursuit he promised Harley that he would tender a 'scheme of an Office For Secret Intelligence at home and Abroad'. He started and returned to the scheme throughout the summer. The proposal he eventually produced contained a sophisticated account of how intelligence could be incorporated into the organs of state, giving Harley as its master newfound power and freedom.

As with the *Review*, Defoe's initial point of comparison in the proposal is France. By his calculation France was vastly outspending England on intelligence services. Their investment produced networks of agents and emissaries in courts and cities throughout Europe. To offset this strategic advantage, England would have to expand its intelligence gathering and correspondence networks rapidly. If Harley placed agents in foreign courts, established better communication with ministers in foreign governments and paid informers nestled in towns and cities on the Continent, England could for the first time truly know the interests and strength of those they confronted at war, in negotiation and through trade. The lack of an established intelligence system had already led to serious diplomatic failures. A case in point was Scotland, where the absence of a 'Settl'd Intelligence . . ., a Thing Strangely Neglected There, is without Doubt the Principall Occasion of The present Missunderstandings between the Two kingdomes'.

The other side of this complacent neglect was that England did not do enough to ensure its own state secrets were kept. Defoe was certain that the proceedings of Queen Anne's cabinet were read out at Versailles. His time under interrogation in Nottingham's office left him with the impression that the aristocratic self-assurance that pervaded the administration left England vulnerable: 'Had I been a French Spye I Could ha' Put in My Pockett my Lord N[ottingha]ms Letters Directed to sir Geo: Rook and to the Duke of Marlebro' Laid Carelessly on a Table for the Door keepers to Carry to the Post Office.'[17] These were letters to England's admirals and generals and whoever ventured into Nottingham's office could have read or taken them.

The scheme Defoe outlined to counter these deficits rests on the maxim that 'Intelligence is the Soul of all Publick bussiness'. It is an animating force. For Harley to channel it, he would need to follow the example of Cardinal Richelieu, whose tactical use of spies and informers laid the way for the consolidation and centralisation of the French administrative state. Or he could take the path of Sir Francis Walsingham, Elizabeth I's feared spymaster, whose command of intelligence staved off threats both foreign and domestic. The crucial difference, though, was that unlike these two precursors Harley would need to be favoured by the monarch *and the people*. Defoe counselled popularity, for in Queen Anne's England the people had taken a far greater right over government – perhaps too great, he conceded – than they did in Richelieu's France or Walsingham's England. Defoe made the case that by knowing the people, Harley could dispense justice and commissions in order to gain a reputation as the people's favourite. Popular approval of this kind carried immense power: 'A States Man Once in the Peoples favor has a Thousand Opportunityes to do with Freedome, what in a Contrary Circumstance he would Not Dare to Attempt'.

Possessed of this freedom, Harley could become a 'Premier' or Prime Minister, a position held in deep suspicion at the time but one that Defoe justified by indexing national interest to a popularity built on the kind of virtue that truly merits the people's love. More influential than the intellectual architecture of such a ministry is the infrastructure Defoe laid out for knowing the country. The Premier Minister would need a system of domestic intelligence equal to its foreign branch. He would need knowledge of all England's counties, cities and boroughs, their gentry, clergy, the leading men and the 'Partyes they Espouse'. Ideally the Minister would have and maintain a 'Table of Partyes, and Proper Callculations of their Strength in Every Respective Part' of the country. He could compile this table by collecting 'Coppyes of the Polls Sent up on all Elections, and All the Circumstances of Such Elections Hystorically Collected by faithfull hands'. In other words, the Minister would have a complete set of electoral data supplemented by opinion sampling carried out by domestic agents.[18]

Defoe's memorandum is surprisingly blunt for someone so dependent. The licence he takes is of the kind that Thomas Hobbes associated with the figure of the counsellor. In a well-functioning system of state, counsellors are not punished for what they advise. According to Hobbes, impunity was a necessary precondition to soliciting forthright and useful advice.[19] It is not clear that Harley ever asked Defoe for anything quite so detailed. The memorandum reads more as a projection. Defoe implicitly casts himself as key agent in the intelligence network he outlines by assuming the freedom of speech that such a position would afford him.

⸸

The scheme Defoe presented to Harley shows the writer's native instincts about the nature of intelligence. He knew how it could be gathered and protected, and he knew its political worth. And yet at the same time he presumed too little of the office of Secretary of State and its new occupant in thinking that Harley would have to build a network of spies from scratch. From the late seventeenth century, Secretaries of State deployed far more professional and organised intelligence-gathering operations than Defoe assumed. They used agents to infiltrate the press and employed writers to present selective intelligence to the public to influence them. Defoe's memo is the work of an intuitive outsider: one who knew that there was no permanently established intelligence infrastructure; that Secretaries of State and other ministers often held loose collections of agents as personal fiefdoms, but who failed to grasp that there was a well-established tradition of professional domestic espionage; that Harley had already begun to run 'spies and inspectors' in 'every office to have a general information of everything' and that his elevation to the Secretaryship would only serve to draw in a raft of new recruits.[20]

To demonstrate the value of his own intelligence (in both senses of the word), Defoe reported an attempt by the Whigs to unite with Nottingham's faction in support of a new bill against occasional conformity. Their intent, as Defoe saw it, was to remove Harley, Godolphin and Marlborough from power. The solution Defoe offered Harley was that the Secretary should bribe the weaker amongst the Whigs to undermine the power of their faction. With this advice, Defoe presents intelligence as a way to perform the dark arts and dirty tricks of politics – justified by those who perform them as a necessity, and then by their opponents as a necessary counter, so that, like two weights connected by a string, they tumble over each other to further depths. This was how Richelieu and Walsingham operated. Defoe was not the only one to make the comparison. Harley's own brother thought that 'no person since the time of Secretary Walsingham, ever had better intelligence or employed more money to procure it'.[21]

Despite Harley's efforts to increase the budget, money for intelligence could not cover his ambitions. His office employed two undersecretaries, Erasmus Lewis and Richard Warre, along with clerks, whose facility with languages helped the Secretary and his undersecretaries impose a degree of order over the rafts of petitions, the foreign and domestic correspondence, as well as the open-source and human intelligence that flowed through the office. The clerks usually began this work late at night and often continued well into the following morning.[22] The problem that confronted Harley in the face of this deluge was access. It would have taken heroic diligence to professionalise his office to the extent necessary to secure its intelligence from hostile actors. Even then, there could be no guarantee.

Harley was a conscientious Secretary, but he was also Speaker of the House. He worked hard enough in the roles he occupied that Godolphin felt moved to express his worry that 'you never take any tolerable care of your own health'.[23] Too often Harley opted for the momentary relief of drink, using it to dull the constant thrum of work: a practice his abstemious father and brother deplored. He was known for staying in London when others would have retired to their estates, even remaining in London during the final illness of his first wife. Harley's overextension, and the fact that he assumed a Secretaryship that for much of its history had run on gentlemanly complacency, meant that leaks and lapses were inevitable. All spymasters live in fear of the leak that might break the dam – and in hope of the leak that will break open a foreign court or ministry.

Growing more adept in the role, Harley began to institute a system designed to silo off his agents. Defoe realised that this was so that none of them could 'know the whole Event of what they are employed to do' – so that Harley alone would see the full picture. In practical terms, it meant that Harley dispatched agents in the field with the barest of instructions, sending further notices only when absolutely necessary.[24] To Harley's detractors, this need for secrecy had shadings of French absolutism. Weighing it above the wants of his own agents tended to have an alienating effect on them. It also saw Harley err on the side of cruelty when dealing with suspected foreign spies.

Le Moyne de Brie, a Frenchman travelling south from Edinburgh, experienced this first-hand when he was tracked crossing the border and arrested in Newcastle. Harley's suspicions were enough to keep him in prison for more than two years. With 'no other hope but to perish most miserable having passed all the winter without fire and candel and almost starved also with hunger', the suspected spy wrote appeals in his own blood, 'crying to the publick for Assistance' as he threw them from the prison's windows in a fraught attempt to plead his cause. Harley's 'cautiousness' kept the bloody letters from reaching beyond Newgate: he had guards outside de Brie's windows who intercepted them.[25] When de Brie's case finally came before a court, he was freed. His time in prison and under torture inscribed the image of Harley as a spycatcher so bloodily in his mind that he assumed Harley's mastery of the world of shadows. Two years later and in need of money, de Brie approached Harley with a proposal to work as his spy at the French Court or at one of France's sea ports.

The figure of Harley as all-seeing and all-knowing was self-perpetuating, allowing him to amass a network of local officials, informers and potential agents. In this way he did indeed resemble Richelieu or Walsingham. All three knew that information was power. All three pursued it with a ruthlessness commanding enough to attract people who were willing (or forced by circumstance) to supply information. All three justified the depths they fathomed to gather and extract this intelligence by virtue of the belief that they acted in the national interest. For Richelieu and Walsingham this interest was embodied in their positions as servants to their sovereigns. As well as being Secretary of State, Walsingham was Principal Secretary to Elizabeth I. Richelieu was both Foreign Secretary and Chief Minister to Louis XIII. Harley, on the other hand, derived his sense of national interest from the middle path he took as a member of parliament. Though he served the Queen, he was the umpire of national interest more than its incarnation.

⸸

Early in his service Defoe angled for a posting on the Continent. Harley had other ideas and resolved to send him to the eastern counties on a fact-finding mission designed to gain the kind of local electoral knowledge that the writer recommended in the memorandum.

Defoe set his disappointment aside by recommitting himself to the task. He prepared horses and arranged for Christopher Hurt, a fellow Dissenter, to accompany him on the journey, securing Hurt a leave of absence from his position as a customs agent. It was at this time that Defoe began to take precautions in his correspondence. He wrote to Harley under the alias Alexander Goldsmith, disguising his handwriting lest any interceptor recognise it. His belief in the need for secrecy meant that intellectually he knew why Harley would keep certain instructions from his agents. But on the eve of setting out, he still had not received any detailed orders. A friend who saw him just before his departure found him 'dejected by the deferring of Hope'.[26] It was clear that Defoe was hurt by Harley's apparent nonchalance in the face of a mission he persuaded himself was uniquely suited to his 'Genius' (his natural disposition or character). In Defoe's mind the vague outline of the mission so clearly aligned with his ideal of service that he pegged the renewal of his sense of purpose to its execution. Even if Harley did not directly acknowledge it, Defoe was convinced that the journey he was about to undertake 'may be the foundation of Such an Intelligence as Never was in England'.

As he set out, he fashioned his own brief, supplementing the fragmentary instructions he gleaned from conversations with Harley with his own ideas. Travelling northeast from London, he would gather intelligence on the political makeup of the counties he visited. He would also begin to establish a network of correspondents. These correspondents would ensure that his intelligence remained current as well as serving as hubs for the distribution of pro-ministerial pamphlets. The overarching aim of Defoe's travels was to know and thereby shape the country's political sentiments. Defoe and his agents would gather the information and distribute the propaganda that could bend these sentiments towards Harley's programme of moderation. This would shore up the ministry's position before the next general election, due to take place the following year. As Defoe summarised it, he would travel England 'Spreading Principles of Temper, Moderation, and Peace ... Perswadeing all People that the Govornment is Resolv'd to proceed by those Rules'.[27] By taking the country's temperature – sampling opinions and building a series of local portraits of politics – he could begin to compose the *Review* as if he spoke for the country at large.

Defoe's breezy description fails to capture the very real fear that motivated him. He was increasingly concerned that the moderate way taken by Harley, Godolphin and Marlborough lacked both political allies and national support. This fear left him sensitive to any possible move against them. In one case, a perceived threat dovetailed so neatly with Defoe's personal resentments that he could not let it go. Defoe was convinced that George Rooke, Admiral of the Fleet, was trying to supplant Marlborough as England's military champion. Defoe thought Rooke was a fabulist who exaggerated his triumphs and turned moments of luck into instances of strategic vision, while covering up his mass of defeats. On a personal plane, Defoe blamed Rooke for the attack on William Colepepper, his lawyer in the seditious libel case. Rooke's ascendence so rankled Defoe that he published a poem attacking the Admiral (anonymously and without Harley's knowledge) and criticised him openly in the *Review* and *Master Mercury*. This one-man vendetta would eventually overshadow his first foray into intelligence gathering.

The route Defoe and Hurt took in building the intelligence and distributional network was oriented by the writer's existing contacts and designed so that he could gather subscriptions for his epic poem *Jure Divino.* From London they rode northeast on the road to Barwick, one of most widely used but worst maintained roads in the kingdom. According to one survey, the first twenty to thirty miles provided a comfortable enough ride but after that travellers were warned that they would need to stop often to repair carriages and rest horses. As the road grew bumpier, Defoe and Hurt would have passed Tottenham, High Cross and Hodison (Hoddesdon), Ware and Puckeridge, before wending slightly west to enter Royston.[28] There is no record of the stops Defoe took before Royston but the wide survey of politics in Hertfordshire he sent Harley suggests that he bolstered any prior knowledge by speaking to locals along the way. Defoe assessed that the parts of Hertfordshire 'adjoyning … Bedfordshire and Buckinghamshire' were 'whiggish and Full of Dissenters', whereas the northeastern parts near Royston, adjoining Cambridge, Huntington and Essex were dominated by High Church Tories.[29]

Royston was a malting town, where large quantities of barley grown in neighbouring Cambridgeshire were brought to produce Hertfordshire malt: widely esteemed England's best beer according to Defoe. Drink vivified local politics. Defoe observed the Royston Club, a group of local Tories who met at the Red Lion Inn on the first Thursday of every month to 'Settle all the affaires of the Country'. The Club distributed Church livings, chose magistrates and sheriffs, and had a heavy hand in maintaining the party's dominance in local elections. All Tory candidates for parliament had to have their imprimatur. Defoe gave his account of the Club in his first report from the tour. Though brief, the letter manages to give Harley a sense of the varied political complexion of Hertfordshire, as well as detailing the mechanics of influence likely to shape the upcoming election. Not all of Defoe's reports survive, but from this one we get a sense of electoral data he was compiling.

From Royston, Defoe rode northeast through 'corn country' until he and Hurt reached Cambridge. Defoe was dismissive of Cambridgeshire but struck by Cambridge itself, a place where university and town are 'Blended together' and yet artificially divided in representation, with each electing its own member of parliament.[30] His main contact in Cambridge was Richard Jardine, a linen draper whom Defoe knew from his days as a hosier.[31] As he built up the network, Jardine would serve as an important distribution agent, disseminating Defoe's writing throughout the city and its surrounds.

The lack of rain made Defoe's trip through a typically wet part of the country a little easier. Leaving Cambridge, he continued northeast in the direction of Norwich, where his friend John Fransham lived. Fransham distributed Defoe's works in the region. He was a linen draper and a Dissenter too. A pattern begins to emerge in Defoe's choice of distribution agents. He selected men who were business contacts, friends or fellow Dissenters. As the network grew, more and more of its members were Dissenting clergymen. Defoe clearly selected agents with the sort of affiliation that might ensure their loyalty.[32]

Defoe never reached Norwich. Though he reported to Harley that he had 'Perfectly Dissected' Norfolk, he avoided its main centre after an event in Bury St Edmunds left him fearful of arrest. Defoe stopped at Bury on his way from Cambridge. Still passing himself off as Alexander Goldsmith, he was there to meet John Morley, a broker whose contacts throughout Suffolk and East Anglia would soon provide the ideal channel for distributing the writer's occasional pamphlets and *Review*.[33]

In Bury Defoe stopped at a coffeehouse to read the news. What he read drew him back from his service to his former life as a fugitive. He was deeply unsettled by the 'Barbarity' of 'an Account, that sundry Persons were taken up in *London* for scandalous Libels, that Warrants were out for *Daniel De Foe*, but he was fled from Justice'.[34] The rumour in London was that Defoe's attacks on Rooke constituted libel and thus caused him to forfeit 'his recognizance for this good behaviour'.[35] Defoe's pardon meant that the question of his recognizance had been settled. But at this stage his pardon was a secret, known at Court but not publicly. Even so, the threat of prosecution and the accusation that he was once again a fugitive were sufficient to throw his plans off course. Defoe was now desperate to hear from Harley, telling the Secretary that without his guidance he would 'hardly kno' how to govorn my Self'. Above all, Defoe feared that 'stirring about may be Dangerous'. The risk was that he could be apprehended, taken into custody and his papers confiscated: a prospect that threatened to reveal his connection to Harley.[36] On the same day that Defoe wrote in utter distress to Harley, Hedges wrote to his fellow Secretary to let Harley know he had enough evidence to seize Nathaniel Sammen, the man who had hidden Defoe during the *Shortest Way* affair. To Hedges, Sammen was Defoe's 'tool'. The fact that he was caught dispersing anti-government pamphlets reveals just how fraught Defoe's attempts to maintain both Harley's protection and his independence could be.[37]

Defoe did not want to abandon his mission. He was wary that venturing into too populous an area might lead to his arrest. Instead of going to Norwich and then onto King's Lyn, he opted to divert his path to the sea town along the Norfolk coast, Lowestoft and Great Yarmouth,[38] before circling back to Bury to await Harley's instructions. His companion Christopher Hurt was agitated that the tour was taking longer than expected, and worried that he might lose his position as a customs agent. The tension between the two wove a pall of dread. Defoe was not one to despair. The threats to his reputation and freedom required a defence. His approach was two pronged. He started by walking back some of his criticisms of Rooke. He then maintained in the starkest terms that he was not a fugitive. He had not '*absconded and fled from justice*', for he '*knows no guilt, for which he has any occasion to fly*'. Indeed, as soon as he saw the report, '*he took care to give Publick Notice to the Government where he is*'.[39] Technically he did let Harley know his location. This attempt to respond in the removed cool of the third person does not capture just how worried Defoe was: so much so that he headed to London for two days.

In London Defoe sought out Robin Stephens, messenger of the press, an agent of censorship tasked with monitoring booksellers, publishers and writers, and arresting those whose works were libellous or threatened the public peace. Defoe heard that Stephens would 'detain him if he could find him'. Though troubled, he had just enough doubt in this report to offer himself up to Stephens in person. Faced with the supposed fugitive, Stephens was forced to admit that he had never received any order '*to Stop, Take, or Detain*' the author. An indignant Defoe promised readers of the *Review* £20 (roughly £2,000 in today's money and far more than Defoe could spare) for any information that could identify the source of the '*Scoundrel, Reproachful and Malicious*' rumour that he 'had fled from justice'.[40]

Though the threat of prosecution evaporated quickly, the confrontation left an impression. Coming so soon after his trial and imprisonment, it brought home the tenuousness of his position. Defoe had a powerful patron but one who kept his patronage secret and who showed scant signs that he would directly intercede on Defoe's behalf. Without such intervention, the decentralised layers of government and the courts remained precariously stacked against Defoe. Spent, he cut short his tour and returned once more to London in time to see the new session of parliament that began on 24 October.

⸸

The session opened in flux. With Nottingham gone, the triumvirate-controlled ministry lost its Tory connection. Yet to secure any Whig backers, moderation in government began to look like a concept without a constituency. Without allies, Harley's Speakership was in jeopardy. Defoe advised Harley to allow an occasional conformity bill to be brought to the House. Knowing it would be defeated, Defoe assumed that the debate would draw the moderate centres of both parties together. In order to consolidate this new base of support, Defoe recommended Harley secure a prominent Whig backer. In his sight was Lord Somers. Though a fierce partisan, Somers was deeply committed to England's war efforts and, like the triumvirate, considered the question of occasional conformity a hopeless distraction.

When the bill was defeated in the Lords, Tory writers were able to perceive the 'snare' Harley had laid.[41] The attempts to fashion a durable bipartisan alliance from this defeat faltered when Harley's overtures to Somers stoked Godolphin's jealousy. Godolphin was blinded by his sense of culpability. He was the one who had advised the Queen to give royal assent to the Act of Security mere days before news of Marlborough's victory at Blenheim reached him. By giving the Scottish parliament the right to choose their own successor to Queen Anne, he had in effect conceded the basic bond of the regnal union in exchange for Scottish support of a war that, after Blenheim, looked as if it had already been won.

Godolphin cannot be faulted for bad timing. The Queen had little choice but to allow the Marquis of Tweeddale, Queensberry's replacement as Lord High Commissioner, to give royal assent to the Act of Security. Anne had been willing to compromise, offering to devolve her prerogative to appoint Scottish ministers and judges to the parliament in Edinburgh. Sensing weakness, the Duke of Hamilton led a motley alliance of Cavaliers and Country opposition alongside some of Queensberry's supporters smarting at his dismissal. This collective managed to tie supply for Scottish forces – crucial to the war and to anti-Jacobite resistance – to the Act of Security, while also pushing for a new commercial treaty. The Scottish opposition successfully exploited England's military ambitions to carve out an audacious course to independence.

In response, the English parliament passed the Alien Act. Receiving royal assent on 14 March 1705, the Act deprived Scots of the right of

English subjecthood and hobbled Scottish trade by embargoing imports of cattle, coal and linen until such time as the Hanoverian succession was settled. An earlier version of the bill included a provision for new Union commissioners. While this provision was dropped, the intent of the Act remained clear. It was designed to pressure Scotland into a parliamentary union, one that would forever solve any question of succession or supply. Because supporters of the Act held it up as a way to repair the Godolphin ministry's mismanagement of Scottish affairs, its passage brought Harley's two roles into conflict. As one backbencher quipped: 'the Scots affair was between two: the Speaker and the Secretary'.[42]

The luck of timing aside, England's disintegrating relations with Scotland now lay at the ministry's feet. Harley sensed from Godolphin's paranoid reaction to the pursuit of new alliances that any further breakdown between England and Scotland posed a threat to the cohesion of the triumvirate. As Northern Secretary he had to find a way to bring Scotland to order; as Speaker, he had to prepare for an election less than a year away. The question looming over these tasks was whether he could chart a course that might mend the growing rift between his two roles – and within the ministry itself.

CHAPTER 4

DARIEN

Captain Thomas Green and the crew of the *Worcester* expected little more than a cursory check from customs officers when they moored in the Leith Road, northeast of Edinburgh, at the end of July 1704. A strong set of southerlies had forced the English merchant vessel to seek land at Scotland.[1] This unplanned stop would be the last before Green and his crew delivered the *Worcester* with its cargo of pepper, cinnamon, turmeric and ginger home to England.

The *Worcester* had been at sea for two and a half years, on a trading venture to the spice-rich Malabar Coast. Despite undergoing extensive repairs at Calicutt (Calcutta), the vessel was sapped by leaks on its return voyage. Fifteen months after setting a course for home, Green guided a ship that resisted his hand through the Firth of Forth. His beleaguered crew had had at last found a firmness underfoot: a stable place to rest and recover, knowing England was not far away.[2]

This stability crumbled almost immediately. Days after the *Worcester* had moored, officers from the Company of Scotland trading to Africa and the Indies (the so-called Darien Company) seized her. Their motive was revenge. Earlier that year one of the Darien Company's vessels, the *Annandale*, had been impounded in England, her cargo confiscated and her crew pressed into service by the English navy. The captain of the *Annandale* was accused of recruiting sailors in London, a direct challenge to the East India Company's (EIC) monopoly. The directors of the Darien Company had little doubt that the greed of the EIC drove them to violate 'the Law of Nations' with such spurious accusations.[3]

At first the *Worcester*'s seizure was a bit of brinkmanship, a ploy by the last men of the Darien Company and the nation who had sunk its fortunes into it against England and the rapacious plutocrats of the EIC. The seizure became something else when the crew were led off the ship and into custody. Crossing the gangplank, the gunner's mate of the *Worcester* was heard to mutter, 'This is the just Judgment of God upon us, for the Wickedness committed in our last Voyage.'[4]

The rumour that shot through Leith was that the *Worcester* had engaged in piracy. Carried on the air of cheap print ballads, news of Green's 'most Bloody crime' gathered details as public attention began to circle around the *Speedy Return*, a second Darien Company ship.[5] The *Speedy Return* had undertaken its own trading voyage to the East Indies. It had been due back some months ago and was presumed missing. A search of the *Worcester* turned up coded letters and a Darien Company seal. Disaffected crew members came forward, willing to testify that, in early 1703, the *Worcester* sighted a ship off the coast of Calcutta crewed by Scotsmen. They claimed that the *Worcester* attacked the ship with guns and subdued it; that Green and his purser Mr Loveday led a party to board this ship; and that, once on deck, they commanded a massacre, slaughtering men of a 'neighbour Nation' before ransacking the *Speedy Return*'s cargo and felling the ship off the coast of Malabar to ensure it would never be found.[6]

The intensity of public outrage magnified each bit of circumstantial evidence, forcing rumour and conjecture into a preordained narrative of English bastardry and gallant Scottish victimhood. The effect was that Captain Green and seventeen of his crew were brought up on charges of piracy, robbery and murder at the Court of Admiralty in Edinburgh. No ship was mentioned in the charging documents. The suggestion of piracy was enough to serve the Darien Company's aims. To seize Green's ship and cargo as direct compensation for the seizure of the *Annandale* would have required far more evidence of the EIC's collusion with the independent *Worcester*. Underwriting the whole episode was the failure of the Scottish colony of New Caledonia at Darien. Its loss brought home the need to redress the disadvantages in trade and empire that England had imposed on Scotland, whose hurt pride and demand for compensation gave impulse to seize the *Worcester* in the first place.

⸸

Harley could not ignore the trial of the *Worcester* crew for the risk it posed to Anglo-Scottish relations. He had a worrying letter from Adam Cockburn of Ormiston, Lord Justice Clerk, the second ranked judge in Scotland. Ormiston told of a perfect storm of ministerial ineptitude, public anger and suspicion. The new Lord High Commissioner, John Hay, 2nd Marquess of Tweeddale, was floundering. Having replaced Queensberry after the travesty of the Scotch plot, Tweeddale formed the New Party out of his allies and friends. Ormiston thought that this group was too insular and failed to solicit the broad base of support necessary for effective government. This was not entirely the New Party's fault. Godolphin had not allowed the amiable Tweeddale to offer places or preferments to induce new allies. The New Party were also hampered by constant undermining from the significant set of parliamentarians still loyal to Queensberry, largely coordinated by Queensberry himself.

The fragility of the new ministry spurred judicial action. Fearing that the government lacked the resolve to address the threat of Jacobites and Catholics, Ormiston tendered plans to disarm all Catholics and confiscate their horses. His particular concern was with the portion of Highland Chiefs who clung to the old religion. Taking away their horses and arms as well as those of their private militias would neutralise their threat. Ormiston also offered a plan to root out Jacobites from the ranks of the Presbyterian clergy. The belief that Jacobites had infiltrated all levels of Scottish life by disguising their corruptions as part of the 'country Interest' was widespread.[7] In this uneasy climate, Ormiston and his fellow judges relished their newly enlarged role as defenders of the nation. Despite sharing Godolphin's and Harley's apprehension that Jacobitism was showing signs of recrudescence, they were 'wholly taken up to find Green and his crew pirates'. Disaffection might make an angry crowd yearn for the old monarchs, but as an early investor and promoter of the Darien Company, Ormiston felt he understood its root cause.

Ormiston's letter did end with reason for hope. The scattershot flurry of public opinion in Scotland was not yet fixed against the Union: 'there is ground to work if there were proper instruments', he assured the Secretary.[8] It was this final point that Harley noted as he passed the letter to Godolphin. The two were meant to meet to discuss the Scottish news but a winter cough had Godolphin feeling his mortality. Fearing that 'the heat of' Harley's 'room would kill me, both while I was in it, and when I should go out of it into the air', he sent a brief response.[9] Ormiston's letter, he wrote, is 'right, in every tittle of it'. Scotland was close to combustion: the sources of rebellion had to be quieted, and the events of the *Worcester* trial and its aftermath needed careful management indeed.

⸸

At trial, seventeen out of the eighteen crewmen were found guilty and sentenced to death. The first set of executions was due to take place on 4 April 1705 but was stayed for a week following a request from the Queen. Anne sent word through her Privy Council that she wanted a reprieve for Green and his men. There were reports that some of the crew of the *Speedy Return* had been seen in London. Green's guilt was in serious doubt. Indignant at this apparent miscarriage of justice, the London papers cast the fate of the *Worcester* as a matter of national pride. Paterson was wary. From the moment the ship was seized, he told Harley he thought that it was 'a malicious, violent, and unjustifiable proceeding'. And though he did not want to intervene, the more he saw the populace inflamed, the more convinced he became that Scotland's peace and happiness could only be achieved if it were 'annexed' to the centre kingdom.[10]

The tumult Paterson observed each day on the streets in Edinburgh increased to the point where it offset the pressure from London. A 'vast Concourse of People' made its way to Parliament Close on the day the Scottish Privy Council met to consider the case, its human mass spreading eastwards to Mercat Cross and westwards to the Tolbooth prison, where Green and the crew were being held. Much of Edinburgh was covered in its throng. In Defoe's telling, the 'Rage of the Common People' thwarted any chance that the Council would grant a reprieve. The crowd that day put him in mind of Jan de Wit, the Dutch politician torn limb from torso by an angry mob in the Hague in 1672.

Inside the West Drawing Room of Holyroodhouse, the Council could hear the cries of the people. They had seen the unruly mass on their way in. But even before the crowd began to assemble, the Council was cowed. Lord Chancellor Seafield had struggled to find the numbers: any member who could find an excuse not to attend did. Those who turned up had neither courage nor political capital enough to deny the anger of the baying mob. Seizing on a technicality – that the request for a reprieve had come from their English counterparts and not the Queen herself – they found the requisite cover to proceed with the execution.

As Seafield's carriage left Holyroodhouse and travelled west towards the Cross, someone in the crowd shouted that the Council had '*Cheated them ... and repriv'd the Criminals*'. The lie ran like 'Wild-fire' from person to person. As the word was passed, it focused their violence. Instead of insults the people now hurled stones. By the time Seafield's carriage reached the Tron Kirk its windows had been smashed. In Seafield's account, it was at this point that the violence of the crowd forced him 'to come out and expose myself intirely to there [their] fury'.[11] Shouting over them, he was able to assure those massed around him that their satisfaction was imminent: the execution would proceed as planned.

Though Seafield escaped danger, his words did little to sate the crowd's fury. They had come to see the English pirates hanged and remained steadfastly in place later that afternoon when Green and two of his crew, Simpson and John Madder, were led through the city to the Leith Sands, the execution site for crimes committed at sea. Even in the dreich Scottish winter, the condemned moved as if weighed by heat, as the hands of the crowd's hydra grabbed at them, each part keen to get a bit of personal satisfaction.

The three men were hanged together. The ropes had no sooner stilled than the crowd had a change of heart. Or so Defoe maintained. In his second-hand retrospective account, the men and women at Leith Sands who saw three lives taken as if they were fish brought on land, lurching and straining as they drowned in air, 'openly regrated what they had done and were ready to tear one another to pieces for the Excess'.[12] This is far too neat a turnaround to be taken as fact. There is evidence, though, that the execution served its purpose – at least as far as settling the people's fury was concerned. Green, Simpson and Madder were the only members of the *Worcester*'s crew put to death. In the following weeks the rest were quietly released, under the nose of public notice.

At the time Defoe was convinced that the execution would provoke the English people. He cautioned readers of the *Review* to remain sceptical, urging them to ignore the reams of print that fixated on the inconsistencies in the case and carried Green's dying protest of innocence. Surely the 'National Justice of *Scotland*, would not Condemn and Execute Men without sufficient Evidence of Fact'?[13] With hindsight, Defoe conceded the difficulty of such appeals. The 'Continual Necessity' to 'set both sides to right' betrayed a complete lack of understanding between Scotland and England (in both senses of the word).[14] The kind of understanding that bonds allies is not just a matter of reason or pragmatic interest but is felt, guided by a sense of shared purpose. The *Worcester* affair exposed this, showing just 'how easie it is to set Nations on a flame, by the Violent Fomenting [of] the Passions and Humours of the People'. For Paterson, it showed that the multitude in Scotland could 'become capable of any ill impression'. By Defoe's reckoning, the 'Animosities on both Sides' were 'raised to such a pitch' that the only possible outcomes were 'a Union or a War'.[15]

Again, Defoe leans towards melodrama. Yet the handling of the case did change things. For one, it hastened the end of New Party rule and ensured the rise of John Campbell, 2nd Duke of Argyll, son of Archibald (Beaufort's patron and Queensberry's ally against the Act of Security) to the position of Lord High Commissioner.[16] The 2nd Duke of Argyll was often spoken of as a military commander and not a politician, but in both realms he was an astute tactician. And while some onlookers thought his rise to the head of the Court party and appointment as Lord High Commissioner marked a break from Queensberry, it is more likely the two worked in concert, with Argyll's rise bringing Queensberry back from political exile. George Lockhart of Carnwath, the Jacobite politician and historian, believed that it was

Queensberry who controlled things, using Argyll 'as a monkey did the cat in pulling in the hot roasted chestnuts'. But the reason Ormiston feared Argyll's appointment had less to do with his connections to Queensberry than the impression that Argyll had too readily aligned himself with popular anger and against the wishes of the Queen.[17] Popular anger had shown its political force. And Ormiston's worry was that Argyll might give in to the campaign of pamphlets and addresses that stirred the people against Green and his English masters: a campaign that had already given the opposition new confidence.[18] The chief source of this anger was Darien.

Defoe's first impressions of Darien came from tales of adventure. William Dampier's *A New Voyage Round the World* (1697) observed the Isthmus connecting the Americas, where one could pass from the Atlantic to the Pacific in three days – though his own attempt took twenty-three.

Dampier left the description of Darien itself to Lionel Wafer, the ship's surgeon. An injury suffered en route had given Wafer a far more intimate knowledge of the place and its people.[19] Wafer and two others broken by the journey made camp at a Cuna village.[20] Using basic Spanish, gestures and what little Chibchan he had managed to pick up, Wafer communicated with the chief. Impressed by how effectively the Cuna had treated his wound, he began exchanging medical knowledge with the tribe. As he recovered and during his attempt to rejoin Dampier, Wafer turned his empiricist gaze to the Isthmus, publishing what he saw there in *A New Voyage and Description of the Isthmus of America* (1699).

Wafer's book rings with promise. Though it does not turn away from his suffering, the floods that swamped the village and nearly drowned him, nor the moments when friendly relations with the Cuna broke down, the book describes a Panama primed for exploitation. There is not 'a more pleasant and advantageous' bay anywhere; 'Perennial springs' abound with ready access to fresh water; there is a 'Good Harbour'; parts of the Isthmus contain 'excellent fruitful land'; other parts possess a land 'so fertile, that upon clearing any considerable part of the woods it would doubtless afford excellent pasture'.[21]

The stories of self-reliance, colonial encounter, and exploration fed Defoe's mind; refining a faith that a 'tour of the world in books' could equip a reader with all that is necessary to become 'master of the geography of the Universe'.[22] It was on this point that he and Paterson disagreed most profoundly.

⸸

Paterson was most likely in Jamaica when the privateer Bartholomew Sharp began raiding Spanish settlements in Central America.[23] It was during Sharp's raids that Dampier first reached the Isthmus. And it was Sharp who found clear evidence that an overland route between the oceans was possible. The excitement this discovery generated in England's Caribbean colony gave Paterson the idea to establish an entrepôt: a point of collection, trade and distribution for the riches of the Pacific and Atlantic worlds. Paterson promoted this idea from the early 1680s. His case became stronger when Dampier and Wafer returned to England a decade later. More than anything else, though, two events coincided to put his plan into action. The first was the incorporation of the Company of Scotland Trading to Africa and the Indies in June 1695 by an Act of the Scottish parliament, with Paterson listed as one of its directors. The second was his presentation in manuscript of works on Africa, the East and West Indies, which narrowed the Company's wide scope for imperial trade to Darien and the planting of a Scottish base there.

Paterson was far and above the most active of the Company's initial directors. As soon as the Act of Incorporation passed, he harried the other directors into meeting. He believed that the energy of mercantilism was self-perpetuating: money begets money, trade begets trade, and the sooner the Company began raising funds, the quicker these funds would be raised. He pushed for the Act establishing the Company to be published and distributed. The time was right 'to strike while the iron is hot', he urged his more reticent colleagues. The 'People here are already as much awaken'd as they are like to be'. Once the subscription books had a few names they would fill fast.[24]

Finding investors for the Company of Scotland was only part of why he wanted regular meetings with his fellow directors. For him, it was just as important that they settle the Company's constitution. If he guided this process, he could shape the politics of Scotland's colonial endeavour, and in doing so, reshape Scotland itself. The Company opened its London subscription book in the autumn of 1695.

Paterson met with resistance from the start. The Act incorporating the Company was passed when William III was on campaign. The initial lack of response gave Paterson too rosy a measure of England's protectionism. The King believed that the Company had formed behind his back with the intent of circumventing the Navigation Acts, which classed Scotland as a foreign nation for the purposes of imperial trade, barring Scots from legally trading in or with the English colonies even though they shared a monarch. To the bristly King, the Company's formation assumed that ultimate sovereignty lay with the parliament of Scotland.[25] William was also reluctant to do anything that might compromise his efforts to negotiate a partition treaty with Spain, one that might prevent Louis XIV from acquiring the Spanish Empire on the death of the heirless Spanish king, Charles II. Once he had grasped the potential effects of this 'interloping' Company, he set out to destroy it; once the English parliament noticed, they too resolved to break 'the neck' of its London base.[26] News of a thwarted assassination plot against the King and fears of a Jacobite invasion of Scotland further skewed William against any effort that might lessen the northern kingdom's dependency. With pressure from William, from the EIC, and the risk of legal challenge and potential impeachment in parliament, the Company of Scotland closed its London subscription books two weeks after they first opened and transferred the base of its operation to Edinburgh.

The question of sovereignty cut both ways. To Lord Belhaven, one of the Company's directors, the English parliament had acted underhandedly by attacking the very 'Independency of the [Scottish] Nation, through the Bowels of the Company'.[27] Forcing the closure of the London subscription books meant the directors had to forgo the £300,000 (roughly £32 million today) pledged by London merchants eager to break the EIC's monopoly. The sacrifice was personal for Paterson. When the Company was initially formed he was offered a reward of 2 per cent of subscriptions and 3 per cent of the venture's eventual profits. With the loss of London as a source of capital, he was forced to relinquish such unprecedently good terms.

Though cut off from the wealth of London, enthusiasm ran high for the Company in Edinburgh and Glasgow and across Scotland. As a Scottish-only enterprise, it became a vehicle for patriotism. The boon was that an exclusively Scottish Company could revivify the Scottish economy, raising the nation so that it could engage England on more equal terms. The risk was that without English investment, England could safely disavow the colony and maintain an imperial policy designed to ensure that England alone benefited from its global trade.

Scottish investment came quickly. The company needed to secure £400,000 (about £42 million today). On the first day they raised just over £50,000 (about £5 million today) in Edinburgh alone. The subscription books opened in Glasgow a week later and within five months they had reached their goal – on paper. Subscribers outlaid a portion of their investment on the promise that they would pay the rest later. To spur subscriptions, Paterson met and worked his enthusiasm on Anne, Duchess of Hamilton.[28] Anne exerted her considerable influence to drive investment, giving potential subscribers a perceived permission to go against the wishes of their King. Her son the Duke worked behind the scenes, lobbying Queensberry to ask the King to embrace and protect a Company upon whose success 'the interest and the honour of the nation depended'.[29] Winning her over was a strategic victory on Paterson's part. The shareholders that followed the Duchess's lead covered a large portion of Scotland. Roughly half came from the landed classes and a quarter were merchants in Edinburgh or Glasgow.[30] The Company had a wide purchase on the nation: professional organisations invested, as did civic authorities in Glasgow and Edinburgh. Burghs and towns across Scotland, from the Highlands to the borders, from St Andrews in the east to Ayr in the West, invested on behalf of their inhabitants. It was not just that the nation as a whole stood to gain; a large part of its people stood to benefit directly.

Wary of any further interference from England, Paterson tried to keep the full measure of his ambitions for Scotland hidden from the English parliament. On 23 July 1696, he arrived at a meeting in

Edinburgh carrying a bounty of manuscripts and books. His fellow directors were overwhelmed by the depth of his knowledge and the pains he had taken to gather the materials. They resolved that the places of trade and settlement that Paterson found 'may prove exceeding[ly] beneficial to this company'. Paterson had in effect found the site of Scotland's new colony. In an effort to keep their plans hidden, lest they attract English or Spanish ire, they further resolved to seal their instructions. If all went to plan, the site would not be revealed until the Company's fleet had reached open waters.[31]

The manuscripts Paterson lodged in the Company's library justified the Isthmus of Panama as the ideal location for Scotland's colony. From later writings we get a sense of how this location supported Paterson's quest for a new kind of imperialism, less centred on simple acquisition and protectionism and geared more to facilitating global trade. In his mind, Spain provided an example of an empire run to its own destruction. Because Spain failed to incorporate new citizens, their colonies depopulated the main and undermined its economic development. Because driven by a desire to spread Catholicism, the Spanish ignored potential trading partners and clung to an exclusivity that limited the benefits their colonies could provide. In contrast, Paterson thought colonialism could be married to liberalism. Imperial power would only be increased if it opened its borders to trade but regulated it in its favour, if it opened its doors to more citizens and gave them a freedom of religion.

The Isthmus of Darien was perfect. Not only was it rich in exploitable resources but its location 'seated between the two vast oceans of the universe' and 'furnished on each side with excellent harbours' meant that it offered one of 'the keys of the Indies and doors of the world'. By claiming and developing this point of connection between the Atlantic and Pacific, Scotland would achieve global prominence and vast wealth. When Paterson later wanted to redesign the Isthmus as a British colony, he went even further, citing Darien as the vital point for 'gaining and afterwards forever keeping the command of the Spacious South sea . . . by far the richest in the world'.[32] He thought it might be feasible to open a channel between the oceans with a canal – an idea that when executed in 1913 changed world trade for ever.[33]

Paterson's charisma carried his proposal over the heads of objections. His confidence set aside all portents: the stories of floods that enveloped whole villages, Dampier's and Wafer's near fatal brushes with the Miskito and Cuna, and the ever-present threat of the Spanish. Paterson and his supporters operated on the presumption that Darien was not part of the Spanish Empire. Despite the fact that Spain had sent soldiers and settlers there as early as the sixteenth century, the Company of Scotland argued that because Spain had not occupied the ground continuously, Darien remained open to other European nations.[34] The directors called on both Dampier and Wafer to give testimony. What they said clearly bolstered Paterson's account: their stories of mineral wealth and branching the two oceans must have outweighed the risk Spain posed.

Paterson offered a further positive justification. Unlike Spain, which maintained 'Tyranny in the Indies', the Scots would be benevolent colonists and would, he claimed, treat the Indigenous people well.[35] The blinders common to the time meant that the Scottish public saw little contradiction in Scotland pursuing freedom from Spain's oppression of the Indians, while actively seeking to participate in the slave trade. The inhuman complacency required to defend a benevolent form of colonisation is on easy display in a poem that celebrates the idea of a Scottish colony, masterminded by 'Wise Paterson', 'Judicious Paterson', a man of 'steddy soul'. Here the fact that the merest idea of a Scottish colony provokes '*English* anger ... proves its excellence', and affirms its design to burst forth from England's imperious control. An animating spirit of freedom is carried through by Paterson, who made it 'evident that Trade by Sea':

> Needs little more Support than being free,
> Freedom's the Polar-star by which it steers,
> Secure its Freedom, and it nothing fears.

'Free Trade' is nation building: it is a solution to Scotland's agricultural and mineral deficits, the path to breaking the nation out of poverty. The poem conveys an idea of mercantile virtue, one that raises all who partake of it, but in teaching 'us what to take and what to refuse' also instils a natural limit to acquisition. It is upon this virtue that the 'Company designs a colony', a place where 'all Mankind' can 'resort', where labourers gain 'an easie Wealth', where 'Black Slaves like bussie Bees will plant them Canes . . . Which boil'd to Sugar, brings in constant gains'.[36]

The 'easie Wealth' and 'constant gains' a Scottish colony promised betrays the notion that imperialism contained a natural limit. Ease and earning came on the burdened backs of the enslaved. In its time the argument that colonisation would free Scotland was convincing. In the streets of Edinburgh, Paterson was lauded as the man who turned a nation better suited to war towards the idea and benefit of trade.

With the English subscription books closed, and Scottish subscribers tapped to their full potential, Paterson would have to go Europe, combining his trip to help procure ships and supplies with a campaign to solicit foreign investors who might pay for them.[37]

⸸

Paterson went first to Hamburg, where the English Resident Sir Paul Rycaut had agents follow him and note down everyone he met. Rycaut had orders to thwart Paterson, and to ensure that the Company 'fell there'.[38] The Resident convinced the Hamburg Senate to ban Paterson from establishing a Company factory in the city. Rycaut also published anonymous tracts aspersing the legitimacy of the Company, discouraging potential investors. When Paterson found out, he felt Rycaut had 'vilified & defamed' the Company.[39] The Resident's report to Whitehall contained a decisive piece of intelligence: it alerted the Secretary of State that Darien was one of several places the Scots had selected as potential colonies. With the cover of secrecy lost, the notion of a Scottish colony took tangible form. As it did, English opposition solidified. An English commission called Wafer and Dampier and interrogated them about Scottish designs on Darien.[40]

From Hamburg Paterson travelled to Prussia and then to Amsterdam where, with three other Company representatives – Lieutenant Colonel John Erskine, John Haldane of Gleneagles and James Smyth – he was tasked with securing more ships and the bulk of supplies for the expedition. The Company entrusted him and his compatriots with £25,000.

Paterson in turn placed his trust in Smyth, a man whose multiple aliases kept his dubious past from the Company's view. Smyth was one of Paterson's epigones and knew how to play on the older man's ego. With the outlay of the Company resting on Paterson's ease in European ports of trade, he took charge, transferring close to £17,000 with which Smyth was to pay the shipbuilders. To Paterson's dismay, the heavily indebted Smyth embezzled the funds. The Company managed to clutch back just over half the losses and a report cleared Paterson of collusion and 'any design to cheat or defraud'. Still, rumours of embezzlement hampered his ability to secure Dutch investors. Paterson never managed to get anywhere near enough money from the Continent to pay for the fleet and had to use the fast-depleting funds of Scottish subscribers: a fact some of the directors saw as trickery, a bit of quick-handed accounting that 'rob[bed] the Company to raise the colony'.[41] Paterson offset some of the outstanding losses from Smyth's thievery with his own money and, desperate to regain his standing, offered to forgo the expedition in order to work in London for the rest. While humbled by his generosity, the report's authors recommended the Company turn down this offer. Paterson would be of more use in the Amcricas.[42] A percentage of the profits he gained there could be returned to the Company's coffers. Paterson understood the project better than anyone, and his 'reputation in several places of America' would surely draw settlers from nearby plantations.[43] The directors managed to cover up the lost funds and were able to assemble ships and supplies. They did not believe Paterson as necessary as the report's authors. The events in Amsterdam had soiled their image of his commercial genius.

The court of directors placed control over the expedition in the hands of seven councillors: Major James Cunningham of Aiket, James Montgomery, Daniel Mackay, Captain Robert Jolly, Captain Robert Pennecuik, Captain William Veitch and Captain Robert Pincarton.[44] Paterson would have to travel as an uncommissioned settler. This loss of status unnerved him. He retained a fierce possessiveness over the Company and its plans, believing that he knew better than the expedition's rulers (and he often did). Though he remained a director in name, Paterson was cut off from the first governing party; he could do little more than express his opinion or vent his alarm as his beloved project set off, casting its fate to the sea.

☩

The directors knew that they needed colonists with experience in the Americas. Unwilling to let Paterson back into the inner circle, they invited Lionel Wafer to Edinburgh in the spring of 1698. Knowing that his presence would confirm the colony's planned location, Wafer travelled incognito as Mr Brown of London. In Edinburgh, Wafer lodged with Andrew Fletcher of Saltoun – the writer, political theorist, politician and fierce Scottish patriot who endorsed Paterson's idea of a trading hub that would carry the benefits of imperial conquest without 'contracting the guilt and blood of Alexander and Caesar'. Fletcher was instrumental in promoting the Company and had been a key driver of Scottish investment, which he saw as a way to raise Scotland from its position as 'the only part of Europe' yet to benefit from global commerce.[45] For Saltoun, the chief benefit of the wealth Darien promised was its guarantee that Scotland would never have to be incorporated into England's realm.[46] In Edinburgh, Wafer furtively met with the directors before cordoning himself off in a secret garret. All evidence suggests that he was prepared to voyage back to Darien. And yet, for some lost reason, he was not amidst the '60 petty officers and 1200 good men' to come aboard the fleet at Leith on 14 July.[47]

Five ships left that day: the *Caledonia*, the *St Andrew*, the *Unicorn*, the *Dolphin* and the *Endeavour*. Paterson was on the *Unicorn*, which was first christened the *Union* but underwent a last-minute name change, rather ominously, to reflect that this was no longer a joint British project. After settling himself in, Paterson went aboard the convoy's lead, the *St Andrew*, to meet with Captain Pennecuik, commodore of the fleet. Paterson found the Captain rigid in his sense of hierarchy and totally unwilling as a result to truck any discussion of his work or domain. When Paterson urged the Captain to call a council in order to canvass the supplies and report any deficiencies to the court of directors, Pennecuik's only response was that he 'knew his business'.[48] The rebuff was brutal for what it forecast. Paterson was trapped in a protocol-forged prison, one that stilled his energy in its course. For a man who prided himself on competence and usefulness, to be treated as an amateur was a bitter insult.

†

The fleet sailed into the North Sea harassed by 'blustering foggy weather' that settled once Scotland faded from sight.[49] Two days into the voyage and Paterson's instincts proved correct. Provisions were short and the already stringent rations had to be reduced further. The seven councillors wrote letters to the directors in Edinburgh for more. The most direct way to get the information home was to send the letters from Orkney. The weather would not allow it: dangerous currents dragged them on and 'fogie hazy weather' obscured any line of sight, preventing the ships from reaching the Northern Isles and separating the *Unicorn* and the *Endeavour* from the rest. It was only after rounding the north of Scotland and sailing southwards from the European main to Madeira, which they reached close to six weeks later, that the ships were all brought back together and the letters dispatched by way of Lisbon and Holland. At Madeira the first set of orders was finally opened and what remained of a badly kept secret was revealed. The ships were to 'proceed to the Bay of Darien and make the Isle called the Golden Island ... some few leagues to the leeward of the mouth of the great River of Darien and there make a settlement on the mainland'. In Madeira the council held an election: Paterson was once again named a councillor, replacing Veitch, who had been prevented from joining the mission by illness.

On 2 September 1698 the fleet left the Portuguese colony to cross the Atlantic. Buffeted by providence, a 'fair gale' drove an easy pace, delivering the ships across the Tropic of Cancer eight days later,[50] and keeping them at a good clip until they reached the leeward islands of the Caribbean, Antigua and Montserrat, at the end of the month.

With the calm, clear waters holding the ships in formation, members of council gathered on the *St Andrew*. The final approach to Darien had to be executed carefully. The councillors decided that the bulk of the fleet would sail northwest to anchor at Crab Island, off the coast of Puerto Rico. Captain Pincarton and Paterson, along with the crews of the *Unicorn* and the *Dolphin*, would be sent to St Thomas, a freeport then in Danish control. The purpose of their trip was to gain intelligence about the state of Darien and to try to find some guides to aid the delicate processes of securing a landing spot and setting the first foundations: a period of intense vulnerability as planters left the defences of the ships for a patch of land yet to have defences of its own. Paterson's familiarity with Caribbean traders meant that the council had no choice but to employ his services. They did so grudgingly. Paterson assumed that, after deferring to the expertise of the sea captains on matters of navigation, the reverse would be true when it came to trade, to staking out and putting down the colony's roots. The men of the sea, whose dispositions Paterson found 'as boisterous and turbulent as the elements they are used to struggle with',[51] ceded little control, deploying Paterson's talents and contacts without taking his counsel. Unable to ignore their mismanagement, Paterson battered against them.

On St Thomas, Paterson and Pincarton chanced upon Captain Richard Moon of Jamaica, a man Paterson had known from his time there. Encouraged that he might secure some much-needed provisions, Paterson took Moon to see the rest of the ships. Moon was unimpressed. The goods the fleet had brought to trade were ill-sorted and expensive. He would not trade. For all Paterson's imploring, the council would not lower their asking price. Dire as their need was, the councillors refused to make a loss. It was as if they were still in Edinburgh, with no hungry people in their charge. They thought only of their ledgers, where Paterson saw the work of numbers in the world. The Company at sea needed to be seen as viable. If Moon reported on the price and state of their goods, it could cut them off. A 'lame account' of the cargo could ruin all prospects. The council failed to see his reason. Ever canny, Paterson persuaded Moon that the way the cargo was arranged obscured the better part from view; he urged the Captain to encourage his friends in Jamaica to send a sloop with supplies to Panama.

⚘

The final passage to Golden Island was a fatal one, hobbling the colonists before they ever touched new land. The first wave of tropical illnesses enclosed the fleet. One of the Company's surgeons assumed that the fevers came from drinking 'unwholesome water'. According to his report, a 'general distemper . . . seized most yea almost all our people'. The men and women of the *Unicorn* were the worst affected.[52] Paterson was surrounded by death, which cloyed at him with the thick humidity of the Caribbean air. His personal clerk Thomas Fenner died just as the ships passed Golden Island and anchored off its coast. Paterson watched as a man he worked closely with, whose skills he counted on to help administer the colony, shivered in violent fits until a deathly pall stilled him.

Golden Island proved less enticing than first assumed. The cliffs were steep, the anchorage poor and the top of the island so heavily canopied in trees that the illness-wearied fleet could barely contemplate its clearing. Sitting off the island, having taken in its scope and scenes, the Scots had their first contact with the Cuna. A periagua carrying a dozen or so men sidled up to the *St Andrew*. The first off the smaller craft was a man the Scots came to know as Captain Andreas. Entranced by the 'gravity of his Cariage', the Scots immediately marked him out as the party's leader. He wore a 'loose red stuff coat on, with an old hat, a pair of white drawers, but no shoes nor stockens'. His garb set him apart from the men following him, who 'were stark naked' except for 'a thread tied around their middles' that kept in place 'a small piece of plate' that loosely covered their penises. Andreas was there to sound the Scots' purpose. He wanted to know if 'wee were friends to the Spaniard'. Pennecuik's answer divulged their uncertain diplomatic position: 'wee had no warr with any Nation; that if the Spaniard did offer us no affront nor injury, wee had nothing to say to them; but otherwayes wee wold make open war with them'. The Scottish were not truly equipped to carry out Pennecuik's threat. This is why the Commodore stressed that their principal 'business was trade': if Andreas and his people 'received us as friends . . . we wold supply them from time to time with such commodities as they wanted, at much more reasonable rates than either the Spaniard or any other could do'. There is a disconnect in how the Darien Company presented itself as militarily non-threatening while pursuing a free trade agenda that could undercut the interest of the Spanish Empire. Pennecuik's tortured navigation of this tension was lost on Andreas, who assumed that the Scots were 'privateers' intent on reaching the South Sea. As a Cuna war captain, Andreas established alliances with European invaders and played them off against each other for his own strategic purposes. He traded in intelligence and would soon convey information between the Scottish settlement and the Spanish ports that surrounded it. His initial assessment carried through: at first the Spanish considered the Scots to be privateers, though they remained wary, lest any hint of permanency signal an incursion into their domain.

With no suitable way to make land at Golden Island, and the mainland directly opposite it sheeted with mangrove swamps, Pennecuik sent the smaller ships out in search of a settlement site. The advance party sailed eastwards, past a promontory that would serve as a good fort, and down the peninsula. Just under the promontory was a marsh and, one skip further south, a cove. This was the place they could at last stake their settlement. The mood amongst the sea-worn travellers was optimistic. The cove, which they named Caledonia Bay, was 'naturally defended from Winds and Storms' by the surrounding outcrop of hills: a landscape that was militarily defensible.[53] The harbour was difficult to enter. Rocks littered the mid-channel. It was even harder to leave, especially during the dry season when strong winds blew directly into the bay.[54] At that moment, though, the thought that they might need an easy way to escape was pushed aside by the utter relief of arrival.

Breezes from land and sea beat lightly as the fleet moved into the harbour and began the process of sending people ashore. Even in this ideal weather, the *Unicorn* struck a sunken rock, skinning off 'some of her sheathing'.[55] Pincarton righted her, and was able to send forty men to join forty men from each of the other ships to begin the process of clearing the land. Paterson worried that the site chosen by the 'sea counsellors' was a 'meer morass'. The nearest source of drinking water was at least half a mile off and the swamplands that surrounded buzzed with life, dispersing fresh crops of mosquitoes that marked the Scotch-white skin of the labourers like jots of unwelcome punctuation.[56]

Each day more men left the ships for the shore. They noticed that the trees were thicker just off the sand on the ground they had to clear to make New Edinburgh than they were further inland. The

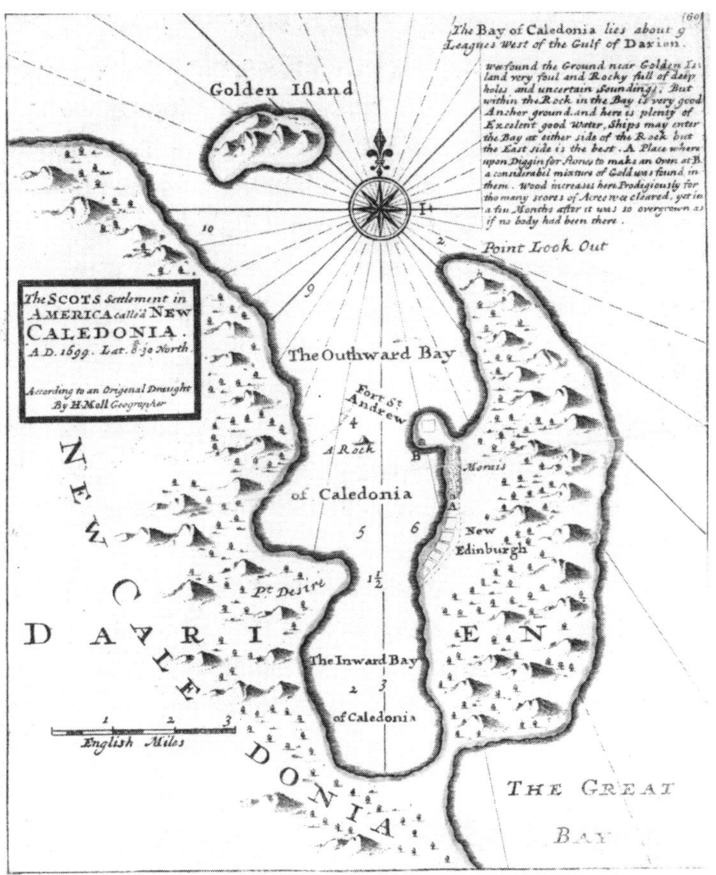

6. The Bay of Caledonia and Scots Settlement, drafted by H. G. Moll after his original (1729).

wind cut the heat to bearable levels; 'on the tops of the Trees' it made 'a pleasant Melancholly Musick'. Ensorcelled by 'the Coolness, Pleasant Murmuring of the Air, and the infinite beauty of a continued Natural Arbor', one colonist was moved to strains of pastoral fancy and began calling the thick canopy the 'shades of Love'.[57] Even so, the task that fell to the healthy amongst the early settlers was grim. They had to build houses for the sick – hasty structures made from foraged wood with the leaves of plantain trees as roofs. For the good of all, the sick had to be taken off the ships and into the dwellings of New Edinburgh as quickly as possible.

Paterson's wife Hannah was one of the first people carried into the new houses. Ten days after first landing, she died, overcome by fever. Benumbed by Hannah's death and without Thomas Fenner's aid, Paterson willed himself into monitoring the development of the colony. The execution did not fit his plan. Even the healthy were 'weake for want of sufficient allowance'.

The first site chosen for Fort St Andrew proved unsuitable. The effort spent clearing the land only to have to relocate and begin the process again depleted the settlers. Energy was a vital resource; to be forced to spend it without gain exponentially increased its consumption. There was no time for the settlers to rest and recoup their strength. A French ship anchored in the harbour brought news that the Spanish 'along the whole Coast are in a wonderful consternation' about the Scots. Their intelligence now signalled that the colonists intended to establish a permanent outpost within the bounds of the Spanish Empire. For Spain this was an intolerable exposure of weakness. The French Captain told the council that the Spanish were preparing ships for an invasion. The colonist's Cuna allies reported sightings of Spanish soldiers. It was yet unclear whether these soldiers formed scouting parties or, as Andreas reported, a full army marching from Panama to Portobello with the aim of retaking the Isthmus.[58] Whatever the case, the life of the colony depended on the fort. Beset by hunger and sickness, the colonists managed to construct a platform for sixteen guns, shielded on the landward side by a parapet with a half-bastion at each end. They dug a canal through the land that connected the promontory to the rest of the peninsula. Eight feet deep and twelve wide, the canal was designed to prevent the scrambling incursion of any invaders. Beyond the canal, the colonists cut back the forest's thickness. Defenders now had a clear line of shot should any Spanish soldiers make it to or across the water.[59]

†

Scotland's image of itself as an enlightened coloniser filtered through the instructions sent with the ships. Once they reached their final destination, the council opened a second set of sealed briefs and found that as the leaders of Caledonia they were commanded 'to take all possible methods to oblige the natives and to enter into a strict correspondence with them, thereby to procure their right or consent to any settlement'.[60] The settlers did not acquire the consent of the peninsula's Indigenous peoples, but they did manage to establish alliances, with varying degrees of formality. Andreas dealt with the Spanish and the Scottish as it suited his needs. Other chiefs like Diego Tucuapantos and Estrara saw an alliance with the Scots as a way to expel the Spanish. These chiefs made the leaders of New Caledonia 'severall advantageous offers to undertake against the Spaniards'. Their reports of Spanish attacks kept the settlers in a steady state of alarm. The sense of mutual need saw Diego put his mark to a treaty of friendship. Solemnised at the newly finished fort on 24 February 1699, the Treaty of Friendship, Union, and perpetual Confederation obliged the Council of Caledonia and Diego's confederation 'to defend the persons, lands, territories, dependencies, and properties of each other by land and sea'.[61]

The terms of the Treaty revealed the disparity between how the framers in Scotland envisioned their sovereign claims to this new land and how the settlers staked those claims in fact. The distance between gaining the consent of the Indigenous peoples to a situation where the Scots increasingly relied on them for defence and supply was felt by Paterson before the rest of the council. Paterson was one of the lead negotiators of the Treaty. He had made the trek to the Cuna villages, had met Diego and appreciated how much of the good relations were built on a mutual antipathy to Spain. The Cuna saw in the Scots a new set of white men who could act against a coloniser whose brutal force they knew far too well.

For their part, the Scots first saw the Cuna as guides. The rumours of mines rich with precious metals were seemingly confirmed by the gold plates that the Cuna wore in their lips and the sparkling beads threaded between the teeth that they hung round their necks. The omens were good. One witness describes how during Paterson's speech the unease of early encounter was broken by laughter when 'A Drove of Monkeys came leaping up and down the Branches of the Trees', throwing things and pissing amongst the people, but doing so by hanging from 'one another's Tails, in a Chain, and swinging in that manner till the lowermost catch'd hold of the Bough of another Tree, and drew up the rest'. For the Cuna, this was a sign of the need for 'mutual assistance'. The monkeys signified something more practical for Paterson, who saw them as another token of the land's natural abundance. The creatures themselves made for 'very agreeable meat'. The negotiating party encountered strange rabbits, 'large as Hares, which have no Tails, but little short Ears, with huge large long Claws' (most likely agoutis), which provided succulent eating, 'much moister than *European* Rabbets'. They also found a rich plant life. There were plantains and bananas, which the Cuna planted in rows. There was maize, which the women cultivated in the 'Savannahs' between forest groves. The settlers who had not eaten maize before described how it 'makes a substantial strong Bread, but it eats something dryer and harsher than our Wheat'. Its chief virtue was its yield: the Scots saw a potential end to their hunger in the fact that 'It produces a wonderful increase, above a Thousand for One'. Around the Cuna villages and between them and Fort St Andrew were Spanish cedar trees – excellent for making canoes and periaguas – pineapples, sugar cane, bell-pepper, red wood and tobacco.[62]

The Cuna had developed agricultural and hunting systems in tune with their land. And while they did in many cases teach the Scots how to hunt local game, and traded food with them, the Scots never developed the kind of competence or openness that would allow them to survive without relief from home. While the yams they dug and planted could have helped, too many settlers believed that they caused illness. Sourcing food relief was a major point of contention for the council. The everyday settlers suffered under their 'scrimp allowances': a situation that was only slightly bettered when Captain Moon finally arrived with a sloop of goods to trade.

One of the councillors, Cunningham of Aiket, grew increasingly 'uneasie'. He became 'possessed ... by so unaccountable conceits and notions' that Paterson and the rest of the council worried he would desert New Caledonia. Cunningham was now a liability, threatening the morale of the colony if he remained, and potentially damaging its reputation if he left. The council toyed with detaining him but resolved to send him back to Scotland 'in friendship'. Their hope was that this would remove his polluting effect while ensuring he kept his misgivings to himself if and when he made it home. Had they trusted Cunningham, they could have used him to carry dispatches and requests for relief to the court of directors in Edinburgh, but his erratic behaviour meant that this was no longer an option. Paterson wanted more councillors appointed to take Cunningham's place, but he was voted down. When it came time to select the person to accompany Cunningham home, Paterson did not have the power to prevent the appointment of Alexander Hamilton. Hamilton volunteered, and the majority of the council agreed, ignoring Paterson's straitened plea that Hamilton was 'their accomptant-generall': he was the only person left who was 'fitt' to manage the 'cargoe', which was then 'in such disorder and confusion' that none but Hamilton could bring it into operational order.[63]

The initial plan was to send Cunningham and Hamilton back on the *Endeavour*, but when the ship was needed for the colony's sea defences, Pennecuik arranged their passage on a passing French vessel. Paterson watched as providence echoed his refusal to let Hamilton go. The French ship was dashed against the rocks that jutted from beneath the harbour and sank before it made it out of the bay. Hamilton and Cunningham were saved by Scottish sailors. The sea may have spat them back but their course was set and Paterson could do nothing to change it. Pulled from the harbour, Hamilton and his charge were placed on a Jamaican sloop and sent homewards, arriving back in Edinburgh three months later.

⸸

Hamilton carried news of a successful settlement, with dwellings and a protective fort. The 'large seal'd packet' he delivered to the court of directors requested aid. At the time the packet was put together, the kind of aid the colonists needed was to help secure what they had gained, to keep them fit until the colony became self-sufficient – and not to save them from destruction. The mood in Edinburgh was jubilant. The directors called the city's leaders to arrange some public 'demonstrations of joy'.[64] Hamilton was feted and received one hundred guineas for bringing news of Scotland's tentative emergence as a true imperial power.

In the three months it took for Hamilton to reach Edinburgh, and in the months after, while the directors organised relief and reinforcement, the pleasant breezy wind of Darien's dry season began to turn wet. As the sky grew dark, so did the fortunes of the colony. Having confirmed that the Scots intended to remain, Spain had little choice but to strike. The Viceroy of New Spain sent forces from Panama to make base at Toubacanti, one of their outposts. The plan was that a Spanish fleet would sail into the bay and attack from the seaward side while the armed force crossed from Toubacanti to rout the Scots on land. The fleet arrived in the Americas in a dismal state and never sailed to Darien. The Scots attacked and overwhelmed one of the Spanish scouting parties. The victory gave the Scottish settlers new confidence: in their first direct encounter with Spain they had emerged triumphant.

The same rain that immiserated the Scots saved them from having to face the full might of a Spanish invasion. Seized in the sloughing mud of Toubacanti, and without adequate food, the main Spanish force never advanced. Scotland's victory was pyrrhic. While Spain failed to lay siege to New Caledonia, her colonial leaders found other ways to isolate the fledgling Scottish settlement.

The Scottish colonists spent the early months of 1699 trying to send trading ships outwards, but voyages planned for Jamaica and New York never made it beyond the harbour. One ship that did manage to navigate the natural enclosure was the *Dolphin*, under the command of Captain Pincarton. Pincarton's mission was modest. He would go to Barbados, trade there and return with supplies. Though the ambition was scaled back, this mission was no less essential than those planned for America. Paterson and the council were devastated when news reached Darien that that the *Dolphin* had hit a rock off the coast of Cartagena and was dragged landwards, her crew left to clamber up to the walls of the Spanish stronghold. The Governor of Cartagena seized what remained of the *Dolphin*'s cargo and imprisoned Pincarton along with the thirty-odd men and one boy who crewed the ship. His professed justification was that they were pirates: the Company knew that this was simply cover for an act of revenge and intimidation.

The loss of the *Dolphin* was one more cut to a bleeding body. The need was now desperate. Pennecuik made it far too widely known that the colony had only a month of supplies left.

Paterson led a campaign to free Pincarton and his crew, writing letters to the Governor of Cartagena, Pedro de Olivera Ordoñez. The letters plaintively but firmly claimed that the Scots of Darien 'are the subjects of the King of Great Brittain, by vertue of whose power and authority granted to us, with advice and consent of his Parliament of Scotland, wee have settled here'.[65]

As evidence, Paterson enclosed the 1695 Act incorporating the Company. It seems that the Governor relished the chance to debate Paterson and the other signatories on the rights and protections owed the Scottish colony. Thanking them for including the Act, he thought it 'very strange that you should so totally misapply the Concessions of the serene King of Great Brittan, which are only for making new settlements in desart places and none possest by any Princes of Europe'. The 'temerity' they showed in settling a Spanish domain threatened the 'univocall peace' between England and Spain. As such, the Scots 'may justlie fear a great many ill successes like unto that which happened . . . to the ship called the Dolphin'.[66]

Within this letter were two unsettling truths about Darien: Scotland's claim to the land stemmed from a false premise; and the colonists did not have the protection of King William, who would not risk any diplomatic breach with Spain. Without such protection, the note that the Company might 'justlie' face other 'ill successes' carried a distinct threat.

Paterson and the council did not secure any justice for the men of the *Dolphin*: Pincarton and the crew were transported to Spain for trial and condemned. It was only long after the Scots left Darien that Pincarton and his officers were released following King William's belated intervention. By that time the rest of his crew had been pressed into lives of hard labour onboard Spanish warships. The broader geopolitical significance of the Governor's letter was that it circulated the notion that the Scottish colony acted without their King. The King's antipathy was widely suspected, but the question of whether William would come to the aid of his Scottish subjects if they faced invasion or starvation had yet to be tested publicly. In his private correspondence, English Secretary of State James Vernon confirmed that he had sent orders to the English Governors in the

Caribbean to 'hold no correspondence with' the Scottish colony, 'nor give them any succour, they having gone upon a design which his Majesty was no way acquainted with, and therefore could not approve of'. An order, Vernon admits, which gives the King some diplomatic cover, demonstrating that 'his Majesty has of himself done all that the Spaniards could have desired of him'.[67] When the orders were received, the lack of royal support for the Darien colony was confirmed in the most desolating way possible: the Governors began publishing proclamations that they would not aid or trade with the Scots, and that no subjects or allies of the Crown should do so either.

News of their abandonment hit Darien when one of the Company's periaguas sailed into the harbour after meeting a Jamaican sloop in open waters. The intelligence they brought was that Lieutenant Governor of Jamaica Sir William Beeston had published a proclamation that 'prohibited all his Majesties subjects from supplying or holding any correspondence with us, upon the severest penalties'. The proclamation was clearly designed to appease Spain. Beeston was no friend of Caledonia. When the Scots first arrived, he worried that any inkling of gold at Darien would draw people away from Jamaica, weakening the English position in the region. When the Spanish worried about the Scottish threat, he had privately assured the Governor of Cartagena that the English King in no way supported the Scottish venture. It is unsurprising, then, that his public proclamation accused the Scots of breaking England's peace with Spain and, as Paterson lamented, disavowed them in such a way as to 'proclaim us pirates'. What truly shocked Paterson was the haste of Beeston's actions. The proclamation was published on a Sunday, an unheard of violation of the sabbath; Paterson suspected it was carried out that morning to stop two ships heading from Jamaica with life-saving supplies.

The proclamation's effects took hold through the resigned talk of the men and women of Caledonia. For his part, Paterson clung to his dream: he refused to countenance the rumour that the Scottish parliament had rejected the asks of the Company, choosing to believe instead that the 'long silence of our countrey' came because those in Edinburgh were 'brow-beaten' by London, and dared not write till they had secured relief. Not all were so staunch or stubborn. The colony was in a state of sheer 'disorder'. The world was closing in. There were reports that letters discovered on the wreckage of the French ship disclosed France's plans to absorb Spanish possessions on the death of the Spanish King, a process that would require the French extirpate the Scots from the Americas. Apparently they had begun to do so by exerting influence on the Cuna to try and stop them coming to Caledonia's aid.[68]

Malnourished, the remaining Scots were easy prey for malaria. Against the heavy wet air, Paterson felt the first clammy signs of the fever that had killed his wife and son. Weak, he tried to argue to the other councillors that their plan to desert the colony was premature. He thought they should simply decamp to the ships, rest and sail to see if they meet with an incoming company fleet. Surely they would. Paterson's febrile optimism did not win support, but nor did he witness the failure of his final argument for the expedition. His position was lost as he slumped into a haze and had to be carried on board the *Unicorn*. Small mercy that, when the first expedition abandoned the colony on 19 June 1699, Paterson was barely conscious.

⸸

The 'long silence' of Scotland that Paterson lamented – the fact that no word from home reached the colonists in their time of need – was the fault of distance and its dislocations, and not a sign of Scotland's indifference. In large part the directors in Edinburgh and Glasgow still viewed the settlement through the optimistic prism of Alexander Hamilton's report when rumour that it had been deserted reached them in September 1699. It was clear, they thought, that the rumour was 'malicious and false', 'contrived on purpose to discourage people to goe to our Colony with Provision &c.'. The directors were appalled when the most outlandish of these stories of desertion were confirmed by the arrival of the *Caledonia* and *Unicorn* in New York (the *Endeavour* had sunk on the journey).

They did not want blame for the 'shamefull and dishonourable abandonment of Caledonia' to redound upon them, and resented reports of 'mismanadgement' circulating in New York, writing to Paterson and the surviving councillors: 'We sent you repeated advices from time to time.' The reports that 'you had not the scrape of a pen from us' since they left were false. Not only that but their asks were heeded. We sent 'two ships, which sail'd from Leith the 12th of May last, with 300 men and a considerable quantity of provisions, ammunition, and other necessaries'. The directors assumed that the ships would 'be within a few days' sailing of the Settlement when you deserted it'.[69] In reality the *Olive Branch* and the *Hopeful Binning* reached the settlement about six weeks after it was abandoned. A previous relief ship, the *Dispatch*, was blown to land off Islay and never made it out of Scottish waters.

Between May, when they sent the two supply ships, and October 1699, when they had confirmation that the first expedition had failed, the directors launched a second expedition, designed to shore up the settlement, supply men and goods, and put down roots for a more permanent society. A hundred women went aboard the four ships that sailed from the Clyde on 18 August, along with around twelve hundred men. Led by the *Rising Sun*, with James Gibson as commodore, the fleet that followed included the *Hope*, another company ship, and two chartered vessels, the *Duke of Hamilton* and the *Hope of Bo'ness*. In sailing from the Clyde, they adopted the route that Paterson advocated, bypassing the treacherous northern waters. In the long term, this decision helped move the centre of Scotland's shipping from Edinburgh to Glasgow; in the short, it made the voyage to Darien far quicker. The second expedition made the passage in half the time it took the first, but with far more casualties. Of the roughly 1,300 who set out, 160 were buried at sea.[70]

The directors deputised surgeon Water Stewart to travel to London, and from there to sail to New York. Stewart's brief was to oversee the refitting of the *Caledonia*, so that it could be sent back to Darien. If he arrived too late and found that the *Caledonia* had already embarked for Scotland, he was to organise a supply vessel for the second expedition. The terms of his mission show that the directors had not countenanced the full scale of the colony's devastation. How else could they assume that the ship was ready to be repurposed or that the councillors, sailors and settlers who had scraped out of the Caribbean could be mustered back?

One witness in New York, who saw the Darien survivors arrive, thought that 'famine and death' could be 'discerned in their countenances'. The *Caledonia* arrived first. She carried 103 souls, 'not above 65 seamen' and more than fifty sick. In the six long weeks it took to reach New York, a hundred people had died and been thrown overboard, though the crew 'reckoned themselves the healthiest ship of the three'. They were right. The *Unicorn* arrived weeks later having lost foremast, topmast and 150 people. The *St Andrew* never arrived. Those who made it to New York were malnourished. The bounty of food struck them with what appeared to be malice: 'from the one extream of want they help to destroy themselves with that of plenty', the same witness lamented: they ate more than their bodies could process and for some this brought on seizures, comas and even death.[71] Across it all, this man remained impressed by how Paterson retained the respect of the colonists. This could only be because 'he hath been both diligent and true to the end'. And yet he was riven by his part in 'this sad disaster' and 'looks now more like a skeleton than a man'. Not all gave Paterson the benefit of his former constancy. Another New Yorker observed his 'crasie condition'; a third reported that he had 'lost his sences, and does not medle in anything'. Paterson had neither the energy nor the inclination to press the first expedition back. As with the vast majority of the other survivors, he was willing to chance the potential ignominy that awaited him in Scotland against the danger of return or the 'unkind usage' they faced in New York, where they lived on a poor line of Company credit and the grudging sympathy of English colonists willing to break the King's embargo. They had not given up on a Scottish colony but believed that this 'tragicall period . . . can never be repaired, excepting only that the Riseing Sunn be arrived at Darien, and keept possession of the place'.[72] Though they did not return themselves, the remaining councillors sent a sloop under the command of Captain Robert Drummond, to give the second expedition their account and some aid. All the while they prepared to sail back to Scotland as quickly as they possibly could.

The second fleet reached Darien towards the end of November. What they saw pitted them with a 'sorrowfull and crushing like

Disappointment'. They had expected 'to meet with our Friends and Country-men'; instead, they 'found nothing but a vast howling Wilderness, the Colony deserted and gone, their Hutts all burnt, their Fort ... ruined, the Ground which they had cleared adjoining to the Fort, all overgrown with Shrubs and Weeds'. Francis Borland, a minister who travelled with the expedition, was put in mind of the *Book of Job*: they were 'confounded because they had hoped; they came hither and were ashamed'.

Much of the dismay Borland spoke of came from the fact that the second expedition was ill-equipped for the work they knew they had to do. They had come to be 'a Recruit and supply to a colony', not to re-found one. And so they spent the first fretful months re-clearing the ground of Fort St Andrew, erecting the bare minimum defences and some places to live. As it was with their voyage, the mortality rate of the second expedition remained far higher than the first. The waves of illness that dragged them under almost as soon as they landed became 'epidemical and raging' in January 1700, taking the lives 'even of our Officers and chief Men', undermining what they felt were natural hierarchies and deracinating those who remained.[73]

Another cleric was driven 'almost to the brink of despair' at the end of January, when the 'pitiful rotten provisions' they had were 'found to be so far exhausted that we were on the very point of leaving and losing this colony'. Vocationally primed to see time pass in cycles of despair and salvation, the Reverend Alexander Shields found light 'in our greatest darkness' when a leaking brigantine stumbled into the harbour in the first week of February. The colonists were able to buy supplies from the ship that providence had delivered them. Within days a second vessel arrived, a sloop from Barbados with enough goods to spare the people of Caledonia. But with light came the shadows of more darkness. On 13 February, the expedition's Cuna allies brought intelligence that Spanish forces were amassing near Toubacanti in preparation for a full-scale land assault on the fragile settlement. Revived by their salvation, the council decided to pre-empt the Spanish. They sent a force of two hundred men, along with at least sixty Cuna warriors, under the command of Captain Alexander Campbell of Fonab. Campbell marched on Toubacanti to find that the Spanish camp was not yet firmly in place. Campbell had surprise in his favour. His attack forced the Spanish to 'run in confusion, leaving all their baggage, nine or ten of them dead, several wounded'. As with the first expedition, the second triumphed at Toubacanti. Though eight Scots soldiers were killed and about eighteen wounded, the skirmish temporarily routed the gathering army. Their ambition swelled by victory over a major power, the colonists began making plans to consolidate their gains, drawing up orders for privateering missions against Spanish ships and discussing ways to take control of lucrative Spanish mines.[74]

⸸

King William's abandonment of Darien provided the Country opposition with a productive source of grievance. Country-aligned nobles and members of the Scottish parliament began to find ways to capture and represent popular opinion in their pursuit of a more independent, self-governing Scotland. They circulated petitions and composed national addresses requesting parliament be recalled – a prerogative of the King. If the Scottish parliament were recalled, it could assert the legality of the Darien settlement. Copies of the address were printed and distributed across Scotland.[75] The Country interest, looser than modern conceptions of a political party, gained a measure of coherence and support by championing the colony, using existing distributional networks from Edinburgh across the Lowlands to disseminate information and collect signatures, as well as employing the communicative channels of the Kirk by calling on ministers to pray for the colony and so corral the backing of their flocks.[76] The King refused to recall parliament. He was unwilling to jeopardise his position with Spain or anger the planters in Jamaica. When parliament did return on 21 May, Queensberry quickly lost control and was forced to adjourn the session after only nine days.

News of the victory at Toubacanti brought the opposition to the streets. As the Country opposition began to cohere around support for the colony, the Duke of Hamilton emerged as a leader the people could get behind. The news itself was far from accurate. The *Edinburgh Gazette* made it seem like the Scottish colonists had defeated a full Spanish army.[77] Such exaggerations only helped Hamilton, who orchestrated a campaign to light Edinburgh in support of the brave men of Darien. The Duke called all in the city to place a lighted candle in their windows, so that the capital would glow with imperial pride. The glow quickly shaded to flame as a crowd gathered, moving through the city's closes and wynds, throwing stones through the windows without candles, and setting on officials they felt did not support Caledonia. The crowd attacked the Tolbooth prison in order to free men gaoled for writing pamphlets in support of the colony but ended up freeing almost all imprisoned there. When they came to St Giles, they hijacked the bellringer, forcing him to play 'Willful Willy, wilst thou be willful still': a swipe at the King.

The Toubacanti riot, as it came to be known, revealed both the power and danger of popular politics, exposing the force wielded by those who represent the people as well as the difficulty inherent in controlling the crowd. On the day of the riot a second national address was published, one that made 'the nation's right and title to Caledonia' the centrepiece of a suite of demands pitched to the security and parliamentary sovereignty of Scotland.[78] Pushed by his powerful mother to take a more active role in coordinating the address, the Duke of Hamilton acted as the point of contact for distributing it and gathering support.[79] To those in the streets, he stood for them against an Anglocentric King. It was a risky position. It gave the Court party room to depict the riot as a Jacobite plot. And it linked the opposition Country party strongly to the colony, which became a key basis for both its popular support and internal cohesion.

⸸

The victory celebrations continued in Scotland long after they did in Darien itself. A mere eight days after the Battle of Toubacanti, Scottish lookouts spied eleven Spanish ships anchored off Golden Island. Spain could no longer tolerate the Scottish outpost in their midst and sent a fleet. Rather than entering and becoming trapped in the treacherous Darien harbour, the Spanish fleet blockaded it, sending the smaller vessels eastwards to Caret Bay. There they were joined by a reassembled land force from Panama. Borland estimated that there were two thousand men in total.

The Spanish attack was efficient and merciless. They cut Caledonia off at the neck of land that joined Fort St Andrew to the main. As they enclosed the Fort, conditions inside rapidly deteriorated. The quarters were so cramped as to be, quite literally, combustible. A store of gunpowder caught fire. The sick who had to be 'hastily pulled out of their Hutts' so that they did not burn alive ended up dying from the exposure. The 'wasting sickness' now spread faster than before; even the seemingly healthy were 'cut off by sudden violent Fevers and Fluzes in a very few days'. At each stage of their steady advance, the Spanish pushed the Scots to surrender, offering a treaty that would see Scots leave with only supplies to sail. They held out to the point of annihilation. But on 31 March 1700, the remaining councillors had little choice but to sign articles of capitulation. The agreement gave them fourteen days to vacate the colony, with nothing but what they needed to 'carry them from this port, Toward *Britain*'.

†

None of the ships of the second expedition made it back to Scotland. The *Rising Sun* was 'staved to pieces' by a hurricane off the coast of Florida; the 112 who sailed on her drowned. The *Duke of Hamilton* made it to Charleston in Carolina when the same storm hit. The ship was sunk but the people it carried reached land. By this point, many of the crew had already deserted the fleet in Jamaica. The last remnants of the Caledonian adventure who wanted to go home found passage on ships from American and Caribbean ports. Borland was one of them. Looking back to the colony's first design 'untill that last dreadful blow upon the *Rising-Sun* and her Company', the reverend calculated that 'Our Nation has lost near two thousand Men in this Undertaking'. The devastating human cost was difficult to contemplate 'besides the Expence and Loss of a vast Treasure bestowed' on the colony.[80]

News of the defeat and ultimate abandonment of Caledonia struck Scotland hard. Kirk leaders called for fast days. Scotland had angered God and needed a spiritual bulwark lest any further disasters beset them in their fallen state. Fasts and the contemplation they enforced had a fairly predictable side effect: the eyes of the nation quickly turned from heaven to the more earthly causes of the colony's defeat. In the press and in taverns, patriots sprayed anger at the colonists who had abandoned the venture and the directors who had failed to support them. A special seething kind of malice was reserved for a King who was not simply indifferent to Scotland but actively kept the nation in a state of dependence. The resentment ran deep. Scotland had been central in the Revolution that brought William and Mary to the throne. Now they ruled against Scotland's interests. William's betrayal drove renewed interest in Jacobitism. More telling, though, was that a man like Lord Belhaven, one of the Darien Company's directors, who had been one of the nobles to personally ask William to take the throne of Scotland during the Revolution, was so appalled that he went in secret to France to convince the exiled James Francis Edward Stuart, son of the deposed James II, to convert to Protestantism and become King of Scotland in William's stead: an act of treason.[81]

In the aftermath of the loss, the Country opposition had legitimate grounds to present themselves as patriots and to attack the Court for kowtowing to England. The way they framed their position and turned to local bases of support, drawing burghs, towns and corporations together in order to speak with the power of an aggregative national voice became their preferred method – one they returned to during their campaign against an incorporating union with England.[82] In response, players within the Scottish Court party and their English backers began to work the methods that would become their mainstay during the push towards union. Unlike the opposition, Queensberry had access to money and could peel off Country support by offering patronage, places and pensions.[83] Writing to William Carstares, he made it known that the £500 provided by the English Treasury had gone to good use: he made strategic payments designed to control the behaviour of Scottish MPs; with £500 more the King could be 'well assured of satisfactory returns'.

In order to prevent the tragedy of Darien forcing a complete break in Scotland's relations with England, Queensberry realised that he had to look beyond the actions of MPs. Because Paterson 'was the first man that brought people here into the project of Caledonia', he was the 'properest person to bring them off from prosecuting it'. Queensberry secured Paterson £100, but found himself 'a little embarrassed', unsure how to give the man his due, 'lest his party in that company should conceive any unjust jealousy of him or himself think I intended a bribe that which is really an act of charity'. Queensberry's act of charity was coercive for its benevolence. The Lord High Commissioner found that Paterson was chastened by the failure of his dream. More cautious than before, Queensberry thought Paterson was 'against moving any thing in this session about Caledonia; and tells me that he thinks he has gained some considerable men to his position'.[84] This was the paradox of Paterson's position. He had been the butt of public shame when he returned to Scotland broken by loss and harrowed by a journey that left him so weak that it took him more than two weeks to ride the sixty miles from Greenock, where the *Caledonia* moored, to Edinburgh. And yet he was still considered a canny thinker, able to persuade the public and those in power.

During his halting recovery, Paterson compiled reports and reflections on Darien. Reading them, it is clear that he was against the Scottish parliament following the reactionary line of the opposition. Without a positive vision for the colony, the opposition offered no means to secure Scotland. Paterson still believed that empire was the solution, and he clung to his plan for Darien, offering it and other schemes to nobles across the Scottish political spectrum, from Queensberry to Hamilton.[85] To him it was the King's proclamation against the legality of the colony that remained the greatest obstacle to its success. He helped drive a petitioning campaign to repeal the proclamation. He also began to reassess the geopolitics of a Scottish colony. One of his reports claimed that he and the other colonists had discovered letters in a French shipwreck that gave evidence of a plan by Spanish colonists and their native allies to declare their loyalty to France as soon as the Spanish King died.[86] This intelligence appealed to William's desire to prevent Bourbon control of the Americas. It also marks a shift in Paterson's thinking. In the first years of the eighteenth century, Paterson reformulated his plan for Darien as a joint British enterprise, one where Scotland and Ireland could invest in and reap the benefits from a trading entrepôt conquered, controlled and regulated by a united British government. Defoe would later lament the fact that Darien had been abandoned. In 1711, when he advocated Pacific exploration as the best path to England's global dominance, he remarked on the lost opportunity Darien presented: 'if we had kept Possession of it when we had it, this new Undertaking would have appear'd to me much easier than I fear now it will be'. With the slip to 'we', Defoe elides the pain Scotland suffered in taking and briefly holding Darien, ignoring the role England played in destroying the colony.[87]

Much of Paterson's plan to make Darien British was written in London, where he moved to escape what he felt was the narrowing scope of Scotland's patriotic glare. This was the plan he would eventually present to the King just before his death. For Paterson, Scotland's access to the world of trade and empire remained the only way to shake the yoke of poverty. In his view it was a 'ridiculous contradiction' that Scotland and Ireland had such different 'circumstances' with 'regard to England'. Glossing over the brutal colonisation of Ireland, and shaped by his experience in Panama, he now believed that the only way for Scotland to become an imperial power – slavers not slaves – was to enter into full and complete union with England.[88]

CHAPTER 5

THE NETWORK

The election of 1705 was fought over two brutal months. Across May and June, the candidates, their backers and the party mobs they stoked engaged in a series of pitched local battles. The strategy Harley's agents carried into the field was elegant for its simplicity. They rode the backlash against the so-called 'Tackers', fomenting public disgust against those High Church Tories cynical enough to threaten the war effort by tacking penalties for occasional conformity to a bill of supply. Harley's aim – endorsed by Godolphin and Marlborough – was to water down the Tory majority, to the point where neither party could dominate. This would shift the balance of power to the Queen's placeholders: loyal servants in parliament who, in Harley's phrase, would act as a 'majority for the Queen and the public good'.[1] As Marlborough wrote to his wife Sarah, if 'neither party might have a great majority … her Majesty might be able to influence what might be good for the common cause'.[2] Her Majesty and the triumvirs.

Defoe's part in the campaign echoed the purpose of his first tour. In three issues a week, the *Review* pulsed a steady beat of moderation. Thanks to the network of distribution agents peopled across the eastern counties, the paper now reached even further. In the weeks before the first polls opened, Defoe devoted an issue to answering a reader's letter about 'our Wounded country'. Defoe popularised the advice column, so it was natural that he would use the form to speak through this one reader to the voters – and to the disenfranchised, whose mood and temper as a collective could nonetheless influence the election:

> If they have any regard to the Honour of God, the Good of Religion, their Safety from Foreign Invasion, the Security of a *Protestant* Succession, the Glory of a *Protestant* Queen, the Success of a Just War, the needful Preservation of Trade, the flourishing of useful Manufactures . . . any Pity to their Families, any Memory of their Ancestors, any regard to their Posterity, and the Liberties of their Innocent Children, to whom they ought to Convey Untouch'd and Unembarrass'd, the same Foundations their Fathers Purchas'd for them with their Blood . . . *they would* STUDY PEACE.

No heartstring is left untugged as Defoe defines the values that unite England. Though it first appears overwrought, the force of the list builds with each clause till it reaches the point where it cannot help but be read as genuine. So staunch is Defoe's belief in the healing power of a 'General Peace, abstracted from the Prejudice of Parties', that he is willing to stake his ethos as a writer and his freedom as a man upon it. Stirred by his own rhetoric, he willingly exposes himself to the 'Fines, Gaols, Pillories, and Exorbitant and Unjust Sentences' that his readers knew he understood first-hand.

As he writes, Defoe asks God to grant him an 'Unresistible Eloquence' to 'speak with Words that should be felt as well as heard, that should touch the very Soul, and make the Blood of the Readers turn within them'. We get the sense that Defoe answered his own prayer in this atypically (and, at times, awkwardly) lyrical essay. Or at least he thought his prayer was answered as he loosed all stores of eloquence on the argument that 'Her Majesty's Safety, the Nations Prosperity, the Glory of *England*, the Establishment of Religion, all depend upon Peace; Peace among our selves, Peace of Families, of Societies, and Parties'. The only possible course for the reader who seeks to mend the nation is to vote for a candidate who eschews petty partisan tricks. This, Defoe declaims, is the path to national healing and personal happiness.

Defoe later boasted that this essay was so widely esteemed that he was asked to print 'five Thousand of that *Review* to be sent all over the Nation to move us to Peace'.[3] Defoe's skills were certainly getting wider notice, with Lord Halifax, member of the Whig Junto, seeking out his services at around this time.[4] Even if this number was exaggerated, few of this now vast readership could have missed Defoe's implication. Peace, union and happiness required some kind of alliance between England and Scotland.

⸸

Looking back on the election results two years later, Defoe viewed the campaign as a triumph. In his mind, the election delivered '*England* the best Parliament this Age can remember'. Had it produced a 'Tacking Parliament' or an 'Occasional-Bill Parliament', the project of an Anglo-Scottish Union would have died in the womb.[5] From Harley's vantage, things were not as positive. Further removed from the kicked-up dust of election riots, he realised that the swing against the Tories was modest. Roughly two-thirds of the Tackers were returned – a result that did not give the Queen's placeholders the decisive control he sought.

There were also some embittering local losses. The most searing: Francis Godolphin, son of the Lord Treasurer and Marlborough's son-in-law, lost his campaign to represent Cambridge. This personal defeat dulled Harley's sheen as a tactical master in the eyes of his colleagues. The centre did not hold as Harley had promised and alliances shifted with the results. Godolphin became more amenable to working with the leaders of the Whig Junto just as Harley withdrew from them. Godolphin's approach won out. With Harley now focusing on his role as Secretary, the campaign to replace him as Speaker narrowed to two: a Junto candidate and a Tacker, a choice that pushed Godolphin further to the Whig side than he wanted.

Defoe was not wrong. A parliament more whiggish in complexion was far likelier to sue for Union with Scotland. But this downplays that the moderate Tories were for Union too. The moderates who remained turned increasingly to Harley for leadership, splitting the base of the triumvirate. What Defoe did not admit was that the election weakened Harley's image as indispensable, the one whose supposedly non-partisan hands were dextrous enough to grasp the nation's best interest from competing forces in the Commons.

⸸

Because Defoe's eastern tour was cut short, it could only ever be thought of as preliminary. At best, it laid the path and outlaid some methods for discerning and influencing the will of the people. To establish a nationwide intelligence gathering and distribution network, he would have to travel more widely and with a more precise itinerary. The journey he embarked upon in the wake of the election did just that. This second tour lasted close to four months and covered at whip speed most boroughs that sent representatives to Westminster, along with the country towns where shire elections were held.

The purpose of Defoe's mission expanded to fit its national reach. As with his first tour, the overall aim remained to win elections by sourcing the data and connecting the distributional nodes that would allow Harley to know and shape popular opinion. But, as Pat Rogers notes, Defoe was also there to conduct a 'post-mortem': he was to report on and quell the protests that arose over contested results, and to refine Harley's campaign operation for the next election.[6] Defoe did not intend for the network he built to lie dormant between polls: the agents he recruited during his journey would stay in place to help Harley manage both country and Commons, giving the politician the intelligence to handle the masses and to leverage those who represented them.

The dislocation Defoe felt during his first tour left a bitter tincture. Before departing London this time, he tried to extract more detailed instructions from Harley. Anticipating both need and danger, he asked Harley to arrange another pass for Christopher Hurt and to supply a certificate from the Secretary's office stating that Defoe travelled for lawful purposes. He did not want to 'be stopt by any Malitious person on the Road — or which may be worse — Search't'.

Supervening his concerns about safety and secrecy was money. Employment did not bring the easement Defoe needed. The more he wrote about 'Peace', he told Harley, the more it seemed that this writing 'Raises war to me'. Old creditors who opposed the line he took in print called in their debts to thwart his ability to publish pro-ministerial works – or so Defoe assumed.[7]

Peace and moderation became even harder to push after the appearance of *The Memorial of the Church of England*. A swingeing critique of Godolphin's ministry, the pamphlet's anonymous author reclaimed the 'true value' of moderation from the dangerous mumblings of Milquetoast ministers: those, like Godolphin, whose attempts at centrism exposed their 'lukewarmness in religion' and 'indifference' to the safety of the Church.[8] The pamphlet infuriated the Queen and brought Godolphin to the cusp of tears.[9] Because it achieved a breakout currency like few other works, *The Memorial* demanded an answer. Harley fixed his spies and informers on the task of finding the pamphlet's author, and encouraged refutations from sympathetic writers, Defoe and philosopher John Toland first amongst them. Defoe's answer, *The High Church Legion*, was rushed to print ten days after *The Memorial* appeared.

Defoe carried *The Memorial* with him as he made his preparations, placing it with the papers he would take on his journey – a totem of the forces arrayed against him. Knowing what he faced but confident in the effect of his work, he asked Harley for more money – enough that he might stave off 'The Necessary Craveings of a Large Family of 7 Children'. Defoe is forthright about the fact that this tour would be more expensive than the last, but cuts the sharpness of his ask with deprecation, adapting a couplet from Lord Rochester:

> That Authors Beggar like, will haunt the Door,
> Where They Received a Charity before.[10]

Rochester was Defoe's favourite poet. A surprising choice given the late lord's reputation as a womaniser, a drunk, a crypto-atheist and an all-out profaner of virtue. The lure Defoe felt was that of a fellow satirist. He admired the boldness and recognised in Rochester the risks he himself took in tearing down the complacent self-satisfaction of his countrymen. To Defoe, Rochester's irreverent example revealed a morality whose first need was a truer knowledge of the self.

There's another line of Rochester's that more accurately conveys Defoe's situation. The poet spoke of 'the after Bribe of Gratitude',[11] the sense of debt more pronounced because bound up with the giver's benevolence. Defoe clearly felt this 'after Bribe' with Harley. As he asked for more money, he tried to mitigate the burden of personal obligation with an ideal of public service. He did not know whether Harley paid him from his personal funds or from the public purse, but his express wish was for the latter. He worked for the state and so felt he should be paid by the state.

There is no indication of whether Defoe's finances were settled or whether he received the detailed instructions he desired before he left London on 16 July. He must have had just enough of each, though, as he rode westwards to Brentford on his way to Reading.

⸸

At Brentford Defoe lodged with Richard Meriwether, one of around six hundred justices removed from their posts by the Tory Lord Keeper Sir Nathan Wright. Defoe realised that the purge of moderate officials presented a major obstacle to 'forming the People into Moderation'. Living in the house of a man brought low by the removal of his role gave a personal dimension to a sweeping programme orchestrated by the most combatively partisan of opponents, Sir Edward Seymour. One of Defoe's tasks was to try and probe the extent of Seymour's dominance in the west and to find ways to overthrow what he called the man's 'western empire'. Seymour's purge meant that before he even set out, Defoe was outdone by men willing to cast all ethics aside to influence national politics at the local level. The injustice of this setback harried him as he rode to Reading, its aftertaste still lingering when he left the town and rode slightly south to Newbury and down to Salisbury and Blandford, where he spent two days, before heading for Dorset.

The first leg of the journey left Defoe 'Extreamly Fatigued'. His pace was punishing. At his back beat a 'violent heat' that stuck him wet to his saddle. Relief only came when he reached Dorchester, and a fresh rain cooled the air, dissolving the bond between his breeches and seat. In each town he passed, Defoe took stock of the election results, compiled a list of local magistrates and clerks, and recruited informants. It was an expensive process but one he justified to Harley in that it provided a 'perfect skeleton of this part of England and a settled Correspondence in Every Town and Corner of it'.[12] The need was plain in a place like Dorchester, where the people were apparently moderate and tolerant. (In taverns and coffeehouses Defoe saw people converse and do business with little heed to party loyalty or confessional affiliation.) And yet the constituency elected two Tories. As a corrective, Defoe's political ordnance survey promised two things: a better understanding of how electoral mechanics were manipulated and a better way to persuade the people of their own interests – as Harley defined them.

The ride from Dorchester to Weymouth and then to Honiton covered some of Defoe's favourite parts of the country. But Honiton itself was in 'Terrible Disorder'.[13] Here Defoe witnessed the effects of mob violence and voter intimidation. The 'Briberies, double pollings, buying of *Voices* and all manner of Corrupt Practices'[14] that had riven Honiton formed a fault line, the contours of which Defoe was determined to trace across the country.

Defoe travelled incognito, as Alexander Goldsmith. This was not always enough to cover his tracks. Hugh Stafford, a Justice of the Peace in Dorset, got wind that Defoe was conversing with all who would listen, 'basely reflecting' on a set of MPs whom he saw as useless: seat-warmers who turned to Tory grandees to tell them how to vote. More sinister, Stafford thought, was that the writer was clearly in this part of the country 'with noe good designe, for he keeps Company with none but presbyterian and Independent preachers, for he has made it his business to visit them almost in every town and parish throughout our County'.[15] Stafford could reconstruct parts of Defoe's journey but not its true purpose. Defoe met with preachers in order to recruit them as distribution agents. These men formed the bones of the skeleton Defoe assembled for Harley.

It was not Defoe's fault that Stafford came to notice him. It was a simple case of mistaken identity that first exposed the writer. As he was travelling the southwest, Defoe sent instructions that any letters for him should be sent to his associate Captain Turner in Weymouth. The problem was that they were delivered to the wrong Turner. The man who received them was a Guernsey privateer. Mystified by the 'Darke and Unintelligible' letters, Turner showed 'them to all the Town'. 'The Ignorant Tarr', as Defoe later called him, returned the letters to their rightful recipient as soon as Defoe arrived. He then joined Defoe and his party, 'Drank a pint of wine with us and Calls for one himself which it seems afterward he went away and Never paid for'.[16] When the landlords demanded he pay for the wine the next morning, the opportunistic privateer 'Vented' about the suspicious letters. The Mayor was summoned. Fearing a '*Presbyterian Plot*', and not willing to meddle with it personally, he put what Defoe called 'all his Hearsays, Supposes, and Drunken Evidences together' and sent them on to Stafford.[17]

Stafford procured a warrant that labelled Defoe a 'Person of ill Fame and Behaviour', and accused him of 'spreading and publishing divers seditious and scandalous Libels and false news to the great disturbance of the Peace of this Kingdom'.[18] Defoe thought it plainly ludicrous that he, a 'Peace-maker' was accused 'of a Phanatick Plot'. According to Defoe, Stafford knew the basis for his warrant was false, and so only issued it once he knew Defoe had left Weymouth for Exeter. It is just as likely that the speed at which Defoe travelled to Exeter and then to Totnes, Dartmouth and Plymouth in his pursuit of more agents meant that he was far gone by the time Stafford made his application. Nonetheless, the warrant was circulated and constables raided the house of Peter Baron, a Dissenting minister Defoe had recruited in Plymouth. By the time they arrived, Defoe had already passed through Saltash, Liskeard, Bodmin and Launceston, evading the grasp of an alderman who bragged that he would have pressed the writer into military service had he caught him. On the ride out of Plymouth he was careful to avoid the damage caused by that week's storm. In his gaze were 'the Wrecks of Ships, and a foaming furious sea': the aftermath of a tempest so violent that the sea's deep roar was only punctuated by 'the firing of Guns for Help from the Ships' moored offshore and 'the Cries of the Seamen' at sea and those 'dash'd in Pieces' ashore.[19]

The law finally closed in on Defoe in Bideford, where, on 9 August, he was seized by a magistrate. As he told Harley, this was 'the first and Onely time I sho'd your Pass'.[20] Apparently, Harley had warned the writer to use the official pass with extreme care. Defoe was released and, though he wanted to stay and defend his reputation in person, he did not want to stay too long in any one place, fearing three legal actions recently taken against him for old debts. Instead, when he reached Tiverton, he wrote Stafford what the Justice called an 'an impudent reflecting letter'.[21] In it Defoe is not as careful with the pass as Harley wanted, boasting about the 'Lawfull' nature of his travels as a way to 'publickly Confute, that Scandalous Falsity affirmed in your warrant of my Lurking in the Country'. Defoe is only sorry, he tells the bumptious Justice, 'my Occasions will not permit me to tell you soe to your face'.

There is an element of bravado to Defoe's threat, which he delivers knowing full well that the two will never meet. At this point, Defoe was running in equal parts on industry and adrenaline. He had bested a pirate, avoided being pressed into the military, and dodged capture and arrest without relaxing his pace. From Tiverton he rode north-east to Taunton, Bridgewater and on to Bristol, covering close to eighty miles in just under four days, before wending gently south-wards towards Bath. Throughout his journey he was accompanied by Hurt and other friends. He was careful, he assured Harley, not to disclose the finer details of his mission to these unnamed associates. It was deeply unsettling when one of his recruits asked him to pass on his regards to Harley: it seemed that, despite his efforts, the nodes of the network realised that Harley was its central coordinating force.

Reaching Bath would allow Defoe time to shore up his cover and turn his full focus back to the network. The plan was that Hurt would head back to London to be replaced by the man Defoe trusted most, his brother-in-law Robert Davis. Davis carried word from Harley as well as funds for Defoe to continue his travels. Common to plans orchestrated through letters, Davis and Defoe initially missed each other. When the two managed to reunite two days later than first intended, each felt a grave satisfaction: Defoe, because he had a dependable sign of Harley's support, and Davis because he found Defoe undimmed and relatively safe and so could shift the freight of his family's worry.

Bath gave Defoe a base from which to make a series of exploratory journeys into the southwest: to Chippenham, Devizes, Bradford, Trubridge (Trowbridge), Westbury, Calne, Malmsbury, Tutbury, Nedbury (Newbury), Cirencester, Bedwin (Great Bedwyn) and Ludgershall. The list as it landed on Harley's desk appeared fairly complete: a point Defoe stressed each time he vaunted the comprehensiveness of his network. There are, however, some important absences: Cricklade and Hindon and all the places that weren't contested in the 1705 polls but would be in future elections. Such limitations aside, the reports Harley received provide operational detail on the 'strange and Unaccountable people as well as practises in the Late Elections': the laws broken; where and how corruption altered the results; the means by which local officials exerted undue influence. Defoe also noted positive cases, where local government was reformed, where corruption was limited, where individual patrons did not control the boroughs, and where popular participation, albeit limited, was allowed. Such cases included Bristol, Gloucester and Bath – cities that not coincidentally elected Whigs and moderate Court Tories.

Defoe's pragmatic observations of an electoral culture that was too tightly controlled by local magistrates, that was fuelled by bribes, and that too often resulted in those standing petitioning and contesting the results, is set against an abiding conviction: that people and voters can be moved by what they read. His patchwork recommendations to remove certain officials and to reform local government are designed to shift the burden of choice back to a voting public, albeit one limited to freeholding men. Defoe's travels revealed a public that was far from apathetic. He saw people who on Sundays 'Devoutly Resort to the News house as they call it first, and then to the Church'.[22] Politics gave them a place for collective emotion and shared devotion. In guiding readers to see the morality of moderation, Defoe, who as a young man turned away from a career as a Dissenting preacher in favour of business, became a preacher in another guise – with a far larger audience.

⸸

In September Defoe pushed north from Gloucester to Tewkesbury, spending a day in Pershore and Evesham, Worcester, Leominster, Bewdley, Bridgnorth, Shrewsbury, Wrexham and Chester. In each place he canvassed informers and gathered electoral histories.

He reached Liverpool on 13 September. Locals noticed him entering and leaving the house of Samuel Done, with whom he stayed for at least three days. Done became Defoe's distribution agent in the city. Reports that he was sheltering Defoe set off talk amongst the merchants who made up Liverpool's Whig political class. The local MP Thomas Johnson expressed his unease to Richard Norris, who had just lost the election to serve in Liverpool's other seat to the Tory candidate. Done, he thought, would have been better to stay well away from someone like Defoe. Defoe's presence in the city became 'a great matter of speculation'. While some thrilled to the gossip, Johnson felt strained. Defoe may well have been an ally but what was he doing in Liverpool? And why was he doing it behind closed doors? 'I do not like such men,' he told Norris, 'let them be of what side they will — it's those creatures' endeavours to influence us.'[23] Sharp political minds like Johnson's could see Defoe was working as an agent of influence. None grasped exactly what he was doing.

Defoe's reports from Warrington, Manchester, Bolton, Rochdale and Halifax were sparse. These towns had no magistrates and were not represented in parliament. The same is true for the next three places he visited: Leeds, Wakefield and Sheffield. Absent frequent elections, he found that the people 'live here in Much more peace with one another than in other parts'.[24] It was not just the elections themselves that fomented discord. Defoe observed that the mandate for elections at least every three years had a negative side effect. Regularity gave three years to those who lost to work against the winner, creating an almost permanent state of contest.[25]

Defoe passed through Derby as the month tapered to a close, noting that though the town was once deeply divided, it was showing early but promising signs that its people were coming together. The reports Defoe sent back to Harley quickly darken after he spent several days in Nottingham, where two Tories were elected despite a popular Whig opposition supported by local magistrates. The situation in Leicester mixed farce and tragedy. Here the election results were overturned first by parliamentary committee and reversed again when the whole Commons assembled. In Lutterworth he reported a violent intrusion into a Dissenting meeting house.

The scattershot of incidents across the Midlands formed a distinct pattern after the events of Coventry, which in retrospect they seemed to foreshadow. In Coventry, 1705 was marred by riots and voter intimidation. The election returned two Tories, but this result was overturned and the MPs replaced by Whigs when the poll was recontested in 1707. In Defoe's account, the 'Continual Zeal and Heat of Parties' allowed by complacent magistrates and encouraged by the campaigns led to 'Railing, Envying, Fighting, and all sorts of Inveteracy and Violence'. Mobs became 'the Decider of Controversies' so that in effect 'Victory in the Street, has given Victory in the Poll'. So entrenched did this system become that the parties themselves formed 'little Armies' – some reports said that there were five hundred people involved in the 1705 clash; others said a thousand. There were incidents of severe injury and grievous harm to people and property. No murders, but Defoe thought this only a matter of time. Grimly significant in and of themselves, Defoe interpreted the Coventry riots as a threat to the peace and unity of England.[26]

The final leg of Defoe's tour took him to Daventry, Northampton, Wellingborough and then east to Huntingdon, Cambridge and Bury, which he'd covered in his first tour. There is a definite sense that Defoe wound things down as he circled back to Cambridge for personal business, and then made the southwards journey to London, surveying the electoral management of Sudbury, Colchester and Chelmsford on his way back home.

One hundred and thirteen days after he first set out, Defoe arrived in London exhausted but gratified. In all, he recruited at least sixty-three agents. He amassed most during the two tours but drew other contacts into the network, presumably by writing to men he knew in the towns and cities not covered by his path. His agents were merchants and Dissenting clergymen – mostly Presbyterians but also some Quakers and Independents. They were booksellers, physicians, one lawyer and two sitting MPs. The network covered more than seventy towns and cities and could blanket the country with Defoe's propaganda. In the first major distribution, Defoe sent between twelve and one hundred copies of a pamphlet supporting the triumvirate to each of his agents, laying a further fifty out in London coffeehouses and giving a hundred to acquaintances. In total, two thousand copies were circulated. If we conservatively estimate that two to three people might have read each copy – more for those that made their way to coffeehouses – then the effectiveness of the network as a means of disseminating information is clear. And this was only part of the network's function. Defoe had before him a staggering base for intelligence gathering. The one risk was that in relying on those sympathetic to his own politics, class and confession, the network might be biased. If Harley's centre of political gravity shifted, these mostly whiggish agents might not be so loyal.[27]

†

Defoe's network was limited to England. While Harley's overarching capacity to manage domestic politics increased, it exposed the gap where such management was most needed: Scotland. Godolphin's ill-timed advice that the Queen assent to the Scottish parliament's Act of Security (which allowed the Scots to determine their own successor to Anne) provoked a sustained backlash in the English parliament. Almost as soon as the Security Bill became law, Somers and his fellow Whig lords began pushing the set of ideas that would eventually settle into the Alien Act. Passed in March 1705, the Act stripped Scots of their established right to be subjects of the English Crown and embargoed crucial Scottish imports into England, like cattle, linen and coal. The removal of subject rights contravened England's naturalisation provisions, preventing Scots from inheriting property in England or its American colonies. This was rightly perceived as an attack on the landed gentry and merchants of Scotland, whose access to empire presented a major sticking point in relations since the collapse of Darien. The failure of Darien and years of poor agricultural yields meant Scotland's economy had no capacity to weather such losses. Defoe himself thought the move was punitive and impolitic. Earlier drafts of the bill reveal the loss of rights and trade were designed to coerce Scotland into a closer relationship with England. Such 'inconveniences' would be removed 'if a nearer and more compleat Union' was reached. These drafts proposed the establishment of new Union commissioners, a clause included in the final Act.[28]

In the wake of the Act, Harley monitored and restricted the movement of horses into Scotland and moved the military to the borders.

These were emergency measures; to get a better handle on Scotland's parliament and people, and prevent the need for them, he sent his first agent to Edinburgh.

The man dispatched was William Gregg. His brief: to monitor the proceedings of the Scottish parliament, giving Harley a less partial account of its debates than he and Godolphin received from Scottish leaders. Scottish born, Gregg was undeniably clever and had a knack for foreign languages. Reckless and impecunious, he admitted that his state would have been 'desperate' were it not in Harley's 'good hands'. Harley's patronage pulled him from a mess of debts – though not entirely. Gregg began to press for more money as soon as his role was settled. In letters to Harley he maintained that an increase of funds was needed to prevent the 'miscarriage' of his task. At a deeper level, an increase in his stipend would further confirm his sense of his own importance. Gregg's unabashed confidence in his own abilities had led him to tout for a position in government; he idolised the man who recognised him with employment, boasting that he would 'sooner forfeit his head' than 'Harley's favourable opinion'.[29] In time he would lose both.

Gregg's confidence was progressively deflated during his first months in Scotland, sapped by his fear that he might be discovered and so 'fall victim to the rage of a boiling nation'. To hide himself he experimented with a cypher.[30] His position as an English spy amongst his own people cleaved him. It is not always clear if his declarations that he is unhappy to be a 'native' of Scotland are a salve to his insecurity or a reassurance of his loyalty to Harley. Isolated from his country, he felt adrift from Harley too, at one point writing eighteen letters before getting a single response from the Secretary. It is not as if he found the writing easy, either. At first he struggled to write at all. He suffered bouts of illness that had a greater effect on his approach than he admitted.

Gregg's Scottish reports are laden with images of disease. There is a sense of febrile heat gripping both his own body and its surrounds. It seeps into the way he conceived of his mission. Repeating a favourite phrase, his role in Scotland, as he saw it, was to take the 'pulse of this boiling nation'. One cause and symptom of nationwide sickness was the unrelenting pull of Jacobitism.

He diagnosed a further 'Epidemical distemper' in Scotland, one that seemed to emerge from a national amnesia. It was as if they had all forgotten the 'fatal isthmus' of Darien.[31] Why else would the nation be seized by a continued desire for imperial possession? Why would the Darien Company be so susceptible to schemes to invade Madagascar and confiscate the wealth of its pirates? And why were so many Scots seemingly eager to send another expedition to Darien? Gregg is mistaken to think amnesia the cause. The schemes to stamp their mark on Madagascar and recolonise Darien, like the schemes floated to increase Scotland's trade and revenue, were less the result of forgetting than the burden of memory. The fatal loss could not be forgotten. Its continued effects cut Scotland off from sufficiency and increased the possibility of its vassalage. This is why Darien was so difficult to blot out and why it needed recompense.

Paterson was more aware of this need than almost anyone. In the time since returning from Central America, as he worked on reforming Scotland's financial system, Darien remained foremost in his mind. He did not think Madagascar a good option but understood why the remaining Company men sought it out.[32] He had other ideas for generating income. Building on the proposals he had shared with the late King, Paterson proposed an expert 'Council of Trade' and a 'National Fund of Money'. The council was designed to streamline the collection of new taxes on land transactions, manufacturing and grain sales, providing £1 million of new revenue in all. The Crown would take a fixed amount and all funds above that would be deposited into the National Fund, which the council would oversee, deploying the money to compensate Darien investors and to employ the poor in various public works schemes designed to bolster Scotland's economy, from increasing salt production to aiding Scotland's flagging fishing industry. It was at this time that Paterson began to work on some of the key union infrastructure, standardising weights and measures and drafting early proposals for what would become the Equivalent: the one-off payment that would offset Scotland's post-union tax burden and also pay off those who lost money with the Darien Company.[33]

Darien remained a difficult issue on both sides of the border. When debate in the English parliament turned to *An Enquiry into the Causes of the Miscarriage . . . at Darien*, a pamphlet that examined reasons for the colony's failure, Harley steered talk away lest old grievances against the Scots rear their heads.[34] In Scotland, Gregg observed a parliament that was fractious because it was cornered. He spent most afternoons in Parliament Hall watching the proceedings. By June he noted that the members 'begin to be sensible of the great loss' that the Alien Act would impose when it came into effect that Christmas. All knew that the import bans would cut the Scottish annual revenue by £80,000 (£8.5 million today).[35] Debates over coin and credit intensified against this backdrop. On one occasion they ended with a duel on Leith Sands. Paterson's plan to establish a Council of Trade that could examine the sources of Scotland's revenue, its legal-economic infrastructure and work to balance imports and exports was enacted in law. Parliament debated restricting English imports and voted to prevent all imports of English, Irish and foreign butter. Grouping England with foreign nations was a direct response to the impending alienage of Anne's Scottish subjects. To Gregg, this was all just tinkering around the edges. Scottish MPs knew that they had to find a way to compel England to repeal the more punitive provisions of the Alien Act.[36] Their best option remained settling the succession.

Queen Anne's letter to the Scottish parliament renewing her hopes for both a dynastic settlement and political union gave some MPs hope that England would allow concessions on trade and monarchic prerogative.[37] Read in parliament, the letter focused the debate around questions of order. What trade and navigation provisions could be struck before settling the succession or suing for a union? Or would pushing for a treaty be the way to settle Scotland's economic and dynastic questions? The opposition wanted all issues of coin and trade settled first.[38] The Court opposed this, in Gregg's view because it would have impeded their hopes of drawing all questions towards the answer of union. On this matter they were joined by the MPs of the Squadrone Volante, formerly the New Party – a grouping of moderate Presbyterians who took on the new name to affirm their position as a free-flying voting bloc, distinct from both Court and

Country. The debate was bitterly tense but made little progress. Until, as Gregg reported, the Duke of Hamilton rose on 16 July to resolve:

> That this House will not go to the nomination of the same Successor with England, till such time as we have a previous Treaty about our Commerce . . . and that we will proceed to such limitations and conditions of Government as may best secure the independence and sovereignty of the Crown and Kingdom of Scotland.

The resolution was approved by forty-three votes. In doing so, the Scottish parliament rebuked the Queen's letter. The major problem to Anne, Queensberry, the rest of the Court faction and the English triumvirs was the nature of the limitations to which Hamilton alluded. Fletcher of Saltoun had proposed twelve such limitations. Fletcher's canon of restrictions included more frequent elections, parliamentary consent for all acts of war and removing the right to choose all offices of state and military from the monarch and placing it with the parliament. Most troubling to defenders of the monarch's prerogative, Fletcher's final limitation had a sting in the tail: if the monarch violated any of the previous twelve limits, then they forfeited the Crown. As Gregg wrote with dismayed hurry to Harley, such limitations would so reduce the Queen's power that she and future monarchs would 'have as little say' as the 'Doge of Venice'. Scotland would become, in Gregg's assessment, a 'Caledonian Commonwealth'.[39]

Harley did not yet have the kind of agent on the ground able to work the press in Scotland. Instead, he deployed his ally William Carstares. Carstares used his personal influence to caution members of the Scottish parliament about the danger an invasion from England posed, the financial impossibility of maintaining Scotland as a separate kingdom, and the risk to the Kirk that would come if the main line of Stuarts – Catholics supported by a Catholic France – returned to the throne.[40] There must have been some relief in Harley's rooms at the Cockpit when Gregg reported that even the hardliner Fletcher was not opposed to an 'honourable treaty' in principle.[41] It depended on the kind of union proposed. Fletcher's preference was for a loose confederal union, with each nation maintaining its own parliament.

He staunchly opposed an incorporated union, one where the parliaments of England and Scotland would be subsumed within a united parliament of Great Britain. His fear was that incorporation would be a de facto loss of independence. Some doubted whether it would even get that far. If the Scottish commissioners asked for too many limits or too many trade concessions then the union negotiations would flounder in stalemate, as had the negotiations of 1702–3. The nature of the union and whether it would happen at all, the concessions Scotland could extract, Scotland's future as a sovereign nation and imperial player: all hinged on the make-up of the negotiating team.

The Country party and Cavaliers believed that the estates that made up the Scottish parliament – the nobility, shires and burghs – should elect Scotland's Union commissioners. They assumed this would be the case when parliament passed an act for a treaty. So when the Duke of Hamilton rose on 1 September and moved the Queen should select the Scottish commissioners, it sent a shock of defeat through the anti-incorporationist ranks. Because Hamilton had waited till more than a dozen Country party members had left the House before making his proposal, it carried – by a mere eight votes. The Duke's Country party and Cavalier comrades could scarcely fathom his betrayal. To Lockhart, Hamilton's reversal marked the beginning of the end: by conceding their right to choose their own union negotiators, Hamilton had brought on 'Scotland's ruine'.[42] He had said as much to Hamilton before the vote, writing to the Duke that unless parliament gives the Queen nominating power, the whole project of union will fail: as Lockhart wanted, and assumed Hamilton did too.

The question of why Hamilton betrayed his own ideals and Scotland's independence is one of the most fiercely debated in the historiography of the Union. Though it scandalised his parliamentary colleagues, it was not entirely surprising to those who knew him best. The Duke's mother worried that her son might cede ground to the Unionists. In the weeks preceding the debate he had written to her to say he thought the Queen should be the one to choose the commissioners. Duchess Anne urged him against this position, and tried to convince him that the commissioners had to be nominated 'in plain parliament': so that process was open and fair, so that the Treaty of Union would not trample Scotland.

There is a gruff but beleaguered note of maternal support in the Duchess' call to her son to 'act the part of an honest and good countrieman'. She had heard from her daughter Lady Catherine, now Duchess of Atholl, that the Queen's representatives had been trying to win his favour: 'all there [their] demand was a Cesse [i.e. supply] and the nomination of the treaters for the union left to the Queen'.[43] Godolphin and Harley certainly dealt with the Duke of Hamilton. Harley had known for months that the Duke was amenable to a treaty. One of his informers in Scotland, who acted as go-between for the Secretary, Godolphin and Hamilton, let the English ministers know that Hamilton was fully aware that Godolphin wanted him to 'make the matter of the treaty easy'. Hamilton just did not know how he could fulfil this task given the utter 'disgust'[44] that his countrymen within parliament and without felt towards the Alien Act.

The speculation that Hamilton's dealings with Harley and Godolphin carried some secret sweetener or bond of clandestine allegiance cannot be substantiated. The fact that the Duke addressed Harley as 'good mason' continues to stoke conspiracists. One of the theories periodically brought up to account for Hamilton's erratic behaviour is that he had designs on the Scottish throne. The lure of favour by the English Court should not be discounted. But the balance of probability is that Hamilton, though no doubt desiring the throne, set his sights a bit lower at this moment. He simply wanted the Queen to name him as one of the Union commissioners who would negotiate the Treaty on Scotland's behalf. Some have claimed that he did a secret deal with Argyll giving the Queen the power to ensure his selection. It is more likely there was no direct deal but that he thought the gesture would bring him the Queen's favour. He clung almost naively to the hope that he would be selected as a commissioner right up to the point it was dashed.[45] As the parliamentary session wore on, Hamilton began to view the factions of the opposition as fighting for an illusory independence. He had serious concerns about the prospect of war with England.[46] Not seeing many ways out, of either parliamentary impasse or war against a greater power, he likely thought that acting as one of the commissioners would give him influence over the kind of union and Scotland's power within it.

This is the most rational explanation. But Hamilton was not known as a rational actor. His aspirations for greater estate in England, his pursuit of self-preservation, and his belief that his power was thwarted clashed in his person against family pressure and the esteem he won as a figurehead of the opposition. This makes it hard to pinpoint the ultimate cause of his about-face. Whatever tipped him to England, there is no doubt that his proposition ultimately saved the Treaty. With the Queen now responsible for choosing Scotland's commissioners, the English parliament moved swiftly to repeal the Alien Act, removing all its provisions except the clause that called for their appointment.

Before Hamilton vested the choice in the Queen, the estates had drawn up a list of their preferred candidates. Even though the Scottish parliament voted to negotiate for a treaty, because of the way power was dispersed across the nobility and burgesses, the men they wanted to select as negotiators were largely opposed to union. In contrast, the commissioners chosen by the Queen were largely in support. The one stark standout was Lockhart, who was selected following pressure from his uncle, the Whig Lord Wharton. Wharton was moved by family loyalty more than political sympathy. He also believed he could win Lockhart to his side. Lockhart himself was shocked and wrote immediately to Hamilton to tell him that he did not solicit the position.[47] He did not want to offend Hamilton. The opposition quickly saw that Lockhart might be useful as a spy: their man on commission, passing them intelligence of its deliberations.[48] Seafield, Queensberry and Mar were commissioners, as was John Clerk of Penicuik. Neither Argyll nor Hamilton was nominated. The latter's efforts to secure the favour of the Queen had not done enough to efface his reputation as an unreliable servant.[49]

Of the thirty-one chosen, about a third had been commissioners in 1702–3. The upshot was that, while broadly in favour of a union, the commissioners had enough of a cohort within their ranks who had pushed for free trade and the retention of some of Scotland's sovereign functions that the group cannot be dismissed as a suite of rogues ready to betray their nation at the first taste of English coin.

The English commissioners were named the following April. Godolphin, Harley and Hedges were amongst them, as were the Whig lords Somers and Wharton, the Solicitor-General Sir Simon Harcourt, the Low Church Archbishop of Canterbury and the Tory Archbishop of York. The English commissioners were far more politically heterogenous than their Scottish counterparts. Harley and Godolphin had wanted more commissioners, but the Scottish side were adamant that the numbers of both countries be even. What Godolphin saw as a mere 'punctilio', the Scottish parliament saw as a vital sign of equity. Though diverse, Harley and Godolphin had a group of commissioners they were confident could be managed. In guiding the Queen's selection, Harley had made sure of it. Godolphin congratulated him for filling 'the blanks very well in the Commission for the Union'.[50]

Part Two

SCOTLAND

CHAPTER 6

EDINBURGH

When Defoe imagined how a spy might infiltrate a foreign capital, he came up with a set of protocols. The agent he personated was successful because he assumed 'all possible Measures for keeping my self concealed': he lived according to the 'Instructions' of his handlers, and took 'a private Lodging remote from the Court', shielding himself from 'all general Appearances of the People'. Once hidden from view, the spy was able to put together a more comprehensive picture of the country: 'I made it my Business to acquaint my self with such Particulars of the publick Transactions' missing from the accounts of other 'private Agents'.[1] The insight borne from Defoe's own experience as a spy was that state secrets cannot be understood in the abstract. A good intelligence system knows its target country holistically.

Defoe could not keep himself concealed in the same way as his fictional spy. John Bell, the postmaster at Newcastle-upon-Tyne who worked for Harley, encountered Defoe on his way north. After sharing a bottle of wine, dinner and three days of conversation, he reported that Alexander Goldsmith was 'a Very Engenious man & fit for that business I guess he is goeing about'. Though Bell is careful to avoid mentioning Defoe's brief, and to use the alias Defoe assumed on tour and in correspondence, he notes that Defoe was not as cautious in person about protecting his identity '& will Owne it at Edinburgh; he says he is so publicly knowne that it would not be prudence [prudent] to goe under an Other name'.[2] Defoe was too well known to adopt a simple cover. He had to find ways to hide in plain sight, unlike his ideal agent, nor could he seek comfort in the bounds of his instructions. When he set out for Scotland, the terms of his mission remained too vague to live by.

Bell was right. Defoe was an 'Engenious man' well suited for intelligence work in Scotland. As a Presbyterian, he shared Scotland's dominant religion and would not be thought of as a tool of the English Church. As a businessman, he was fluent in the economic issues of Union and could establish contacts and source information under the guise of trade. As someone genuinely committed to the cause, he was no mere mercenary either.

The mission stood to benefit Defoe personally. His tour of the country had only delayed his creditors. Since returning, he had spent a great deal of his energy hiding from bailiffs while trying to find more lasting ways to dodge his debts. In January 1706 he contemplated moving to Spain. He also filed for bankruptcy. Because the Bankruptcy Act was so new, Defoe remained deeply unsure whether its provisions would calm what he later called the 'Furious, Subtill and Malitious Opposition' that drove his creditors' pursuit.

The most secure way out remained a posting overseas. From early May Defoe began asking Harley if he would 'please to Send me Somewhere Abroad, Out of The Reach of Their hands'. His 'Reduc't Condition' left him worried for his family. It also threatened his network of correspondents. Plea shades to warning when he tells Harley how his financial woes robbed him of the 'Undisturb'd houres' needed to maintain the network. Without proper finance or assistance, the chains of communication 'Settled by your Order in most parts of England and from which on all Occasions I Could have Rendred you Service, Dyes, and Declines'. Harley had promised Defoe 'a Servant to assist', as well as 'frequent Communication of things to keep Intelligence alive'. Without either, Defoe feared he and the network were 'Rendred Useless'.[3]

Defoe's financial straits and his commitment to the Union dovetailed. Not only did he believe that joining with Scotland would lead to a 'lasting Tranquility' and a 'visible Encrease of the Power, Wealth, and Magnificence of the most powerful Island in the World': he also saw personal opportunities in a constitutional union – both in the increase in trade it would generate and in the role he might claim as a populariser of its benefits. In May he published the first part of an essay designed to remove the prejudices of each nation, a contribution he hoped would 'remove the Mists and Vapours of Imagination, from the Eyes of the People, and prepare Mens Minds for Union'. The prejudices Defoe combats with reason are a mix of historical grievance and future fear. He addresses the English animosity over the role Scotland played in the Civil Wars as well as their fear that Presbyterianism might dissolve the social ties of the English Church. He acknowledges Scotland's pain at losing Darien and how many in Scotland believed that a union would formalise English dominance, forever suppressing Scotland's global ambition, and incurring an irredeemable loss of sovereignty.[4] The strength of the essay is that it takes these prejudices seriously, seeking out their causes without dismissing those who held them – all while making a case for why a union would benefit both countries.

The first part of what would become a five-part essay was targeted to English readers. Anti-Unionists in Scotland later held it up as evidence of Defoe's bias and reprinted it in Edinburgh to expose his irrevocable allegiance to England. But, in April 1706, confidants of the Scottish commissioners, who arrived in London that month to begin negotiating a unification treaty, thought the essay served their purposes: so much so that some Scottish merchants claimed that they commissioned the work.[5] Defoe managed to befriend one of the commissioners, the younger John Clerk of Penicuik, an ally of Queensberry. Penicuik was taken with Defoe's skill as a writer and conversationalist. For Defoe, the friendship offered a point of access. The Union negotiations were unusually well guarded. Serious pains were taken to keep information confined to the rooms of the Cockpit. The commissioners also instituted a self-imposed news quarantine. As far as they could, they wanted to remain unswayed by outside forces.

Except for one occasion, the sixty-two commissioners were not all present at the same time. The Treaty was composed through small negotiating parties in separate rooms. On the Scottish side Queensberry held sway. He and his coterie – Sir David Dalrymple of Hailes, Sir Hew Dalrymple of North Berwick and David Melville, 3rd Earl of Leven – dominated Scotland's position so as to define it. The overarching issue was the form the Union would take. Would it follow the incorporationist model, in which the Scottish parliament would be dissolved and Scottish representatives incorporated into a new united parliament of Great Britain? Or would it be a looser federated Union, under which Scotland retained its own parliament and institutions? Clerk leaned towards the federal model at the start of the negotiations but was gradually won over to the incorporationist side.[6] The concession that brought most Scottish commissioners to the same position occurred when the English negotiators acquiesced to Scotland's demand for 'full freedom and intercourse of Trade and Navigation'. Scotland could access the bounty of England's empire (with the exception of Asia) if they agreed to secure the Hanoverian succession and to be incorporated under a single British parliament; if, as the line goes, they sold their sovereignty for empire.[7]

There were holdouts like Lockhart. Other opponents of incorporation were peeled away as the English negotiators offered to repeal the taxes that thwarted Scotland's economic development: on Scottish coal, salt and cattle. How much Clerk revealed to Defoe during this process is not known. The two talked enough during the three months of negotiations that Clerk was truly excited by the prospect of Defoe coming to Scotland.[8] Accusations that Harley and Godolphin had bribed Clerk and other Scottish commissioners to bring about an incorporating treaty gained credence when the resolution seemed to come about a little too quickly and to hedge a little too closely to England's opening position. If not won by direct bribes, the commissioners were well positioned to benefit from the terms of the Treaty, from access to international trade, the loosening of taxes on Scottish goods and by the provision of the Equivalent. Calculated by Paterson and David Gregory, this payment was intended to compensate Scotland for taking on a share of England's national debt and with it a greater tax burden, which the English insisted was a necessary precondition to incorporation.

For Defoe, the economic implications of incorporation presented 'the most difficult point of the Treaty'. They were complex and liable to stir confusion and popular resistance. To offset the resistance of his English readers, he published a second part to his *Essay at Removing National Prejudices*. He offers an at times disjointed combination of detailed accountancy and folk wisdom. The financial evidence operates at different registers. Some readers likely engaged with Defoe's points on tax and revenue at length. Those who passed over the sums might still have taken confidence from their mere accumulation, seeing them as a bolster to the essay's analytical nub: that the 'Improvement of *Scotland* shall every way be the Improvement of *England*'. While a federal union would allow Scotland to develop for its own ends, Defoe firmly believed that incorporation would lead to the 'mutual inriching' of both nations. London would 'remain the Center of the Wealth of the whole Island' and would grow richer as Scotland itself grew richer and supplied more people to work England's colonies. London would be 'the Fountain from whence, and the Conduit thro' which all that Wealth will be convey'd, and the Ocean into which it all flows will be the People'.[9] National benefit is made distinctly personal. The English people – Defoe's readers – would be amply rewarded by the Union. And this more than justifies the short-term concessions Defoe advocates England make on the grounds of equity: Scotland should not be overburdened by debt or by undue taxes on goods that played an outsized role in the life of Scotland's people and the nation's coffers: salt and malt. It was this even-handedness and concern for Scotland that inspired a belief in some of the Scottish commissioners that Defoe worked on their behalf.[10]

Defoe made sure that Harley knew the extent of his service to the Union cause. His public efforts were easy to display. In May he told readers that the *Review* would now work 'to remove the vulgar [i.e. popular] Obstructions which are industriously thrown in the way and, if possible, Encline all Parties to a Union of Nations, that we may be henceforth one powerful Nation'.[11] With the commissioners having settled on terms by July, the Treaty was now sent to the Queen for approval and to the Scottish and English parliaments for debate and ratification. Defoe recognised that popular resistance could obstruct one or both parliaments – though he worried more about the one in Scotland. Melding two distinct proud countries into 'one powerful Nation' would involve the kind of change that brings the two meanings of constitution into play: altering the frame of law to join the nations would force a new identity on the people. Defoe knew this. And he knew that popular politics would have a determinative effect on the success of the Union, even if the vast majority of everyday people could not vote.

It was not enough, then, to focus only on the good, using essays to counter old prejudices and give voice to a new people. Defoe had to work underground to prevent opposition arguments from gaining currency, cutting them off before the written word was read and passed into spoken fear. Drawing on his contacts in the world of clandestine print, Defoe managed to intercept a manuscript, which he then sent on to Harley. The force of its arguments revealed Defoe's worth in preventing its printing. The manuscript accuses the English Court of 'Machiavillian Conduct' in securing the assent of the Scottish commissioners, but boasts that the 'Scots Parliament' will quash the Treaty. Just as worryingly, it stokes fear that an English-dominated British parliament would 'eliminate Presbyterianism'.[12] Within a week or so of receiving this manuscript, Harley resolved to send Defoe to Edinburgh to report on the Treaty debates in the Scottish parliament. Though Defoe refused to admit he was going north on Union business, the rumour persisted. One gossiper even suspected that part of Defoe's task was to calm public anger, repeating to a friend that 'it is say'd Daniel De Foe is gone into Scotland to apease his dearly beloved the mobb who they say is a little tumultuous upon this union'.[13]

†

Defoe left London for Edinburgh on 13 September, expecting to reach the Scottish capital within two weeks. Beaten by heavy rain, the journey became 'a long winter', full of hazards and inconvenience. He had problems with one of his horses, struggled with the soft crumbling roads and was forced to take an indirect trudge through the Midlands.[14] The energy he derived from his new mission was blunted, too, by the return of a familiar dynamic: no clear instructions from

Harley. The two were scheduled to meet before Defoe departed but some unhappy (and unmentioned) troubles took Harley away at the last moment. For Defoe, this was a 'Perticular Disaster': the Union was an unwieldy endeavour and he needed some clear, definable tasks. He also wanted a greater baseline of intelligence. Without knowing the terms of the Treaty or the characters of the Scots who drafted and negotiated it, or indeed what passed in the English Court and amongst English parliamentarians, he feared he would not know who or what 'to Observe'. The absence of a guideline worried him more than before as the stakes of his mission were higher – for the nation and for himself. Defoe knew that Harley had briefed Godolphin and the Queen about his mission to Scotland: he now had some validation that he was not only Harley's agent but an agent of Crown and state.

On his ride north Defoe retraced the nodes of his network through Cambridge, Coventry, Leicester, Nottingham and Leeds. At each point he checked in with his distribution agents in the hope of finding instructions from Harley. In Newcastle-upon-Tyne, where he met John Bell, at least some of his asks were answered. As Harley's agent for the region and as a postmaster with his own web of contacts, Bell was able to supply Defoe with a new horse and some funds, and to arrange a line of credit for him in Edinburgh. As we saw, Bell managed to make out the vague outlines of Defoe's brief. But he had no instructions from Harley on this matter, either. Defoe had to fall back on the letter he had sent the Secretary, where he defined his own mission, seeking to allay his 'Anxious Thoughts' with some small measure of confirmation. As Defoe saw it, his role in Scotland was:

1 To Inform My Self of the Measures Taking Or Partys forming Against the Union and Apply my Self to prevent them.
2 In Conversation and by all Reasonable Methods to Dispose peoples minds to the Union.
3 By writing or Discourse, to Answer any Objections, Libells or Reflections on the Union, the English or the Court Relateing to the Union.
4 To Remove the Jealousies and Uneasyness of people about Secret Designs here against the Kirk &c.

While he clung to these tasks, he told Harley as he left Newcastle that he felt as if he were 'your Messenger without an Errand'. This remained the case as he rode on to Morpeth, Berwick and into Scotland.

Shortly before or just after he arrived in Edinburgh, Defoe finally received word from Harley. The Secretary's instructions are to the point. Like Defoe's self-fashioned set, they are split into four demands:

> 1. You are to use the utmost caution that it may not be supposed you are employed by any person in England; but that you came there upon your own business, & out of love to the Country.
> 2. You are to write constantly the true State how you find things, at least once a week, & you need not subscribe any name, but direct for me under Cover to Mrs Collins at the Posthouse, Middle Temple Gate, London. For variety you may direct under Cover to Michael Read in York Buildings.
> 3. You may confidently assure those you converse with, that the Queen & all those who have Credit with her, are sincere & hearty for the Union.
> 4. You must shew them, this is such an opportunity that being once lost or neglected is not again to be recovered. England never was before in so good a disposition to make such large Concessions, or so heartily to unite with Scotland, & should their kindness now be slighted.[15]

In Harley's instructions, Defoe's cover and the care he has to take to ensure his communications remain secret are folded into the overall programme. As Harley saw it, Defoe's task was to provide accurate, up-to-the-week intelligence on Scotland and convince all he met that England was both enthusiastic for Union and that such an opportunity, if squandered, would not come again. The method and media of this persuasion he leaves to the resources and guile of the agent.

⚘

Harley had a ready sense of the situation in Edinburgh when he cautioned Defoe to remain covert. Gregg's dispatches from the previous season painted a fractious parliament and combustible nation, prompting Harley to send a series of other agents north. By the time Defoe reached the Scottish capital, Paterson had been embedded there for close to a month. His first report to Harley was sobering. Paterson found 'as much want of temper and more ignorance in the changes relating to the Union than I expected'; his hope was that the Treaty would be met with 'better acceptance' than the national mood suggested.[16]

Though recognised for their reach and genius, Paterson's efforts to establish a Council of Trade that would aid Scotland in developing its financial institutions, raise its credit and reinvigorate its fishing industry proved too expensive to implement.[17] Despite this setback, Paterson wanted to contribute to 'the public services' in Scotland. He continued to work on standardising English and Scottish weights and measures and was angered when it seemed that Harley and Godolphin did not do enough to engage his economic expertise in the Treaty negotiations. As a way in, Paterson allied himself with Lord Somers, one of the English Treaty commissioners and member of the Whig Junto. Paterson tried hard to negotiate this alternative point of access through the Whigs without conceding either Harley's or Godolphin's favour. Hindered by resistance, Paterson tried to resign himself to a smaller role, acknowledging a pain shared by the other agents working for the Union: because it was so monumental a task, those in power 'reckoned [it] too great for little men to have a hand in'. This posture obstructed the best of their contributions and hid from view what Paterson and Harley's other agents managed to achieve.

Paterson's frustration let slip a rare wisp of grievance. He was sure, he told Harley, that had Harley offered him a proper position when he first started supplying intelligence, he could have provided more useful service.[18] Paterson laid out the kind of contribution he could make to Godolphin and ensured that a copy of this memorial was sent on to Harley. In it, Paterson tells how the Treaty commissioners from England and Scotland thought that he should 'goe down to Scotland' to give 'further assistance in the Union, particularly in the matters relating to the Indian and African Company there'. They approached Paterson to promote 'The Aims and Applications of the Equivalent' and to advise 'in what may relate to Trade, or the Publick Revenues', aspects of the Treaty that the commissioners 'seemed to apprehend might not otherwise be so well understood'. When sounding out such estimations of his usefulness, there is none of the resentment that encroached on his letter to Harley. In its place is a heady optimism. Paterson vaunts his 'success even beyond my hope' in 'promoting the Union' and carves out a role that would see him advise MPs on economics, trade and the Equivalent, while also combatting the kind of public misunderstanding of these domains liable to 'Spoil, or at Least very much prejudice the Union'. As counsellor and promoter, he would work to enact the plans behind his aborted Council of Trade, helping the Scottish parliament devise ways to encourage 'Trade, Manufactures & fisheries'. He could also push his view of an expansive Union, one that would eventually draw in Ireland as well.[19] In the final place, he would not simply aid in the calculation of the Equivalent but see that its funds were deployed strategically to bring Scotland into a 'wished for temper', subdued into Union and lulled with contentment after the Union was enacted.[20] The 'noise' Paterson made with this 'long paper' convinced Godolphin. From Godolphin's vantage, it was 'not safe to detain' Paterson in England any longer. As he told a confidant, if the Union were to 'miscarry the not sending him may' turn out to 'be a crime'.[21] Within days of sending the paper, Paterson was deployed to Edinburgh. Tasked with reporting on, and influencing, the debates over economic policy and the negotiations on the Equivalent, he embodied the double life of the spy. He had to reintegrate himself into Scottish society, drawing on the trust and promise of Darien recessed in the nation's memory to present himself as an empathetic advocate for those who lost their fortunes to the colony – all the while doing England's bidding and informing on the countrymen he claimed to represent.

The third agent Harley deployed in 1706 was David Fearne. Unlike Paterson and Defoe, Fearne was not directly involved in promoting the Union. His mission was closer to that of a professional spy.[22] His main task was to gather human intelligence. Because of this position, the weekly reports he sent Harley became a baseline against which Harley could calibrate the intelligence he received from those with a vested interest in shaping how the progress of the Treaty was perceived in London – be they other agents keen to puff their own achievements, or Scottish nobles. One of Harley's spies warned the Secretary that he would never get an accurate picture from the nobles. Their desire to be seen as powerful meant they acted as if 'capable to suppress everything that may arise there of themselves, and this they would have you believe till the disease be past remedy'.[23] The Scottish nobility was apt to maintain an image of control just long enough for Harley and Godolphin to lose it.

Fearne's dispatches from Edinburgh were clearheaded. Perhaps even more important, he sent Harley detailed anatomisations of Scottish parliamentarians, nobles and their affiliations, the position of each on the Protestant succession, their party, their proclivity to Jacobitism, their clan membership and leadership, the shires, counties and burghs they represented, as well as their general disposition and behaviour.[24] Fearne was not an impartial observer. He was an avowed Unionist and deeply anti-Jacobite, yet his relatively straightforward narration of events, coupled with his crib sheet on the main players of Scottish politics, gave Harley the means to monitor his other agents and to understand the perspectives and motivations of Scottish politicians – those in his correspondence, and those who would never write to an English minister.[25]

Fearne's knowledge of Scotland's people and leaders was personal, gathered from his career as an advocate in Edinburgh and sustained by his connections across the country. It was said he had 'Considerable Clyents of the Cheife Nobility and Gentry of the Kingdome and of forreigners'.[26] When his friend Dr William Houston first introduced him to Erasmus Lewis, Harley's undersecretary, he was careful to mention Fearne's position as the nominated tax collector for Orkney and Caithness.[27] Fearne's ties to the west were deeper still. He was a Cameronian, a member of the radical sect of Covenanters who resisted any civil imposition on Presbyterian Church government. His own mother had been forced from her estate for harbouring a Covenanting minister, and much of Fearne's legal practice was devoted to defending 'the oppressed and persecuted Protestants in the west and north Countries'. Despite this radicalism, Fearne was well liked at Court, even by Jacobites, who believed he had once saved the late King James II from a dangerous fall.[28]

Harley came to know Fearne as a 'formal fellow, but very faithfull and in credit with the Kirk'.[29] As fear grew that the Union might threaten the independence of the Kirk, this kind of credit became increasingly valuable.

Fearne's service was tentative at first, and narrowly focused. But as he warmed to Harley, he grew bolder. When the commissioners were in London, he devised ways to bring them over to Harley's thinking. When the Treaty was sent north for ratification, he was well positioned to help smooth its passage. Where he had offered Harley advice without pay before, he expected remuneration when he became Harley's agent – and received it. Fearne understood his value, boasting that 'none other can pretend to know the nation so particularly, the people's constitution, tempers, estates, powers and weaknesses, nor the individual places, their strength and weaknesses'. As an advocate during the Revolution, he rode across England and Scotland; he knew the coast of Ireland too.[30] These travels afforded him the demographic insight and popular tact that Defoe had spent the better part of two years diligently cultivating.

Defoe and Paterson knew that the other was in Scotland and working for Harley. While Fearne may have heard rumours of Defoe's patron, and noted Paterson's public work on the Equivalent, he did not have direct evidence that either served the same master as he did. Neither Fearne nor Defoe knew that the same 'friend' who paid them paid the other, nor that the letters each sent Harley were channelled through the same hub, with John Bell in Newcastle bundling their correspondence together to give Harley a full picture. From London, Harley monitored all those who worked for him, but did not always confide the full roster of his agents to his allies. Godolphin did not know Fearne was Harley's asset until a year into his service.[31] In this way, Harley's network settled into a loose coherence, characterised by inconsistent levels of secrecy and disclosure and an uneven distribution of their findings in England. It is fair to assume that if Harley had imposed a more methodical approach to gathering and reviewing intelligence, less would have been lost across the island and he could have acted on what he received with greater speed and precision. Nonetheless, Harley established a ring of spies able to access the Treaty negotiations in parliament and its committees, who could also live amongst the people of Edinburgh. By instinct, design or a combination of both, he chose men with complementary expertise, backgrounds and wit enough to insinuate themselves into Scottish society and its governing classes.

One agent who remained hidden from the rest was Captain John Ogilvie. Like Fearne, Ogilvie was Scottish. But where Fearne was an unwavering advocate for the Protestant succession, Ogilvie had served in the army of James II: he fought for the deposed King at Savoy and Catalonia and followed him into exile in St Germain. When James II died in 1701, Ogilvie relocated his family to the coast of Normandy. When Queen Anne offered indemnity to all Scots who fought for James II (the same indemnity that brought Beaufort of the Scotch plot back to the British Isles), Ogilvie returned to St Germain to ask for a pass to return home. St Germain denied his request. The exiled Court was unwilling to let their soldier go. Ogilvie had an extensive knowledge of Jacobite networks and the French army and had cultivated diplomatic contacts across the courts of Europe. He was simply too dangerous an asset to relinquish.

Unwilling to pass up the chance at clemency, Ogilvie hired a fishing boat and escaped with his family, sailing from Normandy to the Essex coast. From his actions it seems that he intended to be as frank as he needed to re-establish himself in England, for as soon as he reached Essex, he found the local Justice of the Peace and informed the man who he was and where he came from. A pair of alert Customs House Officers realised the importance of such a defector and alerted Nottingham immediately. Still serving as Secretary of State at this point, Nottingham arranged for Ogilvie and his family to be brought to London at their own expense. He also kept them imprisoned and charged them for the privilege of 'diet and lodging' at such extravagant rates that, in six months, Ogilvie was left with debts amounting to £130 (the equivalent of £14,000 today). Nottingham's intention was to pressure Ogilvie into turning state's agent. It worked. As Ogilvie's debts rose and his arrest for non-payment loomed, he not only gave 'information about the treasonable correspondence carried on between France and England' but offered his services in intercepting such correspondence off the Sussex coast.[32]

When Harley replaced Nottingham in 1704, Ogilvie sought him out immediately, begging for 'some directions . . . to prevent my being put in Gaole for my debts'.[33] Harley saw potential and acted quickly, arranging with Godolphin to pay Ogilvie £100.[34] After being refused a pass by St Germain – when he had served the cause so loyally – and being imprisoned by Nottingham – when he had turned himself in without subterfuge or delay – Ogilvie was overcome by the swiftness of Harley's action. Never, he told his new benefactor, had he experienced such 'honour or genorosetie' from someone he did not serve directly.[35] Godolphin urged Harley to capitalise on Ogilvie's 'good mood', using the ministry's credit to recruit him as an agent. Godolphin was happy for him to serve either on the English coast, in Scotland, Rotterdam or Hamburg.[36] When presented with these options, Ogilvie opted to remain in England. Though he would eventually serve in England, Scotland and France, Harley reneged, denying him the choice and sending him to Holland and onto Hamburg for his first mission – both important hubs for the communication between France and Scotland.

Ogilvie proved the consummate spy and emerged as an essential asset to Harley's Scottish operation. As a former Jacobite, he was able to regain the trust of the exiled Court, along with French courtiers and key European ambassadors. Travelling between Rotterdam, Hamburg and Paris, he began to uncover a global Jacobite underground working to deliver the exiled Prince of Wales to the throne, a plan that required them to obstruct the Union. He had the double consciousness of one eternally watching others. To cast their eyes off his back, he travelled incognito as Jean Gassion or John Lebrun. He begged Harley to 'let nobody see' their more sensitive correspondence, and used an alias for Harley as an extra precaution.[37] To ensure that his messages reached the Secretary, he employed his wife Rebecca as an intermediary. Ogilvie instructed Harley's porter to remove his livery and travel in plain clothes whenever he came to Rebecca's dwellings in Drury Lane, lest her role be exposed. Rebecca's financial dependence on Harley kept Ogilvie in the Secretary's thrall. Ogilvie's fear of discovery pierced his deference, as he lectured Harley on how to maintain his secrecy.[38]

At first Harley paid Ogilvie enough to allow him to mix with the upper echelons of Jacobite exiles.[39] As he did, Ogilvie gained their trust, moving in Jacobite society and through France with such fluency that he was eventually employed as a French secret service agent. The story he gave the French to regain their trust was that he fled imprisonment in England.[40] He remained Harley's man, a double agent with access to better intelligence than almost anyone else in Harley's employ.

To prevent doubts of his loyalty, Ogilvie brought Rebecca and their children back to France, installing them at St Germain, where Rebecca acted as his deputy, keeping track of things while Ogilvie travelled to Versailles and throughout Europe. His early letters to Harley detail efforts to recruit the Duke of Hamilton as head of a French-backed rebellion in Scotland. The French initially kept this plan hidden from St Germain for fear the leaky Court would expose it to England. Hamilton's demurral spurred another plot. According to Ogilvie's sources, the French King and his foreign minister de Torcy wanted to secure a peace with England on condition that Anne did all she could to ensure that her half-brother, the exiled Prince of Wales, succeeded her. Unsure of how this offer might be met, the French continued to amass the twelve thousand troops that would prove their sincerity to potential loyalists in Scotland.[41]

Ogilvie alerted Harley that agents had been sent from France to Scotland to lay the ground for armed rebellion. The threat was real; the Scotch plot proved that. But it was also somewhat abstract. Of more immediate concern were reports that these agents also intended to obstruct the ratification of the Treaty of Union.[42] They were not the only ones. Harley had intelligence that the Dutch had sent sabotage agents too. The fear in Holland was that a united Britain would threaten their trade position and herring fisheries.[43]

When Ogilvie told Harley that with enough support he could embed himself at Versailles, he made the promise to monitor all Scottish visitors, reminding Harley that 'I have been concerned and trusted by them before'. Ogilvie was well placed 'to give you account from tym to tym of what measures may be contravened against the queens Intrest'.[44] The accounts Ogilvie gave were staggering. French invasion of Scotland was a continual topic of discussion at Versailles. Should the Union come to pass, there was a plan to invade then. Even if the invasion itself proved unsuccessful, it would draw English troops away from Flanders and thus cede supremacy to France in the War of the Spanish Succession.

Ogilvie gave Harley the names of Jacobite spies sent to Scotland. He also drew up lists of the 'discontented party' in Scotland, providing Harley with a file on those that St Germain and Versailles saw as potential allies, not least Hamilton, Atholl and Rob Roy. Harley could then corroborate these lists with the ones Fearne provided, gaining a full measure of opposition forces, their local threat and global reach. The lists of both agents fulfilled one of the key aims of intelligence Defoe had outlined two years earlier in his scheme of general intelligence: they gave data on power brokers and their constituencies, details of positions and character of politicians and clergy, and the political nature of particular locales.

Perhaps most significantly, Ogilvie uncovered the traffic of correspondence between Versailles, St Germain and Scotland. He provided Harley with a full map of who wrote to Mary of Modena and her advisors Perth and Middleton. Ogilvie detailed how correspondence flowed through the Scots College in Paris, which acted as a hub, dispersing letters to and from Versailles, St Germain, Amsterdam and throughout Scotland. Thanks to its links to the Scots Catholic Mission, the College had well-worn channels for underground communication. Moving through these clandestine networks of writers and distribution agents was intelligence gathered from England; as Ogilvie discovered, one of Mary's courtiers had 'a considerable salary' to pay informers and spies in England.[45] Ogilvie's immersive work gave Harley enough information to understand how St Germain and Versailles exerted their influence in Scotland. More significantly, the spy's efforts to reconstruct Jacobite chains of intelligence and communication gave Harley ways to intercept and potentially thwart this influence.

This was dangerous work. Sitting behind Ogilvie's insistent offers to return to Scotland before the 'sparks' of rebellion catch flame is the very real fear that he would be exposed. Frances Fox, Middleton's sharpest spy, suspected Ogilvie of double dealing and sought to poison St Germain against him. Perth, who was at once Middleton's chief rival and one of Ogilvie's firmest supporters, worried that Fox's efforts were working and that rumours from England that Ogilvie served two masters would make it impossible for him to ever return to St Germain. Unnerving as they were, Perth's worries abated. The fact that Ogilvie seemed to be trusted by French ministers ensured that he was trusted by St Germain.

Underpinning this trust was Ogilvie's association with Count Belke, a Swede who was then in the French service. Ogilvie had run into Belke when he first arrived in Hamburg and, though he was disguised, Belke recognised him immediately. As a soldier, Ogilvie fought alongside Belke.[46] After the collapse of the Scotch plot, Belke took over the task of organising troops for an invasion of Scotland. Unlike the amateurish and self-interested Beaufort, Belke's commitment to the cause and military nous drove him to recruit support from France's allies as well.

Belke was in direct communication with Torcy. By ingratiating himself with the Count, Ogilvie regained the trust of St Germain, snuffing out talk of his treachery; he also scored what would prove to be one of Harley's most decisive intelligence victories. Belke employed Ogilvie as a trusted messenger to Torcy and so gave him the cypher the French foreign minister used to code his most secret correspondence. Harley's decision to keep Ogilvie in Europe until such moment as 'there was a breach betwixt England and Scotland', when Harley would recall Ogilvie to Edinburgh, yielded unimagined results. With the cypher in hand, Harley and his undersecretaries could easily and quickly translate secret intelligence from France, and no longer rely as heavily on fallible cryptographers to crack the French codes.[47]

As with all theatres in the global intelligence war, Harley had other players in Europe. Monitoring foreign courts was the work of ambassadors and residents. Beneath the access but also the notice of official diplomatic channels were other writers, who provided the Secretary with the kind of intelligence that might slip the proprietary lines of official work. He also had eyes on Jacobite activities in the north of England. Close to Scotland, and a potential weak point, the north needed to be kept as peaceful as possible while the Treaty was debated in the Scottish parliament. For this work, Harley drew on writers within and beyond Defoe's network.[48]

In Scotland itself Harley's was not the only pro-Union intelligence game. The Whig lords Somers and Wharton sent John Shute, a Dissenting theologian, to report from the ground and to try and draw more support for the Union from Presbyterians, especially those who distrusted the English ministry and feared its tack towards its High Church allies. Harley was aware of this appointment and, according to Edmund Calamy, the government supported Shute.[49] The pro-Union Scots had their own agents. Queensberry ran a loose group of plenipotentiaries and informers. So too did John Erskine, Earl of Mar. Mar was one of the Scottish Union commissioners and, in 1705, had been appointed one of Anne's Secretaries of State within Scotland. The report Fearne sent Harley classes Mar as a Protestant, who was probably for the succession but with Country party leanings. In hindsight Fearne's observation that Mar had a tendency to be discontented looks ominous.[50] At this stage, though, Mar was loyal to the Queen and her ministers.

While Mar spent most of his time in Scotland, his undersecretary Sir David Nairne remained in London. The channel between Mar and Nairne was a vital one. The two wrote often, relying on the 'flying pacquett' for urgent communiqués. From Mar, Nairne had current intelligence of the progress of Scottish politics and, in turn, Nairne gave much-needed intelligence on the state of the Union negotiations in England and the perception of Scotland and its politics there. Mar corresponded with Godolphin, and Nairne briefed the Lord Treasurer directly. Mar assumed a sense of personal responsibility for the Union, with Nairne leaving little doubt that Godolphin and the Queen would blame him and Queensberry if any of the MPs under English influence and pay wavered. If they were suddenly 'coole' or, worse yet, opposed Union, Mar's position was at stake.

In an effort to shield MPs from public pressure, Mar employed two agents, Thomas Fullarton and Mr Stuart, who worked hard in Scotland 'convincing people of the necessity and advantage of the Union'. Fullarton was later sent to England to help Nairne report on the 'general disposition to the Union' amongst the English and to perform the same persuasive magic he had done in the northern kingdom. Mar knew that England had men serving secretly in Scotland, but did not know the extent of the ring, nor of Harley's controlling interest in it, reporting to Nairne that 'Defoe is here, but I'm not acquainted with him, so have not seen him. One Mr Shout [Shute], a friend of my Lord Wharton's, is also.' In the same stroke he noted that 'Paterson ... wrote some sheets of paper upon the Union' and showed them to him. Paterson sought the Earl's sanction to publish but did so without disclosing his connections to Harley or Godolphin.[51] The way Paterson cultivated local patrons like Mar, and new patrons in England like Somers, while still maintaining his relationship with Harley and Godolphin, speaks to the enmeshed, complex traffic of intelligence between Scotland and England. Agents often reported to more than one handler; handlers had reports from agents that did not always agree; and, in the cases of Godolphin, Harley and Mar, spoke to each other without always divulging the extent or source of their knowledge – even if they were notionally on the same side. On the ground this knot of information made tracking and intervening in events in Scotland far from straightforward.

From the outset there were signs that the passage of the Treaty through the Scottish parliament would require careful management – of the politicians inside the Hall and the city crowds that surrounded it. The final session of the Scottish parliament had been due to begin in May 1706 but was pushed back, first to June, then July, then September. The impetuous Argyll had resigned as Lord High Commissioner at the end of 1705 when the Queen denied him permission to reward Hamilton with a place as a Treaty commissioner, despite Hamilton's role in vesting the Queen with the power to choose Scotland's commissioners. Queensberry, who had worked with Argyll and retained power as Lord Privy Seal during the latter's tenure, stepped into the breach. Reinstated as Lord High Commissioner for the final session of the Scottish parliament, he spent the time until its delayed opening forming an alliance with the Squadrone Volante, shoring up votes and sizing up the strength of those opposed to Union: members of the Country party,

Episcopalians and Jacobites. When the session finally began in October, the Unionists proceeded carefully. The managers of parliamentary business chose to read through the Treaty articles before opening the floor to debate. To do otherwise would have seemed too hasty, Mar thought, especially since 'the mob of this town are mad and against us'. As support for the Treaty grew in parliament, the opposition turned to the crowd gathered in Parliament Close as a source of resistance. Lockhart circulated the Treaty in the capital before the debate started and so began the process of turning people against it. When the government printed it on the eve of the session, hoping to calm the people, the opposite happened. As Hamilton told Harley, once the articles were printed, 'all men recoiled', causing a 'ferment' beyond expression – not that Hamilton spurned the chaos.[52] Each day, opposition leaders would 'take themselves to the mob and cajol them all they can', Mar reported, stoking their fears and plying them with enough attention to get 'mob and populace on their side intirely'.[53]

As October tapered off, the crowd packed the Close ever tighter, seeming to pin Parliament Hall in its southwest corner. They covered the forecourt and stretched to the curved edge of St Giles' Kirk at the north, forcing members to push their way through the throng to get to the reading of the Treaty. For Queensberry, this meant running a dignity-stripping gauntlet. For Hamilton, who claimed a sprained ankle and was carried through on his chair, the pace was more leisurely, basking even. Defoe witnessed how the crowd followed the Duke, 'shouting and crying out GOD bless his Grace, for standing up against Union, and appearing for his Country'. In a moment of cattiness a few years later, Defoe added a note of mock deference:

> Far be it from me to say, the Duke of *Hamilton* desired or encouraged this Tumulatary kind of Congratulation; That sort of Popularity must be so much below a Person of his Character; and his Grace knows . . . that such things always tend to confusion and to the Destruction of Civil Peace.[54]

Defoe says precisely what deference supposedly checks. Opponents of Union knew that they did not have the votes to prevent ratification. What they did have was the perception that Unionists stood in defiance of the will of the people. Sowing disorder and seeding rumours that the Scottish Crown would be whisked to London, that Scotland would be crippled with English taxes and her Church denuded of its sacral authority, represented an attempt to capture the destructive force of 'the Commonality'. By playing the crowd and delaying parliament's attempts to redress financial and ecclesiastical concerns, they hoped to create an environment where no compromise could be brooked. As the opposition prevaricated, Queensberry pushed through a bill selecting a commission to calculate the Equivalent (to address financial worries of the Scottish folk) and tried to find a legislative solution that would bring into the fold the ministers who formed the Commission of the General Assembly of the Church of Scotland (and so offset fears that Scotland's religion was under attack).

On 23 October the delay tactics worked particularly well. The opposition proposed printing the English book of rates. The Court party argued that it was unnecessary. With one side intent on holding things up, the debate inevitably slogged on past six, when the grey Edinburgh day ticked over into the black Edinburgh night. At this point, clerks were called to light the candles in Parliament Hall. For Mar, this was a bad sign because 'allways in candle light there's a great deal of confusion in the Hall'. Even as the clerks walked by the wooden benches, lighting wicks at every few paces, the source of this confusion remained obscure. The little glowing faces of the candles were overawed by the high arc of the Hall's hammer-beam ceiling, their narrow scope of light blurred at the edges by a penumbral darkness. In the shadows the senses of the parliamentarians pricked to the strange heat that enclosed them. The Hall was crowded. Earl Marischal and Constable deputed fifty men to act as guards. The fact that they were quickly overwhelmed gives an idea of how many people packed the chamber. Members of the crowd had made their way into the parliament, bringing the force of their will beyond the barrier of arcana and privilege meant to channel it towards civil order. As Queensberry tried to bring the question of the rates book to a vote, their energy turned, as if the polar bond of the people within the

Hall sought to pull in the crowd outside. MPs fretted that parliament was about to be breached. Queensberry had no choice but to call an adjournment: he needed to make an escape before the force of the crowd was loosed completely.

The MPs left the Hall to find the Close 'full of mob'. Fending them off long enough to get to his carriage, Queensberry instructed his driver to beat a northeastward path along the High Street. The mob he encountered along the way was unlike that of previous nights; the depth of bodies barely thinned as the carriage crossed through the Netherbow Port, past his private townhouse on the south side of Canongate and on towards his official residence at Holyrood Abbey.[55]

Defoe's attention was fixed on Hamilton that night. He had spent the previous week inside with a 'Violent Cold' and so had not witnessed the full extent of the mob's build-up. What he did see left him convinced that the 'Scots Rabble is the worst of its kind'. Defoe had been warned to take care. Duty and curiosity brought him out. In a borrowed carriage on the way to a friend, he encountered a small part of the crowd. They did not confront him face on but shouted that he was 'One of the English dogs'. During the day the story he told – that he had come to Scotland to remake himself in business and avoid prosecution in England for seditious writings – provided sufficient cover. At night, he was just another Englishman. The 'Dreadful Uproar' he met as he left his friend's house hit him as a personal threat and made him wonder if he should return to London. Having sheltered there till it was dark, he now stared down a High Street 'Full of the Rabble'.[56]

Defoe had no doubts that Hamilton was the prime mover of mob violence. On 23 October Hamilton and his cortege went up the High Street instead of down – towards the residential heart of the city instead of to his residence, in the more sparsely populated suburbs near the castle. The Duke said the change in route was to avoid the mob. Defoe thought it was 'to Point them to their Work'.[57]

There is truth to Defoe's swipe. Whether Hamilton intended the full scope of violence that followed or not, his chair acted as a lodestar. As he was carried out of parliament, it guided the protestors within back into the waiting crowd. Lifted eastwards towards the house of the Duke of Atholl, another key opponent of the Union, it marked a path across the city, drawing people from the closes and wynds which branch off the High Street – each one connected to the system of alleys and staircases that prop Edinburgh up, giving its axial roads the slack to tilt downwards from the fortified castle near its western border. Defoe observed that the crowd now amassed at Atholl's door 'did not Come there to be Idle'. It was far too easy a coincidence that living right by Atholl was Patrick Johnston, Lord Provost of Edinburgh the previous year, one of the Union commissioners, and someone the mob had earlier threatened to 'massacre' for being a 'betrayer and seller of his country'.[58]

The mob's vanguard pushed their way up the stairs to Johnston's front door and, with sledges in hand, attempted a breach. Johnston barricaded himself inside, along with his family and servants. The door held but they were trapped. Frantic, Mrs Johnston took to the window, a candle in each hand to light her cries for help. An apothecary from the town saw her and ran for the guard. Defoe was dismayed by their inaction. Whether they sympathised with the mob or were frightened by it mattered little. In either case, their inertia showed the overthrow of order by the chaos of popular power. For Defoe, the guards were only redeemed by Captain Richardson, a 'brave Resolute Officer' who assembled a party of thirty guards and fought his way to Johnston's house, clearing the staircase, knocking down and dispersing the mob and arresting the handful who would not be removed from the door. Battered and injured, Richardson's guards escorted the prisoners along the same route from which they had come, back towards St Giles, to the Tolbooth – the medieval gaol mere steps from Parliament Hall.

The arrests did not disperse the mob. It was hard to tell how fast the body grew or how far it spread. The protestors quickly put out the street lanterns ahead of them. Without light, the mass moved lithely, a wine-dark liquid filling the gaps in the city's mazy topography. At around 9 p.m. when Defoe left his friend's house to go home, he experienced first-hand their fury, though his accounts of what happened next differ. In his initial report he speaks of how looking out he 'Saw a Terrible Multitude Come up the High street with A Drum at the head of Them shouting and swearing and Cryeing Out all Scotland would stand together, No Union, No Union'. Reaching his rooms, he saw a man below his window say something that angered the crowd, who turned on him. The scuffle was frightening and, again, the man only survived thanks to the intervention of the guards. Three years later, when he wrote his official history, Defoe became the target: he claimed that the mob watched him and followed him home, keen to find where this particular English dog lay. It was only by their ineptitude and God's providence that he escaped assault. Amidst the melee the mob misjudged where he lived and threw stones at the apartment below. In recollecting the event it seems that the very real fear he experienced that night suggested new details to memory's creative working.

Across Edinburgh the smoke of extinguished lamps settled over the streets where those indoors kept their candles unlit, partly because they feared that their windows would be smashed as the mob snaked through the city and partly, Defoe maintained, because they were threatened by members of the chaos who feared candlelight would expose their misdeeds.[59] In the hazy dark the guard units willing to act skirmished with protestors. Though anarchic, the mob had some logic to it. Part of the crowd went for the Netherbow Gate in an attempt to seize it and, in doing so, cut communication between the guards within the city and those in Canongate. Queensberry managed to prevent this happening, sending his own guards up Canongate Street. They retook the Netherbow Gate and, with torches in hand, relit Edinburgh's main thoroughfare.

In securing one entrance, Queensberry's guards left another open. It was just on 10 p.m. when a second mob breached the city through the North Port. Defoe reckoned the group stood between five hundred and a thousand. As the guards attempted to subdue the main body of resistance, this second group made their way along the eastern road from Leith.

Pressured by Queensberry, Sir Samuel McClellan, Johnston's successor as Lord Provost, finally relented and called for more guards to enter the capital. One observer said the 'provost dropt tears when he could not resist, the march of troups into the town'.[60] But they were needed. Fifty troops bolstered the Canongate, another regiment took possession of the Netherbow Port, and a further 150 marched up the High Street to Parliament Close, supported by the Duke of Argyll and his Horse Guards. Their orders were 'to disperse the rabble with violence if there were occasion'.[61] Paterson's report was bullish: the mob was 'totally defeated' by 150 regular troops. With the 'ordinary guards and Militia of the Town' they had entirely 'Suppressed the Mob before Six in the Morning'. He was comforted the next day to find that the troops remained.[62] This was precisely what the Lord Provost feared: order was restored but only because the military made a frightening incursion into the realm of civil power.

Parliament did not sit on 24 October. The Privy Council assembled and issued a proclamation against 'Rabbles and Tumults', a post hoc justification of their forceful suppression of the mob. When parliament resumed on 25 October, Queensberry expected praise for his decisiveness. Opponents of Union were at first reluctant to side with the mob but feared what the use of military force represented. The Earl of Erroll protested that the guards represented an intolerable '*Incroachment on the Rights and Privileges of Parliament*'. There was consensus amongst Hamilton, Fletcher, Belhaven and the Country party that the deployment of the guards and proclamation for further use of force was high-handed. Atholl complained of the 'Guards being sent into town to overaw Parliament'. Their mere presence exerted an undue influence on the estates. Fletcher went further, pitting the guards as a sign of arbitrary government against the protestors, whom he said were the 'true spirit of the country': the same spirit that had carried the Reformation and Glorious Revolution.[63]

Queensberry had the numbers and so parliament approved the proclamation, after which his supporters came to see the events of 23 October in more positive terms. Mar thought it was 'good that this bomb broke in the air': it showed that their 'intelligence was not ill founded', that their early efforts monitoring public sentiment gave enough traction to keep the Treaty debate on task.[64] Defoe came to a similar conclusion, writing that 'this Rabble was a Mine sprung before its Time, which blew backwards and destroyed the Engineers'. Had the opposition waited, had they continued to stir up discontent with the Union amongst the army, Defoe believed that the government could very well have blown up. Though order was maintained, it remained fragile, not least because the events of 23 October raised long-running questions about the power of the people – how it could be limited, represented, deputed and expressed.

For his part, Defoe argued that the 'Parliament was much more likely to be Awed by the Ungovern'd Rabbles of the Streets . . . than by the Forces brought in for their Security'. He perceived no threat because the military remained subordinate to civil power, and was placed in Edinburgh 'to Maintain, not Infringe the Liberty of Speech' crucial to parliament's working.[65] The problem with a parliament sharply divided over the future of Scotland's constitution was that any military intervention was bound to appear partisan. Regardless of intention, the mere feeling of undue influence is taken as evidence that undue influence is being exerted. This perception ran both ways. Mar and Defoe noted that Country lords were bringing Highlanders to Edinburgh. Their presence was menacing because it spoke to an alternative source of military power. When coupled with the assassination threats Queensberry received, the 'unusual' number of Highlanders in the capital left Defoe increasingly ill at ease: so much so, that he sought recourse in lampoon, his preferred métier. He scoffed that it was an 'Absurdity . . . to see a Man in his Mountain habit armd with a Broad sword, Targett Pistol or perhaps Two at his Girdle, a Dagger and staff, walking Down the street as Upright and Haughty as if he were a lord — and withal Driving a Cow'. As he attempts to laugh off the Highlander's comic mismatch with the city surrounds, he cannot help but draw attention to the menace of the man's arsenal.[66]

As the debate in parliament unfolded, it became clear that the 'undue' influence the pro-Union faction most feared came from the people. To Queensberry, Defoe, Mar and others, this original source of sovereign power was being degraded by its unauthorised manifestation in mobs, rabbles and riots. Just as Edinburgh was being settled after October, Mar saw 'emmisarys sent throw [through] the country to get hands to addresses against the Union'. While Mar worried that the emissaries corralling signatures for these petitions and addresses might 'stirr up the country to some foolish irregular thing', Defoe clocked their more basic threat. The opposition had found a way to bring public discontent into the debate. Even if it did not compromise the ratification of the Treaty, it posed dire problems for the endurance of any union.[67]

⸸

The uncanny calm that followed 23 October discomfited some of Harley's allies in Scotland. The Earl of Stair, an advocate, MP and one of the Union commissioners, began to worry that if parliament took a recess to let cooler heads prevail, the exact opposite would happen. A break in proceedings would give opposers in parliament time to regroup. If they could continue to capture the crowd on the street, the collective pressure could easily cause supporters of the Union to 'break us amongst ourselves', Stair warned. Opposers had taken 'too many open steps already' towards raising 'the country in arms'. Stair called for English troops to be stationed in the north and in Ireland, fearing that the army in Scotland 'may be tainted with popular apprehension'. The time was right to intervene forcefully, to show strength without having to use it. This was the only way to save the Union and, with it, Scotland's future, Protestantism and the 'liberty of Europe'. As he told Harley, 'It is easier to stifle ill inclinations than to reduce open rebellion upon popular sentiment.' This wisdom was hard-won. As the official who ordered the Glencoe massacre, Stair knew in his bones the permanent damage caused when popular uprisings were put down with military force.[68]

The Queen shared Stair's concern, asking her advisors at the end of October what precisely they could do to calm the mob.[69] There were no easy solutions. The problem was that 'the mob' was a moving target, as 'fluctuating as the Sea', in Defoe's words. Throughout his career Defoe devoted significant time to theorising the place and function of popular power. In his reasoning, mobs were dangerous because they drew authority from the idea that *the people* hold original sovereignty – an idea Defoe supported – and in certain circumstances could revoke this authority and so bring down a government. In *A Hymn to the Mob* (1715) he captured this notion in brief, speaking to the mob as he proclaimed:

Kingdoms and Empires to thy Center tend,
In thee they all began, in thee they all shall end.[70]

The lapse in most cases was that the mob constituted on the street was not a legitimate representation of the people and so greatly overstepped its authority in wielding sovereign power. What unsettled Defoe was that various bodies laid claim to such representativeness and built themselves up as if they spoke for the people. As troubling as the rabble in the street was, Defoe was more concerned with those who fed the rabble and were sustained by the heat of popular support that came off it. As he told Harley, the mob of 23 October was just one mob. There were two others: the mob in the governing body of the Scottish Church, and the one 'within the house it Self', in parliament.[71]

In calling opposers in parliament a mob, Defoe works against the notion that parliament was a representative body. His implication is that MPs were not speaking for the people when they raised questions about Scotland's sovereignty, independence, finances and place in the world – all areas legitimately within parliament's purview – and they were, in fact, manipulating the people against their better interests. The Commission of Assembly (the Church leaders) had a similar hold. The Commission had its own factions, pro and anti-Union, Court and Country. Hamilton and the confederated opposition pressured members to call a national fast. Had they been successful and had parliament failed then to give civil sanction, it could have severed the connection between Church and state, roiling the Treaty before it was even considered. Under the guidance of Carstares, the moderates won out. Instead of issuing a national fast, the Commission sent a circular letter to the individual presbyteries, leaving it up to them whether they would call for a fast day within their bounds.[72] While many Kirk leaders saw such fasts as necessary, a moment of solemn contemplation to bring divine guidance to the most momentous of decisions, Defoe saw them as a tactic. Fast days gave ministers and opposition MPs time to prepare 'Tumultuous addresses', marshal signatures and mobilise a national campaign against the Union, aided by the publication and distribution of anti-Union pamphlets. What worried Defoe was that if this loose alliance of opposition MPs, Commission members and writers continued to gain support and amass addresses, they would form a contiguous mob of state, Church and folk that might come dangerously close to speaking for the people.

Defoe faced a popular movement with powerful institutional holds and support from England's enemies abroad. According to his biographer, Paula Backscheider, in order to respond Defoe had to pioneer methods of 'counterinsurgency', finding ways to denude a movement that, though organised, had no single head or centre.[73] He had to infiltrate institutions, gain contacts and access, dominate the press and write to sap the opposition's main source of strength by bringing the people onto the side of Union. Defoe was uniquely fluent in moving between the various commissions of finance and Church and adept at insinuating himself in parliamentary business. He was a seasoned propagandist, but he was misguided in the belief that he alone had to address all objections to Union – economic, religious and political – while rooting out plots of violence and counteracting foreign infiltration. This blinkered view was probably what Harley intended. Defoe did not know the full extent of what the other agents did. From Harley's vantage, the network was arrayed to meet the demands of an insurgency, though he would not have used the term. Fearne had valuable connections to the Kirk and a line of intelligence on the Equivalent. Even if the latter fell through, Paterson was so deeply immersed in calculating and promoting it that Harley would remain ahead of things. And while all agents in Edinburgh reported on suspected Jacobite activity, Ogilvie's position on the Continent was designed to apprehend any plot at its source.

⸸

Defoe was impatient with the pace of the debate. Each lag pulled at the tethers of his restive mind, which moved and darted as the voicing of the Treaty called in forces beyond parliament and connected religion, finance and the fundamental principles that ordered the country. Defoe had to find a line through competing constituencies and issues and hold this line in public writing so that he could gradually pull from the mobbish mass a *people*, at once governable and ready to be unified. The mob violence removed any illusions about how difficult this task would be: frustrated by continued Presbyterian opposition to the Treaty, he told Harley that he found the Scots were 'a hardened refractory and Terrible people'. Galvanised by the challenge, he began to settle into a routine. Each day, he visited and observed parliament, reporting to Harley what he saw. Each night, and well into the early mornings before parliament sat, he met with members of the Church Commission. He gave advice and counsel, explained the Treaty and behind closed doors began to exert what he called 'Secret Mannagement', building alliances and gaining the trust of ministers so that he could gradually turn the churchmen towards supporting the Union. Though many churchmen did support Union, according to Paterson their 'diffident carriage' in failing to voice this support was as harmful to the cause as those who preached against Union.[74] In Defoe's presence the ministers seemed modest and careful, but he knew that when they stood in presbyteries around the country 'they Enflame the people'. Turning them could turn the nation but any effect he had was going to take its time filtering from Edinburgh to the west and north, to Glasgow and St Andrews, where opposition was building.[75]

Defoe's 'Secret Mannagement' extended to other sources of influence. He drank in the alehouses of Edinburgh, walked its streets and socialised with its merchants and politicians. He found an ally in the younger John Clerk of Penicuik, whose literary affectations drew him to the writer. Thanks to the young laird's intimacy with Queensberry, Defoe wheedled his way into Queensberry's circle, befriending the Dalrymple brothers, who were then serving at the highest points of the Scottish legal system. Defoe also began to seek out members of the Edinburgh Society for the Reformation of Manners, eventually joining the grassroots moral reform movement.[76] Perhaps most consequentially, he developed relationships with the printers and booksellers of the city, winning the favour of Agnes Campbell Anderson, widow of Andrew Anderson and inheritor of his patent monopoly on printing the Bible in Scotland. Because of this monopoly Agnes was one of Scotland's richest and most powerful printers. Defoe engaged her to print the Edinburgh edition of the *Review*, the profits of which helped sustain his mission.

Defoe devoted the little time he had between spying on parliament and building a base of influence in Edinburgh to writing. In short, concentrated bursts he wrote letters, three issues of the *Review* per week, poems and pamphlets, as well as continuing his series of essays aimed at removing the prejudices between England and Scotland. His essays now turned to Scotland's advantages and directly addressed the volume of anti-Union literature in circulation. Defoe did not work alone. Queensberry and the Court party had a team of writers. Defoe's output is, however, significant in volume and industry, and because of how precisely it was targeted. Connected to the work he did undercover, Defoe's writing in Edinburgh was designed to appeal directly to constituencies whose opinions he had sampled and analysed. In his mind's ear there was a pleasing harmony between the work he did in secret, fashioning constituencies and reporting to Harley, and the work in the open, what he called the 'Publick Intelligence' of pamphleteering and publishing.[77]

By November, parliament had finished reading through the Treaty and came to debate and vote on its first article: the mandate to join England and Scotland by incorporation. There were 'murmer[s] being spread' that another mob attack on parliament was imminent.[78] In the Hall opponents of Union continued to delay. They argued for a break in proceedings to consult their constituents, the freeholders, or risk parliament's fundamental representative authority; they raised questions about the sequence of the process – why agree to full incorporation before the other articles were considered? And they pushed for an explicit guarantee that the Scottish Church would retain its autonomy. The worry that religious pluralism could not be maintained if Scotland had to share an English parliament in which bishops sat alongside uncompromising High Churchmen was real enough that, to offset concerns, the Court faction promised to introduce an Act securing Presbyterian Church government immediately after article one passed.

Defoe witnessed the debate as it dragged on from ten in the morning till past eight during the first nights of November. A sharp tactician himself, he grasped that the anti-Unionist's prevarication bought them time enough to make the nation constitutionally resistant to Union – to spread ideas and discontent that could easily undermine his own work creating a shared British consciousness. Nothing was confined to the Hall: both sides spoke far beyond parliament's doors, publishing and distributing key speeches. MPs often argued along the same lines as the writers who supported them – and in case of Penicuik for Union and Hamilton against it there is evidence they directly coordinated their messages with the writers who backed them.[79] When the opposition could delay no further and the article came to be debated in earnest, they raised their first objection: incorporation violated Scotland's Claim of Right. The Act confirming the succession of William III and Mary to the Scottish throne vested the Scottish parliament with authority beyond its English counterpart. James II of England and VII of Scotland fled England, allowing the English to claim he had abandoned the throne. Because he had not fled Scotland, the Convention of Scottish Estates had to find other means to justify replacing the King. They turned to key Scottish precedents for popular sovereignty: the Declaration of Arbroath (1320) that located sovereignty in the community, and the writings of George Buchanan, in which he outlined how a popularly constituted body entered into contract with a monarch and how that contract could be revoked.

Defoe called the invocation of the Claim of Right a 'Surprizing blow', but it really wasn't. By the time it was raised in parliament, Defoe was busy answering in print anti-Union polemic from George Ridpath and James Hodges that reverted to the theory of representation the Claim endorsed. Ridpath's work affirmed the rights of freeholders against a Union that, in his argument, abridged those rights.[80] Hodges argued for a federal union in part because an independent Scottish parliament was the only way to retain the rights of the people. Defoe believed that Hodges' work was sponsored by Hamilton and the Country Party.[81] He saw how his book *The Rights and Interests of the Two British Monarchies* was 'industriously spread over the whole kingdom', doing 'more Mischief than a thousand men'.[82] He was right. Hodges received financial support organised by Hamilton. He also gave the Duke and others like Belhaven advance warning of his publications, so that they could effect a symmetry between opposition as it played out in the press and in parliament.[83] The addresses and petitions that confronted Defoe daily drew their authority from native Scottish ideas of sovereignty; from the idea that an assembly of freeholders holds the power to limit the actions of parliament. Defoe, who had championed popular sovereignty in England, found himself on the other side. Rather than dismiss the idea outright, he wrote around its edges, asserting that the addresses were not representative. They were confected by discontented Jacobites and, as such, Ridpath had no basis for asserting that the majority of freeholders were against the Union. Ergo, parliament did not violate their will by ratifying the Treaty.

Though necessary, Defoe's contortions on constitutional theory had limited appeal. (They were better received, though, than Paterson's answers to Hodges.)[84] Sentiment drove the anti-Union case. It was hard to say that an expression of popular will was not genuine when so many saw the mass of people assembled, signed and witnessed addresses and read a growing body of work expressing the popular anti-Unionist case. In parliament itself the speeches delivered on article one laid out the case for and against Union. But it was the opponents who seemed to capture this state of national feeling. Defoe and Paterson were in the Hall to witness their efforts. Defoe noted how Hamilton 'Rav'd', speaking loudly and forcefully against Union. Paterson found Fletcher of Saltoun more compelling.[85]

It was, however, the speech given by John Hamilton, Lord Belhaven, that caused the most lasting concern for the agents, as it did for Harley, Godolphin and the Scottish Court faction. Despite the fact that the speech was mocked in the parliament, was full of 'dismal stories' and delivered with what Defoe thought was sickly, bathetic aspect,[86] Defoe could see its reach. He was not the only one. Seafield reported to Godolphin that while Belhaven's words had 'no great influence in the House', they were clearly 'contrived to incense the common people'. Roxburghe thought the speech was targeted to 'cobblers and tailors'.[87] Belhaven's speech works better on paper, confirming the suspicion that it was designed for immediate printing.[88] It opens with a series of paragraphs, each beginning 'I think, I see'. Belhaven conjures a vision of a '*Free and Independent Kingdom*' never conquered delivering up the power to manage its affairs to another nation. It is a vision of a national Church 'founded upon a Rock', secured by a '*Claim of Right*', giving up its 'strictest' legal protections and thus descending to 'an equal level with '*Jews*' and '*Papists*'. It is a vision of a peerage giving up what their ancestors defended, reducing themselves to a level where English tax collectors will garner more respect. Belhaven's vision casts over Royal burghs, judges, soldiers, tradesmen, right down to the lowly ploughmen: all of whom are embroiled and degraded by a Union, which he likens to an act of patricide – a killing of the fatherland. Working himself to such a pitch that he had to take a moment's pause – an act that Court MPs scoffed at in the chamber but when written induced the sympathy of readers – his portrait culminates with an image of '*Ancient Mother* CALEDONIA', like the assassinated Caesar in the senate 'Covering her self with her Royal Garment, attending the Fatal Blow, and breathing out her last with a Et tu quoque mi fili [And you also, my child]'.[89]

Defoe's answer to Belhaven's overwrought speech was lampoon. On the night of the speech, after parliament rose, he returned to his lodgings and wrote *The Vision, A Poem*. He copied it out and circulated it to MPs, ensuring they had read it before the vote on article one was called. He then had it printed and quickly distributed throughout the city.[90] The poem's first lines echo the words of Squadrone leader Lord Marchmont, who quipped as the still tremulous Belhaven returned to his seat: 'Behold he dreamed, but lo! When he awoke, he found it was a dream.' Defoe calls on 'Dreamers of Dreams . . . So[o]th-Sayers, Wizards and Witches' to witness a more outlandish vision than they could dream. As he does, he follows Belhaven's anatomisation of Scottish society, moving from Church to ploughmen, soldiers to merchants, to render each of Belhaven's predictions ridiculous. When he finally reaches the image of Scotland as assassinated Caesar that was Belhaven's pièce de résistance, he thanks him for a simile that better serves his case than the Scottish lords', asking 'Was Simily e're so unhappily brought?' when it was Caesar who betrayed his country and Brutus the noble assassin who defended Rome's liberty.[91]

Defoe was pleased with the reception the poem got, boasting to Harley that it 'has made Some sport here and perhaps Done More

Service than a More Solid Discourse'. Harley agreed.[92] Belhaven responded with a poem, which Defoe then answered by sarcastically praising Belhaven's talent as a poet.[93] The fact that Belhaven met Defoe on his chosen field – verse – proves Defoe's effectiveness at turning the argument. But Belhaven did not know that Defoe was the poet in question. He was convinced that a Scot and an Englishman had written the poem together, another sign of Defoe's capacity to slip in and out of voices, as he did genres and modes, employing the 'More Solid Discourse' of the essays when the occasion called for reason and deflating with wit and humour the attempts of anti-Unionists to tap the nation's emotions. This orchestrated heteroglossia was key to his cover. Though the bulk of Defoe's works were published anonymously, he did attract suspicion. In the *Third Essay* he addressed the rumour that he was an 'Emissary', or spy, which arose when his authorship of earlier essays was revealed.[94] When some thought his attacks on Belhaven too sharp, he wrote a second poem, *Caledonia*, more direct in its praise of Scotland. Anodyne as it was, *Caledonia* proved his loyalty and earned him some much-needed money. At the same time, it spun pro-Union sentiments into jaunty verse in an attempt to make them ring in the ears of everyday Scots. This was typical of Defoe's work in Scotland. His writing made him known, but never completely. As one work threatened to expose him, he wrote another, and another, never giving time for a singular image to stick.

Writing also gave Defoe access. In moments when he could no longer dodge suspicion by referring to his debts in England or his prospective business ventures in Scotland, he started telling folks that he was writing a history of Scotland and the Union. This project may have begun life as a cover story. But, as cover stories go, it was brilliantly effective, for, in the act of researching the history, Defoe was eventually granted access to parliamentary registers and minute books, yielding significant intelligence.[95] It was, however, his reputation as a writer on trade that arguably gave him his most significant entrance to closed-door negotiations. On 4 November, Defoe was in parliament to see the first article passed by a vote of 116 to 83. With incorporation settled, the financial and ecclesiastical implications that opponents warned about gained the force of impending reality.

Parliament dodged the bulk of the financial concerns by deputing the Committee formed to calculate the Equivalent to consider all matters of customs and taxes. On 5 November, the Committee called Defoe to 'assist' them. Fearne had a secret source on the Committee, but Defoe's invitation was a breakthrough for Harley's network. Paterson reported that the commissioners, who were drawn from lords, barons and burghs, were 'all of the Union interest'. In his partial view, he did not think that they had much to do on the Equivalent itself, given that he and David Gregory had already done the maths. On other issues, including questions of drawbacks, taxes and trade, he thought they were poised to do 'considerable service'.[96] Paterson's condescension provoked hostility. One Scottish politician called him a 'blockhead' and could not fathom how Godolphin could trust him. Nairne worried that because Gregory and Paterson were 'men of letters and figurs' and not enmeshed in everyday business, their attempts to address matters of taxes and customs alienated everyday Scots.[97] The Committee invited Defoe for this reason. His talent in formulating and communicating policy was needed. In exchange he not only gained admission to secret negotiations – sending them in 'Draft' to Harley – but was able to shape them. As he told Harley, 'I am in their Cabinet by some Mannagmt and can Influence them more than I Expected.' As advisor and unofficial press secretary, he could bring his writing to bear on policy designed to offset financial objections to Union – policy that in some cases he helped create.[98]

Defoe publicly defended the Equivalent as the 'best Means in the World' to ensure the equality of the Union. He did not share Paterson's belief that it was a completed project. Because it underpinned all the articles, he felt that it needed to be a dynamic, open entity.[99] The question Defoe faced was how to make this happen. In his *Fourth Essay, at Removing National Prejudices* he somewhat dismissively left the broader philosophy of tax to Paterson, choosing to focus instead on brass tacks: those areas where the Equivalent, taxes and tax drawbacks (the reimbursement of import duty paid once the goods were re-exported) had clear and widely graspable impact.[100] This was an inspired approach. The Committee had wide leeway to settle financial matters, which Defoe was keen to exploit, steering them towards the kind of solutions and small adjustments that would prevent the need for any new Treaty article or significant amendment – both of which would slow the ratification process indefinitely.

Defoe's mind was clearer than it had been since arriving in Edinburgh. Bell had finally sent him a payment from Harley of £52.10s.6d.[101] He now had funds enough to work and live, though the work remained expensive. In the Committee and in writing he devoted his attention to five commodities that exercised Scots, freeholders and ploughmen alike: beer, linen, salt, fish and coal. It was on beer that Defoe's tough-minded pragmatism had the most lasting effect. English excise regulations had two tax rates for beer: a low rate on 'small beer' (that which sold for six shillings or less a barrel) and a higher rate for 'strong' ale or beer. On the other hand, Scotland had a single rate. The two rates became a source of outcry – a compelling case in point for how the Union would immiserate Scots, unfairly taxing a substance that was both sustenance and pleasure. If the English rates prevailed, Scotland's national drink, the Tippony ale, would be taxed as a 'strong' beer. In effect, Scots would pay more for their national drink than they currently did and more than the English paid for theirs. Defoe rightly assumed that 'the Clamour of the people would be Intollerable' if this came to pass.[102] And so in the Committee he proposed an elegant solution. He assessed that the Tippony ale was about two-thirds the strength of English strong beer, and argued that there should be a middle tax rate devised to bring the English and Scottish taxes into compromise. This rate was added as 'explanation and addition' to the Treaty. In practice, tax on Tippony ale was restricted to two shillings a barrel, bringing it into line with the English tax on small beer.[103] Defoe made it so that a key question of excise could be settled without an amendment or new article. For him this became a sign he touted widely, that the 'middle way' was the 'only method to do Justice on both sides, and make both Parties easy, which is the True End of the Union'. As he took care to tell Harley, a lesser advisor such as Paterson, who 'converst with but few' and spent time with numbers not people, could not reach this solution.[104] The Tippony ale gave Defoe a potent piece of evidence that careful negotiation could bring the two nations together fairly. As he told readers of his *Fourth Essay*, '*Scotland* will desire nothing Unreasonable, and small Explanations on the Articles, will make all the just Objections reconcilable'.[105]

Religion remained a major point of contention. It was clear to Nairne that Fletcher, Hamilton, Atholl and their supporters were fanning fears about the Church in order 'to make the Kirk the cause of delaying the Union'.[106] Fearne's report on the opposition leaders confirmed that men like Atholl were dangerous because they were both easily discontented and carried with them large clan followings. Harley had a letter from Carstares that made this danger vivid. Despite the support in parliament, Carstares 'tremble[d] at the thoughts of what may be the consequences' if the Treaty miscarried. He had no doubts that if the Treaty did fail, the cause would be religion. He sought affirmation from Harley that 'the Parliament of England will agree to any security that can be reasonably demanded by us for our ecclesiastical constitution'. He was sure they would, he said, yet still felt the need for Harley's word. He also reported the two main objections to incorporation raised during the Commission of the General Assembly. Members had serious worries about the English abjuration oath, which excluded non-Anglicans from the succession. They also objected to the English Test Acts, which, by mandating Anglican communion as a precondition for office, would exclude Scots from most levels of civil service. On the whole the Commission could not allow a united parliament to impose oaths that clashed with the principles of the Kirk. It was not just a matter of answering these objections rationally, as the promised Act of Security of Scottish Church aimed to do: Carstares gave warning about the ambition and approach of the opposition and the 'pains' they took 'to possess the minds of well-meaning people with such prejudices against the Union'.[107]

Godolphin received a similar warning through Nairne and Mar, who told him that the 'humor against the Union in the country is augmented' and 'ministers are most to blame for it'.[108] John Shute monitored the discord in the Church, reporting to the Whig Lords. The English MPs who favoured Union understood that the Kirk could cause major problems for their project. For one, the Presbyterian

Church was not as stable as it presented. North of the Tay, Episcopal holdouts maintained their churches and congregations.[109] If Scotland was governed by a united parliament that included English bishops, the fear amongst some commissioners was that the Scottish Episcopalians would be empowered. If the more radical faction of the Commission led by the synod of Glasgow and Ayr acted on this fear and gained majority support, the Kirk would in effect centralise opposition forces. As one historian put it, the Kirk was the only institution in Scotland able to mobilise national opposition to incorporation.[110] The Duke of Hamilton knew this. Using Robert Wylie, his local minister and his mother's ally, to probe the anti-Union sentiment amongst other ministers, Hamilton conducted a one-man opinion-sampling mission. The results gave the Duke some confidence. Wylie told him that if parliament acts righteously, brethren ministers will join; where ministers were previously 'under a tepid unconcernedness', they are now 'awakened' – ready to counteract whatever the 'treaters at London have had the confidence to promise in the name of ministers'.[111] The Commission had at their disposal a national network of ministers able to preach against the Union. By calling on parliament to institute nationwide days of fast and prayer, they could delay proceedings and marshal popular resistance, using their authority to coordinate and circulate national addresses to give this resistance form.

Carstares held the moderate line as Defoe met with individual ministers on a daily basis. With tact and persistence he managed to convince enough of them to support the middle way.[112] It was thanks to Carstares and Defoe that the Commission was able to resist pressure to call a national fast or take any action of address that could have centralised the anti-Union position. The disorganised attempts of Hamilton and others to gain ministers to their side did not succeed as they could have. Wylie and other opponents of Union did not come and attend the Commission. And so Hamilton blamed him for the fact that the Commission never emerged as an anti-Union base.[113]

In effect, Carstares and Defoe, the chaplain and the spy, managed to decentralise Kirk opposition, sending it back to the localities and thwarting Hamilton's attempts to use the national Church as a base of support for the anti-Union campaign in parliament. Defoe echoed his private diplomacy in writing by answering questions about the Church in his *Third Essay*. Less focused on the granular details than his discussions with individual ministers and theologians, the *Essay* cuts straight to first principles when Defoe asks readers how opponents to Union in Scotland and England can both claim that their respective Church is under threat. Both cannot be true and so, in Defoe's argument, neither is. To show that this is the case he writes about constitutional protection in the sentimentalised idiom of shared Christian values: '*In Union*, Love, Peace, Charity and Mutual Assistance, are natural consequences; And can those pull down any Church?' Reciprocal protection is a virtue but also deeply self-interested, for if either side intrudes upon the other, 'The Fundamental is distroy'd, the Government dissolves, and the whole Island becomes a Mob, one Universal Rabble'.[114] In one stroke Defoe frames popular resistance as a threat and places the Churches of England and Scotland as links in a chain which, if broken, cause the whole island to descend into a state of nature. This is solidarity created by Hobbesian fear. It was clearly effective, as pro-Union MPs held *The Essay* up in parliament to answer all who claimed incorporation was incompatible with the Kirk.[115]

The Act of Security for the Scottish Church was designed to give the protections the force of statute. The Act took seriously concerns and offered guardrails in place, guaranteeing that 'the *Worship, Discipline* and *Government* of this Church, should be effectually and unalterably secured'. It affirmed the protection offered by the Claim of Right and it allowed Scots to serve in civil office in Scotland without conforming to Anglicanism. As Defoe told his readers, the Act gave 'equal Security and equal Establishment' to the Scottish and English Churches.[116] Such protections were intended to quell opposition in the Church, cut off a source for inflaming the public and create a permission structure for parliamentarians who supported Presbyterian Church government to assent to the other articles of the Treaty. Opponents of Union knew how effective this would be and so did all they could to hinder its passage. Atholl pushed for a delay by bringing the Cess (the supply for army and civil lists) up for debate and secured its passage in the hope that once this had been done, the Court party and England would have fewer reasons to keep the parliament in session. Queensberry took the win and kept going. Hamilton, Belhaven and others then attempted to add clauses that might cause England to reconsider. The changes they managed to get through were minor. And though they voted against it, the Act passed on 12 November.

At first the Act seemed to work. Defoe reported to Harley that 'The Ministers are quieter here now than before'.[117] The Earl of Stair confirmed this report, telling Harley that his initial prediction that the lack of protections for the Church in the Treaty 'might lose us the populace' would not eventuate. Stair now predicted that tensions would abate. Once 'the Ministers find themselves safe, they will soon make the people easy and quiet'.[118] Lockhart was dismayed at the turn, lamenting that ministers now 'preached up what not long before they had declared anathemas against'.[119] It was as if 'the trumpets of sedition began to fall silent'.[120] Queensberry seized on the quiet, pushing through article two of the Treaty, which guaranteed the Hanoverian succession in Scotland and article three, which united the two parliaments into one parliament of Great Britain. Yet, despite the success in parliament, Defoe sensed trouble. In the Hall things were 'Right Enough, but Really Every Where Else the Nation is in very strange Confusion'.[121]

Within a week it was clear that the Act had not tamped popular sentiment as he had hoped, nor had it moderated the most ardent of the Kirk's defenders. Protests broke out in Edinburgh. They were exceeded in severity by those in Dumfries and Glasgow. The disjunction was all too vivid for Defoe. With each article passed, the two nations were drawn closer together in law. Yet as the bonds tightened, their grip intensified the resistance, which spread faster and with more fury than the central governments in Edinburgh and London expected – or could allow.

CHAPTER 7

GLASGOW & HAMILTON PALACE

By mid-November, Defoe's letters to Harley split their focus between a parliament powering through the Treaty and an opposition turning to the nation at large to find any means to resist it. Defoe dutifully noted each article passed. Yet he could hardly stifle the sense that the Treaty was becoming a way to paper over a growing divide within Scotland itself. This sense came from the country around him. In Glasgow, on 7 November, James Clark, a minister at the Tron Kirk, preached a sermon that called his congregation to action, telling them '*Addresses would not do, and Prayers would not do, there must be other Methods*'. Defoe interpreted this as a call to arms but stopped short of blaming Clark for the riots that followed.[1] By Defoe's own account there must have been some coordination beforehand, for the people left the Kirk wearing hats emblazoned with the words 'No incorporating union' and marched to the beat of a rebel's drum from the Trongate through a city that Defoe thought was the second 'best built city in *Britain*' after London: neatly arrayed around four main streets, full of stone buildings and doric columns – a city that reflected the sensible mercantile ethos he typically admired in its inhabitants.[2] But not then. At the end of 1706, this famed Glaswegian pragmatism was absent and the 'Rabble' was hot. On 8 November, Glasgow's deacons met with the city's Lord Provost to urge him to prepare and endorse an anti-Union address. When he refused, the deacons turned to the streets and lit the flame: the crowd seized upon the Lord Provost and the rioting began.

On one of his daily walks through Edinburgh, Defoe found a man who had come from Glasgow carrying a warning that placed these riots in a more distressing context: there was talk that Covenanters from the southwest were being summoned. The plan was for them to join Atholl's Highland supporters, marching through Hamilton to advance on Edinburgh. The threat of armed insurrection was keen enough that the English soon moved some of their forces to Northern Ireland and the Anglo-Scottish border. Defoe did not know of the troop movement, but he saw how the violence of the nation echoed in Edinburgh: Queensberry was 'Threatned with Daggers, pistols'; people threw stones at him each time he left and entered parliament, and on at least one occasion the crowd managed to seriously injure his guards. For Defoe this was a sign that 'At last … downright Insurrection and Rebellion' encircled Scotland. Any misstep and the country might rise 'to Blood, Civil War, and all the terrible consequences of an enraged and divided nation'.[3]

When Defoe's sources told him that all the west is full of 'Tumult' and 'Glasgow is mad', he planned to venture westward to attempt to duplicate the work he was doing in Edinburgh – sampling opinion on the street, seeking out the sources of discontent, infiltrating the institutional backers of popular unrest, winning allies and reporting to Harley those figures who, with the right incentive, could be turned to the Union. He was stopped by 'honest people flying' from Glasgow, who warned him that it was not safe. If he were to go, he would have to be entirely undercover.[4]

South of Glasgow in Dumfries, a seaport on Scotland's west coast in Paterson's home county, the protest adopted the starkest symbolism. Around two hundred men marched into the marketplace at midday on 20 November and burnt the articles of Union alongside the names of the Treaty commissioners. They set fire to the document that would enslave them and immolated the names of the traitors who sold out their nation. As the fire burned down, the Dumfries folk nailed a paper to the market cross that outlined their reasons for opposing the Union – a paper Defoe classed as 'Seditious'.

From his vantage in the capital, Defoe saw an opposition doing all it could to make the collective strength of the resistance known. He sought out people who had joined protests in an effort to discern the reasons for their action. At the same time, he tried to disabuse them of the prejudices that led them to the streets.[5] The protests worried the Court: 'Wise Men began to give the Design of the Treaty for lost', thinking that the protests and riots represented the honest view of the people. Defoe was suspicious. The protests were just a bit too coordinated to be spontaneous expressions of popular will. His conversations with participants led him to believe that the protesters were 'Tools' of the opposition; that Country party figures and Jacobites had manipulated the folk into acting against their own interests.[6]

Defoe found that the worst pockets of resistance gathered 'about Hamilton and that Side of the Country', which he ascribed to the fact that the people there are 'Dayly Deluded by the party of that family'.[7] Defoe's suspicions were well founded. Outmanoeuvred in parliament, the opposition thought that mass demonstration, both peaceful and armed, could provide a strategic countermeasure to the Treaty's onward march.

Anne, Duchess of Hamilton, saw mustering troops as a good means to inspire fear in lawmakers – a way perhaps to turn the course away from incorporation. In late November she wrote to her son the Duke, telling him 'we have frequent Rendezvous here' – a nod to the men assembled on her lands – before sounding the defiant note: 'as long as we have Law for it, Lett them say what they will of me, I will encourage them'. The 1704 Act of Security gave legal cover for arming local militia. Mustering troops was already common but increased once the Treaty was before parliament.[8] One of Queensberry's spies worried that mustering gave ordinary men 'such Perfection in Discipline, that they could exercise by Beat of Drum, and perform their other Parts as well as the regular Troops'. For this spy, mustering was more than a show of force: it was the creation of an alternative Scottish army.[9]

A brilliant political mind, Anne realised there were gains to be had in wedding her hereditary power to the growing mass movement against the Union. She had no misgivings about the anti-Union message. This was a 'Cause wherein all people are concerned', she wrote, and so there was every reason that 'Every Body should Joine together'. If she could organise a leadership phalanx amongst the hereditary peers and magnate families, the popular protests might gain the kind of organisation and legitimation that could make the anti-Union movement an effective opposition force: one that might disrupt the ratification.

⸸

Anne was a formidable player who had the power and reputation to cause significant trouble: a fact Harley was quick to appreciate. Her estate was an important base for independent Scottish power. The troops mustered there were well armed, thanks to the establishment of armouries in Hamilton and Glasgow in early 1705.[10] As early as 1704, Harley convinced Godolphin of her 'inclination and influence' over her son, whom he identified as a potential weak point. As Duchess in her own right, head of a magnate family and closely related to others, she had the ability to maintain or split aristocratic power. In her kith and kin were two of the most consequential figures in the anti-Union opposition: her son the 4th Duke of Hamilton and her son-in-law the 1st Duke of Atholl. She was also an important intermediary between the opposition and the leader of the Court faction: her nephew the Duke of Queensberry. The English ministry were wise to keep watch over her work.[11]

Anne began her life in England close to – but not fully a part of – the Court of Charles I. She was the second daughter born to a family that longed for a male heir. The passing of her mother when Anne was only eight set off a cascade of deaths that ended Anne's childhood prematurely. Within a few short years, Anne's three brothers perished and the Civil Wars broke out. Because her father served as one of Charles I's Scottish advisors, the onset of war meant he could no longer care for her. And so Anne was sent to Hamilton Palace, southeast of Glasgow, to live with her grandmother, Lady Anna Cunningham, Marchioness of Hamilton.

Lady Anna ran her estates with unflappable practicality. After living with her courtly, English-aligned father it must have been a thrilling – if not a confounding – transition to now live with so fierce a defender of Scotland. When Charles I tried to impose a new prayer-book that threatened to reshape the Presbyterian liturgy, Lady Anna joined the resistance movement, signing the National Covenant pledging to defend the Scottish Church. When her own son (Anne's father), who fought alongside the King, tried to land his cavalry on the Scottish coast, Lady Anna personally led the forces against him. Riding at the head of a Covenanting troop, she carried a pistol and threatened to shoot him herself if he dared come ashore.[12]

Though austere and stiff-backed, Lady Anna was also charming and fun. She loved music and fine jewellery. The young Anne warmed in her care, finding stability and a role model for the kind of self-governed life that few women in that period could achieve. The bond between grandmother and granddaughter, Anna and Anne, grew as the world around them was riven by war.

While on a trip to Edinburgh with her father James, news reached them that their imposing mother and grandmother was close to passing. Death continued to stalk Anne. Within days of returning from Edinburgh, her father, who remained loyal to Charles I, left on a hopeless mission to rescue the King, one that ended with him executed at Whitehall, just as Charles I had been.

With the deaths of her grandmother, father and her uncle's subsequent passing, Anne returned to Hamilton Palace as heir. By right the family's holdings should have made her the largest landowner in Scotland. Her late father's lands stretched from the Isle of Arran in the west to the castle of Kinneil in the east, from Hamilton Palace southeast of Glasgow most of the way down the rich valley forged by the River Clyde. But the estate was decimated by the debts of her father and uncle and Cromwell's occupation of Scotland. The palace itself was commandeered by one of Cromwell's colonels. This left Anne scant land and less money, though her duties remained. As the head of her family, she had to care for her last surviving sibling, a younger sister, as well as four cousins. Taking one serving woman, Anne and her charges relocated to a small house in the woods adjoining the palace. There she spent the Interregnum in the shadow of her former home – a place that had flourished under the imperious care of her grandmother. Cut low by fortune, Anne did not let her despair override her responsibility to her family, nor her hope that she could regain what was hers.

Anne's status and the sleeping promise of her stolen estates meant she could marry well. William Douglas, 1st Earl of Selkirk, held lands adjoining Hamilton's. Douglas had to renounce his Catholicism before the two could wed. A mercurial character, Douglas was quick to anger and at times selfish. But even those who disliked him had to concede that he was a 'great master in the knowledge of the laws, of the history and of the families of Scotland and seemed to have a regard to justice and the good of his country'.[13] Driven by love and sustained by an innate sense of justice, William and Anne managed to recoup the funds needed to reclaim Hamilton Palace. The two successfully fought off all legal challenges to the estate. With the restoration of Charles II in 1660, Anne recouped money owed to her late father and persuaded the new King to grant Douglas the use of her title, making him Duke of Hamilton – a rare instance of a husband taking on the title of his wife.

The Duchess and Duke of Hamilton had a productive and happy life together. The Duke served as a powerful advocate for the family's interest, gaining entrance to the institutions denied to Anne because of her sex. She fashioned his politics, guiding him towards a more favourable view of the Covenanters and ensuring that he acted as an ardent defender of the Scottish Church. In thirty-eight years of marriage, they had thirteen children. When the Duke died in 1694, Anne was devastated. She had lost a true partner, the man in whose company she had remade her family's fortune and restored their place atop Scottish society. Without him she had to turn to her sons to represent the family publicly.

☨

As matriarch, Anne drew on her children and their spouses to gain intimate knowledge of parliament, the military, the English Court, the Kirk and the kingdom at large. Her fourth daughter, Catherine, married the Duke of Atholl. Her third surviving son Charles, Earl of Selkirk, was an army officer and courtier. Her fourth son John was Earl of Ruglen. Her fifth son, George, 1st Earl of Orkney and the first British soldier promoted to the rank of Field Marshall, was a hero of Blenheim and Marlborough's close confidant.[14] Anne was a deeply involved mother. With the help of her secretary David Crawford, she was also an excellent correspondent. She made her views known and exerted her influence over her children. In a country where 70 per cent of parliamentary seats were held by noble landlords, her position as head of one of Scotland's oldest and most powerful families meant that this influence had tangible legislative power.[15] As a patron, she wielded similar force. Hamilton's local minister, Robert Wylie, was an influential member of Commission of the General Assembly of the Church. He was also adept at sampling and shaping the opinion of ministers in presbyteries throughout Scotland – often at the Duchess' request.[16]

It fell to Anne's first son James to act as the family's chief parliamentary representative – a position conferred by accident of birth order and not because he was constitutionally suited to the role. James was named after the Duchess' father – and was freighted with the legacy of a man whose violent death at the hands of an English parliament remained scorched in her consciousness. When he was reckless (as he so often was), when he acted for himself above his family, or bent towards the English, this legacy only intensified Anne's disapproval. To less sympathetic observers the two Jameses shared something else: an ability to play both sides. The first Duke managed to stay in the favour of the Covenanters right up until the moment he fought against them.[17] The younger James was profligate. He had a quick temper, duelled, philandered and ran up huge debts. According to Hanoverian spy John Macky, he was 'very extravagant in his manner of living' and, because of this, 'grows covetous'.[18] This proved intolerable to his mother, who by graft and enterprise had painstakingly restored the family's fortune. In some respects, the divide between mother and son was generational. But shading the common complaint of prudent parents about their spendthrift scions was an uneasy co-dependency. James owed his title as Duke to Anne. French secret service agents suggested that he owed much of his 'credit' and popularity with the Presbyterian folk to her as well.[19] Without him, Anne could not live the public life for which she was uncommonly suited. The nature of their dependence is revealed at the moment when Anne first granted James the title of Duke of Hamilton. As she wrote to her son, then aged forty:

> I am willing to resigne the title of Hamilton so that you may be in a capacity to represent the family, which I wish you may doe for the interest of king and Countray, as your father and predecessors have done, Since I give my consent to this sooner, than otherways you might have had it, if you act otherways it will be a great grief to me.[20]

Anne expected James would represent the family's interests as she defined them. Brandishing her 'grief' as guilt, she presumed that he would write often, giving her news of parliament and ensuring that the votes he took and the speeches he gave aligned with her wishes.[21] To the new Duke's dismay, the title came alone. Anne did not cede control of the family's lands or fortune. She did not trust James to maintain what she had rebuilt. For years, the Duke felt his mother did not do nearly enough to help him financially.

The Duchess was often embarrassed by the way Hamilton carried himself. She could scarcely believe she had to censure him for 'beeing overtaken with drink' in front of his fellow MPs. Of greater concern was that she could not always fathom his motivations. When she could find no reason for his erratic behaviour in the wake of the Alien Act and saw his weakness as a threat to the opposition's upper hand, she cried out. 'As for your pollitícks,' she wrote, 'truely I understand none of them; and your brother Selkirk knows as little.'[22] Anne and Selkirk (the son who was closer to her in belief and interest) did not understand the Duke's actions. Anne was unwilling to believe what others assumed: that Hamilton's financial straits had left him open to corruption; that he had been bought off by Queensberry and his English allies. Clerk of Penicuik thought that Hamilton's erratic behaviour – the fact that he appeared opposed to the Union in public speeches but did little behind the scenes to unify the opposition in Church and Estates – had to be a result of an alliance, formed 'in secret with the Duke of Queensberry', with whom he met 'every night, or at least 2 or 3 times in a week'. A French spy reported that Hamilton met with both Queensberry and the Earl of Stair, and that Atholl had confronted the Duke over this apparent treachery. Harley's spy Ogilvie confirmed the meetings too.[23] At first Hamilton denied it, but when Atholl produced proof of the meetings, his retort was that they were designed to 'intimidate or gain the two chiefs of the English faction': an excuse that neither Atholl nor the spy believed.[24]

Hamilton was hard to read. On one hand Jonathan Swift described him as a man out of his depth: a '*good natured person, very generous, but of a middle understanding*'. Macky found him open too, but not because he was simple or good natured: he was 'very forward', Macky thought, 'and hot for what he undertakes' because he was 'ambitious and haughty'. Macky had observed that, since the accession of Queen Anne, Hamilton had 'made strong efforts to get into the administration'.[25] He even tried to ingratiate himself with the Duchess of Marlborough as a way into the Queen's favour.[26] To some it seemed that his ultimate ambition was to dislodge Queensberry as the principal magnate in Scotland.[27]

To others it was Hamilton's supposed interest in the Crown that explained away his actions. As a descendant of James II of Scotland, he had a definite – though distant – claim to the throne. The way he entertained it unnerved his family. Stories that he had toasted to William III's damnation during the last reign had worried them. They saw a man whose sense of his right veered too close to treason and was liable to bring the whole Hamilton clan into disrepute. Their concerns grew during the debate over the Treaty of Union. His brothers Ruglen and Selkirk were disturbed by 'a very hot report' circulating in London in November 1706. The whole city heard how Hamilton 'protested' before the first article was voted on, lest the formation of Great Britain should prejudice or impinge upon 'the right' his family had to the Crown. Ruglen was so worried about the effects such a protest might have on the family's standing that he made 'haste to waite upon her Majestie in her Closet', where he insisted that the whole report was 'made up'. He begged his brother to tell him that it were so – for, as he left the palace, he had the pitting feeling that Queen Anne remained 'in doubt'.[28]

Hamilton never raised the protest, as much as he wanted to. Duchess Anne discouraged it, and the power she exerted as head of the family eventually overwhelmed him.[29] The fact that London and the Queen herself believed he had insisted on his claim to the throne shows how clearly he telegraphed his intentions, perhaps as a response to his mother's intervention. When Hamilton sent Duchess Anne the text of the protest for approval, her response was unambiguous. Though she 'thought much on it', she resolved that raising it would 'neither further, nor obstruct' the family's 'access to succeed to the Crown', which itself was 'not very probable'. Raising the objection would only 'expose me to be laughed at', she told her son. When Hamilton pushed his mother to reconsider, she found herself 'more and more against it'. Concerned that he might go against her, she sent a threat in the form of an apology: 'I should be sorry if you did any such thing without my allowance, because if you doe, I shall be obliged to declare against it, and beside will take it very ill from you.' Chastened, Hamilton reserved his right to differ privately, perhaps nursing the distant hope that he might be crowned King of Scotland should the Union fail.[30]

7. Anne, suo jure Duchess of Hamilton, after Sir Godfrey Kneller (1679).

The back and forth over the aborted protest reveals two very different political operators. Duchess Anne thought long term. Because she saw her role as protecting the legacy of her family, she could never shake her consciousness of posterity – nor would she have wanted to. James was more immediate. Keen to seize any opportunity for wealth or advancement, he did not always reckon with the consequences of his actions. Where Anne kept tables on political players in England and Scotland, James was often paranoid, warning his mother that their enemies were looking out for faults and weak points in each of them.[31] And so while Anne saw no lasting gain in raising the family's claim to the Scottish throne, James thought it might bolster his status. His belief was genuine, but not unshakeable. For as much as he relished his lineage and prided himself on Jacobite support, there were credible reports in France that he had taken money from Hanover and would support their succession in the end, even at the expense of his own.[32] He had already shown a willingness to accede to the succession, and to negotiate directly with Hanover, if it meant putting off the Union. It is hard to separate governing principles from short-term tactics. Defoe for one believed that Hamilton's willingness to negotiate with Hanover cleared him of the imputation that his actions were guided by his pursuit of the Crown.[33] The upshot was that Hamilton came to be known for his inconstancy: his tendency to change tack as it suited him made it hard to discern any underlying philosophy of rule. This had implications for the opposition more broadly. If his mother could not understand his politics or motivation and his brothers were forced to moderate his public image, could his allies ever trust him?

⸸

Harley, Godolphin and their partners in Scotland grossly underestimated the initial reaction against the Union. But once it was clear that the anger of the people could undermine the progress of the Treaty, they quickly began to seek ways to denude the crowd. Mar advised Godolphin that the 'best way is to lett them cooll in the same skinn they grew hot in … and after the stirr is over to punish the ringleaders'.[34] Queensberry took a more tactical approach. Instead of punishing some of the mob's leaders, he sought ways to turn them.

An opportunity fell upon him when he was approached by Major James Cunningham of Aiket. Cunningham, who led an armed protest in Glasgow, was the former councillor of the Darien Company sent home by Paterson when he suffered a breakdown in Panama and began to speak against the colony's leaders. The same anti-authoritarian ravings that made Cunningham such a liability in Darien drew him to the anti-Union movement. It seems he was looking for direction. Though he stoked rebellion in the west, he came to Queensberry after an apparent volte face and offered to 'go among these men & by pretending to be their friend to dissuade them from dangerous measures'.[35] Queensberry secured Cunningham as a double agent by offering him £100 from the funds that were set aside for bribes and gifts to ease the Treaty's passage. Queensberry had other agents embedded in the crowd, providing ground-level insight into the anti-Union protests. It was not enough to infiltrate the movement on the street, or to turn or punish the leaders of the mob: Queensberry, Harley and Godolphin also had to seek the secret springs that moved the crowd. It was obvious to all three that Defoe was right: the Hamilton family bore ample responsibility for firing the 'Engines' of dissent.[36]

One of Duchess Anne's backers took encouragement from the fact that the people needed 'no bodie to inflowence them'.[37] Popular opposition was genuine and free flowing. While Anne drew strength from the people, she did not think that a bottom-up movement was enough. Her role mustering military displays led many to believe that she had also personally seeded the protests and uprisings in Lanarkshire. When it became clear that parliament would do its best to push aside protests and rush through the Treaty, she stepped up her efforts to seek out those points of influence that could unite the protests and fashion a cohesive opposition. Her first step was to shake the branches of her family tree, writing to her son that parliament's steady march left 'the people hereabouts ... in a ferment as I believe they are all through this nation'. Such an opportunity should not be wasted, she implied with all the subtlety of a disappointed mother: 'I neid say no more only It's sad to sitt still, and be ruined.' Duchess Anne did say more. Her letter carried a clear message that James should drop his silly dynastic games and rash attempts to gain administrative office and instead unite all 'dissenters' in a public address to the Queen that would acquaint her of how 'the Nation is disposed against this Union'.

The Duchess' strategy was self-fulfilling. In showing strength, the opposition would gain it; by presenting a united front, they could achieve it.[38] The clean thrust of this public front belied the fiendishly difficult task of uniting those who opposed Union. Putting aside the personal and political differences of those leaders able to influence the people on the street, the opposition itself was divided, not least because they opposed the Union for often contradictory reasons. The Jacobites were motivated above all by a desire to reverse the gains of the 1688 Revolution by installing the main Stuart line. The Episcopal clergy joined Catholic Jacobites on the belief that a second Stuart restoration was the best way to restore Episcopal Church government. The Covenanting Presbyterians, whose abiding desire to preserve Scotland's political and ecclesiastical independence was set out in the Solemn League and Covenant, could not accept a Catholic monarch, nor Episcopal Church government. They associated Catholicism with arbitrary rule and vaunted the unique status of their covenanted nation, believing that Presbyterianism entailed a degree of egalitarianism that was alien to England. The most radical wanted to extend their reformation and its social gains south to England. Duchess Anne's efforts to bring these forces together reveals the extent and effectiveness of the opposition to Union. In her work we also see the opportunities the anti-Union actors missed, and how Defoe and Harley's other spies successfully sabotaged the resistance.

⸸

At the end of November, Defoe wrote to Harley to tell him that 'the war here is begun'.[39] The Glasgow town officers had barely quelled the riots that began at the start of the month when they reignited. One of the earlier rioters, a tobacco-spinner called Parker, had been imprisoned for his role. The crowd that reassembled to protest his detention quickly tuned violent, seizing upon the Lord Provost and stealing arms and munitions from the houses of the city's magistrates. The Lord Provost was pursued by a mob into one of the city's tenements and only escaped death by secreting himself in a fold-up bed. The mob was led by George Finlay, who set up a guard overlooking the centre of Glasgow in sight of the cathedral's main doors. To Defoe, Finlay's choice of location made it seem as if he and his men 'were in Opposition to the Town Guard'. From this alternate locus of authority, Finlay and the rioters held the city. They 'Beat their Tatoo round the Town like a Garrison', and indeed they were like a military company for, as Defoe noted, 'they had the City in their full Possession, and every Bodies Life and Goods at their Mercy'.[40] The rebels knew that reinforcements for the guard had to be closing in. But their spirits were firmed by accounts of risings in Stirling, Hamilton and Angus. It seemed that the nation had finally rallied the will to oppose the Union with force.

Finlay had military experience and his swift overpowering of Glasgow convinced him that he could spearhead an armed rebellion. So while the main column of the uprising remained in the city, Finlay led a small group of between forty-five and a hundred east across the Lowlands. Defoe reported to Harley that their intent was to join with the other Lowland risings. They would march first to Cadder and then to Kilsyth and Stirling, gathering more men and arms before marching on to Edinburgh to 'raise the Parliament': to tear down the body on the cusp of betraying their country.[41] Finlay expected to be joined by masses of people at Hamilton. Cunningham of Aiket was reportedly gathering followers to march on Hamilton. He would be aided by Atholl's men who would clear the pass at Stirling. Wylie encouraged his congregants to join the forces, and there was a keen sense that Hamilton himself supported the rebellion and would muster his own men.[42]

Finlay's departure did not calm things in Glasgow. The main mob still controlled the city. Realising their impotence, the city's magistrates turned to the national government for help. Queensberry's first instinct was to find a political and legal solution. The one he settled on opened the possibility for military action should it be needed. On the last day of November, parliament issued 'A Proclamation Against all Tumultary and Irregular Meetings and Convocations', which declared any gathering that stoked resistance 'to be open and manifest Treason'. They also passed an Act that repealed provisions of the

Act of Security, which permitted armed musters. When the Act and Proclamation were read in Glasgow two days later, it seemed that they would do little. The messenger and magistrates of the city tasked with reading the legislation were harassed as they came to the Glasgow Cross at the centre of the city. According to Defoe, the messenger struggled through his reading of the Act and 'hardly read the Title of the Proclamation, when the Stones came so thick' that he retreated.

The magistrates ordered one of the town officers to get up and complete the reading, calling in the town guard for cover. He too was met with 'Volleys of Stones' and 'driven off by the Fury' of the crowd. Trying to bring things to order, the head of the guard commanded his men 'to fall upon the Rabble with the Clubs of their Musquets'. Some did, while others could not bring themselves to beat their own people and deserted. Their ranks depleted, the guard was unable to stem the chaos. They retreated, chased back to the guard house by the mob. '[F]lusht with victory', the crowd now loosed itself on the streets, storming the Tolbooth – the prison and courthouse – where the city's main stock of arms was stored. They brought ladders so they could bypass the mason-bordered doors and breach the less-fortified windows on the second floor, seizing 250 halberds once inside. The crowd was in control. According to Defoe's sensationalistic report, they roved from house to house, plundering private stocks of pistols and swords and committing a litany of outrages as they did. Defoe shares unverified accounts of men disturbing the sick and dying and forcing pregnant women out of their beds, ostensibly to check underneath for hidden pistols. While no blood was shed, Defoe was confident in his assessment that the Glasgow crowd 'acted the Exact part of an Enraged Ungoverned Multitude'.[43]

As the crowd ransacked Glasgow, Finlay and his band headed from Cadder to Kilsyth. Scouts and spies tracked their progress, following them as they passed the Antonine wall, the crumbling symbol of an empire's outer reach. The spies gave Queensberry the intelligence to cut the rebels off before they reached Edinburgh. The militia's number was not concerning, but the fear was they would draw more people in. As one of Harley's confidants in the Scottish parliament wrote – too confidently – at this stage, nothing could prevent the Treaty's passage but 'violent and open Rebellion'.[44] Questions of public safety aside, for this reason alone the government could not allow the rebellion to grow. Queensberry ordered a detachment of dragoons and some horse grenadiers under the command of Colonel Campbell to head to Glasgow to intercept the rebels and retake the city. English warships were also sent to the west coast as a further bulwark against unrest.[45]

Defoe took it upon himself to turn public sentiment against the rebellion, seeking to isolate the group from potential partners before they could form a broader coalition. By his assessment, this task was made easier by the group's leaders. During the rebels' march to Hamilton, Andrew Montgomerie and Captain Boyle joined Finlay as self-appointed generals. It was Finlay, though, who drew most of Defoe's scorn. Montgomerie was merely 'another of the Knot, but Famous for nothing that I ever heard of', Defoe later wrote.[46] Finlay on the other hand was a 'mean scandalous scoundrell fellow', an 'Abject Scoundrel Wretch, that openly profess'd himself a *Jacobite*'. In Defoe's mind this open avowal would prevent him from uniting with the second set of insurgents Defoe and Harley's network were then monitoring: the Covenanters in the west who were also plotting ways to rebel against the making of the Union, but whose staunch Presbyterianism meant they could not ally themselves with a movement driven by Jacobites.[47]

Shortly after arriving at Kilsyth, Finlay, Boyle and Montgomerie were informed that three troops of dragoons and a squad of the Queen's guards were on the way to intercept them. None of the bands of rebels, whose rumoured coming Finlay used to entice his men to march, had arrived. Atholl was less willing to take up arms than he pretended. Cunningham of Aiket was probably already in Queensberry's employ. The abrupt abandonment of his rising suggests that Queensberry may have been able to use him to expose areas of resistance in order to suppress them. The death of the rising came when Hamilton withdrew his support at the last minute. Lockhart could find no clear reason why Hamilton pulled his support but aired the speculations of others. Some said Hamilton capitulated to the Court. Lockhart also heard that he was afraid to risk his English estates. Others said that Hamilton knew of troops stationed on Scotland's borders and believed that more troops 'could be wafted over from Holland' and would decimate Scotland if civil war broke out. But if that was the sole reason, why had Hamilton apparently continued to entertain armed rebellion? Finding little clarity, Lockhart concluded that withdrawing when he did was the act of a dog. Hamilton should have 'advertised his friends' of his intention when they had time to reassess, not when they had already raised arms, and when their failure would discourage others from taking up their fight.[48]

In a final effort, Finlay sent one of his men back to Glasgow to draw more people from the main uprising. Finlay had heard that there were around four hundred ready to leave. No doubt anticipating military backlash, the four hundred '*Thank'd*' Finlay's man '*and stay'd home*'.[49] Finlay and his troops needed time. And to get time they needed protection from the force of the Queen's army. For that, they marched towards Hamilton Palace.

The march south that took the ragged band of rebels to Hamilton tracked the River Clyde, following it down as the marshes and bogs around Kilsyth gradually gave way to rich green fields. Approaching Hamilton Palace from the north proved a heady experience. The Duchess' main residence, which she casually called 'the house', was intimidating. Behind its colonnaded front stood three storeys of libraries, halls, bedchambers, sixty-two hearths, a series of kitchens, offices and multiple nurseries (many of them housing the Duke's children, who Anne complained were left there without regard by the Duke's flighty second wife). The grounds around the Palace, lovingly improved by Duchess Anne and her late husband, matched the house for grandeur. Kilometre-long avenues of trees met travellers as they passed the deer park, orchard and through the gardens. Duchess Anne had a private garden under her bedchamber. There she did much of her thinking on a seat set amongst the venerable firs that sheltered her ancestors.[50] Because she had encouraged musters and was seen to support the earlier riots, many in England assumed that Anne backed the Glasgow militia. The report was that the men who led the march to Edinburgh were 'servants or Retainers' of her family.[51] This was not entirely true. Finlay, Montgomerie and Boyle had no association with the Hamilton family. But two of the Duchess' servants were implicated in the riots and march. In a mark of her power and political affinity the true leaders of the uprising did turn to her for aid, seeking her protection to preserve what was in the end the most significant act of violent resistance against the Union.

The Duchess' reaction was not what Finlay's company expected. She was 'ill pleased' that they came to her. It is not that she didn't sympathise with their cause; it is just that she saw no way they could succeed. To back Finlay openly would jeopardise her standing and close off avenues of resistance that had a better chance of obstructing the Union. But she did not want to abandon Finlay's men, either. Her tenants and the people of Hamilton largely supported armed resistance. Her secretary David Crawford noted that in Hamilton and its surrounds a man 'Is in hazard of his life, if he doe not speak against the Union'. And so Duchess Anne allowed the rebels to make camp on her land. To maintain order, she commanded fifty of the townsfolk to keep watch over the camp and placed others as sentries throughout the town. The rebels could stay as they waited for the two companies they desperately hoped would join them. But they could not recruit men from Hamilton. The Duchess wanted their stay to be as brief as possible. Crawford did not know where they'd go next. All he could do was repeat to both Duchess and Duke what the rebel leaders had told him: that they 'will never part with Religion, Liberty, Independency, and Crown'.[52]

The Duke fretted over accounts that there was widespread disorder in Hamilton, fearing his mother had somehow encouraged the rebels. She quickly put him straight. She had maintained strict order, she said. Had she not 'prevented it, the same things might have bein done through this shire as was done at Dumfries, and perhaps worse'. She actively stopped people joining Finlay and forbade those under her charge from engaging in their own protests.[53] Defoe admired the 'prudence' of her actions, noting to Harley the fact that she 'Threatned her Own Tenants with Disposessing them if they presumed to Appear in Arms': a threat that apparently offset the efforts of local ministers who read a paper supporting the uprising in thirteen parishes across Lanarkshire.[54] Ultimately, Anne saw these acts of resistance as too narrow. She had word from her son Orkney. Back from campaign and in London, he kept her apprised of the progress of Scottish politics there, writing that Anne's view of Scotland as a nation in a 'distracted condition' was not shared in the English capital. In fact, the English believed one faction caused all Scotland's troubles and 'once the Unione is Gained all that ferment will be Allayed'. While glad that Anne did not write to the Queen to tell her about the state of the nation, Orkney concedes that 'politicks' is 'very much out of my province'. As a military man, he cannot see what action could be taken to throw the Union off course. On this he defers to his mother's judgement. The message she seems to have taken from his commentary on the London scene is that the opposition to Union had to be seen as national if it was to prevent Union or steer it away from incorporation. Anything short of that and it was too easily dismissed as factional: the domain of a disgruntled few.

Finlay and the Glasgow rebels remained at Hamilton for three days. When no reinforcements came, they had little choice but to turn back towards Glasgow, trekking through Ruglen, where they took a final vote on how to end things. The safest way was to shrink back, disbanding and turning their arms over to the deacons of their guilds rather than the city magistrates in the hope of more lenient treatment. Meanwhile, the dragoons made their way through Glasgow. A lieutenant and two other dragoons rode ahead to Finlay's house. By the time they had seized him and Montgomerie, the whole body of the troop had pushed itself into the city. As Defoe tells it, they 'March'd down to the Cross' at the centre of the city and 'Drew up there on the Street, where they sate still upon their Horses, it Raining very hard all the time, which was about three Hours'.[55] The stark presence of 220 heavily armed horseman sat at the city's crossways was enough to disperse the mob.

Once the soldiers felt sure of calm, they departed, retracing the rebels' steps by riding to Kilsyth to round up any remaining insurgents. In Defoe's opinion the dragoons left Glasgow too early. As soon as they departed, the mob rose again 'as furious as Ever'. This time they took all of Glasgow's magistrates prisoner, sending two of the captured on to Edinburgh to propose a potential exchange for Finlay and Montgomerie. Defoe thought the move a gross overreach that would 'Force the Govornment to Hang these Two Men and to send the Dragoons back'. The Edinburgh Council were unsympathetic, sending the Glasgow magistrates back with a high-handed note to 'take better Care of the peace of the Citty'.[56]

In prison, Finlay informed the colonels of the grenadiers and dragoons that one of the men they sought was a servant of Duchess Anne. In fact, he was not, but two other targets were directly associated with the Duchess. Dragoons returned to Glasgow to keep peace, and then went on to Hamilton where they arrested Mr Porterfield, Duchess Anne's servant, and James Weir, town treasurer of Hamilton, for their alleged parts in the uprising. Porterfield was accused of encouraging the muster. Weir was accused of supplying the Glasgow rebels with funds.[57] Their arrests greatly distressed Anne – especially that of Porterfield. As she told it, Porterfield 'was born and bred up in my family and has been my servant ever since'. He was 'but a tender lad' and Anne feared what would happen if he was imprisoned. In her experience Weir was a 'sober and substantiall man', who was serious about his duties and not likely to be guilty of 'treasonable practices against the government'.

Duchess Anne allowed Porterfield and Weir to be seized out of respect for Queensberry, who signed the warrant for their arrest. But she was deeply suspicious of the government's motives. She believed that the arrests had been orchestrated 'only to make a noise and to see if they can putt a lash on me'. She remained 'confident' that nothing more could come from this attempt to control her, telling her son that neither Porterfield nor Weir 'can say nothing' that would implicate her. It seems that the spies and traitors that the Duke warned of had supplied the government with the information they needed to undermine Anne's efforts. As she told him, 'I wish those that are spys amongst us were discovered and if they tell but truths it were little matter but that is not the design of such.'[58] Anne was likely correct in assuming that the design was indeed sabotage; that Porterfield and Weir were arrested in part to impose control over her and those loyal to her. Porterfield was not charged and Weir was discharged without punishment. The Duchess believed that the government's ploy was successful: in the aftermath of the arrests, fewer people left Hamilton for Glasgow, fearing that any involvement in a popular resistance movement might land them in gaol. A failed rebellion, especially a 'rash and foolish one', most likely suppressed the desire for other attempts.[59]

Though predictable, Finlay's failure put the Duchess in a regretful mood and turned her mind to other strategic failures in the movement against Union. Writing to Hamilton, she lamented that he and his allies had missed an opportunity when they did not leave parliament during the debate over the first three articles. Their absence might have delegitimated the formation of Great Britain, the imposition of the Hanoverian succession and the creation of a single unified parliament, enacted thereby. Her advice to him now was that he arrange a walkout during the voting on article nineteen, which retained the Scottish court system but made it subject to regulation from the parliament of Great Britain. She knew that Atholl had planned to protest article twenty-two, which mandated that Scotland would be represented by forty-five MPs in the new Commons and sixteen peers in the Lords. Anne thought that opposing article nineteen was a more 'popular' cause: in her view, the independence of the Scottish courts was 'every bodys concern'. A protest against subordinating the Scottish courts would not be seen as MPs standing for their own interests alone. As Fletcher and others pointed out, representation was a matter of national interest: to reduce Scottish representatives so drastically while leaving English representation unchanged was an assault on the power of Scotland and its people. Anne did not agree. She capped her advice to her son wistfully, adding 'I am very sorry there is not a better understanding and concern among you [Hamilton and Atholl]'. The line indicates that she intended to redouble her efforts to unite the main opposition, and seek out parliamentary and non-violent solutions that would be 'every bodys concern' – that could legitimately demonstrate Scotland's opposition to Union and give England some second thoughts.[60]

†

With hindsight, Defoe speculated that the rebellion 'might have been Fatal enough' to the Union had the opposition succeeded in 'getting the poor People to arms in other Places' – had the mass of armed rebellion not been confined to Glasgow, Dumfriesshire, Stirlingshire and Lanarkshire. At the same time, he thought that the government acted too harshly in the aftermath of the violence. As the opposition regrouped and turned their energy to arguing and addressing against the Union, Queensberry remained in militaristic mode. Defoe thought this was a tactical error, writing that it was 'very backward to Punish the Exorbitances of the Tongue, at a Time when they were Inviting all the People to Unite'.[61] There is a tinge of self-interest in this reflection. It implicitly frames Defoe's own approach to the rebellion as the more productive one. In some respects he was probably right. Rather than stymieing speech and legislating against the freedom of assembly, Defoe attempted to seed dissension, targeting and distributing quickly written pamphlets designed to split an opposition that was already ruptured by deep ideological and confessional differences.

As the dragoons prepared to return to Glasgow to once again quell the rioting there, Defoe wrote and published *A Short Letter to the Glasgow-Men*. Scotland had proved more expensive than he anticipated. He made a special point of telling Harley that the money he received was spent 'in the True Service I came here for'. Of the thirteen guineas left from his last payment, he planned 'to lay Out' six of them 'for the Effectuall spreading this letter at Glasgow and Over all the West'. To ensure that his message cut across the opposition stronghold, Defoe planned 'to print about 2500 of them and send them to Glasgow, Lanerk, Hamilton, Sterlin and Dumfreis'.[62] The calculation shows that Defoe treated Bell's payments as both personal remuneration and a fund for government business. He continued to publish extensively in Scotland, even at moments when his own funds were low, suggesting that he probably agreed to give publishers all profits in exchange for printing his works. The *Letter* is a deft piece of writing. Targeted to the Presbyterian majority, it reinforces Glasgow's history as a redoubtable Kirk bastion and defender of Scottish liberty: both of which are threatened by each person who joins a rebellion led by

Jacobites and Catholics. Defoe browbeats potential rebels on the grounds that to riot in support of Finlay is in effect to rebel against their own Church. To follow a Jacobite is to tear down the gains of the Glorious Revolution and violate the Solemn League and Covenant. As the prose tips towards hyperbole, Defoe tells potential rebels that they are 'digging Graves for your Children among the Rubbish and Rottenness of Popery and Idolatry'.[63]

To put himself on the side of Glasgow, Defoe invokes the commonplaces of Presbyterian sermon culture, measuring out his screed against a Jacobite-led opposition with enough explicit invocations and latent references to the Old Testament to place him amongst the pious. Though the writer thinks Glasgow should support the Union, he does not deny the right of the royal burgh to make its opposition known. He only asks that Glaswegians do it legitimately, through their representatives and by petitions and addresses. Violence is only justified, he argues, if there is a clear majority who believe that their representatives are acting against them and need to be restrained. By exposing some of the rebel chiefs as Jacobites, and peeling his readers off their cause, Defoe casts doubt on whether such a majority exists. At the same time as he encouraged Glasgow men tempted by violence to take the moderate path of addressing, he was working to delegitimise addresses on other fronts. This two-pronged approach was highly effective in closing off potential avenues for popular resistance. Defoe knows the people of Glasgow: he had agents in the west. With their intelligence, and from his own conversations with people who fled the city, he manages to produce a public-facing work (and to spread it to trouble zones using distribution agents) that in effect cuts the opposition off from the source of their greatest power – the people of Scotland. Defoe was patently happy with the results. He told Harley that contacts in Glasgow 'flatter me it has done a great Deal of Service here', and he republished the *Letter* in the *Review* during the final push towards ratification when anti-Union violence bubbled again.[64]

⸸

The support for Finlay and the ringleaders persisted after their arrests, showing that there was still an appetite for active resistance.

This is why Defoe's work turning people back into their houses – and dulling the allure of the throng – was so important. On the opposite side, Duchess Anne kept faith to the belief that there had to be consolidation amongst the leadership if resistance was to have any effect. She had to find enough common ground so that leaders in parliament and amongst the peerage could embrace resistance fulsomely. Only then could the opposition fashion a collective response, one that would prevent counterinsurgencies like Defoe's from using their individual sympathies or religio-political identities as a means to alienate grassroots constituents. For the Duchess, consolidation was a family matter. It hinged on her ability to bring her son the Duke of Hamilton into a productive working partnership with her son-in-law, the Duke of Atholl.

Before the Treaty of Union was committed to paper, Duchess Anne expressed the desire that 'the country party would unite' behind the man whom she hoped would act as its unifier, her son. If the party gathered behind him, she believed 'they could prevail over their opponents'.[65] Her desire for unity took on greater stakes after the events of the Scotch plot turned Atholl against Queensberry. With Atholl now casting himself as the leader of the Cavaliers and seeking a role as leader of the opposition to rival Hamilton's, the divisions in the opposition were made more apparent. But with Atholl's rise the anti-Union movement had the potential to achieve a greater reach than it could under Hamilton alone. Atholl could bring in the Jacobite support that Hamilton lost after he gave the Queen the right to choose the Union commissioners – and could do so without putting off the Presbyterian mainstream. Though Presbyterian himself, Atholl came from an Episcopalian family and was likelier than Hamilton to appeal to those Episcopalians who saw Union as a threat to the reimposition of Episcopal Church government that the Stuart restoration promised. The fact that a united parliament would contain the English bishops who sat in the Lords – a major impediment to some Presbyterians – was not enough to shake the majority of Scottish Episcopalians from their loyalty to the main line of the Stuarts. Atholl's willingness to tack between these Episcopalians and the anti-Union Presbyterians 'induced many to doubt the sincerity of his professions' according to

Lockhart. But on the whole, it was successful in giving him a wide base of support.[66] If Hamilton and Atholl found a way to lead together, they could weave the various, conflicting strands of the opposition into a formidable force, one that could countermand the Court and the English – or so the Duchess intended.

In the month before the Glasgow riots broke out, Duchess Anne had urged her son and Atholl to 'concert measures together', insisting that their alliance 'cannot but be for the publick advantage'. She tracked each man's movements and acted as a point of triangulation, trying to arrange meetings between them when they were both in Edinburgh. While public interest carried some persuasive force, it was not always enough to overcome the obstacle of private interest. The competition to lead the opposition was a battle of egos. And Atholl's sense of his destiny was only affirmed by his utter distrust of Hamilton.[67] After Finlay's and Montgomerie's arrests, when Duchess Anne redoubled her efforts to forge a unified opposition party, Atholl's view of Hamilton became obvious. Atholl would not even trust Hamilton to deliver a letter to the Duchess. The rebuke was intense. Hamilton complained to his mother that it showed just how 'weak' he was in Atholl's mind. Because of the lack of 'confidence' Atholl had in him, Anne's attempts to bring the two men together crumbled. They could find 'neither consert nor agreement'.

It is easy to see why the two did not get along. Atholl had the zealotry of a convert; after Queensberry accused him of treason in the Scotch plot, he became 'all of a sudden a violent Jacobite'. Newly staunch, he was galled by Hamilton's inconstancy. The Cavaliers – who represented the Jacobite interest in parliament – were drawn to Atholl, not least because he had a stronghold in the north, was popular across the shires of Fife and Angus, and had significant landed influence in Highland and Lowland Perthshire. Moreover, Atholl had the ability to muster six thousand troops. And because his estate was relatively small, he was less likely to be elevated post-Union, and so less likely to chance his fate by siding with England. According to Lockhart, Atholl remained committed to armed resistance and would have 'gone to the field' had others shown the same boldness and resolve. But even the sympathetic Lockhart had to allow that Atholl lacked the temperament to lead: the man could truck no alliance, for 'his vanity and ambition extended so far that he could not suffer an equal, and did therefore thwart the Duke of Hamilton's Measures'.[68] Atholl's haughty coldness isolated Hamilton. After repeated attempts to draw him closer, Hamilton told his mother:

> I am soe weary that I profest wish I were any where rather then heer for I serve for nothing but to bear the blame of other peoples faults; I have to let reason & not humour Governe me but it's hard to be Blamed by the Court & not to satisfie others.[69]

As debate over the Treaty reached its final stages, it was increasingly apparent that neither side saw Hamilton as an honest broker. He was left resentful of Edinburgh and hurt that others did not esteem him as highly as he estimated himself. Hamilton's growing listlessness further hindered his mother's desire for a working alliance amongst the opposition's leadership. The upshot was that, while public energy built against the Union, its collective force was arrested: every time it burst forth it was drawn back to the limits of those who deigned to lead the movement.

The familial infighting affected the opposition's action in parliament. In the Hall, Fletcher remained at the vanguard of a principled resistance. As successive articles of the Treaty were voted on and approved, Fletcher grew more distressed not just with Hamilton but with his parliamentary colleagues at large. Fletcher was rigid in his perceptions and struggled to believe that either the Scottish or English parliament would approve the Treaty as it was written. When this perception was disproven, his dismay was that of a man deceived. He attacked the negotiators for having 'betray'd their trust'.[70] Unlike Hamilton, who fed on approval, Fletcher seemed to actively repel it. Paterson reported to Harley that Fletcher's righteous anger led him to act in a way that risked censure by parliament.[71] Fletcher clearly felt that he had to exhaust every possible measure to prevent what he believed was a fundamental breach of the laws of Scotland, even if it estranged him from the parliament that he had spent so much of his life trying to enter. Fletcher reverted to the same limitations on the

Crown he had outlined with the Act of Security, essentially proposing that no one could succeed to the Scottish throne without guaranteeing frequent elections and relinquishing some monarchic prerogatives to the Scottish parliament. He wanted to break the 'influence of English ministers upon our government' that stemmed from the monarchic control on appointing Scottish officials. For Fletcher, the centralisation of state in London was the prime cause 'of our present ill condition'.[72] His opposition colleagues again floated the prospect of voting on the succession instead of the Union with Fletcher's limitations statutorily enforced. England had word of this, and knew that Fletcher and Hamilton were likely supporters, and that the Marquis of Annandale would be the one to propose it. Godolphin also had good intelligence that the measure would fail because the Squadrone Volante would vote with the Court against it. When it was raised, Hamilton broke parliamentary protocol by addressing the Commissioner directly, urging him to see that 'the humour of the countrie' is against this Union: this much was made plain by 'the addresses' that were flooding the parliament. If Queensberry called a recess, then he could guarantee opposition support for 'settling the successione'. Fletcher, Belhaven and Atholl joined the chorus. It turned out that Godolphin's intelligence was right. Queensberry had the numbers and could push this ploy to the wings.[73]

Fletcher tried to delay proceedings by arguing that the voting order on articles should be rearranged and proposed amendments to the Treaty that England could not accept. In some actions he was joined by Hamilton. The most significant of these saw Hamilton put forth the proviso that Scottish members of the united parliament should have a veto over all Union business. This was too great a concession and it directly confronted Defoe's assurance that once united, the parliament could not act against Scottish interests, for to do so would void the basis for Union and for its own existence.[74] Fletcher had Atholl's support on more amendments than he did Hamilton's. For unlike Atholl, Hamilton was unwilling to vote against any article that concerned the Equivalent, fearing he would not get the share he so coveted. Fletcher desired still more support from Atholl in parliament. But it was Hamilton's increasingly apparent self-interest that truly galled him. Each time Hamilton voted for an article that stood to benefit him economically, opposed an amendment or was absent, Fletcher saw it as an act of bastardry, a notch on England's staff as it beat a man he once considered his leader into submission.

⸸

Hamilton might have been a disappointment domestically, letting Fletcher and the Scottish Jacobites down in equal measure. Globally, he was still perceived as a real threat. The geopolitical stakes of ratification could not be avoided. When parliament debated the shared tax burden post-Union, MPs objected to the greater taxes needed to fund the War of the Spanish Succession and argued for an exemption to last its duration.

On the Continent, Harley's agents continued to scan for foreign interference in Scotland's affairs. From Ogilvie's dispatches Harley knew that a Franco-Jacobite invasion remained a topic of conversation at Versailles and St Germain, and that despite his inaction on invasion and openness to Hanover, Hamilton was still seen as a potential leader. Hamilton had lost trust with some, who interpreted his giving the Queen the power to choose the Union commissioners as a sign that he was playing both sides. Historian Daniel Szechi has made the case that Hamilton dangled his support for armed uprising as a way to keep Scots Jacobites onside and to sabotage any invasion attempt from the inside.[75] If so, the plan worked better on the Continent than in Scotland. For as Scottish Jacobites grew increasingly dissatisfied with Hamilton, Ogilvie reported that St Germain continued to send agents to the Scottish Duke in an effort to recruit him to lead a Jacobite revolt. Some clearly still trusted the Duke – or at least saw him as their best hope. The agents of St Germain delivered little. Though they offered him enticements, including making him Duke of Châtellerault as a counter to any English bribe of titles, the most that the agents were able extract from Hamilton was that he supported the restoration of James Francis Edward Stuart, but that, as before, he was unwilling to do more until it was clear Stuart had widespread support.[76] Hamilton's ego was puffed by these continual overtures. But he was at best a reluctant military leader. He feared the

English forces. Not only did he not want to confront them head on: he was so concerned that they might march north after the Union to capture its opponents that he asked his mother to prepare him a set of rooms in the deserted Avondale Castle, where he could hide from any incoming troops.[77] When their agents were unable to firm up Hamilton's offers to lead, St Germain toyed with sending Perth himself but, as Ogilvie told Harley, they backed down when faced with the difficulty and danger of such a mission.

Ogilvie moved between Hamburg, Rotterdam and France. He returned to England briefly in June 1706, ostensibly on business from his patron Count Belke but in fact to meet with Harley. Their meeting was brief and, from Ogilvie's perspective, frustrating. He felt he could not get his side across, so he wrote to Harley to make his case. The costs of his mission were getting too high and support from Harley did not cover his expenses. At stake were his life and the lives of his family. His mission was so dangerous that he genuinely feared he might be executed. He worried that his 'cunning' wife, who had been such a good source of information at St Germain, would be left at the mercy of those she spied on. If ever the Jacobites found reason to suspect him, he told Harley, 'they will put her up and my children also in a monastery to keep me to my good behaviour'. The mission itself was at an impasse. It had yielded good results. Ogilvie had ingratiated himself with the Countess of Erroll, a key figure in the Jacobite underground. He had also identified the stream of agents flowing from St Germain to Scotland and England. Yet, as he continued to insist, the only real way to know 'anything' of 'the affairs' of the agents sent by St Germain was for him to return to Scotland.[78]

†

With risings in Glasgow and the southwest under control – for now – and the plans for a Franco-Jacobite invasion percolating in the background, Duchess Anne, Hamilton, Fletcher and Atholl returned their attention to addresses, the one arena in which anti-incorporationist actors had successfully demonstrated the strength of their support. This was the last arena where even the distrustful amidst the opposition could link in a show of unity. In Defoe's analysis the addresses presented were interchangeable with petitions.[79] Their framers maintained a distinction, insisting that addresses had a more corporatist character and were less driven by personal grievance. Their function was similar, however. Addresses tendered formal arguments to Queensberry and parliament that confirmed their own support by virtue of their signatories. The opposition were very good at deploying addresses to show that vast swathes of the country opposed the Union. As the Treaty was considered and debated, eighty-five addresses were delivered to parliament from over a hundred associations: royal and baronial burghs, parishes and presbyteries, bearing at least twenty thousand signatures.[80] The power of addresses rested on the idea of a sovereign people; that original power derived from freehold, and that this power should inform the actions of government. This was a line Defoe himself took during his days leading petitions against the government and this history was thrown in his face when he tried to argue that the election of MPs was all the consent needed for them to govern for the people of Scotland. Fletcher and the minister for Hamilton, Robert Wylie, were amongst those who pushed for more consultation. When parliament did not allow breaks in the debate to consult with constituents, addresses became a way to show Scots that entering into a Union denied them their rights, and England that this Union was forced on a population largely opposed to incorporation.

Historian Karin Bowie has uncovered new evidence revealing that the addressing campaign was more centralised than previously assumed. Led by members of the parliamentary opposition, addresses often used a standard text that was carefully designed to cut across divisions of rank, position and affiliation to bring the country together against the Union. The basic text ran that 'incorporating union' is 'contrary to the honour, fundamental laws and constitutions of this kingdom, Claim of Right and rights and privileges of the barons and freeholders and burrows of this kingdom and church'. It then urged members to reject incorporation and 'preserve entire soveraignty and independency of crown and kingdom', to keep the rights defended 'by our heroic ancestors for the space of two thousand years' so 'that the same may be transmitted to succeeding generations'. With this sweep, the addresses took in all the organs of Scottish government, the national Church and all who had a claim to share in Scotland's sovereignty – past, present and future. The text was then adapted to suit the specific nature of the corporation doing the addressing. This strategy had the best of both worlds as a result: coordination from above and participation from the grass roots.[81]

As Hamilton saw it, the addresses were a natural reaction to a moment with no parallel in history, 'when a nation in general is so averse to a thing that the representatives will have no regard for their constituents, but in spite of their teeths and contrary to their repeated instructions they will proceed in a matter where so much aversion is shown'. As the representatives voted, he told his brother in London, 'Addresses come in from all corners daily.'[82] It was not that the addresses were spontaneously flowing in, though Hamilton cultivated this impression for strategic reasons. More than one-third of the local addresses came from Lanarkshire, within the domain of the Hamilton family.[83] From November, Hamilton pushed for shire-wide addresses. His mother agreed to help him, though at that point she believed targeted parochial addresses might be more effective. She was nonetheless active in securing signatures and was informed at each stage by the progress of the addressing campaign.[84] Atholl helped circulate the text for addresses, drawing lairds and nobles into the campaign. He also strongarmed many of his vassals into signing them. For his part, Fletcher called for breaks in parliament and drew attention to the addresses coming in, allowing the opposition to coordinate the subject of particular addresses, keying them to the articles debated as a way to bring popular support to bear on their parliamentary position. The reaction in parliament was often dismissive. Hamilton told his mother that some MPs laughed the addresses off.[85] Whether this laughter was provoked by haughtiness or insecurity is not clear; what is clear is that the addresses needed to be addressed, by parliament and by Unionists beyond its doors.

The issue for Unionists was not simply that the addresses demonstrated opposition support; it was that they generated it. When published in newspapers, read and talked about, the addresses had the effect of making their positions open: their intent being to draw people beyond their list of signatories to the cause. In doing so, they fed other forms of opposition. In one instance that caused particular unease, rank-and-file members of the army addressed their officers, stating their unwillingness to enforce an unpopular Treaty on their countrymen, publicly undermining the threat of military force in the process.[86] The fact that Unionists did not fight addresses with a significant addressing campaign of their own is a tacit admission that they could not match the opposition's numbers. Instead, they waged a counterinsurgency by pushing the position first articulated by the Earl of Mar: that the addresses 'were procured by people mostlie disafected to the Government, and they had been industrious to misinforme people of the termes of the Union and aver'd manifest falshoods'; they were not representative but engineered on false terms to exaggerate anti-Union sentiment. People had been 'forced to signe'. And no one should think that these addresses make the 'nationes inclination' known.[87]

Defoe was characteristically industrious in apprehending and responding to the addresses. His contacts in the north and west sent him copies of a few before they were delivered to parliament, giving him a momentary advantage. He boasted that arguments he distributed, especially those in his *Fourth Essay*, had already 'stopt Three addresses which were Comeing Out of the North and that a Gentleman Reading it among about 20 that had Resolvd to address they all layd it aside'. His approach was to take the addresses seriously while working to render them illegitimate. To do so, he cast them as unrepresentative: as he saw it, the addresses excluded great parts of the population and magnified others disproportionately. Their tone and approach also breached petitioning rights. In letters to Harley he noted the total exclusion of women from the list of signatures: this despite the coordinating role Duchess Anne played and the fact that Presbyterian women constituted a natural bloc of opposition to Union.[88] In the *Review* he attacked particular addresses, like that from the convention of royal burghs, arguing that it was driven by Jacobites and Episcopalians and that the signatories did not represent a majority of burgh representatives, a point he reiterated in his *Fifth Essay*.[89] He proclaimed that he would 'undeceive those people, who are imposed upon' by such addresses 'to think that the universal Cry of the people of *Scotland* is against the Union'. Widening his scope a week later, Defoe rooted out the cause of this deception, telling his readers in Scotland and England how the 'the whole Interest of the [Country] Party, by Books, Pamphlets, Rabbles, Speeches, Emissaries . . . had been employ'd to incense the poor unthinking People in the Country against their own Happiness, and bring them in to address their Governours against the Union'. He was troubled too by the way the addresses 'are magnified' in England, selectively printed so that they appear 'extravagantly greater than really they are'.[90] With the first line he attempts to cut off claims to public support in Scotland; with the second he assures English readers that reports of a widespread opposition are grossly exaggerated.

The pace and volume of Defoe's writings on addresses gives a measure of the risk they posed. Having dealt with them in his *Fifth Essay*, he attempted to have the last word on the subject with *Two Great Questions Considered*, the sixth and final *Essay at Removing National Prejudices*, where he devotes half the work to the rights and responsibilities of petitioners and the petitioned. Here he affirms the right to petition but also the right of parliament to reject a petition. In addition, he sets some limits to what a petition or address can do. For one, it can ask but not make a claim on power. It certainly cannot threaten those it petitions with their removal if they choose not to accede to the petitioner's ask. To tamp the power of addresses required some finessing given Defoe's own history. In his reasoning, the Kentish petition, which he supported, was legal in form and delivery but was presented to a government that acted scandalously. By contrast, the Scottish parliament was too patient given that the addresses presented to it breached norms of content and delivery, asserting too much power and encouraging illegal assemblies.[91] The criticism remained that Defoe could be bought; that he changed his position with the masters he served, and now tried to overturn in Scotland the very rights he helped establish in England.[92]

Though it danced around hypocrisy, Defoe's smear campaign hit an opposition nerve. Lockhart later inveighed against 'that vile monster and wretch Daniel Defoe' and the 'other mercenary tools' who aspersed the genuineness of the addresses. While Lockhart admitted that the addresses emerged from a coordinated opposition, he was indignant at the suggestion that 'any sinister means were used to bring in subscribers'.[93] At an overarching level, the battle over how the addresses should be received – whether they were an authentic expression of popular sentiment and what the parliament owed such expressions – gave Queensberry and the Court faction enough cover to reject the demands of the addresses against incorporation. One ground for this was that they asserted they had no means of verifying the signatories.

The opposition had one way to answer, but it was risky. They could bring some of the signatories to Edinburgh. In the winter of 1706, this is what they did. In a rare moment of unity, Lockhart, Atholl, Fletcher and Harry Maule concerted to bring to Edinburgh landowners from across the country who had signed addresses to ask parliament to respond. As Hamilton told his mother, he was not one of 'the original contrivers' but went along with the scheme at Atholl's request. Lockhart contradicts the timidity of this account, writing that Hamilton 'relished' the scheme. The plan was for the landowners to call on Queensberry to lay aside the Union, or 'at least grant a recess until they had informed the queen of the present temper and disposition of the nation'. Whether this succeeded or not, they would then present to the Queen herself one final address objecting to the Union and calling for a new election. By focusing on landowners, the planners made a direct claim upon the originality of sovereign power; they also invoked a precedent for its exercise, echoing the National Convention of 1638 that rejected Charles I's impositions on the Scottish Church and set off the war against him.[94]

The flaw in the design was that Edinburgh was a relatively small place. Agents like Defoe were intimate with the people who walked its streets. So, when the city began filling with strangers, many of them armed, he alerted his handler in England. Harley passed the letter on to Godolphin, who responded that 'De Foe's letter is serious and deserves reflection. I believe it is true and it ought to guide us very much in what we are doing here, and to take care in the first place to preserve the peace of that country'.[95] The mob on the street was one thing. A gathering of heretors (inheritors) represented a far more powerful base and both Harley and Godolphin realised the problem the collective could pose to the Union. Queensberry did too. He ordered arms and horses valued over '100 merks' to be seized, and tasked the magistrates of Stirling, Leith and Queensferry with sending lists of travellers bound for Edinburgh, so as to keep track of the gathering body.[96] Within days, Defoe had gone fully 'Incognito' and 'gotten into the Company of Some of the people', successfully infiltrating a group of heretors linked to the Duke of Gordon. Ensconced within the group, he was able to send details of their plans to Harley and, through him, to Queensberry who, Defoe claimed, was until then entirely unaware of the movement amassing against him. This was not true. Queensberry had received a copy of a circular delivered throughout Lanarkshire calling the heretors to the capital.[97] Defoe's work was nonetheless important. He used his new associates to try and get a copy of the national address. The intelligence he gained gave Harley a secret view of the opposition and positioned Defoe to sabotage their national address from the inside.

Defoe spent much of his day in conversation with his new associates, trying to unsettle them and the other landowners in an effort to thin the gathering out. This work proved easier than he first imagined. Defoe found that the flipside to the strength the heretors sought in numbers was that none were willing 'to venture their Own heads in the Fray', a failure that stymied their action.[98] Defoe's programme of sabotage was also aided by circumstance. Edinburgh was expensive and those heretors who were unwilling to pay good coin for miserly lodgings went home before any national address could be agreed upon. Still, Defoe was proud of the role he played in undermining what Atholl and Fletcher hoped would be the last best stand against the Union. Writing to Harley, he boasted, 'In This Little scheme of their Affaires I have Acted a True <u>spy</u> to you.'

As a true spy, he recruited informants admitted to the inner workings of the opposition. From them, Defoe secured intelligence on the three private meetings held by Atholl, Hamilton, Fletcher, Lockhart and their comrades. He also had eyes on the more general meeting held before a quorum of the landowners. It was during the private meetings that Hamilton put forth a plan for one person to go to

Queensberry 'and beg him to give Them Time to address the Queen'. Hamilton knew that if the heretors ventured to Holyrood as a group, they would be denied entrance.[99] The sticking point was that nobody wanted to be the person to wait on Queensberry. Defoe heard that at another meeting the group raised the prospect of using force to extract their demands but resolved that the position of English troops made this foolish. During the public meeting, Hamilton once again seemed as if he'd turned on his putative allies at the last minute by insisting that they add a clause to the address offering to settle the succession on Hanover in exchange for England rejecting the Union. The reasoning he gave was that this would give English Tories a stronger foundation for opposing the Union in their parliament. The clause presented an insuperable obstacle. Atholl could not agree without jeopardising his Jacobite constituency. As negotiations dragged for three days, more and more country gentlemen left the capital and the fragile compact of Jacobites and Presbyterian anti-Unionists crumbled.

Working on intelligence he had of the letters calling the landowners to Edinburgh and the reports of their meetings, Queensberry issued a proclamation 'discharging unwarrantable and seditious convocations'. Even if the opposition managed to reknit their frayed alliance, they now had no legal way to assemble their show of national strength. As Lockhart recounted, Atholl and Hamilton were now 'so jealous and out of humour with one another' that he despaired for the fate of the country and the party. As the opposition turned on itself, the Court saw through the passage of articles sixteen, seventeen, eighteen and nineteen: instituting a common currency, customs duties on import and export, trade regulations and taxes, and the preservation of the Scottish legal system under Britain's control. By the time the national address collapsed, Defoe predicted that the full ratification of the Treaty of Union was a mere two weeks' away.

⚘

A year later, when Hamilton looked back on the opposition's failure, he felt the need to justify himself to his mother. For the past twenty years, he insisted, it had been his aim 'to preserve peace in my countrie'. He had served this aim right up 'till thos pretended patriots deserted both it and me'.[100] There is credible evidence to suggest that Hamilton played both sides. His secret meetings with Queensberry are suspicious. His debts and the funds he took from Hanover certainly suggest that he could be bought. But it is also likely that he was stopped from openly declaring rebellion by self-interest and cowardice. By appearing to support and then withdrawing from risings and from the heretors' address, he sabotaged the opposition at key times, never allowing its strands to coalesce around the set of core principles most of the disparate factions and actors agreed upon. Whatever the particular alchemy of his motivation, his acts of self-sabotage rendered the opposition vulnerable, creating an opening for Defoe and other agents to exploit through a successful counterinsurgency. These agents presented and exaggerated the opposition's divisions in order to undermine their strongest argument: that the Scottish nation and its people were united against the Union.

CHAPTER 8

FURTHER WEST AND INTO THE HIGHLANDS

People from across Scotland came to Edinburgh for business. Defoe moved freely amidst them. To his mind, he attracted little mistrust from any group, bragging to Harley that 'I am Perfectly Unsuspected as Corresponding with anybody in England. I converse with Presbyterian, Episcopall-Dissenter, papist and Non Juror, and I hope with Equall Circumspection . . . I Have faithfull Emmissaries in Every Company and I Talk to Everybody in Their Own way'. Employing informants and gathering intelligence allowed Defoe to infiltrate all levels of society. But amongst merchants, Defoe was with his own. He did not need to contort himself. His conversations with them did not give him the same frisson of deception. He could be more open and genuine. In business, the line between cover and life was blurred.

Defoe spoke the language of commerce to trade-minded MPs, proposing a joint venture in a salt works with one, and, the next day, a partnership in a glass manufacturer with another. To the traders beyond parliament's doors, he was even freer with his cover, promiscuously shifting his putative plans to appeal to the local business interests of burghs and towns across the country. 'With the Glasgow Mutineers I am to be a fish Merchant,' he nodded to Harley, 'with the Aberdeen Men a woollen, and with the Perth and western men a Linen Manufacturer.' With all groups he drew the conversation back to the Union and the gains he expected it would yield for the industry he'd adopted that day. Defoe's tactics were astute. He did not offer general economic blandishments. Instead, he used his expertise in business (better in conversation and writing than in the ledger book) to foster solidarity and appeal to the self-interest of merchants and manufacturers. As a reader of mankind, he knew that personal profit was one of the few drivers that could work against the current of patriotic sentiment turning Scots away from the prospect of incorporation. Besides, few groups could disperse Defoe's ideas more widely than merchants. They were well represented in parliament; they had significant local clout, and could move freely through the burghs, towns and villages, the presbyteries and parishes where they worked and worshipped, across the Lowlands and well into the Highlands.

⸸

It was not enough to turn those who came to Edinburgh. As effective as this was with merchants and heretors, Defoe and the Scottish Court faction needed a more reliable way to seed ideas and monitor potential insurrections. To this end, they engaged agents of influence. These agents were particularly necessary in the southwest and Highlands, where bonds of local trust provided the only access to volatile populations who spread beyond the reach of Defoe's existing network. In the southwest, Defoe employed John Pierce. It was Pierce who passed the word in Galloway and Dumfries that Finlay was a Jacobite – a message designed to prevent the anti-Union forces there joining his rising.[1]

The southwest had a proud history of resistance to state control, largely stemming from its demographics. The region was home to the highest concentration of staunch Covenanters: the most radical sect of which were the Cameronians. The Cameronians refused to return to the fold in 1690 when the Presbyterian Kirk was established as Scotland's national Church. Their grounds for separation were that the Kirk did not renew the terms of the National Covenant and Solemn League and Covenant (not least the promise to reform England and eradicate prelacy there too), nor did the parliament make subscription to the tenets of the Covenant necessary for the holder of the Scottish throne. The Cameronians rejected all parliamentary control over Church matters – and refused even to pay taxes. They pursued what they believed was a pure – because uncompromising – Presbyterianism. They held their meetings in secret. Their practice was one of rigorous castigation – of self and others – performed before an Old Testament god, who dangled the souls of sinners as if they were mice before a spitting flame. The fear at Holyrood and Westminster was that the group would ally with the Jacobites against the Union. Their total unwillingness to compromise made this unlikely.

A second more moderate group, the Hebronites, presented a greater threat in this regard.[2] Led by John Hepburn, who preached in the yellow tinted fields of Kirkcudbrightshire and its surrounds, the Hebronites wanted the Covenant renewed, but were otherwise amenable to the doctrines of mainstream Presbyterianism. Like the Cameronians, they opposed the Union. Unlike the Cameronians, they were willing to engage in the political process. The so-called 'Cameronian address' that declared the impossibility of uniting with a nation that had violated the terms of the Solemn League and Covenant was produced by Hepburn. Defoe tended to conflate the two sects, which only increased his fear of a Cameronian–Jacobite alliance. In truth, there was a longstanding animus between Cameronians and Hebronites.

Defoe and so many others failed to distinguish the two sects because of their secrecy and shared intensity. At the time Defoe was deeply worried that Hepburn, a 'Mad Man (that is Mad in Zeal)', though disowned by the mainstream, was now influencing those ostensibly more moderate ministers: 'They Talk his Very Language Now Every Day in Their Comon Discourse.'[3] Years later, Defoe told a story about a walk he took with Queensberry that began at Drumlanrig Castle, Queensberry's estate, and continued into the surrounds of Dumfries and Galloway. In the fields, they came upon Hepburn preaching to a gathering of '7000 people, all sitting in Rows on The steep Side of a green Hill'. Hepburn 'held his Auditory, with not above an Intermission of half an Hour, almost seven Hours', and this was despite the fact that many 'had come fifteen or sixteen Miles to hear him, and had all the Way to go home again on Foot'. Defoe could not help admiring the zeal of the congregation and Hepburn's capacity to hold them in awe. If the English churches had such power, they would be 'more throng'd, and our Alehouses ... less throng'd on the Sabbath-day'.[4] As much as the story seeks more from English churchgoers, in illustrating the commitment of the Covenanters it shows why the southwest and its leaders had to be subdued. In Galloway and Dumfries, Lanarkshire and Ayrshire, there were people who had an unmatched commitment to their faith; at the say of their preachers, they could be formed into a formidable bloc of agitators and fighters. These were men whom Queensberry's spies reported 'fight as they pray, and pray as they fight, making every Battle a new Exercise of their Faith'.[5]

Defoe warned Harley that 'Management' of people by their priests 'has done Incredible Injury to the Case', singling out the 'West' as the place where this manipulation was most severe. Bullish as he was, Carstares had to admit the same: parts of the country were in a 'distracted state'. Carstares added a caveat. Yes, some ministers 'preached against the Union', but the influence went both ways: '[t]he plain truth is that in some places the ferment of the people upon false notions of the Union is so great that ministers for their safety are obliged to go further in complying with them than they are of themselves inclined to.' This was the challenge facing any agent sent to the southwest. The source of anti-Union animus was not always clear. To combat it, they had to confront the resistance at both ends, turning preachers from the extremes and calming the temper that seethed amongst the people.[6]

†

The Hebronites were largely responsible for the burning of the articles at Dumfries. After the act, Hepburn sent a delegation to Edinburgh to seek leadership. He wanted the burning to have far-reaching effects and sought guidance on how the efforts he coordinated in the west could contribute to the broader struggle against the Union. Defoe got wind of the delegation shortly after their arrival and alerted Harley that there were plans afoot for a rising in the west country.[7] At first Defoe wanted to head west on his own. But his committee work on the Equivalent held him back. He considered himself indispensable. He could do more good by resolving the outstanding questions of incorporation in the city, he reasoned, than in settling the discontent amongst the Covenanters. Harley had other agents who could take up the latter. Paterson came from Covenanting stock. Fearne was a Cameronian and had good contacts in the community. But Harley did not manage his agents at a granular level. Defoe was the one who deputised the mission and delegated money from his own meagre stock to fund it. He did not know Fearne was employed by Harley, and his always competitive relationship with Paterson had devolved from begrudging alliance to outright hostility. Defoe disputed Paterson's calculations in public and traduced him in letters to Harley as a man of 'Unperforming Numbers', who has done nothing for the cause and who is spoken of in Edinburgh 'in Terms I Care not to Repeat'.[8] And so Defoe turned to Pierce, an agent who was not vying for Harley's favour and would have no qualms reporting to Defoe himself.

Defoe was confident that Pierce was the man for the mission, reassuring Harley that he is 'Very well known among' the west-country folk and 'Very Acceptable to their ministers who are the firebrands'. Even so, it was a dangerous ask to infiltrate a community famed for its secrecy and intolerance. In order to 'Cool the People', Pierce had to make it past their 'first fury', an obstacle that left Defoe 'in pain for him'. Knowing that difficult missions were rendered impossible without clear support and instruction, Defoe sent Pierce with his own servant, horses and set of papers sketching out a set of arguments designed to 'Open their Eyes' – to reason the Covenanters away from outright rebellion. By providing Pierce with the kind of supplies and instructions he wished were more forthcoming from Harley – and making a point of telling Harley how he did so – Defoe implicitly conveys the affinity he felt for Pierce. Defoe told Harley that (like himself) Pierce 'is Sincerely Zealous for the Public'. He (too) 'will merit a pardon for what has past if he performs this service, whether he has success or no'.[9]

Pierce's past crime was the distribution and suspected authorship of *Legion's Humble Address to the Lords* (1704), a petition he likely worked on with Defoe. But where Defoe dodged the charges, Pierce was forced to flee to Scotland in June 1704.[10] Accounts of Pierce note his extremity, but differ on its sort: he is depicted variously as a High Churchman, a Republican and a Covenanter.[11] Given his history, Pierce was most likely a former radical turned moderate, one who did so without expunging his core belief in a sovereign people – much like Defoe. Whatever his politics, Pierce was in Scotland. Defoe trusted him. He was staunchly pro-Union and may have even written propaganda for the cause. More so, as Defoe tells it, he readily volunteered for the mission – despite its clear perils.

⸸

In December, Pierce set out for the Hebronite heartland at Dumfries, going, in Defoe's admiring words, 'where No Man but himself Durst go at this Time'. From Dumfries, he followed Hepburn and his flock to the mountains of Galloway, sidling Merrick and the dented peaks of the Uplands. Passing himself off as Allen, Pierce worked his way on Hepburn's 'Most Resolute' disciples. He too was struck cold in admiration of their fervour. Pierce stood in a field amongst 'a Vast Congregation, Severall of which Came 24 Miles on Foot to hear' Hepburn. They remained in the minister's thrall as he preached and prayed 'without Intermission near 7 houres'. The 'first fury' that Defoe feared the Covenanters would exhibit to outsiders must have abated as Pierce was able to talk at length with some of Hepburn's most prominent and powerful followers, arguing with them about the improvidence of a western uprising and forcing them to see that any attempt to ally with Jacobites constituted a violent betrayal of their ideals. Most impressive of all, Pierce was able to spend a full three days with Hepburn himself.

⸸

Defoe hungrily awaited Pierce's news as the city around him observed Christmas. Feeling powerless, and perhaps a little jealous of his adventures, Defoe sought to aid Pierce's mission by gathering letters from Dissenting ministers throughout England – tapping into the same group who acted as his distribution agents. Working the network, Defoe sent missives on to Hepburn 'to quallifye and perswade him not to peace Onely but to perswade his people alike'. If he could move the shepherd, he would move the flock. But Defoe was distracted. The city felt tight with tension. The presence of Highlanders continued to menace him. He was certain that there were 'Some Secret Designs on foot'. Everything teetered, and he was not sure which way it would tip: as he told Harley, 'it will be Either a Union or all Confusion in a few weeks more'.

Besides, the cover he worked so hard to maintain was slipping. His fierce advocacy for the Union convinced many that he was a tool of England and the Court. For this, he was 'Openly Threatened to be the first Sacrifize'. Defoe was spooked. The threat was credible enough that he set about finding new lodgings, ears pricked to the first signs of danger. At the same time, he received news from London that threw him into further 'Disorder'. His father James Foe had died.[12] A tallow chandler by trade, but a merchant in daily business, James had risen to become a freeman of the city of London. He had ensured that his son had the education to make him a Dissenting clergyman. When Defoe set this path aside and went into business, he had James as a model of probity and guild-esteem: his father was in many ways the ideal tradesman that Defoe would later valorise in print. When Defoe went bankrupt, when he switched and changed ventures, he strayed from the path James had laid down. When he added the nobiliary French 'De' to the solid English Foe, he gave the sense that he sought something above his father. The betrayal inherent in making his own way – in seeking more than his father offered him – sat uneasily with Defoe his entire life. He raised his sense of sonly guilt to high art in *Robinson Crusoe*, which begins when the hero ignores his father's advice and chooses to go to sea. Throughout the novel, Crusoe looks back on his father's words and comes to see his turning away from them as something unnatural. When his slave Friday finds his own father, a primal longing chokes Crusoe, who can barely 'express how it moved me to see what Extasy and filial Affection had work'd in this poor *Savage* at the Sight of his Father'.[13] In life and in fiction the Prodigal son returned too late, arriving home after the father's will has been opened and read. In the novel, Crusoe's family had long presumed him dead and left him nothing. In life, Defoe was made executor of his father's estate but was restricted by provisions that ensured what he spent furnished his children's needs and not his debts – the caveat a final note of paternal disappointment.[14]

†

When Pierce returned in the last days of December, Defoe was still disjointed by grief and regret. Nonetheless, he was thoroughly impressed by Pierce's accomplishments. In Defoe's estimation, Pierce did 'Such Service there as No Man in Scotland but himself Could have done'. In the three days he spent with Hepburn, he managed to break through the fear and prejudice that isolated the preacher and rendered him a source of terror. Pierce 'Opened' Hepburn's 'Eyes' and, in turn, showed Defoe (and, through him, Harley) that Hepburn had been 'Misrepresented' to the world. As these barriers broke down in the minister's company, Pierce became increasingly confident that there was no longer any 'Danger' from Hepburn; 'Unless', that is, 'Some New Artifice Succeed to Inflame' his followers. The result should not undersell the difficulty of Pierce's mission. Indeed, Defoe's spy found that Jacobite agents had reached the Hebronites before he did and had almost succeeded in forging a Jacobite–Covenanter alliance. With support from France lacking, the Scottish Jacobites turned to the Covenanters as an alternate source of men and money.[15] Pierce's own assessment was that Hepburn was 'Mad man Enough' to brook this marriage of convenience. But under Pierce's persuasive hand, he turned away from it, publicly disavowing the Jacobite overtures. Hepburn's subdual was so complete that Lockhart believed (without corroboration) that the preacher had been turned Court spy by Defoe's man in the west.[16]

In public, Defoe extended Pierce's work by downplaying the rebellious inclinations of the Covenanting sects. His intent was to lessen the hazard of a western uprising in the process. In an issue of the *Review* in early January, he assured his predominantly English readers that 'you will find no more *Presbyterians* led by the Nose in a Snare, and if the *Jacobite* Party expects any thing from ... *John Hepburn* ... they will find themselves mistaken'.[17] By telegraphing the newly established unwillingness of Covenanters to ally with Jacobites, he takes the gust out of any potential alliance.

In the backstairs of power, Defoe tried to leverage Pierce's success for his own benefit. Pro-Union Scots like the Earl of Leven were impressed by Pierce and wanted him to return to the field to keep the tumult of the west at bay and to cut the Covenanters off from any incoming Franco-Jacobite force. As head of the military in Scotland, Leven believed that the counterintelligence work Defoe coordinated was needed to help secure Scotland from uprising and invasion. Defoe was willing to dispatch Pierce once again. But to keep this vital node of his intelligence (and now sabotage) network up and running he really did need more supplies from Harley or the Scottish Unionists. As he had found in England, it was easier to get support for establishing the network than to find the means, energy or interest to maintain it.

It is unclear what happened with Pierce. It does seem that Defoe's failure to secure more funds caused him to find other employers. Barely two months after extolling his achievements, Defoe could not even bring himself to write Pierce a letter of recommendation when the agent returned to England, telling Harley, 'Since Some who were fond of haveing an Agent here Employ'd him Out of my way . . . I have Not Recomended him to you.' Though he knew the difficulties of working without sufficient pay, Defoe still expected complete loyalty.[18]

⚘

The prospect of a Jacobite–Covenanter alliance unsettled Queensberry. Not willing to leave Scotland's protection to England alone, he dispersed misinformation agents to Jacobite strongholds to pass the message that the Union would re-establish Episcopacy and clear the way for James Francis Edward Stuart to succeed Anne as monarch. This whisper campaign was less than successful.[19] The message was too obviously intended to dupe. For the most part, Jacobites remained strongly opposed to the Union. As we saw, Queensberry also sent agents west to infiltrate potential Cameronian rebellions, chief amongst them Cunningham of Aiket. If his own account is to be believed, it was another of Queensberry's putative agents who played the most decisive role in preventing anti-Union forces from aligning themselves with England's foreign enemies. John Ker of Kersland took credit for disrupting a Franco-Jacobite-Covenanter league that, if it came together, would see the Scottish parliament 'raised', Britain descend into 'a Field of Blood' and 'Liberties' all over Europe decimated.[20]

According to Harley's spy Ogilvie, Ker was considered a 'rogue' by his fellow Scots.[21] An Ayrshire man who married into a prominent Cameronian family, Ker styled himself a leader of the sect – though few Cameronians ever followed him. Two decades after the Union passed, he published a memoir apologising for his role in bringing it about. The apology has none of the humility of the genre. Ker aggrandises his role, telling of how he infiltrated Cameronians at Queensberry's request, boasting that he was chosen by the Commissioner because he was the only one 'likely' to 'prevail' with the sect. He tells of how he was with the Cameronians when they burnt the articles at Dumfries (in fact it was the Hebronites), and alerted Queensberry that in order to maintain his cover he would have to take part in burning houses of pro-Union Scots. However, his key achievement – or the key reason for regret – was that he went with the Cameronian delegation to secret negotiations at Sanquhar in Nithsdale. There, the radical Covenanters met with Highlanders, who sought an alliance. The plan formulated by Jacobite agents sent from Versailles and St Germain was to 'Snare' the Cameronians. These agents encouraged the Highlanders to downplay their Jacobitical motivations and get the Cameronians to march on Edinburgh from the south at the same time as the Highlanders marched from the north. The pretence was that the force was simply intended to prevent the Union and remove the government. As Ker saw it, the march and the alliance behind it would give encouragement to the French, who would finally have sufficient backing to invade and install the putative James III and VIII as King. At the meeting, Ker exposed this trap and managed to persuade the Cameronians that the fight for true independence needed a broader national coalition, one that could not simply remove the current government but rebuild one. The Cameronians backed out and the plan crumbled.[22]

Historians have found no record of the meeting at Nithsdale, where one should really exist.[23] Queensberry's allies doubt Ker was ever employed by the Duke.[24] Ker was chronically indebted and though he claims 'Money was never my Master' and not the mover or 'Motive' of his actions, it certainly gave him good motive to puff his story for sales.[25] Even Lockhart, who was inclined to believe some of

Ker's tales, had to admit that the supposed spy 'found means to ingratiate himself with several people of no great rank, from whom he picked up stories'.[26] It certainly looks like Ker took accounts of Cunningham's work for Queensberry and fused them with rumours about Pierce's very real contribution. Ker rightly identified that preventing an alliance between Covenanters and Jacobites in the Highlands was crucial to the passage of the Treaty of Union. Defoe's instincts about Scotland – honed by the intelligence he gathered from human and open sources – led him to recruit and deploy a spy who was able to do just that.

Ker was an unabashed fabulist. But that is not to say there is no truth to his *Memoirs.* One fact, verified by Harley's own spies, was that Louis XIV and the exiled Court at St Germain looked at the rumblings in the west and Highlands with an eye to turning the 'Commotions' to their 'Advantage'. To exploit the tensions and make a play for global power, France 'sent some Agents and Emissaries ... in order to increase the Flame, and lay a Foundation for a new Revolution'.[27] The most dangerous of them was Colonel Nathaniel Hooke.

⸸

Traditionally the Highlands encompassed everything above the line that crosses from Helensburgh on the northern reach of the Firth of Clyde to Stonehaven, just south of Aberdeen. For the government in Edinburgh, this vast cut of country presented a problem. Separated from the south by language, the Highlands resisted all forms of centralised control. Though not monolithic in politics or religion, the region remained the country's firmest redoubt of Catholicism and Jacobitism. It was home to a significant Episcopalian population too. The demographics and culture of the region meant that the Highlands was the place that kept the promise of the auld alliance with France burning brightest. A further challenge for Unionists was that clan loyalty was still a principal affiliation: in the Highlands, military power cathected to local war lords and was not easily brought to heel by feelings of national sentiment.

The Highland clans were well armed, hardened by geography and inspirited by a glorious military history. Ogilvie warned Harley that these were 'resolute' men. From 1705, when the spy first heard of French plans to invade Scotland if the Union passed, he reported that all French attempts would hinge on the Highlands. French troops would land in Scotland's north and enter the British Isles from there. Even if the French were defeated, they could 'retire into the Highlands where they could always defend themselves or make a good capitulation'.[28] During Defoe's own tour through the region many years later, he found a place filled with noble seats, many of them sympathetic to the Stuarts. The sympathy and shared purpose between clan government and the Stuart monarchs was born, as Alan Macinnes has shown, from a complementary sense of paternalistic rule. Just as the clan chiefs were entrusted with the customary protection of their lands and people, so too was the House of Stuart the 'rightful trustee of Scotland'. The clan patrimonies in the Jacobite view were bonded to King and land. The loyal chiefs could no more forsake their rightful King than give up their own birthright.[29] Between the chiefly estates and the towns that gathered around them were rock-cropped mountains difficult to traverse, and dense pine forests that entangled travellers in their growth. The Highlands, as a result, were hard to penetrate but easy to defend, a fact that had been borne out since the Romans first ventured north. Defoe's own guide through the Highlands noted as much when he reached the Firth of Tay in the northeast. This was the point of the Roman Empire's 'utmost Bounds': their best general, Julius Agricola, made it further 'into the Heart of *Highlands*' than all before him. But even he stopped at the Tay when he saw no 'End of the barbarous Country', nothing but an indomitable wild of men and mountains.[30]

When Harley and Hedges scooped intelligence that Hooke was headed to the Highlands, they had to act. In late August, the Secretaries of State got word that their agents had captured a spy from St Germain. Upon interrogation, the man revealed that a certain Captain Carron, 'a midlle siz'd man, of a flushy complexion, with freckles' and wearing 'a light periwig', was currently acting as a courier between the exiled Court and the Scottish Jacobites, ferrying men and messages across the North Sea. Harley warned Queensberry to be on the lookout for Carron. The English spymaster had 'verry good information that

Colonell Hooke is sent from France just now a second tyme to Scotland to negotiate affaires with the discontented there, and to hinder the Union'.

It was assumed that Carron would sail up the north coast of Scotland, making land at Cruden Bay in Aberdeenshire, so that he could take Hooke to Slains Castle.[31] On its east side the mortared granite of Slains is moulded into the sheer cliff, giving occupants a good view of the North Sea and all incoming vessels. On the west, the moss-topped cliff drops off into a deep gulch, as if the sea had hewn the castle a moat. Slains belonged to Anne Hay, Countess of Erroll, the sister of the Duke of Perth, a principal courtier at St Germain. The Countess was a Jacobite agent and was in contact with Mary of Modena.[32] By 1705 she was part of a group that called themselves the Juncto. Other members included her son, Charles Hay, Earl of Erroll, along with Earl Marischal and David Murray, Viscount Stormont.[33] The Countess used Slains as a way station, welcoming agents from France there before moving them inland to Delgatie Castle, another of her properties. Delgatie had specially designed secret passages that could keep someone like Hooke safe before the Countess sent him out across the Highlands and Lowlands. That Harley knew about parts of this underground track suggests a good countersurveillance operation. That he tasked Queensberry with intercepting Hooke, despite acknowledging his danger and importance, suggests that Harley had limited manpower so far north. The most he offered the Scottish Commissioner was a warning: Hooke 'is a bold, dextrous man, and if he could be taken knows very much'.[34]

Harley's assessment was right. Hooke was bold and shrewd. He knew much because he had reached the highest echelons of the French secret service. As one of the few truly professional spies of the period, he gained a reputation for being 'as cunning and as designing a fellow as any in Europe'.[35] Born in Ireland in 1664 to an English mother, Hooke's background did not foretell a career as a Franco-Jacobite agent; if anything, it promised the opposite. Like Defoe's, Hooke's family were nonconformist in confession and whiggish in their politics. After a privileged schooling that reflected his parents' aspirations more than their means, the future spy left his place at the mainstream Protestant Trinity College Dublin for institutions more open to religious and political dissent, studying first at the University of Glasgow and then at Sidney Sussex, Cambridge – Cromwell's old college and still the training ground for English radicals.[36] At Cambridge he was drawn to the Earl of Shaftesbury. When the Whig grandee fled to Holland to avoid a treason trial after his unsuccessful attempt to exclude James Duke of York from the line of succession, Hooke followed him.

With Shaftesbury as its political nucleus and John Locke as its tutelary spirit, the exiled community in the Dutch Republic became the centre of English radicalism. It was there that plans took hold for a more militant attempt to remove the newly crowned James II from the throne that was led in England by the Duke of Monmouth. When the rebellion collapsed, Hooke was spirited back from the battlefield of Sedgemoor to the Netherlands by a clandestine Whig network, moved through an underground channel of safe houses and transports from London to continental Europe.

Hooke was pursued through the political wilderness by James II's agents. After Monmouth was executed for treason, Hooke's fate became clear. With few options left, Hooke had his damascene moment. He converted to Catholicism. Despite the circumstances, it does seem that the conversion was genuine. In later years when it would have been far easier to return to the Protestant fold, he kept to the old faith. In the eyes of the cynics, Hooke's conversion served its purpose. Shortly after renouncing the religion and politics that had been his family legacy, Hooke received a pardon from James II and entered his service.

James' triumph over Monmouth did little to stem the growing movement to replace him. As ferment thickened into revolution and parliament invited William and Mary to accede to the throne, Hooke went home to Ireland to fight with his King. Serving as both soldier and spy, his main function was as a messenger between Irish troops and English and Scottish Jacobites. As useful as his knowledge of the Whig underground proved in the countersurveillance aspects of this role, Hooke could not escape the force and fervour of William's agents. Determined to rout out all Jacobite lines of communication, when William's men uncovered Hooke in Cumbria in 1689 they arrested him and took him to the Tower of London.

It was in the raven-ringed prison where Hooke first met Hamilton (at this time known as the Earl of Arran). Arran had been sent there the previous November for a characteristically imperious act. The young Scottish lord fought with James II right up until he left England. Returning to Whitehall, he met William but refused to acknowledge him as King. Arran's rebuff pushed William to display his monarchic power. The new King sent Arran to the Tower. The gossip traced back to Jonathan Swift is that Arran's father (perhaps guided by Duchess Anne) advised William to lock away his errant son as a means to bring him to line.[37] Whatever the case, the surroundings gave Hooke an inflated sense of Arran. Blocked in by dismal grey, the young Scottish noble looked every bit the political prisoner. Hooke struggled to shake this sense of him, even as Hamilton continually disappointed the hopes of Jacobites.

When Hooke's brother, a lawyer, managed to secure a writ of habeas for his release, Hooke did not slink back into London life, though it would have been easier to do so. Instead, he returned home to Ireland once more, to serve James II as both spy and solider. He fought alongside James at the Battle of the Boyne, where the former King suffered a defeat decisive enough to force him to flee. Hooke followed his deposed leader to France. In the hardscrabble world of exile, Hooke distinguished himself. The spy's knowledge of England, his experience on the battlefield and in the world of cloak and dagger impressed French foreign minister de Torcy – so much so, that the minister inducted Hooke into his own league of spies.

†

Hooke repaid Torcy's favour with the energy of a man redeemed. Moving between his roles on the battlefield and in the field of espionage, his first missions in 1703 were geared to aiding France's war efforts. In particular, Hooke looked for ways to weaken the Anglo-Dutch alliance. On the English side, he initiated lines of communication with politicians susceptible to his influence: first amongst them the Whig lord, John Somers, who had sought Hooke out through a contact in London. Hooke took Somers' overture as a sign that tensions over the Hanoverian succession were ripe for manipulation. He relayed to Torcy that the Hanoverians had sent money through the Duke of Argyll to gild the advent of a new hereditary line. Though he advocated French funds to counterbalance this, Hooke sensed that the Hanoverian investment reflected a deeper rift. To turn this division to France's advantage, Hooke approached both Whigs and Tories.[38]

Hooke tried to get Whig support for a second Stuart restoration. His intent was to persuade Somers that the return of the self-proclaimed James III and VIII – with limits to preserve the Anglican kingdom – was the best path for his party. Fearing Godolphin's influence, his plan was to appeal to Marlborough personally by framing the Stuart return as a way for the General to add to his coffers. A Stuart return would mean peace with France. But even if Hooke failed, the divisions he stoked in the process were likely to weaken England militarily and geopolitically.

When the battles of the war paused for winter at the end of 1703, Hooke took himself to Aix-la-Chapelle, where the generals and higher officers on both sides gathered. There he met with Marlborough and Orkney (Hamilton's brother), adopting the cover story that he was in France under duress. In Aix-la-Chapelle, his attempts to sound out English and Scottish officers had some success. There were Scots interested in supporting an invasion. But for the most part, the officers were more interested in engaging him as a double agent. One recruiter was a little too loose, blurting out that a series of English nobles had approached James Francis Edward Stuart with false shows of support to distract the exiled prince from any attempt against England's rulers. This explained Somers' overture and why Marlborough seemed so open. Realising that the duper had become dupe, Hooke redoubled his efforts on the one aspect of the plan that still looked workable: an invasion of Scotland.[39]

Hooke told Torcy that 'four thousand men' sent from France 'with a good quantity of weapons' would rouse 'the Duke of Hamilton and other lords' into a concerted force, the combined strength of which would make the exiled prince 'master of Scotland in a very short time and would put him in a position to enter into England'. Hooke believed that the only way to unite all the Scottish factions to take up arms 'for common cause' was to publish a proclamation and distribute it at the head of the invading force. The statement needed to emphasise that the Scots had tried to live with the English but that certain parties in England were now trying to colonise Scotland. The only way to protect Scotland's independence was to take up arms. Hooke advised his French masters that the statement would have to downplay the Jacobitical impetus for the invasion.

The plan was interesting but it had to be filed away. After the exposure of the Scotch plot, there was little appetite in France for a Scottish adventure. But things soon realigned. The Franco-Bavarian army was defeated at Blenheim and France needed a new way to regain the kind of military advantage that would allow it to sue for a good peace. The trial of the *Worcester* crew brought Anglo-Scottish tensions to the brink by force of public outcry. The passage of the Act of Security showed a Scotland willing to break from England and gave leave for nobles to muster arms and men. Hooke and his French handlers agreed in 1705 that now was the time to put it to action.

Before he departed, Hooke travelled to St Germain to get Mary of Modena's blessing. Versailles officially left the management of Scotland to the exiled English Court. And yet the Court was so leaky and inept that Hooke had to keep St Germain briefed without divulging any information that if leaked could hamper his mission. When Hooke told Mary he would soon travel to Scotland, he asked her not to tell even her closest advisors that Louis had trusted him with the Scottish affair.

Endorsed by Torcy and Louis himself, Hooke's mission was preparatory. He had to see if the country was 'united' enough to supply a credible military force; and he had to chart the path this force could take southwards to England. Crucial to his mission was to win allies in the Scottish leadership. The French King hoped Hooke could make his way through the Scottish parliament. At the very least, he should confirm that Hamilton in particular and Jacobite nobles more generally had the 'courage to free themselves' from the 'yoke of England'. A frigate, *L' Heroine*, was arranged by the foreign minister. Hooke would leave from Dunkirk as soon as the winds blessed it.

The winds did not favour Hooke. It was August before his frigate finally made its way. Carrying letters from Louis XIV to Hamilton, the Jacobite Duke of Gordon and Earl of Erroll, Hooke arrived at Slains, where he was to meet the group of lords who had slowly and secretly built the base for a potential rising. When Hooke met Gordon and Erroll, the impression he got was that if France offered support, these peers would rise to the occasion. Hamilton was the exception. The reports Hooke had from the Scottish nobles and from his other sources tarnished the image of Hamilton he had formed in the Tower of London. The Duke was apparently tetchy and reticent, more concerned with protecting himself than defending Scotland's independence.

In the most fulsome attempt yet to bring Hamilton back to the cause, Hooke undertook the dangerous trip to Edinburgh – hoping to confront the Duke directly at his residence. Hooke dodged enemy agents and slipped through the capital to Holyrood. For the final part of the journey he was escorted by a Jacobite agent codenamed Madame de Largo, who brought him into the Palace by a 'circuitous' route, carefully avoiding rooms occupied by Queensberry and Argyll – lest the spy fall into the hands of the Union's leaders. Harley knew of the path Hooke took after the fact. The English spymaster was able to anticipate Hooke's steps in 1707 when he repeated his mission, again trying to firm up Scottish support for invasion. In 1705, though, Hooke went largely unimpeded.

Hamilton met Hooke in the dark, explaining to the spy that 'he trusted no one'. Those alerted to Hooke's mission would ask Hamilton if he had seen the French agent. If they met in darkness, Hamilton could swear an oath that he had not. Even in the shrouds, the first meeting was warm. Hamilton seemed pleased to be visited by the man he called his 'prison comrade'. The Duke was 'touched by the honour' that Louis had shown him in sending Hooke directly. He was pleased as well with the French King's letter, leaving the room briefly so that he could read it in the light. He would take his time and offer a proper response later, he told Hooke. Hooke thought nothing of it in the moment. Over the course of his meetings, as the Duke parried any attempt to put name to deed, Hooke could not help but see it as yet another means of prevarication. In that first huddled meeting, Hamilton complained about the state of the opposition. There was 'no union' against the Union and 'even less vigour'. Queensberry had money from London and had bought influence. The only way to counterbalance it, he told Hooke, was for Louis to send Hamilton an allowance, which he could then use to buy the favour of the burgh representatives. With this group under his influence, he was confident he could prevent the Union.

Hamilton spoke with 'fire and speed'. Hooke could not wedge a word in. When he tried, the Duke simply repeated himself, rehearsing the reasons for his hesitancy. To wit, Hamilton worried that the Scots campaign was merely a 'diversion', and that France would turn away from Scotland once the mission had yielded its tactical gain. Hooke tried to reassure him that this was not the case; that it was time 'to take advantage' of England's predicament. The nation had 'so great a war on its hands'; 'its troops so far away'. Never would Scotland be in a better place to strike a blow 'for its independence and its freedom'. As the two talked into the night, Hamilton seemed to soften to Hooke's position. The spy could not budge the Duke to sign on to the final course of his plan: the restoration of James III and VIII as King of England and Scotland. Hamilton's resistance was troubling. It seemed only to confirm the suspicions Erroll voiced to Hooke: that Hamilton wanted two separate kingdoms for the simple fact that he might then rise to Scotland's throne.

Between meetings Hooke and Hamilton exchanged letters, deploying de Largo as their courier. Reading them, Hooke mused to his French handlers, 'I believe I had a sense that to make the Duke of Hamilton Act, I should not insist too much about what concerns the King of England [i.e. the exiled prince].' Hamilton took the line that all plans should wait until the death of Queen Anne. Again, the two sat without light, their second meeting dragging until four in the morning. Hooke's tone was conciliatory. He tried to assure Hamilton that France did not want to interfere but simply to help them preserve their sovereign rights. The Duke clung to the self-justification that in his mind shielded his hypocrisy and talked constantly about the Jacobites, whose 'impudent zeal' split the opposition and alienated allies. Hooke was more wary now. He knew that this back and forth over the form of the invasion would serve only to delay it. Before Hooke slipped into the frosted morning air, Hamilton set him the impossible task of bringing Jacobites to his position, one where uprising did not automatically result in the restoration of the main Stuart line.

Frustrated with Hamilton, Hooke continued meeting with other Scottish nobles. Because Hamilton insisted that Hooke keep their meeting secret, he prevented the agent from strengthening the bonds of the opposition. Thinking that Hamilton had not met Hooke, the other Jacobite nobles grew even more distrustful. They were willing to commit to Hooke's plan but they insisted on one condition, 'that there be no other hidden intent'. They did not want to be Hamilton's 'dupes' or tools. If he did not trust them and throw his full weight to the cause, they would pursue a restoration without him. The distrust went both ways. Hooke had given Erroll money to defray his expenses. Hamilton assumed that the spy had a similar amount for him and was withholding it. Hamilton suspected (falsely) that, like his family, Hooke was trying to manage his finances – to prevent him from funds that he believed were rightfully his.

In their final meeting Hamilton finally agreed to candlelight. Aside from dropping the precautions, nothing else had really changed. Hamilton still vented at the Jacobites, claiming in a phrase that Hooke saw as a projection that 'they will speak a lot, but nothing will ever come from their talk'.[40] Hooke had turned: he would pursue the other Jacobites, keeping Hamilton at a remove, waiting until he did something that affirmed he could be trusted. As he left Holyrood on the final leg of his tour through provincial Scotland, he hoped there would be a way to bring this popular figurehead into the arms of rebellion. It was not to be – just yet. A day after the final meeting between the spy and Duke, Hamilton went to parliament and put forth the fatal proposal that gave the Queen the right to choose the Union commissioners.

Returning to France that week, Hooke delivered his report to Torcy and the King. Largely positive, despite his failure to acquire Hamilton's endorsement, the upshot was that the people of Scotland stood against the Union. A select group of nobles could lead them. Indeed, he had signatures and firm commitments from amongst others Erroll, Panmure, Stormont and Drummond.[41] The uprising at the head of a French army could in the best case restore their ally James III and VIII to the throne. And in the worst, tear England away from the European fronts. Ever the strategist, Hooke advised that it was better to avoid places like the west where Presbyterians opposed a Jacobite restoration and focus on parts of the Highlands and border counties where support for the cause was strongest.

⸸

There was little action on the Scottish front until 1706, when the Grand Alliance led by Marlborough continued its streak of victories against French armies. Increasingly desperate, the French foreign council re-examined Hooke's plan and eventually accepted it. As the Union was about to pass, Hooke was ordered back to Scotland, to once again survey the conditions. This time, however, he would be followed by French troops – or so he was promised. The spy's new task was to channel resistance to the Union towards a war on British soil.

Harley's intelligence led him to believe that Hooke would return to Scotland that year. Talk spread that James III and VIII – 'the Pretender' to the throne in Hanoverian eyes – was poised to land near Aberdeen in the final months of 1706. Another version maintained he had already landed in the Highlands. Carried on the wings of hope – and fear – these rumours tensed the Scottish government into high alert. Patrols were increased. Some significant Jacobite assets were intercepted crossing the North Sea.

In reality, French reluctance to commit fully to an invasion plan – coupled with difficulties coordinating Versailles, St Germain and Scotland – meant that Hooke was only dispatched in March 1707. The spy left behind a pregnant wife. Always the professional, he told her nothing of his mission. Not where he was going, nor when – or if – he would return.

Hooke must have felt a sense of déjà vu as he retraced the steps of his old mission. As in 1705, in 1707 the winds were against him. One difference this time was that Hooke was accompanied by Moray, a lieutenant colonel in the French service, who recruited his brother for the mission as well.[42] The rationale was that the two relatively unknown agents might move more easily in certain parts of Scotland than Hooke could. As they waited in Dunkirk, Hooke adjusted the plan, sending Moray's brother to Holland or Ostend so that he might find a boat to England and from there make his way north, engaging Jacobites in the border counties before crossing to Scotland.

When Hooke and Lieutenant Colonel Moray finally landed at Cruden Bay and took the steep climb to Slains, it was evident that things had changed. The passage of the Act of Union to the 'great discontent and despite the will of the nation' galvanised the Juncto. The Countess of Erroll told of how the group was now willing to proceed without Hamilton. The Juncto had managed to draw to their cause Lockhart and others who earlier looked to Hamilton. At first Hooke was unsure. He had remained in correspondence with the Duke and still saw him, despite his manifest unreliability, as a necessary player in any uprising. The Countess' response to Hooke's demurral was to warn him to proceed carefully. The Juncto had good reason to suspect that Hamilton passed intelligence to London.[43]

Harley's spy John Ogilvie infiltrated the Juncto after the fact, gleaning intelligence from the group about Hooke's mission. As he reported to the English spymaster, Hooke was hosted by the Countess of Erroll, using Slains as a base for a cross-country operation. In Ogilvie's startled phrase, Hooke 'did travel up and down boldly as an English drover from place to place'. Hooke spent the time negotiating with sympathetic nobles over funds and troops. Worryingly for Harley, Ogilvie noted that Hooke was willing to promise that the would-be James III and VIII could accede to the throne while maintaining the established religion. Hooke now had the power to offer something that might remove the barrier between Presbyterians opposed to the Union and Scottish Jacobites.[44]

While the general outlines of Ogilvie's brief were correct, Hooke's mission was far more delicate and subtle than Harley's spy allowed. For one, he did not boldly traverse the country. Hooke was deeply reluctant to enter Edinburgh this time. After the parliamentary session was brought to a close, the city emptied out. A stranger would have been gravely conspicuous. The problem Hooke faced was that

Hamilton remained in the capital, making it difficult for Hooke to reach him. As his time in Scotland drew on, Hooke increasingly suspected that this difficulty was intentional, that Hamilton's excuse that he was too ill to travel might have been a ruse. Hooke moved between Slains and the estates of Viscount Stormont, a Juncto member, and the Earl of Strathmore a fellow Jacobite, whose residence was near Scone.

Though he could not drive throughout the country, he and Moray still managed to cover a lot of ground. Because Moray was too well known south of the Tay, Hooke sent him north 'to make progress with the Highlanders'. This left Hooke free to pursue negotiations with the leaders of the northeastern families. Their tactic to 'split the kingdom' was motivated in part by a desire to move away from Hamilton.[45] With Hamilton's betrayals ever more patent, Hooke noted that the loyalties of Scots across the classes gradually turned to Atholl in the north and the Duke of Gordon in the south.[46] An alliance with Gordon would carry the added benefit of his formidable wife, Elizabeth Howard, who had spent considerable time and diplomatic effort winning over the radical Presbyterians of the southwest.[47]

The mission was more successful than that of 1705. But Hooke remained cautious. He kept in steady contact with the captain of the frigate that brought the spies to Scotland, readying him for a quick escape. Much of Hooke's diplomacy was carried out on paper. Hooke deployed the Countess of Erroll as a messenger, trusting her experience with coded letters and her expertise with invisible ink. He also relied on her confidants, particularly Mr Hall, a priest, who acted as go-between for Hooke and Hamilton. The chief aim was to bring together disparate groups of Jacobites (the Juncto, Hamilton's followers and Catholics), Episcopalians and Presbyterians who opposed the Union. In writing and in conversation, Hooke worked to break down barriers between them: 'I made them see . . . the impossibility of freeing themselves from slavery while these jealousies persisted'. Now that the Union existed in fact, circumstances did a lot of this work for him.

Hooke's work gained the speed of success as he met with Catholics and with Jacobite lords sympathetic to the Juncto. The reports he got from the latter gave him a sense that their vassals were asking for 'permission to rise up, reproaching them that the nobility allowed the homeland to be sold and ruined'. Hooke still wanted Hamilton's support. He recognised that the Duke was 'the soul of the whole affair',[48] and so appealed to the Duke's better nature through Mr Hall, sending a letter that implored Hamilton to rise to his destined heights, for 'it was now in his power to cover himself with immortal honour, and to render himself greater than any of his ancestors'. Hooke emphasised that the moment to act and redeem himself was now and 'it would never return; that he would ruin not only his country but himself, the English having been too much irritated by him not to crush him'. Hooke was astute in pointing out that Hamilton was wrong to hang his hopes on English preferment. Convincing as Hooke's rhetoric was, the only response Hamilton mustered was that he was ill.[49]

Hooke proceeded with 'great restraint', not knowing if Hamilton had lost all currency with the Presbyterians of the southwest or whether his mother's connections still bought him their support. He still had some backers amongst the nobility and Hooke was unwilling to cast off any potential allies. In delicate negotiations, Hamilton asked France for ten thousand troops, far more, Hooke knew, than Louis was willing to commit. Though Hooke carried letters from the putative James III and VIII, Hamilton claimed this was not enough to confirm St Germain's backing. The Duke demanded a letter from Mary of Modena as well. Hooke was now convinced that the Duke was playing him, telling Torcy that if the exiled Queen had written to Hamilton, 'he would have no doubt imagined some other cause for complaint'; that Hamilton knew all too well that the prince would not have written without his mother's permission. It was at this time that Hooke learnt Hamilton was not nearly as sick as he had made out.

And so Hooke sidestepped the Duke, firming plans without him. He received assurances from Presbyterians in Clydesdale, Galloway, Aire, Kirkcudbright and Tweeddale that they were 'resolved to take up arms' against the united government 'and raise thirteen thousand men'. More importantly, they had the means to 'sustain them'. Their offer was contingent on Hooke's promise that any invasion would preserve the established Presbyterian Church. Hooke also secured backing from Atholl, who, sources told him, was in military terms 'absolutely the most powerful Lord in Scotland'. The Jacobite lords began to circulate a memorandum outlining their commitment to a rising backed by a French invasion. Sensing his exclusion, Hamilton and his allies were outraged. One, Viscount Kilsyth, confronted Hooke, arguing that he had purposefully sidelined Hamilton: 'I replied that I had no such intention', that the Duke 'excluded himself'. He added that the nobles 'are resolved to act without him if he continues to play them as he did'. The goad was not entirely truthful as many in the group refused to send the memorandum to Hamilton, anxious he would leak it to Queensberry or England.[50]

Fearing irrelevancy, Hamilton finally agreed to meet with Hooke. To the Earl of Erroll it was clear that the Duke was 'afraid that the design would succeed without him'.[51] In a series of letters and messages carried by Hall, Hamilton asked for more men than before, this time requesting fifteen thousand troops. He also advised Hooke that the Jacobites should turn their focus to the political tensions in England between Marlborough, Godolphin and the Whigs and should perhaps seek a new alliance with the Whigs who were on the rise. When pushed on why he had increased his ask, Hamilton asserted that 'no one will suffer more by the Union than himself'. Hooke's retort was brutally swift. He reminded the Duke that this was not the case, as post-Union he was now entitled to the privileges of English peers who, unlike their Scottish counterparts, could not be arrested for debt.[52]

When Hooke asked Erroll to raise a signal at Slains, calling the frigate back to Cruden Bay, he had not yet had a reply from Hamilton. What he did carry back to France was a firmed-up plan. His scouting told him Leith was the best landing place for the French fleet. He had commitments from Atholl of six thousand men; Gordon offered a further four thousand, the Marquis of Drummond and Count of Breadalbane three thousand, Erroll and Marischal put forth a further six hundred horses and dragoons, Stormont sixteen hundred horses and dragoons to serve near the English border and fifteen hundred in Angus. Perth offered four thousand infantrymen and four hundred dragoons with horses. Hooke was also increasingly confident that the Presbyterians of the southwest would put aside differences that before the Union seemed insuperable and join a force able to undo the Union before it took proper hold. He was confident, too, that this force was finally enough to bring about a commitment from Louis XIV's most hesitant advisors. If they sent five thousand troops and arms for a twenty-thousand-strong Scottish force, France could drive its greatest foe to the depths of civil war.[53]

CHAPTER 9

THE ACT OF UNION

Disappointed by the unruliness of the Union debate, Paterson produced his own, publishing the minutes of the fictional Wednesday Club: a group of enlightened merchants whose methodical discussions were designed to offset any final objections to the Treaty. Released in 1706, the Club's proceedings were meant to style the content and tone of extra-parliamentary dialogue – to allay concerns before merchants in London and Edinburgh took them up with members of the Scottish Estates. Unlike Defoe's polemical dialogues, Paterson's did not give sufficient air to the opposing position. In attempting to short-circuit the argument to his favour, Paterson exposed the fragility of his optimism. Nowhere was this more evident than on the question of the salt tax.

Article eight of the Treaty allowed seven years' leeway on taxing salt, after which the tax would double the price of a peck for the typical Scottish buyer. Adopting the persona of Mr May, Paterson dismissed the worries of other Club members, making the unsupported claim that salt employed in fisheries would be essentially free from tax and that salt producers 'will have a great deal of benefit by the Union, since it will create a much greater consumption and demand'. Skirting the perspective of the average consumer, May's view won out.[1]

Not everyone was so serene. In letters written to the Earl of Sunderland in December 1706, Mar confessed, 'There is nothing of the Treaty I'm now so afraid of here as the salt.' Resistance to the tax was fierce enough that Mar feared it would turn MPs against 'the Union in generall'.[2] The occasion for the letters was Sunderland's appointment as Secretary of State. Marlborough lobbied for the Whig lord to replace the malleable Hedges after the latter was tempted away from his position by a judgeship. The Queen opposed the reshuffle, fearing that Sunderland would shift the balance of ministerial power towards the Whigs. Marlborough triumphed, and Sunderland was made Harley's colleague, a move that isolated Harley. Mar's instincts were right. Salt became a sticking point in the Scottish parliament because it was another area – like beer – where the equity of the tax system was brought home to the people. Because of this, article eight was vulnerable to amendment.

Both Paterson and Defoe saw attempts to amend the Treaty for what they were: part of a last-ditch scheme by anti-Unionists to insert changes that might in small or cumulative ways prevent the Treaty from passing – if not in Scotland, then in England. Despite this, Paterson and Defoe clashed over the best way to push the final articles through. Paterson took Defoe to task for his willingness to compromise – a breach, he thought, of their express instructions to resist any changes to the Treaty. Defoe was affronted that Paterson dared 'Caution' him against encouraging Scottish demands for drawbacks on the export of beef and pork. Buoyed by a letter from Harley that praised his work, Defoe felt justified in his flexibility, moving and stretching according to his best judgement. Both he and Paterson had been invited to attend the Committee for calculating the Equivalent, to which parliament remitted all the thornier excise adjustments. But as Defoe snarked to Harley, he hardly saw Paterson there at all.[3] The implication is that Defoe was closer to the ground, that Paterson assumed the world was like that of the Wednesday Club and that a high-handed diktat would win out. Defoe, on the other hand, knew that the volume of Scottish imports (of beef and pork) paled against those from Ireland, making the drawback an economic non-issue. For him, the concession had to be set in the context of England's global trade. When it was, it emerged as an easy way to get the last bits of the Treaty through the parliament.[4] Looking back, Godolphin agreed. Paterson was too rigid; Defoe's approach was right.[5]

As much as beef and pork were important, both Defoe and Mar saw them as a diversion from the 'main point', which remained the tariffs on salt. When it became clear that the Scottish parliament would not pass article eight as it stood because of these tariffs, Mar and his Court partners met at Holyrood to change tack. Their aim was to persuade enough 'doubtfull members' to join them. They worked with their allies on the Committee to find possible amendments that might juice the vote. Defoe was in his element. He later boasted that he had the

> Honour to propose and draw up, by Order of the Committee of Parliament in *Scotland*, several, if not most of the Calculations, Proportions and Allowances of the Customs, Excise, Draw-backs, exemptions from Taxes, *&c.* and was particularly at the Debates in the said Committee, upon those of the Salt and Malt Taxes.[6]

This is likely an overstatement of his role, although he certainly made significant contributions. He was part of the group that proposed an exemption on the malt tax for the duration of the War of the Spanish Succession. And he was one of the thinkers who set forth two related concessions on salt. The first was that Scotland be allowed to use domestic salt in the curing process, bypassing foreign tax. The second took the Country party's demand that Scotland be exempted from the English tax on salt on the grounds that two-thirds of it was used to pay back EIC loans and qualified it, establishing that this exemption should only last seven years.[7] With these concessions, Mar and Queensberry were able to push the vote through.

Defoe was useful because he was so quick on his feet. He was able to deduce the wishes and interests of his handlers in England even when those wishes went against previous instructions. The simple fact was that Harley did not brief him often enough. Even if he did, the communication delay meant that no agent who clung to the letter of their handler's instructions could act with the speed negotiations necessitated. Beyond speed, Defoe was able to move between parliament and the Committee. By watching debates, analysing the motives of MPs, speaking to them in private, he could move the Committee towards changes that could affect the votes in the House. For Defoe, politicking of this kind was a game of shillings and pence. Some of the concessions proposed were small change and could be rationalised, even when they complicated or undermined the calculation of the Equivalent. The justification that freed him from the ledger was that most of what the Committee offered and the parliament approved could be fixed or even undone when the united parliament of Great Britain assembled. What mattered in the moment was less the precise calculation than the perception of fairness. The Scottish MPs had to feel they were getting a good deal, but not one so good that the English MPs and lords rejected it.

Defoe's actions in the Committee carried the heft of his intelligence work. He understood the business of the country and the nature of its people. From this he could easily perceive what interests brought MPs to line, and where others might be induced to act by the right bribe or promise. Though Harley did not respond as often as Defoe needed, the 'true spy' kept his master briefed up to the minute on these tactics. Defoe ensured his effectiveness in the final negotiation with this posture – and it did not go unnoticed in Whitehall. As internecine conflict in England looked like it might weaken Harley's hold, others began to seek out his man in Edinburgh.

⸸

Defoe had a longstanding relationship with the Whig leader Charles Montague, Baron Halifax. Through his brother-in-law, Robert Davis, Defoe contacted Halifax 'to offer my Service'; in particular 'to Accquaint him with Matters here'. Harley had a good working relationship with Halifax, despite their political differences. He approved of Defoe's sending him intelligence, on the condition that Defoe did 'not by any means let him imagine, You correspond with any one here, or have any motive, beside Your selfe for Your going thither'. If Defoe could keep his service to Harley hidden from Halifax, maintaining that he was in Edinburgh for personal reasons, then Harley promised him 'I will find a way to make it useful to You'.[8] Despite his distance, Harley still wanted control over the flow of intelligence and to keep the full extent of his agents hidden so that if needed he could manipulate Halifax's position on Scotland by controlling what Defoe sent him. This kind of reserve power worked well enough with potential allies, like Halifax. But within the ministry itself, the practice lost its tactical edge as Godolphin came to know more about Harley's agents in the field. Godolphin certainly felt no compunction sending Defoe his own instructions via Harley, even seeking to foreclose Defoe's freedom to move on the Committee during the final negotiations.[9]

The jostles to define Defoe's work were part of a broader play for power, in which Scotland was drawn into a fight over control of the English ministry. Godolphin, who had long relied on Junto support in the Lords, pushed for the appointment of Sunderland against the wishes of both Harley and the Queen. Compelled by the Duke and Duchess of Marlborough, Godolphin supported the appointment of Whig bishops and academic chairs. The Queen took this as an incursion on her prerogative. The triumvirate cracked, but not uniformly. Marlborough and Sarah moved further away from Harley than Godolphin did, but the division was nonetheless clear. The Marlboroughs and Godolphin thought Harley was trying to install a Tory ministry.[10] Harley feared that the duumvirs would ally with the Whigs and exclude him from power. Harley, however, had a powerful ally in the Queen. In a successful scheme to water down Marlborough's influence with the monarch, Harley installed his relative Abigail Hill at Court, priming her to supplant the Duchess of Marlborough as Anne's favourite. With Hill as his emissary, he hardened the Queen against the Whig-ward lean of her Treasurer and General.

The Court intrigue in England reached Scotland at the speed of gossip. Ever more distrustful of Godolphin, Harley had his spy Ogilvie intercept intelligence from Godolphin's Scottish connections. As Ogilvie later put it, he gave Harley 'a full account of what passed betwixt my Lord trasoror [Godolphin] and him [Seafield]', the Lord Chancellor of Scotland, allowing Harley first view of Godolphin's Scottish manoeuvrings.[11] Harley's principal fear was that the image of a Whig party in ascendence would draw Scottish MPs to their side. Though such a transfer would not have threatened the Treaty, it would have allowed Sunderland and the Whigs to sweep in and take credit for Harley's work on the eve of its completion. Harley had already seen the Squadrone – a decisive voting bloc in the Scottish Estates – drift towards the Junto; he wanted to prevent any loss of his own clout that would follow as others jumped on the bandwagon. Hamilton ventured to Hooke that perhaps the Jacobites might be able to exploit the tension between Harley and Godolphin and form an alliance with the English Whigs.[12] Hamilton's gambit was naive, but it does speak to how the shift in power in England ramified northwards, rippling across the surface of Scottish politics. As Harley and Godolphin drew further away from each other, they increasingly used Scotland as a proving ground for domestic politics, taking opposing positions on trade interests, rights and loopholes in the late stages of the negotiation to claw power from each other at the very moment the Treaty came into effect.

⸸

In parliament there was a tentative optimism amongst the Unionists. With the passage of articles eight and thirteen, the drawbacks on salt and malt were resolved. The body could now move on to article fifteen, which outlaid the Equivalent. This was the one article that, according to Defoe, 'has of it self made more noise in the World, than all the other Articles'. In his assessment, conditions were finally right to broach this final economic barrier. The '*Glasgow* Rabblers' were imprisoned 'in the Castle of *Edinburgh*'; all other 'Mobs and Rabbles ... had been suppress ... the Meeting of the Heretors ... had been Discharged by Proclamation' and the clause in the Act of Security that allowed musters 'had been repealed'. There was 'now no Room ... for violent Methods, except by open and actual Rebellion'.[13] The Equivalent was designed to paper over national divisions with money. The sum was meant to offset future contributions to national debt, ease Scotland's eventual tax increases and act as a stimulus for the nation's industry. It was also to contain reparations for the loss of Darien – a payment that mandated the dissolution of the Company. Of the £398,085.10s settled on (roughly £41 million today), nearly 60 per cent, or £232,884, was to be paid to investors in the Company of Scotland.

During the final negotiations on the Equivalent, Defoe touted his most audacious cover story. By telling all who would listen that he was 'goeing to write the hystory of the Union in folio', he managed to get 'warrants to Search the Registers and parliament books'. Defoe had proposed writing a history of the Union before, and did end up producing the first full account of the Union in 1709. By initiating the process of acquiring subscriptions for the work as the Committee wrapped up its duties, he put himself in a position to access materials that could at once inform his interventions and strengthen the factual basis of the intelligence he conveyed to Harley. When he reflected on his contribution during these pivotal final months, he revelled in the front his story offered: 'Under pretence of writing my history I have Everything Told Me.' But it was not a passive process either, as he elaborated in his boast to Harley: 'I act the Old part of Cardinall Richlieu. I have my spyes and my Pensioners In Every place, and I Confess tis the Easyest thing in the World to hire people here to betray their friends.' There is a bold shift in this analogy. Where once he compared Harley to Richelieu, it is now Defoe with his sub-agents and emissaries, distributors and informers, who acts the part of the spymaster.[14]

The formula the Committee settled on was that the Equivalent would be paid over seven years and taken primarily from customs and excise duties. As Alan Macinnes points out, because the fund was raised by increased duties on Scotland, Scotland essentially paid its own compensation, echoing Sir Walter Scott's charge that 'Scotland herself was made to pay the price given to her legislators for the sacrifice of her independence'.[15] Along with reparations, the fund helped offset the costs of standardising coinage.[16] Defoe charted the ways that the government in Scotland accounted for English coin already in circulation. Fearne kept Harley informed on the proposed means to prevent 'the bringing in of foreign coin to clog the Equivalent'. The debates acted as prelude to article sixteen, which in an effort to standardise coin in Scotland, proposed replacing Scottish silver coins with those minted to the sterling standard. In his dispatch to the English spymaster, Fearne also detailed how anger was fast turning to Paterson, for his role in promoting the Darien Company. In Fearne's report, 'All people that subscribed to the said company (except some happy persons, masters,) exclaim now against . . . Paterson [and the others] that put them upon that project.'[17] To subscribers stung by personal losses, it was clear that the nation's loss as a whole had forced Scotland's hand to Union. The anger of the country made Paterson defensive. In a series of open letters circulated privately, he pushed the idea of the Treaty as generous, depicting its terms as if they offered more than recompense for any losses, future or historical. Their access to free trade would, he argued, 'be much more than compensation'.[18]

In London, Scots watchers sat poised awaiting any bit of news or intelligence on the final articles. Mar's undersecretary Nairne found himself in a 'world of truble', combatting the rumours and misinformation that shot through the city's 'chocolate and coffee houses'. Nairne saw how doggedly Mar worked as an unofficial government manager of the negotiations, alongside Seafield and Stair, and wanted to ensure that his southern flank was sufficiently covered. He was not the only one. Whig agent John Shute returned to London, as did Mar's agent Thomas Fullarton. When he arrived, Fullarton found that the English people generally supported the Union, even with the amendments. What unnerved him was that there was an undeniable set of detractors who manipulated latent animosities in the service of the Scottish Country party. The main set of detractors were High Tories who showed a condescending prejudice against the Scots and an inveterate bias against Presbyterianism. More troubling still was that this underground opposition that 'obstructed secretly from hence' also sought to impede Mar's work 'from the other side of the water'.[19] Harley perceived the same and recalled Ogilvie to Scotland, moving his most valuable asset behind Jacobite lines back to his native land.[20]

Ogilvie's new task was to monitor, uncover and sabotage both Jacobite and Dutch interference during the final passage of the Treaty. The Jacobite threat was apparent, but Harley was now also concerned about Dutch intrusion. Writing to George Stepney, envoy-extraordinary and plenipotentiary at The Hague, Harley noted how the Union was being 'misrepresented in Holland', especially by *The Flying Post*, a newspaper written by 'a disaffected Scot', which was 'translated at Leiden'. Harley was aware that in a climate of misinformation, 'natural Envy to see any other State flourish is very readily turned into jealousy'. Fearing a challenge to their commercial strength from a united Britain, the Dutch were ready to act. Harley had good intelligence on this, telling Stepney he had 'very positive Informations that the [Dutch] States have remitted to Scotland a very considerable sum of mony to obstruct or hinder the Union'. To offset any potential obstruction, Harley asked the envoy to monitor all correspondence between Scotland and the Dutch states.[21]

Holland's interest was laid bare with the passage of article sixteen which, in standardising coinage to sterling, facilitated a better exchange and supply of currency and in the process moved Scottish merchants away from using Dutch currency as an exchange standard.[22] With the Equivalent finally agreed upon, the final economic articles passed quickly. Articles seventeen and eighteen passed on 31 December. Article seventeen standardised weights and measures and article eighteen ensured fiscal regulations and commercial law were uniform across the two nations. In Defoe's telling, 'The Seventeenth Article required no Debate at all, being what every Body acknowledged to be needful. The Eighteenth Article was so well worded, and every Thing that related to *Scotland* so well provided for, that there was very little Room for Objection.' Mar's account largely corroborates Defoe's. There was little debate on article eighteen, though Belhaven did raise the fear that its provisions would allow a British parliament to 'impose a sacramental test on Scots men', forcing them to conform to the Anglican Church in order to hold civic office. Court supporters quickly dismissed this, saying it was dealt with in the Act of Security for the Church. Belhaven's intent in voicing this fear was to delay the vote. When the Court-aligned MPs quickly added a clause further protecting Scottish religious freedom, he was outmanoeuvred.[23] With the passage of article eighteen, all the economic matters of the Treaty were settled. A major impasse had been cleared. The Scottish parliament had only the administrative aspects of the Treaty left before them. On 2 January they passed article nineteen, which preserved the 'Being and Constitution' of Scottish courts but brought them under the regulation of the united parliament. On 6 January they passed articles twenty and twenty-one, preserving, respectively, the organs of local government by maintaining heritable jurisdictions and the rights and privileges of the royal burghs.[24] Stair,

Mar and Seafield kept proceedings brisk, steering debate towards the Court's position. As they did, a nervous excitement built. There were only four articles left on the table. As each one passed, options for parliamentary resistance narrowed. It was now going to be ratification, revolution or, as it turned out, a combination of the two.

†

Money was essential to managing the vote. Whether this amounted to bribery or fair remuneration depended on one's point of view. Opponents of the Union saw every piece of money paid by the government or pledged in the Treaty as a bribe – including even the Equivalent and its reparations for Darien. Proponents of the Union, the beneficiaries of Queensberry's largesse, saw the money as fair remuneration – even as the pretexts for payments grew flimsier. Scotland was asked to sell its sovereignty on the promise of trade and empire, the benefits of which were in prospect more than in hand. The English ministry and Scottish Court party knew they had to offer some more immediate inducements to ensure the Treaty was ratified.

During the negotiations themselves, the Jacobite Lockhart assumed that the Equivalent was itself both a bribe and a cover for more extensive bribery, recording how 'a sum of money was necessary to be distributed amongst the Scots. And this distribution of it amongst the proprietors of the African Company was the cleanliest way of bribing a nation to undo themselves.' Lockhart sensed other bribes afoot. The parliament had been sitting for too long and so had degenerated 'many of its members corrupted by bribes, pensions, places and preferments'. Five years after the Union passed into law – when exposure no longer threatened the Treaty – Lockhart uncovered evidence of what he long suspected: 'that money was remitted to Scotland from England and employed in bribing members of Parliament'.

Before the final session of the Scottish parliament, the Queen ordered Godolphin to lend Scotland £20,000 (£2.1 million today) from the English Treasury, sending it to Queensberry and the Earl of Glasgow, ostensibly so that they could pay salaries still owed to the Scottish civil list. As per the Queen's instructions to the Lords of the

Treasury, the money was to be 'disposed by you . . . in such a manner as you shall find fit for our service'. Realising that the sudden injection of English money would look suspicious, Queensberry and Glasgow wrote to Godolphin asking him to cover the money's trail. It was essential, they wrote, to keep the Queen's letter to the Treasury from being read into the public record. They proposed that Nairne receive the money personally. He could pass it to the two Scottish lords, who would then distribute it off-the-books. Not only did this allow them to escape notice at the time but, as Lockhart reflected, this secrecy was doubly perfidious for it made Queensberry and Glasgow 'absolute masters' of the fund, able to distribute it 'to whom, after what manner and to what purposes they pleased'.[25] Glasgow later conceded to Harley that 'if it had been known that there had been a farthing sent from England to Scotland it would have totally disappointed the carrying on of the Union'. He was sworn to the 'greatest secrecy and privacy' by Queensberry, for had the money been discovered in the last throes of the final Scottish parliament, 'the Union had certainly broken'. Though in the end he felt some regret, Glasgow clearly supported the distribution of money at the time, advancing £6,000 of his own money so that the funds (or bribes) could be handed out efficiently.[26] After the Union came into effect, he gave an account to Godolphin about how the money was spent, begging him to burn the letter after reading.[27]

In Queensberry's hands the money became a useful tool for consolidating the pro-Union voting bloc. Of the £20,000, Queensberry kept just over £12,000 to pay his own expenses. A further £2,854 was dispersed to five members of the Squadrone, with their leader Tweeddale receiving £1,000. Queensberry's agent Cunningham of Aiket received £100.[28] It is difficult to gauge the direct effects the money had. It certainly seems as if only one or two members like Lord Elibank and the Earl of Glencairn changed their position to vote for Union; in Elibank's case for a mere £50.[29] Still, Lockhart maintained that 'the money was designed and bestowed for bribing members of Parliament'. It had to be, for 'all the persons (excepting the Duke of Atholl) on whom it was bestowed did vote for and promote the Union'.[30] Lockhart's logic does not consider how these members would have voted without being bribed. Indeed, the vast bulk already supported the Union (some more recently than others). The £1,000 given to Atholl is interesting. P. H. Scott has speculated that because Atholl was by then the most influential opponent to Union, it was worth at least attempting to win him over.[31] Set in a broader context, though, and we see that payment was only part of the £1,500 owed to Atholl. Atholl was also deeply in debt to his brother Lord Dunmore. By passing the payment on to Dunmore, Atholl could keep his hands clean: he could vote against the Union while his brother, whom the payment benefited, voted for it.[32]

But bribery is not simply the exchange of money for votes. The £20,000 bolstered existing support. The strategic distribution of funds to members of the Court helped secure Mar's hope that the 'several members' whose support was peeled off by the widespread opposition on the streets 'will come about again'.[33] Money also carries its own assurance. The payment of arrears sounded a promissory note for the spoils of office. Settling the debts gave Queensberry, Mar and Seafield room to offer more. They used it to foreshadow the benefits the Equivalent would bring and to signal future office, making promises to far more than sixteen lords that they would be amongst the sixteen Scottish peers due to sit in the Lords.

In 1707 the lords would be selected and incorporated along with forty-five MPs nominated from the last Edinburgh parliament but would have to face elections the following year (the MPs in their constituencies and the lords by the body of Scottish nobles). The promise of places was particularly useful when it came to attracting the support of the Squadrone. Though depleted to roughly twenty, the group could still prove decisive in a close vote. The payments to Squadrone leaders Tweeddale, Montrose (£200), Roxburghe (£500) and Marchmont (£1,104) were significant in and of themselves. But they betokened a wider effort led by Mar, Queensberry and Godolphin to bring the party to heel. Squadrone members were assured that they would be 'great men and favourites' at Anne's Court once the Union passed. Godolphin's longstanding policy of keeping the group 'on ice' – separate from both sides – underwrote this promise, which was designed to ensure the group remained bound to him personally.[34]

Squadrone members were also appointed as managers for dispersing the reparations due to the Darien Company. But as soon as the Treaty passed and it came time to actually mete out the money, Mar reneged on this offer.[35] By keeping the final members of the Squadrone united by the promise of advancement, the English ministry and Scottish Court party ensured that when the group came out for Union, the balance tipped decisively in its favour.

✢

By promising places in the Lords, Queensberry and Godolphin chanced a high-risk gambit. The level of Scottish representation in the united parliament had not yet been settled. In reality the number of representatives outlined in article twenty-two remained the final hurdle to ratification. Making Scottish nobles feel as if they would be rewarded with a place in the Lords enticed them to confirm the article. The promised rise in personal power served to offset the radical loss of Scottish representative power as a whole. For Defoe, opposition to article twenty-two centred on the idea 'That it was Dishonourable to *Scotland* to lessen the Number of her Representative, while *England* retained her entire Parliament'. Defoe believed that the number was equitable, having been calculated according to a formula that set Scotland's share in total tax and its number of people against those of England. The brute force of the arithmetic left little room for nicety, or national pride. It seemed that Scotland was being treated as merely another of England's counties. The common refrain was that Cornwall had forty-four MPs, only one less than the number proposed for Scotland.

Paterson's answer to the charge that Cornwall has 'about five times the people in the Representative it can Claim by the Proportion of Taxes' was that the calculation took place when the county 'furnished all the known world with Tin'. The 'Inequality' was not, therefore, nefarious or designed but merely a result of the 'vicissitude' of trade. He urged all to see that 'Scotland hath more allowed in the Representative, than any other part or district of England'. Though in large part accurate, Paterson's rejoinder was not all that convincing, especially when one considers that the Union was sold on the idea that it would increase Scotland's trade. Scotland was set to join a lumbering chamber at the lowest point of its projected wealth. It could very well prove Cornwall's opposite: as the nation's revenue grew, its voting power would remain the same.[36]

The selection of the peers divided Scottish nobles, scrambling one of the opposition's most potent lines of attack. In a letter to Duchess Anne, Atholl speculated that her son, the Duke of Hamilton, would be made a peer of Britain. This troubled Atholl, who complained that, despite their relationship, he was appalled by Hamilton's 'politicks and ways of attaining his designes'.[37] Precisely which side Hamilton was on remained in doubt as the opposition gathered in clandestine meetings before the vote on article twenty-two. The hope was to plan and execute one final decisive act of parliamentary resistance.

The barrelling inevitability of the Union united the disjunctive factions of the opposition like nothing before it had done. A majority of Presbyterians and Jacobites (in parliament) were willing to cast aside their divisions for the moment and unite behind Hamilton as the putative leader of a Country–Cavalier alliance. As leader, Hamilton volunteered to propose a bill that would confirm the Hanoverian succession in Scottish law – conceding one of England's key drivers to Union – on the condition that the Treaty of Union was set aside. They predicted that Queensberry and the Court party would reject this measure. When they did, the entire opposition would walk out of parliament, delegitimising any further attempts to ratify the Treaty's final articles, and threatening civil war. One of the few to object to the plan was Atholl, who could not agree to the Hanoverian succession on principle, nor overcome his suspicions towards Hamilton.

Atholl was pessimistic but others believed that this scheme might just work. In Lockhart's telling the scheme 'caused a universal joy' amongst the opposition. As word spread about their plan, 'great numbers of gentlemen and eminent citizens flocked together' in Parliament Close. They were there to assist the walkout, defending the MPs as they forced their way out of the Hall. The crowd waited for Hamilton. But Hamilton remained at the Abbey, claiming he had a toothache. Still clinging to the bill as the last hope against Union, his allies rushed to his residence. They cajoled him at first and when this didn't work they inveighed against his 'double dealing and wavering', which could only convince the world of the worst of him. At last they were able to drag a reluctant Duke to parliament to 'prosecute the measure'. But when he got there, Hamilton balked. In the Hall, Hamilton asked his allies who was going to stand up and deliver the protestation. They faced him down with flattery: 'there was none so proper as his grace'; he was 'the person of the first quality and most interest of the nation'. They begged him for leadership, 'assuring him they would stand by him with their lives and fortunes'. Hamilton's response was to prevaricate. He told those clustered around him that he would support the measure but not propose it. In a compromise that suited no one and preserved nothing but his own sense of affiliation with the opposition, he would second the measure. The backroom fight was carried out in hushed tones under the full glare of parliament. And so Seafield and Stair simply moved things on. Time was lost, and so was the opportunity.

The succession gambit failed before it could be launched. This was all the more disappointing, as Lockhart later wrote, because Seafield told him that had Hamilton raised the proposal, Queensberry 'and other ministers of state had resolved to prorogue the parliament and give over the prosecution of the Union'. The question of why Hamilton backed out at the last minute is easier to account for than some of his earlier betrayals of the opposition. To reconnoitre support for the bill, the anti-Union opposition had to let knowledge of their plan spread. Queensberry quickly got word of their intent and sought Hamilton out. According to Lockhart, Queensberry told the Duke 'he had intelligence of what was in agitation, and could assure him if it was not let fall England would lay the blame of it upon him and he would suffer for it'. Clerk of Penicuik corroborates this account, confirming that Queensberry threatened Hamilton, most likely with legal backlash against his English estates.[38]

The backstairs machination filtered through the webs of intelligence that stretched across Edinburgh to reach England. Fearne sent Harley a report of a secret meeting between Hamilton and Queensberry, which had lasted four hours. He had also seen Hamilton meeting 'very frequently' with Seafield.[39]

The Scottish public did not need evidence to suspect secret dealing. Hamilton's 'behaviour . . . gave occasion for people to talk far and wide, that he had made his terms with the Court and betrayed the Country party'.[40] The sputtering end to the parliamentary resistance dispersed this talk beyond Hamilton to other members. Defoe tracked an impression that began within the opposition but soon took wider hold: namely, that 'Bribes of English Money . . . frighted or Debaucht the Parliament from their Duty'; that Scotland was 'bought and sold' and would soon 'be Enslav'd to the English'.[41] Carried later by the bardic song of Robert Burns, this view has both folklore and history behind it, and remains prominent in popular understandings of the Union.

Hamilton's family were dismayed. His brother Selkirk wrote to the Duke on behalf of their mother, who could not bring herself to raise hand to a letter: 'you will not beleave what impression this has upon my lady [Duchess Anne] who is more then can be expressed against this Union which is I am affrayed irrecoverably intailed upon us'. The reason the Union was now inevitable is clear to both brothers, even if Selkirk cannot muster himself to blame Hamilton directly. The English parliament will not delay, he tells the Duke, as the Scottish parliament gave them no reason to: 'wee did not bring the succession a greater length & did not make our protests & leave the House in a body'.[42]

⸸

Without a mass walkout, the House swiftly moved to debate and vote on article twenty-two. The tensions within the estates that would later teem were by this stage already bubbling. The main clash was between the barons and upper nobility over whether the eldest sons of peers should be eligible to stand for election to the Commons. The jostling eventually led the barons to make a trade with the burgesses, giving them fifteen out of the forty-five seats in exchange for supporting exclusion. The other point of contention was the oath of abjuration required of English office holders that in effect excluded Presbyterians from the throne. Some MPs proposed that anyone who wanted to hold office in Scotland should take an oath to affirm the Presbyterian Kirk, but this was quickly shut down. Though Defoe was discomfited by the abjuration oath, he worked behind the scenes to intercept and prevent some of the more incendiary pamphlets that whipped fears about the oath and the obligations against conscience that would allegedly obtain in the new united state. In parliament the debate was intense. Atholl, Lockhart and Buchanan led the protests, with each raising their objections as individuals disgusted by their new subjection, and not as a powerful united block. The session dragged into the afternoon. It was capped, in Defoe's telling, by an 'Extraordinary speech' from the Earl of Stair.

After the House had risen for the day, Stair travelled home depleted. At four he spoke briefly to his wife, before sloughing off into a weary sleep. Stair died that night, with doctors chalking the cause to apoplexy. He had spent the last four months guiding the articles through parliament, a loyal servant to the Queen, who had brought him back into favour after the massacre at Glencoe. The mood in parliament was sombre and resigned. The Court had lost a man Defoe called 'one of the best in the Nation'.[43] When article twenty-two passed a day after Stair's death, the opposition knew that the Treaty would be ratified in its entirety.

As the opposition's hope withered, Duchess Anne received news that severed the last connection between its two most prominent actors. Lady Catherine, Duchess of Atholl, had died. Duchess Anne had lost a daughter and confidant, Atholl a wife he respected and Hamilton a sister who cared for and chided him. Hamilton knew what this death meant. The condolence note he sent Atholl is baldly self-interested and painfully insecure. Its opening line, ' I hope you'll alwaes believe whereon you are concerned, I shall have a tender regard', sets the tone of a letter in which Hamilton calls Atholl his 'brother' and 'friend' more times than any true brother of friend ever would.[44]

Broken by his loss, Atholl withdrew to his estate. It was clear to all that any prospect he and Hamilton would work together was incontrovertibly lost. With the opposition thus scattered, the final three articles passed with little resistance. Article twenty-three standardised the rights of peers across the kingdom, article twenty-four inaugurated a new seal for Great Britain and article twenty-five voided laws in either kingdom that were inconsistent with the preceding twenty-four articles. Leven told Harley that there were still outstanding questions, not least how the Equivalent would be distributed and how the forty-five Commons places would be divided between shires and boroughs, how the peers would be appointed and which MPs would be asked to stand in the first election for the united parliament. But as 'these things being what only concerns' Scotland and 'not England', Leven was confident that Scots would 'incline to finish the Treaty before we take those things under consideration'. After the final articles passed, all that remained was a vote on the Treaty as a whole. Leven had agents scattered across the country 'to observe what's adoing'. He was happy to report to Harley that 'by all accounts I have all is quiet and the ferment amongst them is much abated'.[45]

⸸

On 16 January 1707, Defoe wrote to Harley 'with Joy'. The Treaty had passed. Queensberry touched it with the sceptre and rendered it the law of the land. The Scottish parliament had voted itself out of existence and acceded to join England and Wales as the United Kingdom of Great Britain. Defoe's brief first impression was that 'an Universall Joy of the Friends of both Nations Runs thro' the Citty'. He reported to readers of the *Review* how the canons fired from the walls of the castle boomed over Edinburgh. As the sound touched his ear he heard in it 'the articulate Expression of UNION, UNION'. As 'even the Thunder of Warlike Engines cry Peace', Defoe felt the reverberations of what had been achieved: 'what is made to divide and destroy, speaks out the Language of this Glorious Conjunction!' Defoe was mocked for this moment of pathetic fallacy, but it is hard to begrudge him the release. The Kirk leaders debated but reneged on a final address, satisfied at least for the moment by the protections offered the Kirk in the Act concerning its security and those folded into the Treaty.[46] With pensive breath let out, and time to reflect, Defoe marked this the day that '*English* and *Scots* Valour' would 'Unite together, to Overthrow their Foreign Adversaries'. Had they been united sooner, 'perhaps *Europe* had paid Honours enough to Us before now, as the greatest Nation in the World'.[47] This was the age for British triumph to make up for the squandered time of internal conflict.

Fearne's account of the ratification had none of Defoe's prospect or promise.[48] On the contrary, he found Edinburgh 'barren' after the ratification, as the city emptied out of business and politics. Still, he remained grateful that Harley updated his orders and renewed the finance for his mission.

There was no reason for Harley to bring his agents in from the cold just yet. While the Scottish parliament may have finished its work, the English one was yet to begin. And while protests had tentatively been suppressed, there was still a sense of unease. Harley's quick eye would have easily noticed that Defoe's 'Universall Joy' had a hollowness to it. It lacked the author's fluent way of writing the crowd into teeming presence. Amongst Harley's agents, there was nonetheless a feeling of accomplishment. The successful ratification brought its many fathers out of the shadows. In desperate audacity, William Gregg, the first agent Harley sent to Scotland, whose work there ended before the Treaty reached Edinburgh, took the good news as occasion to ask Harley for more pay. Gregg was deep in debt and would try anything.[49] Paterson put into the world that he wanted employment in recompense for his service. Defoe was none too subtle, either. In the same letter that he announced the ratification to Harley, he added, 'It is not my bussiness to Recomend persons. I wait now your Instructions whether to stay or Come away.' What Defoe awaited was an indication not simply whether he would stay in the field as Fearne was to do, but whether his service might now translate into something more official, more open and more stable than espionage. With the mission drawing to its close, he found a new forthrightness in reminiscence, confessing to Harley, 'I have had an Uneasy Post here Under so Many frequent Feares of Murther, Tumult, Rabble &c, but I Resolv Not to be Uneasy in Any of your Commands.' He stood ready, despite the dangers, waiting for a note or encouragement about what he was to do next.[50]

†

On 18 December, two days after the Union was ratified in Scotland, Queensberry sent the Act down to England. The men of his circle vied for the honour of carrying the document to London. Not willing to pick a favourite, the Lord High Commissioner sent it by ordinary courier.[51] This monumental act, one that would forever alter the constitution of England and Scotland, cut an inauspicious path south to the English capital. The parliament was not sitting. And so the Act lay with the Queen until the end of January, when she addressed both Houses, urging Commons and Lords to ratify it.

It took five weeks for parliament to ratify the Act. When Defoe looked back on this time, he swept the process up into a moment of English ascendency, setting the making of the Act against French defeats in the War of the Spanish Succession. The Earl of Peterborough had forced the French to end their siege of Barcelona, Marlborough had triumphed at Ramillies, and England's allies Savoy had won victory over the French at Turin, all of which was 'enough to Overthrow the greatest Empire in the World' and turn the mood in England. In Defoe's telling, England's people were 'made Glad and Easie in Hopes of a speedy Peace'; so much so that they 'were prepared to Grant almost any thing which the Queen in Reason could ask'.[52]

The triumphal flourish of Defoe's history belies the machinations required to bring the two Houses to heel. In the Commons, Tory opponents of Union rehashed some of the same techniques the Scottish parliamentarians had employed. They tried to delay vote on the first article until the others were passed. They attempted to bring the minutes and records of earlier attempts at Union to the floor for debate. With characteristic deftness, Harley was able to shift consideration of amendments from the full House to a committee. There was still opposition within it. One member rose to say that the Union was 'like marrying a woman against her consent'. The common metaphor of Union as marriage (that Scots critics attacked for the subordination of their nation to the status of a wife) is made brutal to expose how 'union was carried on by corruption and bribery within doors and by force and violence without'.[53] Despite his own growing misgivings, Harley stood firm, guiding the Treaty to full passage by February. In the Lords, Godolphin took on an opposition led by Defoe's old foe Nottingham. Nottingham's resistance stemmed more from the rise of the Junto than from any principled objection to Union itself. He was wary of Godolphin's management, and the alliance he formed between the Court and the Junto in order to ram the bill through the Lords. As Godolphin moved further towards the Whig grandees, the already marginalised Harley came to regard ratification as yet another signal of the shift towards a whiggish government and away from his own moderate position. It was the Junto who pushed the Treaty through the Lords.

When news of the ratification reached Edinburgh, Queensberry wrote to Harley to express thanks that the 'great affair passed so cheerfully with you'. The Scottish peer lamented that it had been such a traumatic delivery in his own parliament. At this stage he could only 'wish this nation had been as wise and embraced it as readily'. In a letter to a man whose share in the triumph of Union was increasingly complicated, Queensberry added, 'I hope the advantages of it will soon convince many of their mistakes.'[54] The Scottish parliament had voted itself obsolete, and Queensberry was worried about how to control the magnates and commissioners, barons and burgesses who were not included in the united parliament in London. His hope was that the advantages of the Equivalent and trade would keep this floating constituency in line.

In March the Act of Union passed the Lords and in May it was touched by the Queen into law and sent back to Scotland.[55] In her speech to the two Houses after the passage, Queen Anne signalled the Union as the lasting achievement of her reign. But even as she sat enthroned before the Lords, with members of both Houses crammed into the chamber, she acknowledged just how difficult this achievement had been:

> I consider this UNION as a Matter of the greatest Importance to the Wealth, Strength and Safety of the whole Island; And at the same time, as a Work of so much Difficulty and Nicety, in its own Nature, That, till now; all Attempts which have proved ineffectual. And therefore I make no doubt, but it will be remembered and spoke of hereafter, to the Honour of those who have been Instrumental in bringing it to such a Happy Conclusion.

The MPs who had supported Union would have basked in the honour the Queen bestowed. Defoe and his fellow agents took pride, too, as those 'Instrumental' in bringing the two nations into one. In the *Review*, Defoe echoed the Queen's words by directly relishing that he is one of '*those that have been instrumental*'. Not willing to leave it there, Defoe published the speech in full in his *History of the Union*, careful to include the Queen's final hope that her subjects in both nations 'Act with all possible Respect and Kindness to one another, That so it may appear to all the World, they have Hearts disposed to become one People'.[56]

Part Three

THE UNITED KINGDOM OF GREAT BRITAIN

CHAPTER 10

UNSETTLED NATIONS

Harley scarcely had time to mark the Act's passage before news reached him that the Union's establishment in law had not achieved what the Queen had hoped. There was no sign that the fact of Union had turned English and Scottish hearts towards one another. In Scotland, it seemed the opposite was true. One of Harley's associates travelling south from Edinburgh felt compelled to report that in the capital and north of it, the people 'cry so bitterly against the Union, cursing those great men of theirs that gave consent to it'. Particularly perturbing was that 'They do not this in private, but in taverns and along the road when they meet anyone'. In the taverns and on the roads, at markets and in squares and closes, the Scots were not just cursing the Union but crying out to the 'pretended Prince of Wales as the true heir'. People turned to Jacobitism as a way to cast off an association that so chafed against their sense of self and nation that many openly wished to see Marlborough and his English forces defeated in battle. In Scotland's south, the traveller noted a 'more moderate' temper. Even so, in his experience, 'one may see fifty men before one that is for the Union in South or North'.[1]

Harley had a fuller view of Scotland than this writer and other outside observers knew. Godolphin thought that, if anything, Defoe's Scottish dispatches had become habitually pessimistic. As Defoe continued to voice the threat of Jacobite scheming, the Treasurer told Harley, 'I have often observed that he gives you the worst side of the picture.'[2] In the aftermath of the Act's passage, Defoe begged renewed leave from both men to express things freely. It was not that he wanted to give a 'Melancholly Account of Things' to 'Enhance' his handlers' 'Opinion of my Services', nor to shirk from their dangers. It was simply that he wanted to give an accurate picture of what was happening on the ground. What he and other agents noticed in Edinburgh was that 'The Ferment Runs Every Day higher here, and the ill blood of This people is So much Increased that there is No Speaking among them but with the Uttmost Caution'.

Defoe began to sense the change underfoot straight after the Act passed, when he seized on a group of Presbyterian ministers of a nationalist bent. These were 'a Restless Uneasy people' who, as he warned Harley, could all too easily set the tone of the country. Defoe's approach to 'Mannage Them' was to apply 'Tender Usage and Cool Counsels'.[3] His *Fifth Essay* tried to settle things, but his footing was increasingly tentative. The spy quickly found that he could not move as easily through the city as he done a mere month before. He was made cautious by the anti-English sentiment that sat heavy on the town. There was a personal element as well. Defoe was increasingly seen as a hack for pay, a writer who, as one of the nationalist clergymen put it in print, 'Patronize[s] not the best Cause, but the wealthiest Client'.[4]

The closing in of Edinburgh society on Defoe was confirmed by another of Harley's spies. After years of agitating to return home, Ogilvie finally made it back to Scotland. In Edinburgh, Ogilvie encountered 'Mr Defoe' but observed that 'nobody would suffer him in their company except the anti-monarchical men, for they believe he is sent down to be a spy over them and that his flight is only a pretence'.[5] Suspicion, as Defoe himself admitted, made his work more difficult and dangerous.

Much of the difficulty arose because the uncertainties surrounding the Union's effects redounded on the man who had promoted it. Any injustice or slight by England and Defoe complained that the people of Edinburgh 'Come Crowding about me Reproaching me ... with what I have said of the Honour and justice of the English Parliament'. Making things worse was Harley's silence, leaving Defoe without the information he needed to answer the charges. The man famed for his ability to dismember an opponent's argument could now 'make no Answer', and folk in Edinburgh noticed.[6]

Defoe pushed through his apparent change in status. To offset the 'Clamourous Clergy', he once again turned to personal diplomacy, seeking out the most influential amongst the group and trying to persuade them in the hope that their influence would cascade downwards. The work took its toll, as did his separation from home. His infant daughter Martha had died earlier in the year, and Defoe began to ask with growing insistence to be allowed a trip home. The news he received that in part accounted for Harley's silence only made his situation feel more parlous. The Secretary was ill. He had suffered bouts of apoplexy in the early months of 1707 and appeared physically strained in parliament.[7] In the midst of his own pleas to return, Defoe called down a prayer that yoked Harley's fate (and his own) to the completion of the Union project: 'God almighty in Mercy to These yet Unsettled Nations preserv a life So Necessary to Their Imediate felicity.'

Without Harley's direct instruction, Defoe had to reorient his mission on his own terms. His efforts to tamp down the influence of nationalist clergy appeared successful insofar as the General Assembly of the Church of Scotland never became a locus for resistance, as some feared it would. Defoe took from this success a new commitment to combatting what he believed was misinformation about England and its intentions. In the face of his dwindling funds, and the exposure of his cover, he recommitted himself to do everything to 'push the Great work of Reconciling the minds of this People to One Another and to the Union'.[8] In Scotland he published a suite of pamphlets that redressed attempts to split English Dissenters from their Presbyterian brethren. For the principally English readers of his *Review*, he offered a series of essays that aimed to marry 'the Spirit of Union' to Union in law: to 'joyn' the two nations in 'Interests, Charity and Temper', to convince them that while each place preserved its own distinct ecclesiastical polity and legal system, Scotland and England were now possessed of 'one Politick Heart, thro' which the Blood of the whole united Body circulates'.[9]

Throughout his time in Scotland, Defoe's writing complemented and built upon his secret service. He continued to source information from his 'spies in the Commission, in the parliament and in the assembly' and to use the writing of his *History of the Union* as 'pretence' to 'have Every Thing told me'.[10] This cover shifted as he embarked upon writing the *History* in earnest. After the passage of the Act, the fight to define the events of Union began, with Defoe's work opening a front that still endures.

†

The Union imposed on Scotland a British administrative state, largely run through London. The process of bringing Scotland into its clutches was messy. Defoe later remarked that the negotiations it entailed 'opened afresh the Mouths' of those who opposed the Union 'and furnished them with matter of new Clamour'.[11] As the Treaty's provisions were worked out in public, the lumbering edifice was exposed. So too was the discontent that ran through Scotland. The question of representation still had to be resolved. The pact between the barons and burgesses to restrict the sons of peers from sitting in the Commons was not enough to overcome Queensberry's 'Dextrous Management'. By mid-February, the vote to allow the sons of peers scraped in by eighty-five to seventy-two. The election of the sixteen peers required a subtle hand, too. Due to be carried out through an ostensibly open process attended by the entire body of the Scottish peerage, Queensberry had to find ways to steer the group towards a list of people tractable to his own interest. Working against him were clan loyalties, internecine fights and a deference to the position of magnate families. But as Queensberry made very clear to his allies, appointing Hamilton, as his rank and position seemed to demand, 'wou'd not be acceptable above'. Though his actions had pushed the Union forward at decisive moments, Hamilton's playing both sides left him without a home in either. Queensberry strongly implied that the Queen did not want him in the Lords. Mar and his other Court allies got the message and 'ever since we have taken pains to prevent his being chosen'.[12] In the end, the selected lords were entirely pro-Union. There were two from the Squadrone, Tweeddale and Roxburghe, and the rest were of the Court, amongst them Queensberry, Seafield, Glasgow and Leven.

Marrying two tax and customs systems created substantial loopholes. In February Defoe sent Godolphin a letter outlining the attempts of merchants to exploit them. Defoe wrote to Godolphin because the Lord Treasurer was now the clear head of England's government. Created 1st Earl of Godolphin the previous December, his elevation pushed Harley further aside. With Harley weighed by illness too, it was resolved that Godolphin would take over as Defoe's direct employer. The supposed benefit was that Defoe's service would be less reliant on Harley magicking up funds: he could be paid directly from the Treasury. Personal loyalties died hard. Even though Godolphin was his official employer from the passage of Union to 1710, Defoe wrote most frequently to Harley throughout this time. In the first of his surviving letters to Godolphin, Defoe reports that Scottish merchants are poised to manipulate the nation's current 'Open Trade with France', something their English counterparts had no access to because of the war. The Scots merchants were 'Buying up Wines and Brandys' and other commodities at a volume that Defoe found 'Incredible'. Ships were arriving at Leith often twice a day. The Scots merchants' plan, as Defoe easily deduced, was to stock up before 1 May, when the Union was due to come into effect, and then simply move the goods duty-free to England. Though Defoe is censorious about the practice in his letter to Godolphin, he was not above capitalising on this loophole himself. Barely two weeks later he offered to buy Harley 'a Ton of Rich Claret' on his 'Own Risq'. The second loophole that merchants in both kingdoms seized on concerned the drawbacks. Between the passage of the Act and its coming into effect, merchants imported goods that would attract a drawback (tobacco, especially) from England with a view to draw-back the duties they paid before they re-exported the goods to Europe. Powerful London merchants were outraged. They directed their indignation in ways that risked the last bare threads of comity needed to weave the Union into being.

The London merchants petitioned the Commons to close the loophole. The bill the members came up with would impose tariffs on French goods arriving via Scotland. Harley worked behind the scenes to support it. At stake in the public debate was whether or not there would be exceptions for Scottish merchants who lived in Scotland. If none were made, Defoe told Harley, 'It will make ill blood here and they Talk loudly here that the Union is Broke before it is begun.' If exceptions were made, Defoe thought it would open the door to 'Inumerable frauds'.[13] Defoe did not know that Harley supported the bill and so in the *Review* tried to downplay its need, telling English readers the potential for fraud was low.[14] In truth, the fraud unnerved him and the situation in Scotland left him frightened. He feared that all the work he had put into the Union was 'Unravelling' and that his safety was at further risk, warning Harley that if news did not reach Edinburgh that efforts to close the loophole were dropped, 'I shall Need No New Orders from England about Staying Or Returning, for Really Sir [t]here will be No staying here for me nor hardly any English man.'[15] Paterson was far more sanguine, insisting (too optimistically) that these trade quibbles were not a threat to the Union.[16]

The whole episode was galling for Defoe, who anticipated the trade issues that arose from the lapse in time between ratification and enforcement.[17] His main concern now was that if the loophole were closed, then Scots would see it as a violation of the Union's free-trade provisions and would reconsider the compact. The issue dragged on, disaffecting merchants in Edinburgh and London as it did. In the end, the Lords was not willing to risk the Union and so rejected the bill. However, the issue was far from settled, with Defoe forced to attack those people who, to 'amuse, terrifie and disorder the People, spread false Reports', the most malicious of which was that '*Lawyers*' in England 'have found out a Method wholly *to stop the Importation*' of French goods through Scotland.[18] Defoe came round to the Lords' position, advising Harley and Godolphin to let the question of fraud slide for fear that any prosecution would alienate the people. By August he felt confident in these tactics for, as he told both Godolphin and Harley, the 'Clamorous Party Are Now Turning their Tongues to Other Subjects'.

The months leading up to 1 May 1707, when the Union came into effect, and those that followed it, directly exposed a gulf between the Act as a quasi-constitutional document and a structuring principle of everyday life. Agents and operatives like Defoe had a unique vantage on this gap and were the first to grasp what it meant for the future of the Union. What Defoe, Fearne and Paterson witnessed was that the pain of uniting with England was felt most sharply when the Equivalent failed to live up to its promise.

In early March, Defoe told Harley that of all the things turning Scots against the Union, 'The Equivalent is the Main Disgust'. From his point of view, its use as a mechanism to control the populace was being perverted. Too many people had 'swallowed large Morsells of it in Expectation', and Defoe feared that those controlling its distribution were not allowing enough of the funds to 'go as Designd'.[19] Distributing the Equivalent was fraught from the outset. When Defoe first reckoned with the question, he assumed that investors in the Darien Company would be paid first, and then private individuals would be compensated for losses incurred in the process of reducing Scottish coins to the English standard.[20] He later detailed the public debts it would be used to cover. If the Equivalent was insufficient for these purposes, the Treaty allowed the increased customs revenue to be put to those debts for a period of seven years (so that Scots paid for part of their compensation themselves).

Looking back, Defoe noted that when the Treaty was being negotiated, many saw the Union as 'so mean a prospect' that they sold their shares in the Darien Company for 10 per cent of what they had paid, despite the fact that the Treaty stipulated that the stock would be repaid with interest.[21] Those who retained or bought shares stood to do well, especially since the Company still had roughly £200,000 left on its books. The dynamic of uneven benefit and exchange, where some paid their own compensation and others stood to profit, meant that the jostling to get one's share of the Equivalent was frenetic. The Treaty commissioners wanted the Equivalent to be used to offset expenses they sustained during negotiations. Fearne feared that the Equivalent was in danger of being consumed entirely by such 'private uses'. The danger of the contest over the Union meant that there were agents everywhere. As Fearne put it, 'The public offices are pestred with secret spyes and intelligences', who were all now vying for payment, taking money that would otherwise be used to win public support.[22]

Paterson was in a deeply uncomfortable position, as both figurehead for the benefits of the Equivalent and someone whose own solvency depended on its payout. Even when the distribution had only just started to wend its way through the bureaucracy, Paterson already felt the cold shoulder of Godolphin's neglect. In a letter to Harley he feigned blitheness. When telling the Secretary the 'Lord Treasurer has taken no notice of me above twelve months', he made sure to add the untrue 'nor I of him'. And yet Paterson was entirely preoccupied with pushing his own methods to distribute the Equivalent to Scotland's advantage. Foremost amongst them was his proposal to offset any delays by putting the Equivalent 'into a regular fund'. That way, when 'poor people' were not given the principal owed them immediately, they 'may at least have interest of 5 per cent. For a year, two or three.' It was a good idea.[23] The full settlement of the Equivalent took the better part of two decades. As it dragged on, Paterson increasingly saw the money not just as his entitlement but, as he told Godolphin, as 'a recompense' for his work on the Union.[24]

In 1707, there were already signs of trouble. The Equivalent was meant to arrive in Scotland on 1 May, the day the Union came into effect. The first instalment only left London on 16 June. Anti-Unionists took 'Great advantage' of the delay, according to Defoe, stoking fears that England would renege on the payment. Defoe even reported a rumour to Harley that Hamilton had marched to Mercat Cross at the centre of Edinburgh and 'protested' that 'the Union was broke'. Though Defoe gave little credence to it, he warned Harley that such 'reports Joyned with the want of Money makes a great Deal of Ill blood here and Does Unspeakable harms'.[25]

Things did not settle when the money arrived at Edinburgh Castle towards the end of June: the Bank of England made a serious miscalculation in failing to consult 'either the Temper or the Circumstances of *Scotland*'. The wagons the bank sent north carried only £100,000 in 'ready Money'. The remaining £298,000 was in Exchequer Bills. Defoe witnessed how the reliance on paper credit 'raised a new Clamour in Scotland'. People unfamiliar and as a result suspicious of these bills thought that 'the *English* Trick'd them'. In fact, because the bills did not accrue interest, they violated article fifteen of the Treaty. Of more immediate concern for the majority was the fact that they were 'payable 300 Miles off'; and 'if Lost or Mislaid, or by Accident Burnt, were Irrecoverable'.[26] The government in Scotland took brisk action. Seafield convinced Godolphin to send £50,000 more funds in gold. The commissioners distributing the money were given wider latitude, to give cash but also to treat those who accepted bills more favourably. They could pay them earlier than they were due, and the bills could now be drawn from and were thus payable in Edinburgh. Even so, Defoe's reports remained stark. The bungled distribution boiled 'ill blood' and 'Revived the Old Heats' to such an extent that, if the Union were negotiated now, Defoe thought 'it would be Impossible'.[27]

Defoe exposed a plot to rob the wagons that carried the money. Though none was stolen, the people hurled abuse at the guards delivering the gold, even attacking their horses. In the throng, he heard people cry out that the Equivalent was 'the Price of their Country'. Defoe sensed the pernicious influence of 'Subtill Jacobites' and nationalist Kirk ministers. In the *Review* a year later he imagines a conversation with a young boy turned by Jacobites. He asks the ten-year-old why he cursed and stoned the Equivalent; the boy replies, 'Because it was the Price of Our County and it ruin'd us all.' In his *History of the Union*, Defoe implies that Hamilton encouraged the protest against the Equivalent. This is unlikely as Hamilton was more concerned with taking his family to their estate at Kinneil. In his last dispatch from Edinburgh, he made the point of complaining to his mother of 'shoals of English excise men and other officers coming hither'.[28] It was ominous that the first sign of Union was the arrival of tax collectors. This was not the warp and weft of two nations woven together, but the creeping tendrils of English power.

Defoe was alert that these officials would at once attract and concentrate the ire of the Scots. He begged Harley to urge all men sent north on government business 'to use all the Courtisye, Civillity and Calmness possible'. It would have taken heroic levels of civility to endear English excisemen to the Scots they were charged with taxing. The English officials became easy targets. Lockhart called them 'the very scum and canalia [rabble]' of England. He delighted in telling a story about a Scottish merchant travelling through England. The merchant feared that he would be robbed. His landlady told him there was no reason to worry; that the area had no highwaymen. When he asked why, she answered, 'They are all gone to your country to get places.' The pirates were now privateers, taking roles as surveyors, collectors and officers of custom. The deeper problem was that the hatred towards excisemen was easy to exploit. Defoe reported that one of the 'Artifices' Jacobites used to 'Enflame' was to recruit men to impersonate English officials. These ersatz excisemen would go 'about the streets and Crye Out Upon Scotland, and Call the Brewers Men, Scotch Rogues, and Scots Dogs'. The effect, Defoe lamented, was that they ended up 'Refounding a Nationall Aversion which is the Great thing we hoped the Union would have worne off'.[29]

⚲

Lurking behind Defoe's critique of English custom agents is his own self-interest. With real justification he positioned himself as a man whose knowledge of Scotland would allow him to impose the new laws with a sensitivity to local mores absent from the current crop of officials. His time in Scotland had given him a gnawing double consciousness. He thought and acted with his secret employer in mind. He was also keenly aware that his ability to move through Scottish society was dependent on Harley's largesse. Godolphin's taking over as his official employer was meant to provide more consistency and security on this front. The fact that it did not pushed Defoe to seek employment out of the shadows. In his sights was a position as a customs official.

Defoe was not the only agent who felt that the shift from Harley to Godolphin hindered their stable employment. In the European field John Toland complained to Harley that he 'silently endur'd the greatest hardships imaginable'. Through it all he kept the state secrets entrusted to him – or so he claimed. Toland knew Harley had paid him 'from your own pocket' and so clung to him; more now as it seemed that Godolphin did not want to employ him. The political calculus, as Toland put it, came down to a 'maxim with certain ministers to consider men no further than they may be useful or hurtful to their own designs'. Toland's experience gives insight into the happenings in Scotland, where ratification accelerated the drive for official employment amongst Harley's agents. Fearne wrote that once the Union came into effect, secrecy crumbled and 'all suspicion of English influence is now out of doors'. His implication is that he can no longer work as a secret agent and requires a more official position. And so he begs Harley to know 'whether there be any further use for me here, or whether I should return'. Like Defoe, Fearne's situation was abject: 'under God my dependence for earthly matters is upon yourself', he reminded the Secretary. In the same moment as Fearne appeals to Harley's generosity, he invokes his service to the Scottish Court, telling Harley, 'If Stair had lived, he had seen me provided for after the Union in government.'[30] Agents within a loose network prove difficult for their handlers once the main task of their mission is completed. Often these agents had served more than one interest or master, and their work gave them access to sensitive material and secrets of state. The calculation as Toland had it is not just what they could do in government but what might happen if they were excluded from it. In Fearne's case, the arithmetic was clear. He was still needed as an agent in Edinburgh, especially since Defoe was planning to leave the city for a tour of Scotland. In Defoe's case, the calculation required far more thought from Harley and Godolphin.[31]

When Customs House Officers were proposed, Godolphin left Defoe's name off the list. He did not think appointing him would pass muster with William Lowndes, Secretary to the Treasury. As the man who arranged some of Defoe's secret service payments, Lowndes knew a bit too much of Defoe's work as an agent and the deceptions involved. Harley could have intervened in Defoe's favour but did not.[32] As people he knew were named to jobs, Defoe became increasingly bitter. When Paterson was recommended in March for a position on account of his service, Defoe was utterly demoralised. For his own ego, he had to find reason why Paterson was chosen over him. The only thing he could come up with was that he had maintained his secrecy a bit too well. Defoe speculated to Harley: 'if my Labour had Not been always to Conceal my Self I might have had the Same honour — but I have No body to Recommend me Sir but your Self, to whom I leav it. I am Sure he [Paterson] has the Credit of a good stock in the Face and is Applauded for Some things I Actually did in the Committee. I beg Sir I may not however be forgotten.' The man who brought him to Harley, and whom he outshone in Scotland, ended up taking credit for his work. Harley showed the letter to Godolphin, who largely agreed with Defoe's assessment of Paterson's service.[33]

A mixture of guilt and obligation moved Harley to respond. In June the Secretary sent his agent a letter, the first since that January, in which he recasts a commonplace of Defoe's by hoping, 'I have not been an unprofitable Servant'. Harley's levelling must have succoured Defoe. Here in ink was a promise to serve Defoe with a reward befitting his own service. It is a striking letter but, like much of Harley's prose, gives little away about the precise nature of his intentions. Though his relationship with Godolphin was at this point strained to breaking, the two did come together to offer Defoe a role as Commissioner of the Customs in Scotland. We only have Defoe's side. From his perspective, the position was offered with a caveat: Godolphin implied Defoe could still be of better service as a spy. When he turned the position down, Defoe took satisfaction that Godolphin will be 'pleased with the Choice I have Made'. Years later, he reminded Harley that he forewent the position because it was Harley's 'Opinion as well as his Lordship's [Godolphin's] That I Might be More Servicable in a Private Capascity'. More than once Defoe came to regret this risky personal choice. He rejected a sinecure to continue his secret service, even though it promised uneven financial rewards and little security. Defoe chose to continue as an agent, and to work settling the Union, rather than to take his rightful reward for helping to birth it.

⸸

As Defoe began preparing to travel around Scotland, Harley was ever more isolated at home. Though he still had the support of the Queen, he was out of step with the ministry. The imposition of Sunderland as the other Secretary of State against Harley's wishes marked Godolphin's growing dependence on the Whig Lords for support in parliament. The split between Godolphin and Harley – who remained convinced of his own ability to forge a moderate coalition – affected the agents in the field. Defoe was ostensibly Godolphin's agent, yet he still provided Harley with far more intelligence than he offered the Lord Treasurer.

The added complication was that Harley continued to use Scotland as a means to unsettle Junto–Whig alliances. When Harley supported the merchants who wanted to close the trade loophole, he knew that doing so would impede the Junto's efforts to forge partnerships in Scotland, and even cut off a potential source of their power in the impending united parliament. Harley's manoeuvrings angered the Whig Lords. The guileful Sunderland countered, putting Harley the trickster in the rare position of another's snare. In early 1707, Defoe sent Harley a gauzy letter to say Sunderland had approached him.

> I have had Severall Letters and Some hints I guess from the Other Newly alter'd part of an office Near you Sir which I long to give you the hystory of if you please to Command it; I presume you will Suffer nothing of that to be to my prejudice, and permit me the freedome of takeing yor honour for the Concealmt from all Eyes or Eares but your Own.

Harley was struck silent. He did not immediately advise Defoe to cultivate the connection; he did not deploy Defoe as he did when Defoe served Halifax and, to a lesser extent, Godolphin, to shape their views of Scotland for his own ends. Defoe's biographer Maximillian Novak reads the letter as a lucently cloaked threat. Defoe wanted to demonstrate that he was in demand and could be employed by others who might take more care to support him. The distrust between agent and patron that Sunderland wrought turned, too, on Harley's fear that Defoe might return to the whiggish bedrock of his own principles and seek new patrons more aligned with his beliefs, especially as Harley increasingly turned to the Tories as allies in government. Harley's fumbled silence left Defoe caught between patron and paymaster, buffeted with requests but stranded with no instructions. And so, once again, he had to embark on a tour without a defined mission from London.[34]

On 25 March 1707 the Scottish parliament settled the final business of the Union. As per the Treaty, when they rose, the body was dissolved. Defoe stayed in Edinburgh to witness the conclusion of Union business and to see the end of the last parliament to sit in Edinburgh until 1999. Filing out of the hall with the ministers, Defoe returned to his lodgings to gather himself and prepare for a tour to Glasgow, Stirling, Wemyss, St Andrews and Aberdeen. His mission as he had to define it was 'to preach Peace & Good Manners to the preachers of Truth and Sedition'. He wanted to win over holdouts within the Kirk, whose aggregative national influence threatened to undermine the Union at the point of its inception. Before he departed, he had some unfinished business in Edinburgh, also intended to keep the Kirk in check. Throughout March and April he attended the meetings of the General Assembly in Edinburgh, as well as meetings of the synod of Lothian. They were quieter than expected. Nonetheless, Defoe stuck firm to his programme of persuasion, writing and distributing pamphlets to the ministers. The volume of work justified his asking Mr Bell for more funds.[35]

Defoe left for Glasgow in early May. With their principal agent absent from the capital, Harley and Godolphin had to rely on Fearne's intelligence. Despite Godolphin's clear position as Premier Minister, Harley still referred to Fearne as 'an agent of mine' and all the intelligence the operative gathered passed through Harley as spymaster. Fearne continued to provide his reliable and unembellished reports. Characteristically, Harley kept him in the field without due acknowledgement. The Secretary did not increase supply or furnish updated instructions. Fearne was underutilised and felt undervalued as a result. In one report he complained to Harley that he was 'doun right ruined, lying idle here'. Deprivation bred paranoia. He did not know that Harley had a wholly positive image of him and began to suspect that he was being 'misrepresented by some envious or malitious person; or that you [Harley] have taken some offence unknown to me'.[36] Fearne wanted to return to London. His experience bespeaks a wider problem. By mid-1707, Harley's entire Scottish network was underutilised and poorly supported. The spies in the field were exhausted and they began to lose heart and hope at the precise moment they were needed to guide Scots to accept the Union in its early form – tentative and vulnerable to attack as it was.

Defoe's tour confirmed that some things had settled post ratification. Defoe was pleased that he could now go to Glasgow, 'where I Must have been Torn to pieces if I had Gone before'. Still, he moved with the stealth of someone who sensed danger. He was deeply unsettled when he caught signs that his letters were being intercepted (his letters to his wife were delayed and appeared to have been opened). As he pressed northwards, he was sure that some wider 'Mischief' was at play. He had little doubt that Jacobites were behind it. Though he had set out with the prime intent of winning over Presbyterian nationalists, Defoe's tour confirmed the 'Intollerable boldness of the Jacobite party'. This was especially true in the Highlands, but as Defoe's travels revealed, the Jacobites were amassing power in some Lowland provinces too. He warned Harley 'that Unless Some Speedy Care is Taken to prevent Their Disorders The Consequences Can not but be fatall'. At a local level, Defoe gathered witness accounts of how Jacobites and Episcopalians fomented attacks on Presbyterian meetings, staging assaults in Dingwall so as 'to make the World believe it was a *Natural Tumult*'. The aim was to alienate the Presbyterian mainstream: to make it seem like the Kirk government was under attack because of the Union; and, through this ploy, to spread the idea that 'the UNION can be broken'.[37]

Of greater worry was the intelligence Defoe gathered that linked these machinations – these confected outpourings of Episcopal support – to a campaign that aimed to alter the terms of the Treaty of Union by calling for toleration of Episcopacy. Such a move would rock the civic foundation of the Church of Scotland. As Defoe and Harley's other agents gathered, attacks on the Kirk constituted one strand of a concerted assault that would culminate in a French-backed invasion. Ogilvie's deployment to Scotland signals that Harley was keen to this threat. Though he scoffed at rumours from Hanover that the Prince of Wales was moving incognito through London, Harley had accounts to corroborate Defoe's: on his desk were letters that accused the Duke of Atholl of engaging in a 'hunting' (a party designed to amass troops). Defoe passed on an account that affirmed that the Jacobites 'have 30000 Men Ready at a word': a good piece of intelligence, as the mastermind of the plan Nathaniel Hooke predicted the same number. In Harley's trove of correspondence were reports that Hamilton was 'picking up large horses'.

The word whipped through Scottish and English Jacobites that 'King James VIII will be On shore Quickly'.[38] When Defoe returned to Edinburgh, he found the town 'taken Up with a Discourse of Severall people landed in the West of Scotland From France and Captain Murray Apprehended'. Robert Murray, brother of the Captain John Murray who followed Beaufort to Scotland in the mission exposed as the Scotch plot, had been arrested. Ogilvie, who was pursuing Jacobites near Perth, noted the arrest too, although in his account to Harley he presents it as something of a missed opportunity. Robert Murray was seized in Glasgow, not at his lodgings where he kept papers and likely had evidence of the wider plan. Ogilvie rightly assumed that Robert travelled with his brother John (now a lieutenant colonel in the French service). Indeed, there were warrants for John's arrest, and Godolphin assumed as Ogilvie did that it was John who was the senior partner.[39] The failure to stop John worried Ogilvie. To him the blunder exposed that the new British state lacked the will or method to stave off a threat that was both internal and external. Scotland was an undeniable weak point: Ogilvie's treks through the Highlands gave him the impression that 'whole kingdom is disaffected and if France were but able to send them 10,000 men ... they would rise infallibly'. Ogilvie counselled Harley to try find a way to disarm the Scots. While Defoe had far less access to the Jacobite encampments and military manoeuvrings, he was an excellent reader of world affairs and was deeply concerned that the recent success of the French in the Battle of Almanza – and the ground they gained thereby in the War of the Spanish Succession – would motivate them finally to act on this long-rumoured invasion.[40]

Like Fearne, Defoe was depleted. The intelligence he provided drained him, both physically and financially. Because he did not know that Harley had Ogilvie enmeshed with the Jacobites in the Highlands, he felt the immense burden of reporting on the rising in the north and the invasion that might support it. This responsibility paralysed him. He could not quit his post without permission from Harley or Godolphin. And yet he could not remain, either. He simply had no money left. In a letter he later regretted as 'Importunate', he likened the five months he had spent without adequate supply, with no orders to return, and only one letter from Harley and Godolphin to that of 'a Man hang'd, Upon an Appeal, with the Queens Pardon in his Pocket'.[41] Defoe sent his brother-in-law to appeal to Harley in person. Realising that perhaps his worth as a spy in Scotland is what made Godolphin and Harley reluctant to call him in from the cold, he proposed a scheme that would see him spend eight months a year in Scotland, three in London and one travelling. With the knowledge that Defoe could be redeployed before the upcoming election, Harley finally relented. In November, Mr Bell sent Defoe £100. After more than a year in exile, Defoe had funds enough (and presumably orders) to return home.

⸸

Within days of Defoe's return, Harley faced a true and immediate crisis. The events and machinations that brought Harley to the brink involved, as one contemporary noted, 'so many intricate pipes which lead up to it, that we must at present lodge it amongst the mysteries of State'.[42] Paterson would have approved of the metaphor. When one masters the plumbing of state and gains systemic control over the channels of information and favour, they can bring the unwieldy organs of power to yield. On the other side, when the labyrinth of the system crosses and overlaps beyond sight or influence, the former master can drown in a flux of shit.

The hope that Harley would bring the united parliament to order rested on a belated idea of his administrative command. By 1707, the moderate coalition that had been the base for his power was fraying. Unusually for the Secretary, he spent much of the recess at Brampton Bryan, gathering himself before returning to London on the cusp of the session. When Godolphin nervously reminded him that the parliament faced a series of questions that had to be resolved, Harley could no longer mask his contempt with deference: 'The little experience I have had,' he shot back, 'inclines me to think that they never succeed so well as when they are directed. The people will follow somebody, and if your lordship will not think fit to explain your own thoughts, others will make use of your authority.' The threat is there, but so is the concession that, in symbol if not in deed, Godolphin retained the kind of authority to lead a ministry.[43]

Harley was ill at ease because he rightly perceived Godolphin entering domains that the duumvirs had traditionally left to his oversight, including the management and appointment of clergy. Harley tried to hold supporters of the ministry together in parliament, corralling them against the developing alliance of convenience formed by the Junto and opposition Tories. In an attempt to win the Junto over, Godolphin acceded to their choices for the bishoprics of Exeter and Chester. The problem was that Harley and the Queen had already promised both sees to Tories. Contrary to Godolphin, Harley wagered that the best path to maintaining a moderate ministry was to engage the Tories in parliament. Unlike the Whigs, the Tories lacked a ruthless and efficient leadership. By Harley's reckoning, they were thus less likely to turn parliamentary support into ministerial jockeying, as the Junto had already done with the appointment of Sunderland. The Duchess of Marlborough had informers at Court and attempted to keep her husband apprised of Harley's manoeuvrings. Sidelined by Harley's agent Abigail Hill, and on the outs with the Queen, Sarah did not deliver the duumvirs intelligence or leverage enough to work against Harley and the Queen, who secretly installed their candidates.[44] Denied in the Church and outgunned in the backrooms, the Junto turned their ire against Harley, delivering a series of parliamentary defeats that saw Harley and Godolphin lose control of the legislature and, with it, the infrastructure they needed to control Scotland.

The Junto and their Tory confederates launched a series of inquiries into the maladministration of the navy. Harley was able to offset most. This was fortunate, as the inquiries targeted Admiral George Churchill – for the purpose of embarrassing Marlborough, his brother – as well as setting their gaze on Prince George, husband to the Queen. Closer to home, the inquiries could also have exposed the loss of ships that stemmed from Harley's failure to act on intelligence from his agents in France.[45] Harley had less luck against Junto-led attacks on the Scottish Privy Council. The Scottish Privy Council was the chief administrative arm of law and government in Scotland, essentially acting as the executive branch. The Council played a crucial role overseeing elections and adjudicating any controverted contests. For Harley, the Council and some of its members – Queensberry, Stair, Cockburn of Ormiston – provided intelligence. Despite its mixed composition (Atholl had a seat), the Council was seen as aligned with England. As a result, it was abidingly unpopular. Godolphin and Harley wanted to retain the Council. It would be hard to manage any election without it. The Council possessed the kind of data and knowledge of constituencies that Defoe advised Harley accrue in order to dominate electoral contests. But Harley, sensing that he did not have the votes to preserve it, took the gamble of changing his position.[46] To Godolphin's horror, he ended up supporting dissolution. Harley's hope was to negotiate the date the Privy Council would be dissolved, so that it could be retained long enough for him to stage manage the election in Scotland and, in doing so, shape the composition of the new united parliament. The Junto and the opposition Tories simply had more votes. In committee and then on parliament's floor they repeatedly outflanked Harley, who first called for the Council to sit until 1709 and then scaled back his ask to just after the election. Godolphin saw all controls slipping and spoke often at the debates. He tried everything he could to overturn the dissolution – but to no avail. There would be no delay. The Council was slated to disband on 1 May 1708, the first anniversary of the Union and mere weeks away from the election.

Godolphin was proven right. Harley did not have the same control over parliament he had once had. This was not for lack of trying. The incorporation of the forty-five Scottish MPs and sixteen peers nominated by the Edinburgh parliament allowed Harley to offset any Jacobite gains until the general election of the following year. But the Squadrone members drifted towards the Junto, as did the parliament on the whole. The rift between Godolphin and Harley widened in defeat. In parliament those who opposed the Court began to exploit it for their own gain. Tory backbenchers began to question the management of the war with Spain, the issue that held Godolphin's ministry together. The documents they tabled revealed to the House that the Exchequer had received £631,213 for maintenance of 29,395 troops, but at the time of the defeat at Almaza, there were no more than 8,660 troops in the field. Godolphin and his allies felt that Harley did not do enough to prevent the parliamentary inquiry. Falling back on the one arena where he still had sway, Harley began meeting with the Queen to complain about the 'mismanagement' of his fellow ministers. It was also at this time that writer Joseph Addison recorded a bit of gossip: there was talk that 'Mr. Harley and his friends had laid schemes to undermine most of our great officers of state and plant their own party in the room of 'em.'[47]

⚘

Complicating matters was that in January, just as Harley was called to defend the government's actions over Almanza, and as he was beginning to form plans for a new ministry with himself at its head, William Gregg, his junior clerk and the first agent he sent to Scotland, was arrested for treason. Since returning from Scotland, Gregg had found the duties he was assigned in Harley's office 'a perfect drudgery'. The work seldom began before eleven at night and it carried on long into the morning. Gregg confessed himself 'happiest' when he could leave early, escaping the onerous process that Harley used to keep track of his correspondence. Letters were taken in shorthand, before being written out in full. They were then sent to the York buildings for Harley's signature, before they were returned to the Cockpit for clerks to copy them into the record books. From the start, Gregg wanted to be redeployed to Savoy or elsewhere on the Continent. He told Harley his 'mind was depressed by his debts and desired to be thrown abroad'. Though, like all of Harley's agents, Gregg's sense of security was eaten away by the Secretary's silence when he was in the field in Scotland, he nonetheless looked back on the work fondly. He had designed his own task and created his own cypher. Not only did his mission in Scotland rise to his belief in his own talents but, looking forward, foreign deployments were better compensated than a clerkship in Harley's office.

Despite the status and pay of the work, as a clerk Gregg had access to intelligence of the highest order. Before him lay secrets of state: he could read all Harley's correspondence. In the mills of paper that enveloped the office were the cyphers Harley used to encode his most sensitive letters. Seeking money and most likely thrilling to an inflated idea of his former work as a spy, in October 1707 Gregg began writing to Michel de Chamillart, the French War Minister. At first Gregg sent little more than open-source information, news that any French agent in London could have gathered. But with Chamillart's prompting, he began to copy and send confidential papers secreted from Harley's office.

Gregg was not a very good spy and was entirely indiscreet. When not in Harley's office, he spent much of his time in the Cross-Keys tavern in Covent Garden. Ale made him bombastic, as did the need for esteem. He bought favour with his merchant drinking partners by working to secure them passes to France, so they could engage in illicit trade. In an act he later admitted was 'downright madness', he boasted about how easy it was to pass secrets to the French. In the office itself Harley's secretaries and undersecretaries noticed odd behaviours: Erasmus Lewis found on Gregg's desk letters he knew he had left on the desks of other clerks. Others reported that Gregg liked to peruse certain French letters because he found them 'entertaining'. He was especially interested in the letters between the captured French general Marshall Tallard and Louis XIV's wife Madame de Maintenon. As an English prisoner of war captured after his defeat at Blenheim, Tallard's letters were conveyed through Harley's office. Before they were sent out, Gregg enclosed his treasonable correspondence. His smuggled enclosures detailed proceedings in parliament about troop augmentation. They contained secret communication between Westminster, the Queen and courts of the pro-Habsburg alliance. Most damning, Gregg managed to send a copy of the Queen's private letters to her ally Prince Eugene of Savoy, head of the Holy Roman Empire's armies. The letter was in draft with Harley's and Godolphin's emendations. Had it reached Chamillart, it would have exposed the innermost workings of Anne's government.[48]

Jonathan Swift later defended Harley, claiming it was he who discovered Gregg's treachery and brought the clerk to justice. Swift's defence came soon after Harley had employed the satirist to join Defoe amongst his cadre of propagandists.[49] The truth is that the suspicions of Harley's secretaries and undersecretaries did not prompt them to turn him in. Gregg's furtive correspondence was only discovered as it made its way through Europe. Postmasters in English pay at Rotterdam and Brussels noticed his letters almost simultaneously. The postmaster at Brussels sent the copy of Queen Anne's letter to Prince Eugene on to Marlborough.[50] Gregg's residence was then searched and copies of further letters found wrapped within a quire of fair paper hidden in Gregg's closet.[51]

Gregg was arrested on 1 January 1708. On 3 January he was examined by Sunderland who committed him to Newgate, charging the clerk with 'high treason for compassing the death of the queen' and 'adhering to her enemies'. Six days later he was escorted from the prison to the Old Bailey. The trial was brief. The evidence was incontrovertible and Gregg pleaded guilty. As expected, he was sentenced to death. The events obsessed Harley, who fixated on the smallest details of the proceedings, hoping to read in them the extent of his own liability. Throughout the trial, Gregg remained steadfastly loyal, telling the court his debts were the sole reason he was moved to betray his country. No one in Harley's office had suborned treason, and certainly not the Secretary himself. Still, there was reason for Harley to worry. The days were long in Newgate. A man awaiting his death might take any step to shake free its final throes. It was well within the realm of possibility that the Junto could dangle a reprieve to coerce Gregg into implicating Harley in treason.[52]

⸸

Harley had to act quickly. He continued meeting with the Queen and kept watch over her through his cousin and agent Abigail Masham (née Hill). Harley's brother noted that the Queen's growing reliance on Harley caused an 'incurable jealousy' in Godolphin.[53] With their relationship frayed, Harley was now sure that Godolphin would tack further towards the Junto as a way to ensure the Court interest in parliament held. Harley could not tolerate such a move. As he told Defoe, he believed the Junto were 'reall Atheists & pretended Patriots' who needed to be unmasked for the good of the nation.[54] And so, contra Godolphin, he set in motion a scheme that would accommodate the Tories, reshaping the ministry and retaining the moderate way with them as his base of parliamentary support. The major question was whether Harley could get Marlborough to sign on to such a scheme. With the war still hot, the champion of Blenheim was indispensable to any new ministry.

The delicate negotiations were made more difficult by the pressures of haste. For a man who so tightly controlled his image, Harley lacked sufficient time to cut off rumours and close down leaks. His inability to parry attacks on Almanza had not only tarnished his reputation but cast doubt on his loyalty to his ministerial colleagues. It is also likely that parts of his plan to remove Godolphin escaped the seals of his office. It is unclear which of these incurred the 'displeasure' of the duumvirs. But in late January, when news reached Harley that Marlborough and Godolphin were upset by him, Harley saw his plans and future unravel. In a desperate effort to correct the 'misrepresentations or misconstructions' that turned them, Harley met with Marlborough to explain himself. He hoped to do the same with Godolphin. In a pleading letter soliciting a face-to-face meeting, Harley offered a solemn 'protest', affirming, 'I never entertained the least thought derogating from your lordship or prejudicial to your interest.' Godolphin's response was swift and unforgiving. In a mark of its resolution, he delivered the letter by hand to Harley's rooms in the Cockpit. While Godolphin was sorry to 'lose the good opinion I had so much inclination to have of you', he had no reason to doubt his altered view of Harley: 'I cannot help seeing and hearing, nor believing my senses. I am very far from having deserved it from you. God forgive you!'[55]

A week later Marlborough tendered his resignation to the Queen, having tried and failed to convince her, he said, 'of the false and treacherous proceedings of Mr Secretary Harley'.[56] The following day the Queen met with the Duke and Duchess of Marlborough and Godolphin in a room adjacent to where her cabinet sat. The three coordinated their approach for deepest effect. First Godolphin rose to resign, telling the Queen he could no longer serve 'with one so perfidious as Mr Harley'. Queen Anne gave him a day to reconsider in deference to his service. Then the Duchess did the same. Finally, Marlborough came to do in person what his letter had already called down. He rose to resign the sword of his command. Like Godolphin, he could not continue to serve in a ministry with 'so vile a creature as

Harley'. The actions of the three old friends in effect dismantled the Godolphin ministry on their terms (or at least threatened to), side-stepping the Queen's prerogative to choose and dismiss those who served her.

Marlborough's resignation struck deepest. The Queen's fear, which she expressed in the room, was that their enemies would use Marlborough's resignation to reach a peace disadvantageous to England. But Marlborough was unmoved. As he pushed the resignation, the Queen turned to him: 'Let me tell you your service I have regarded to the utmost of my power, and if you do, my lord, resign your sword, let me tell you, you run it through my head.' And yet Anne held firm. The Queen did not dismiss Harley.

The chaos loosed from the meeting carried into the cabinet room where ministers called for Harley's dismissal. Still, the Queen held firm. Until, that is, the next day when the parliament turned on the Secretary. The Commons left a bill of supply on the table, a threat to the smooth running of the nation and its war. In the Lords, the Junto moved to initiate an inquiry into the Gregg affair, proffering a body of examiners led by seven Whig lords, three of them leaders of the Junto itself. The intent of the inquiry was unmistakable: to 'bring in Harley as a party in that business', Swift remarked, could only end in 'impeachment'. Harley knew his time was done. On 11 February 1708 he resigned as Secretary of State.[57]

⸸

Defoe rushed to the York Buildings as soon as news rang through London that the Secretary had resigned. He must have known that Harley would not see him. The impulse to wait on his patron was something deeper than a loyalty performed and habituated over time: as he put it, he was joined to Harley in 'The Bonds of an Inveiolable Duty'. Defoe later admitted he was 'lost'; that in the moment he assumed – despite his working for Godolphin – his career as an agent was over. If nothing else, he believed in the political maxim that 'when a great Officer falls, … all who came in by his interest fall with him'. A complicated sense of grief and indebtedness suffuses the letter he left at Harley's doorstep. 'Others Sir Compliment you On The Accession of your Good fortune,' he wrote. 'I Sir Desire to be The

Servant of your worst Dayes.' And these were Harley's worst days. The letter found in its reader a man levelled in the prime of his working life. After twenty-seven years in parliament, having been Speaker of three consecutive parliaments and served as Secretary of State for four years, he was sent down the to the backbench, where he began, pitted of ambition and purpose. Defoe seeks comfort for Harley. In loss there is deliverance, Defoe assured him: 'you are Delivred From a Fategue', from 'Wasting your Houres in the Service of Those That Understand Not how to Vallue or Reward in proportion to Merit'. Defoe's final consolation seems designed to brace both reader and writer: 'Perticularly you are Delivered from Envy and I perswade my Self you Are Removed from a Toterring Party That you may Not share in Their Fall.' Defoe almost convinces himself that Godolphin's ministry will end and that Harley – pushed from it early – might as a result stand poised to return to power.[58]

†

The threat of an inquiry into the Gregg affair helped drive Harley from office. Once he was gone, the Whig lords carried it on, confident that they could heap more soil on Harley's political grave. Their intent was obvious. They extended Gregg the hand of mercy on the proviso that he offer a full report. The questions centred on Harley; had Gregg given 'pertinent answers to them' – answers that implicated Harley in treason – 'he might have saved his life'. Gregg held to the line that he 'knew no more than what he had already confessed'. When pressed, all he could add was that he was 'tempted' to commit treason 'by the devil, and the hopes of getting money'. Much to the committee's dismay, Gregg was resolute that he did not receive 'advice or encouragement' from Harley or anyone in his office. The lords went over records of Gregg's service. They heard about a cypher he had used, 'which they wanted mightily to see', hoping it might hold the key to a wider conspiracy. When Lewis presented it to them, their disappointment was palpable. The cypher was the one Gregg used in Scotland, a page with a simple cryptonym: 'H. for Hamilton &c'. A friend of Harley's brother reported that the cypher, much like Gregg's testimony, was 'of no service to their design'. He took particular glee to note that the sum total the lords found by their investigation

> was that he [Harley] came late to the office and things were done in haste and letters taken down in short hand and obliged to go to his house to have them signed (whereby the clerk's shoes were worn out, a great prejudice to the Government) and such other enormous crimes.

To the sarcastic observer, a messy office did not treason make.[59]

Clinging to their intent, the Whig lords wanted to read dysfunction in Harley's office as a sign of something more sinister. And so they broadened their focus to Gregg's earlier crime of counterfeit, taking it as evidence that Harley did not properly vet those he allowed into the inner sancta of state. They also examined Harley's employment of two French agents, Alexander Valerie, aka Alexander Clerk, and John Bara. Harley employed the two men at the port cities of Calais and Boulogne-sur-Mer, using them to monitor the movement of both commercial and naval vessels. In parliament the two were exposed as double agents, who had duped Harley and given the French intelligence that threatened the English navy. Perhaps even more damning was that they revealed that Harley failed to act on the one piece of good intelligence that Bara provided in order to win his trust. Had he passed Bara's plotting of French ships on to the Admiralty, Harley could have prevented some of the losses of English convoys that the parliamentary examination of the navy condemned. Not only did Harley let double agents in, but he failed to realise and capitalise on the kinds of intelligence that could aid the war effort. The Lords' inquiry culminated with an address to the Queen calling for reforms that would see the 'papers and letters of the greatest importance be kept private from the clerks and under officers'. Designed to embarrass Harley, the recommendation that, 'in order to put a stop to this pernicious correspondence', the Queen should personally intervene to professionalise the office of the Secretary was not a bad one.[60]

Those on the committee could not help but feel that the address would have had more force had they broken Gregg. Yet he remained loyal. On his way to the scaffold, Gregg left a paper with the sheriffs that cleared Harley. As he stood at Tyburn, facing down the crowd, he turned to the sherriff to give final words that all could hear: 'Mr Harley is perfectly innocent.' The scene was too composed – as was Gregg himself. Almost immediately people began to speculate that Harley had orchestrated the performance. Perhaps he had also pressed a hidden hand in his own investigation: had he used Lewis to control information and steer the inquiry away from his office's worst excesses? The chatter was muffled as the Gregg affair was eclipsed by a greater scandal. The nation at large was drawn into a French action, 'the most bold and daring attempt' they had yet 'undertaken this war'.[61]

⸸

Harley's formidable spy John Ogilvie continued the mission he was set on before his handler's troubles had begun. Having dismissed Edinburgh as an intelligence desert, Ogilvie crossed the Lowlands. The journey induced a kind of magical stupor. Ogilvie could not quite believe what he saw and heard: the portrait of the nation he sent Harley was like that of 'an Italian necromancer'. The finding that shocked him into an altered state was that rumours of planned French invasion seemed to be true. They were true enough that 'most of the kingdom is entered into an association with the King of France'. The Scots anticipated the arrival of troops, from France and the Irish Corps, and they expected the Pretender himself would land soon. From what Ogilvie could gather, it looked as if the invasion was first planned for November 1707 but had been delayed. Ogilvie believed the rumours but for Harley's sake pursued confirmation. Riding north to Perthshire, he began visiting estates that bordered the Highlands to seek out and disrupt Jacobite networks at the moment they tried to extend their influence southwards. He spoke to nobles across the county but it was James Drummond, son of the exiled Earl of Perth, he most sought. From Drummond, Ogilvie could extract the intelligence needed to expose the intertwining plots of St Germain and Versailles that stood behind invasion of Scotland.

Ogilvie spent significant time cultivating Drummond's trust. When he was in Europe he befriended him. An incisive judge of character, he saw that Drummond was far more cautious than his father. When St Germain had wanted to use Drummond as a messenger, he demurred, fearing it would expose him. As Ogilvie moved between Rotterdam, St Germain, Hamburg and Paris, he was able to keep Drummond on side, even leaving his own agent Dennis Connell in Drummond's service. When spycatchers spotted Connell near Gravesend, they noted his outlandish clothes and that he 'had the King of France's head cut in steel tied to his watch'. The picture is of a roguish fop, an all too obvious Jacobite trinketed with the steel image of loyalty. It was a costume. Even so, Drummond and his father were convinced.[62] Connell returned with Drummond to Scotland before going back to St Germain, where he shadowed Perth, keeping Ogilvie informed of the happenings of the exiled Court. By recruiting Connell and other informers in Scotland, as well as France, Ogilvie in effect fashioned his own node within Harley's network, one that was uniquely able to infiltrate the Franco-Jacobite compact and expose its workings to the English spymaster.[63]

When Ogilvie came to meet Drummond in Perthshire, he took extra precautions. It was not just for his own safety: displaying the effort he took to shroud himself immediately set the cautious Drummond at ease. The two arranged for Drummond go on a hunt. While he stalked the woods that bordered his estate, Ogilvie would make his approach. The two men ended up speaking for three hours. The central thrust of their conversation confirmed what Ogilvie feared: Hooke had indeed been in Scotland while the last parliament sat and had left convinced that after the Union passed the Scottish Jacobites were ready to take military action. The Jacobite spy had taken this message to Louis XIV and returned to Scotland once again, earlier that year, to 'treat with the nobility and gentry'. This time he carried a set of instructions from the French King committing ten thousand troops, arms and money and a declaration promising to maintain Presbyterianism as Scotland's established religion. Ogilvie conveyed these instructions to Harley in haste, but not before seeking a final few points of corroboration. He confirmed Drummond's story with the Earl of Breadalbane. He confirmed that Panmure had met with Hooke. And in his conversation with Stormont, a member of the Juncto, he perceived a man ready to rise.

With this, Ogilvie sent Harley definitive evidence that France was planning to invade. Louis' war council had finally committed money.

They were willing to make tactical concessions to Scotland's established religion in order to draw Presbyterians in and, by promising an elevation of status, they had a way to entice vassals away from any lords who remained loyal to England. Ogilvie's time in Europe primed him to see an increase in French 'tampering' in Scotland's affairs. From his informers at St Germain he heard too that the 'the Prince of Wales is become very vigorous', steeling himself to return.

Immured in domestic intrigue, Harley was even more distant than usual. Ogilvie was 'uneasy here', he told Harley. Not least because he feared for his family in London. Though Ogilvie needed instructions and knew his work would be more effective if guided from London, he did not sit idly in wait. He was a resourceful agent and once he had established the invasion was imminent, he set about finding ways to afford the Queen's government the upper hand in both espionage and military campaigns. He redoubled his ride across Scotland, sending his brother north to Aberdeen to cover ground he could not. As they traversed their land, the two exposed Jacobite agents and French spies. Ogilvie relished the job of spycatcher. As he told Harley, 'there is nothing like a thief to catch a thief': a man who had been in the French service and pretended he remained so was able to 'snap' agents of France, including Catholic priests and recently returned Scottish exiles. He was 'no stranger to their haunts'. He had lived their lives and knew their ways.

Ogilvie provided Harley with details of military build-up in the Highlands and west country. He found a colonel he had served with in France, who had been at Slains when Hooke was there. From him, Ogilvie extracted fuller details about French troop preparations, including that they planned to leave Dunkirk by light frigate. Most worryingly, when considering their own forces, he found that a large part of the Scottish army was likely to join the rebellion.[64] As a countermeasure, he urged Harley to send the Scots soldiers to other fields in Europe and replace them with English troops. These troops would need someone with knowledge of the country, who had plotted rebel strongholds and knew who to target in order to dismantle the war-entrenched factions. For this, he offered his own services. He wanted to be an officer once again, a move that would give his family greater security and force him out of the shadows – out of the French secret service but also out of Harley's.

Alert to any signs that rebellion would spring before the French arrived, Ogilvie passed Harley intelligence about a plan to attack Edinburgh Castle. In his telling, the plan was 'put off till they have encouragement from France'. What he did uncover was that Ker of Kersland was 'at the bottom of it', but that his movement between London and Edinburgh raised the suspicions of other plotters, who believed that he was there to 'trepan' them, to bore in and undermine their rebellion. In Ker's account, he did infiltrate the plot but dissuaded his co-conspirators from attacking the Castle on the reasoning that any premature uprising might impede the arrival of James III and VIII. At this point, Ker had a Royal Licence that allowed him to associate with Jacobites 'in order to gather intelligence'. Notwithstanding, Ker's recount of events needs to be taken with caution. Ker claimed that it was he who captured the cypher that allowed the English to crack all communiqués between Scottish Jacobites and France.[65] As we have seen, it was Ogilvie who was given this cypher by Torcy, and who thereby allowed Harley's office to interpret secret correspondence from France. Ker's overreach casts serious doubt on his presentation of his other achievements as a secret agent. As he tells it, he found himself drawn deeper into Jacobite 'Labyrinths', running his own spies and offering men to fight in the invasion: an offer that Hooke mostly corroborates. The idea that Ker became a central Jacobite agent is not borne out by Ogilvie's manifests. But Ker did pass intelligence to Godolphin, alerting him that the French fleet had left Dunkirk on 9 March.

In a familiar pattern, Ogilvie and Ker worked largely without adequate support. Had a broader and more centralised coordination existed it would have given Britain a true advantage at the start of what became the Jacobite spy wars: the extended efforts of sleepers and secret agents to restore the main line of the Stuarts, an espionage campaign that supported the invasions of 1708 and 1715 and culminated in 1745 when Bonnie Prince Charlie led an uprising that came within 200 miles of London. In 1708 the French invasion gave Whig lords a point of blame. Here was another piece of evidence that Harley's office missed vital intelligence.[66]

It is not fair to lay the blame for the bungled response on Harley. Harley did have early reports of a potential invasion from Ogilvie and from Defoe, who noted the September prior that France could 'Do a great Deal of Mischeif' with minimal men and funds.[67] However, Harley did not keep this intelligence to himself. He passed Ogilvie's dispatches on to Godolphin. Moreover, Ker reported to Godolphin about the invasion.[68] And Marlborough had a letter from a member of the council of state at Brussels that warned him too.[69] Looking at the spies in the field, the process of infiltrating Jacobite networks was honed, but hampered by the fact that too many masters and not enough funding produced competition rather than proper cooperation between the agents. The fact that intelligence flowed through the offices of the Secretaries of State, who were also in competition with each other at this point, raised another impediment. Even if Harley had devoted all his energies to the intelligence from France and Scotland, the administrative state lacked the impersonal and objective mechanisms to funnel intelligence to action. All had to go through Harley, who was no longer a viable conduit. He was distracted by the Gregg affair and campaign to remove him. In any case, his relationship with Godolphin and Marlborough had deteriorated far past the point of trust.

In the end Harley was not Secretary when the French fleet departed. The problem was that his agents still reported to him and not the office. Had Harley still been in power when the French sailed, Ogilvie speculated: 'I should have either lost my life or you should have known all the particulars both of their ships and numbers of their troops and I fancy I could have been very useful to you after they had landed.' But with Harley gone, Ogilvie promised never again to 'venture my life or my honour' for espionage.[70] Despite bouts of coldness and irregular pay, Ogilvie's loyalties (like Defoe's) lay far more with the man who had rescued him than the organs of state surveillance he built, but from which he was now completely estranged.

⸸

In spring 1708 the French fleet was ready to depart Dunkirk. Heeding Hooke's advice, the main body was made up of frigates: small, fast vessels – twenty-three in total. Accompanying them were five men-of-war, larger ships with heavier arms. Together, the ships carried six thousand French troops. The fleet was commanded by the Chevalier de Forbin. Forbin had little enthusiasm for the mission. He had wanted to stage an attack on Amsterdam and felt that with this assignment he was being dragged away from the main theatre of war.[71]

Unlike a battle in Europe, an invasion of Britain meant Forbin had to contend with St Germain. Two of Middleton's sons joined his force. The greater complication was that fleet had to carry the would-be James III of England and VIII of Scotland. Even before they left, the putative King caused problems, forcing Forbin to delay the fleet's departure as they waited for him to recover from a bout of measles. The French council of war was wary of the Stuarts. Hooke's main task as he travelled with the fleet, as both soldier and spy, was to ensure that the invasion did not break loose from French control; that the 'rightful' King (the Pretender) remained a tool rather than true ally. The French needed James III and VIII as a figurehead to rouse Scottish forces. As a tactical imperative, they had to ensure that in the field he remained under French control.

Despite forewarning, the English response to the invasion lagged. Once it was clear that invasion was indeed inevitable, there was a scramble. Marlborough brought troops back from Europe, sending part of the force to buttress Leven's army in Scotland and another to the northeast of Ireland – ready to launch a counter-invasion. With the military stretched by a protracted war, this movement came at the expense of depleting his army in Flanders. At sea, Marlborough coordinated with the Admiralty to deploy ships under the command of Admiral Sir George Byng to blockade Dunkirk. The English parliament perceived the threat. They voted through supply and authorised a war footing, suspending habeas corpus. In Scotland itself, Anne sent warning and authorisation to the Scottish Privy Council. Facing down the end of its existence, the Queen emboldened the Council: its final act was to keep the peace using any and every means.[72]

By mid-March it seemed like the hand of Providence had finally stretched to France's favour. Rough winds broke Byng's blockade. Forbin seized the advantage and launched the fleet. Carrying the freshly recovered James III and VIII, the French ships made directly for Scotland. At this point Hooke's recommendation proved astute. The frigates fast outran Byng's ships, reaching Scotland two days before the English navy got sight of them. The problem was that the same northwest gale that had allowed Forbin to slip through the blockade now blew him off course. The French fleet was meant to land at Leith where, according to Hooke's plan, James III and VIII would be in position to 'immediately make himself master of the capital'. Seizing Edinburgh would 'strike terror in the hearts of [his] enemies'.[73] The city was perfectly positioned to launch an invasion of Britain: it drew in roads from the north along which Highland forces could travel; to its south it led the army's way to England. Instead, Forbin touched land around a hundred miles north, near Aberdeen – a mistake that Defoe came to think of as 'a Deliverance'.[74]

As Forbin's fleet doubled back to Edinburgh, Byng regrouped in pursuit. Unbeknownst to either commander, a French vessel, the *Proteus*, arrived at the Firth of Forth at two in the afternoon on 23 March, half a day before the rest of Forbin's ships. Suffering damage from the storm, the *Proteus* had turned back when the fleet first set out. When it resumed its course, it sailed directly. Following the initial plan, the *Proteus* made its way up the Firth towards Leith, where it was met by Scottish pilots who guided the ship to harbour. As Hooke later reported, the *Proteus* was greeted by a ready and impatient people, whose whole country 'has expected the K— of England these three months'. Fishing vessels and small boats stood poised to flood the firth and bring the troops ashore. There was no doubt that James VIII would 'be received with the utmost demonstrations of joy'. There was even word that the slippery Hamilton had amassed troops and awaited his King's arrival.[75]

When Forbin arrived that evening, his experience was entirely different. Though he sighted the entrance of the firth, he did not carry on to Leith. He sent a signal from aboard. When one was not returned on the ground, he assumed the support that had so fulsomely greeted the *Proteus* was simply not there. The winds that carried the *Proteus* now blew against the incoming vessels. Forbin held the fleet in a waiting position in the stretch of sea between the mouth of the River Forth and the Isle of May while he assessed his position. By this time Byng had made it to the Firth, cutting off all Forbin's chances of making land there. With Forbin in sight, the strategic instincts trained into Byng took hold. The Admiral turned to the French. Alarmed, Forbin 'immediately weighd' and 'got under Sail', as Defoe later chronicled. In the chase, Byng recaptured the *Salisbury*, a vessel earlier taken from the English.[76] The rest of the French ships sped through, pursued by the English navy as far as Buchan Ness. At that point Byng ceded to their speed and so turned back, anchoring his fleet off Leith in a position designed to defend Edinburgh.

For Defoe, the contrary winds and Forbin's moment of indecision saved the fledgling Union. Defoe was certain that had the French landed, '*They would with very little Opposition have been* Masters *of the whole* Country.' His reasoning was premised on the conditions when Forbin sat off the mouth of the River Forth. At the time Scotland's fortifications were 'out of Repair'; the nation's magazines were empty, 'The *New Government* Unform'd' and 'The *People* Divided'. In words that uncannily echo the aims of Hooke's plan, Defoe knew that had the landing been pulled off '*in two Hours*', the French and Jacobites '*had been Masters of* Edinburgh'.[77]

Having abandoned the landing spot Hooke thought best, Forbin's fleet sailed up the coast in an attempt to salvage their mission. The King on board wanted to disembark. Forbin counselled him against it as they tacked up the Aberdeenshire coast. When they reached Inverness, the wind beat them out of a safe landing. With that, retreat turned to abandonment. The invasion was scuppered and Forbin turned his course back to Dunkirk. The invasion was costly and embarrassing. While Hooke's choice of frigates gave the French the advantage of speed, they were small. They could not carry sufficient supplies and lacked accommodation for troops. Many of the soldiers had to travel on deck. Without enough food and exposed to the elements, nearly four thousand of them perished.[78]

Defoe's view that the King of France would not '*Embark in a Design of so Great Consequence*' had he '*not received Invitations from* Scotland' was widely shared.[79] In the aftermath of the aborted invasion, the government rounded up suspected conspirators, amongst them Fletcher, Belhaven, Hamilton and Atholl. The Privy Council investigated both Hamilton and Atholl. Hamilton was arrested at his estates in Lancashire and imprisoned at Edinburgh Castle, before being transported to London. Atholl was called before the Council. Despite Lockhart's claims that Stirling and Edinburgh castles and 'all the prisons in Edinburgh, were crammed full of nobility and gentry', the prosecution of the upper echelons was relatively short lived. After the Court rebuffed Hamilton's pleas for bail, he turned to the Junto, who secured it on the condition that he support them in the upcoming election by allying himself to the Squadrone and against Queensberry's faction. Atholl never came before the Council. When summoned, he sent a doctor in his place to testify that he was too sick to attend. The Council then ordered dragoons to seize Blair Castle, his ancestral home in Perthshire. They called the order back when they had confirmation of the gravity of his illness. After that, Atholl suffered no further prosecution. As with Hamilton, the fact that the sixteen representative Scottish peers would be elected as part of the general election meant politicians in England considered him as a potential ally in the new parliament – and certainly someone who could use his influence amongst the nobility to determine who was returned as part of the sixteen.[80]

For Lockhart and other Scottish Jacobites, the failed invasion was a sign that Louis XIV was not truly concerned with restoring James III and VIII but had simply used the mission as a diversionary tactic in a larger war.[81] It is true that diversion was probably France's main aim, but it was also in the Bourbon interest to install a King who in exile had become a French vassal. The underlying motivations do not diminish the significance of what could have been. Historians have shown that even though the Pretender already established never touched Scottish soil, the mere attempt caused a massive decline in English stock prices. If the invasion had rolled south, it could have cut off London from Newcastle's coal, dulling the city's power. At the time Defoe pointed out that Scotland was 'naked' and vulnerable to attack. Hiding in plain sight, he staked before English readers a particular authority on Scottish affairs: 'The Intelligence, I have establish'd in *Scotland*, enables me to speak sometimes what every Body does not hear.' What he told them was that they should take seriously Scotland's vulnerabilities and support buttressing its military defences. In the same issue he also counselled readers to ignore pernicious rumours that opponents to the Union had coalesced behind the Pretender – and that Presbyterians were driving this process. It was in England's tactical interests to make it seem that the opposition in Scotland remained divided and had not come together to the extent they did. When the French retreated, Defoe allowed himself a moment of triumphalism:

> And so the *French* are gone Home again, are they? And all the mighty Project is come to nothing.
>
> *Their numerous Fleet with seven thousand Men*
> *Went out to Sea, and SO came Home again.*[82]

Free from the immediate risk, Defoe's assessment a year later was even starker. Had the Pretender landed, it would have '*Ruin'd Scotland*' and '*Brought the* Seat *of* War *home to our shores*; it would have diverted forces from Flanders, where they were needed and, in doing so, '*exceedingly protracted the* War'. Only by 'the immediate *Interposition of a* Divine Power' was the invasion snuffed. The cascading series of missteps, accidents and bad weather turned Providence's favour back to England. And for this, Defoe was humbly thankful, knowing that a successful invasion would have '*at once Unravelled all this happily finished* Constitution'. It would have undone his work in bringing the Union about. It would have split two nations in war at the very moment they were set to choose the men who would represent them in the parliament of the United Kingdom of Great Britain.[83]

CHAPTER 11

TWO ELECTIONS

Defoe arrived back in Edinburgh on 17 April 1708. The trek north was the worst he had experienced. It might just have been 'the Severest Journey That Ever man had'. The rain beat continuously. The roads quickly passed from clogged to flooded. The 'Depth of The Wayes' caked his poor horse's legs, forcing each movement into a slow deliberate pull from the brackish mire. Defoe worried about how these conditions would slow the passage of intelligence and make his reporting on the election that much harder.[1]

Defoe was uneasy continuing as a government agent after Harley's fall. With hindsight, he was thankful that Harley had urged him to continue working for Godolphin. Defoe recalled how Harley pressed the writer to recognise that Godolphin 'will employ you in nothing but what is for the publick Service', while also reminding him that in a larger sense 'it is the Queen you are serving'.[2] The reflection is a little rosy. As Samuel Johnson quipped, after Harley fell 'he lost his power but kept his enemies'.[3] Defoe's image of Harley graciously passing him to Godolphin is suspicious. Most likely it served to justify the writer's change in allegiance after the fact. It might also reflect how he shored himself up at the time. Defoe did not have a personal connection to Godolphin. Though he was closer to Sunderland in politics, his service to him was limited. The cross purposes of the two ministers came to complicate Defoe's communication with each. His fear that he would be accused of 'Maintaining a Counter Correspondence'

– acting as a double agent – increased as Sunderland emerged as Godolphin's chief electoral antagonist.[4] It is easy to see how holding on to a broader ideal of national service helped define his purpose. But it too was darkened by Harley's shadow. Defoe remained faithful to Harley and his moderate vision, making it difficult to work for a ministry that had not just felled him but as it fractured seemed ever more intent on undoing his work.

⸸

The election had to be held in 1708. While Defoe publicly supported regular elections, shortly after arriving in Scotland he complained to Godolphin that enforced regularity 'has This irreparable Mischief in it, That it Keeps alive Our Divisions'. Defoe's momentary lurch away from defending the franchise speaks to the fractious situation that confronted him on his return to Edinburgh. Compounding things was a deep concern that Godolphin's aloofness might leave him with even less support than he had under Harley. With all due deference, he reminded his new patron that 'In the Affair of the Union My Lord I was placed here with assurance of Support', that 'I did my Uttmost' and 'I had my Share of the Hazard of the Union More Than any man', and yet 'Every man more or less (but I) reaped some share of her Majesties Bounty'.

The state of politics in Scotland dismayed Defoe. The forces arrayed against the ministry had cynically abandoned their party principles in favour of a kind of electoral gamesmanship that made it so

> they that would be call'd the *Whig* Party vote for profess'd *Jacobites*, *Whigs* set up *Tories* against *Whigs*, and *Jacobites* take the Oaths to quallifie themselves to vote for *Whigs*, and *Tories* set up *Whigs* against *Tories*. In short, it is all a Game of Parties, the Squadrons jostle in Politicks where they joyn in Principle, and joyn in the Means where they are Opposites in the End.[5]

The task Defoe assumed fell to him was to sift through this confusion of alliance and principle to give Godolphin first off and Sunderland, too, a way into the thickets. It was clear to Defoe that Godolphin and the Court had some disadvantages. The disbanding of the Scottish Privy Council just before the election limited ministry control over how the election was run. The final pages of the Council's minutes have been torn out, forever shielding from view their last actions. What can be seen is that the Council's demise served the Squadrone's efforts, but only in the very short term. The Court lost its managerial advantage but Scotland as a whole lost a body that coordinated intelligence, monitored dissent in MPs and clergy, and oversaw military defence. Though eliminating the Scottish Privy Council was designed to standardise local government, ironically it made Scotland less amenable to centralised government, and even more prone to Jacobite risings.[6]

The Junto's support for abolishing the Scottish Privy Council helped firm their alliance with the Squadrone. Because the Junto had been the ones to secure Hamilton's bail, he was corralled into the pact and tasked with promoting an alternative list of peers. If the Junto–Squadrone alliance could get some of their own lords selected they could gain an important source of power, setting the tone for the election of the lower house that had begun by the time the lords were chosen on 17 June, but continued well after. Queensberry had been made a British Secretary of State for Scotland and worked with Godolphin to prepare their list of sixteen. The Court party still had favour and patronage at their disposal and should have triumphed. But Hamilton was able to draw significant support to the Squadrone's list. In the weeks before the election of the peers, Duchess Anne finally managed to broker a peace between her son and Atholl. Though Atholl was still under guard and too ill to travel, he sent in a proxy with his selection.[7] With the opposition figures united and joined to the Squadrone and their Whig allies, Hamilton firmed up a bloc of nobles to counter the Court's list. The only person on both lists was Hamilton's brother Orkney. Despite the Court considering him a viable prospect, he ended up supporting Hamilton and working to elect Squadrone members. The Court returned eleven representative peers and the Squadrone six (with Orkney counted for both). Hamilton was elected. He joined lords like Mar and Leven appointed in 1707 and returned now. Though the Court party had a small majority, the fact that the Squadrone managed to elect six lords represented a significant shift in power. For Godolphin it was a major loss; for Hamilton a 'Glorious victorie'.[8] It portended well for a party keen to exploit the weakness of the incumbents to knock Queensberry and Godolphin from the perches on power they had held for much of Anne's reign.

Edinburgh after the election of the peers was in a state of 'Combustion' according to Defoe, who likened it to 'the City of Naples after a Vesuvian Erruption'. Working the campaign, he reported its early results to Sunderland, noting how fortunate it was the Franco-Jacobite invasion had failed: most of England was completely unaware 'how much Averse to English Government A large party Even of our Friends are here'. Sunderland was now running Shute as his agent and had a better sense of things than Defoe allowed.[9] The fact that Defoe did not shield from Sunderland his contempt for the Squadrone's abandonment of the Court exposes the limits of Defoe's intelligence. It was Sunderland who helped break the alliance and Defoe's lack of awareness no doubt led the Secretary to dismiss the value of his work as a spy.

The Whig campaign that Sunderland helped coordinate certainly indicates that the party was open to exploiting the invasion as a way of fomenting for their own gain divisions within and between England and Scotland. Sarah Churchill played an important role in this campaign. The Duchess of Marlborough had a good nose for polemic. In 1705 she had anonymously sent Defoe funds when Marlborough had featured positively in the *Review*. In 1708, she oversaw the work her private secretary Arthur Mainwaring did producing *Advice to the Electors of Great Britain*. The pamphlet took as given that the '*French* receiv'd Encouragement' to invade from both Scotland and England. When it came to speculate the source of this encouragement, it pitted the two parties against each other. Was it the Whigs who invited the Pretender? It was unlikely, given that their raison d'être was preserving the gains of the Revolution Settlement. Far more likely was that the Tories called the Pretender to British shores given that above all the party worked 'to make a Government as absolute and lawless as possible'.[10]

Alongside the propaganda campaign, the Whigs engaged in a series of highly effective dirty tricks. Sunderland, his Squadrone partners and Hamilton pushed rumours that the Queen was on the cusp of rejecting Godolphin and Queensberry in favour of the leaders of the Junto and Squadrone. They leaked letters as evidence: their intent was to sap Godolphin and the Court of the electoral cachet that came from royal support. The second rumour they spread was that Godolphin had purposefully neglected Scotland's defence during the invasion. The implication was that Godolphin was a crypto-Jacobite. As far as accusations went, it had enough sticking power to shake him. Without Harley, the bristly Godolphin was ill equipped to fight back. At the polls in Scotland, the Court was outmanoeuvred by the Junto who worked locally with the Squadrone to back their candidates. In the first elections for the united parliament, the Junto had effectively broken the Court-Squadrone voting bloc that had delivered the Union. In a move that troubled Defoe for its preferencing tactic over principle, the Junto and Squadrone opposed candidates backed by the Court, even appealing to Jacobites to do so. The hypocrisy of tacitly endorsing Jacobites in order to stave off the threat of Jacobitism left Defoe in fear for the future of the new United Kingdom.[11]

†

Defoe was 'on the Spot'. He wrote propaganda and used his network to oppose Jacobites. And while he felt he did quite well, the fact remained that a set of radical Whigs were 'not asham'd' to 'Vote even those Men into Parliament, who were at that very Time lock'd up in the Castle of *Edinburgh*, for favouring the Invasion of the Pretender'. He faced down a slippery campaign that played both ends. The Junto used the invasion to tar Godolphin and his allies and yet at the same time allied themselves with people who openly supported invasion. The obviously paradoxical campaign worked because elections in the early eighteenth century were narrowly localised affairs: across different constituencies heteroglossic and even contradictory arguments could be plied to the same party ends. In Scotland in 1708 forty-five seats were contested. The Treaty assigned fifteen to burghs and thirty-three to counties, meaning three alternated. This complicated the returns which throughout the period were already often disputed, with controverted seats adjudicated by the parliament itself in a process that more often than not reinforced the incoming majority.

Elections required the kind of management at which Harley excelled. Targeted local campaigns called out for the data-driven, opinion-sampled infrastructure and political demography Defoe provided during his tours of England and Scotland. That is not to say that the result would have been different had Harley remained as Secretary. The counterfactual cannot be proved. It is likely, however, that Harley would have had a better countercampaign, one designed at the granular level to offset the swing away from the ministry and Scottish Court. Even though he was no longer Secretary, Harley still kept close watch. He received a full account of the nobles and how they were likely to vote on the representative peers. His former under-secretary Erasmus Lewis also kept him updated on Hamilton's movements. His lurch to the Junto, which Defoe read as brazen, was in Lewis' report 'a hard morsel' for Hamilton to take 'but he was forced to digest it' to gain his freedom.[12]

The election of Hamilton and Orkney was not the sum total of the family's push for power. Their youngest brother Archibald stood for two seats: Great Marlow in Buckinghamshire as well as Lanarkshire, the family's Scottish stronghold. Duchess Anne ran much of the strategy, though she left the day-to-day electioneering to her secretary David Crawford. Her son and political crony Selkirk ostensibly stood back as well, lest it seem he was unduly influencing things. However it appeared, this was Anne's election. She attempted to talk a potentially formidable opponent out of the running. And, when this failed, Crawford made plain that the votes she commanded out of personal loyalty, especially in Glasgow, would be enough to sway Lanarkshire her son's way. Crawford was right: Archibald was elected to the Scottish but not the English seat.[13]

Another candidate who needed the sort of backing the Hamiltons provided was Paterson. His position as a customs agent had given him the stability Defoe so deeply desired. With this small berth came a chance to catch himself, and to revive some of his plans. At the start of 1708 he believed that the best way for him to shape the nation with his ideas was through elected office. This compelled him to run for a seat in the Dumfries burghs against William Johnston. Both Paterson and Johnston were elected on a double return, sending the result to parliament for adjudication. The well-connected Johnston won out and Paterson never took his seat. The loss was a 'great mortification' to Paterson and, according to Harley's son Edward, 'an unknown loss' to parliament at a time when there was a 'pinch for money' and an 'able projector' might have been rather useful. Denied once more an entry into a place of power, Paterson slumped into 'a long and dangerous fit of sickness'.[14]

Of the forty-five MPs for Scotland, nineteen were backed by the Squadrone and twenty-six by the Court: a good result for the Squadrone. In England and Wales, the Whigs triumphed. For the first time in Anne's reign the party achieved an outright majority. And yet their capitulation to the Jacobites had long-term effects that, in Defoe's analysis, they never adequately countenanced. The party had ushered in a group of Jacobites who 'not only stood their Ground against their Patrons, but overthrew' Whigs of all kinds in the coming sessions, moderates and radicals alike.[15]

⸸

In the face of an electoral loss orchestrated by his alleged allies in the Junto, Godolphin's laissez-faire approach to agents in the field lost some of its command. The Treasurer did not seem to have the same high hand of control he once did. Sensing this, the ever-opportunistic Ker travelled to London in March 1709 to claim payment for his secret services. According to Lockhart the initial payment of £500 increased to 2,000 guineas after Ker threatened to expose Godolphin's connections to the Jacobites. Such connections were common to the ministry and were a regular aspect of the traffic in intelligence. The fee Ker extracted was likely exaggerated. But the story illustrates a growing problem. The agents deployed for and against the Union were left in the field, mostly without support or instruction. The Union and the aborted invasion of 1708 altered the grounds of debate so that Jacobitism emerged as the natural home for Scottish nationalists. This newly ennobled cause looked good to many of these capable and often unscrupulous spies.[16] Still loyal to Harley, Ogilvie tracked the work of Jacobite spies who were sharper than Ker and chased more than personal gain: these spies pushed schemes that would involve Marlborough and thereby legitimise efforts to place the Prince of Wales on the throne after the Queen died.[17]

Defoe remained committed to the Union and proud of the work he did bringing it into being. When sent back to Scotland in August 1709, he slipped back into a city with a new kind of ease. Though he did not take for granted the stability of the political settlement, he was able to live more of his life north of the Tweed. The stories that had once given him cover now marked his integration into Scottish life and business. He brought his son Benjamin to enrol in the University of Edinburgh. As a parent to a child adult in all except responsibility, Defoe ostensibly gave Benjamin his freedom while keeping watch from afar through his network of friends, who kept close track of Benjamin with especial focus on what he spent. The year 1709 marked a new phase in Defoe's work. He was too established in Edinburgh and too well known to infiltrate any Jacobite network. That fell to Ogilvie. Defoe's skills had other uses. His main brief was to colonise the Scottish press. His intent was to acquire the machinery that could move the Scottish public away from rising or rebellion. To that end he started an Edinburgh edition of the *Review*. With aid from his friend John Russell, Defoe won rights and privileges to publish the *Edinburgh Courant*. Defoe also began working with David Fearne, another of Harley's former agents, contracting out to him the rights to publish the *Scots Postman*. Had the Scottish press remained Defoe's focus, the stable of titles would have given him an agenda-setting mandate.

⸸

As immersed as Defoe was in his Edinburgh life, his eyes and mind were fixed on London politics. In the city things were shifting. The Junto were not the partners Godolphin had wanted. Soon after they had triumphed in the election, they began 'forming schemes, and preparing accusations' against Godolphin and Marlborough. Their intent was to wrest the ministry from the duumvirs. They were bent on exposing Godolphin's financial mismanagement. Wharton and Somers employed Paterson to audit the nation's finances. Paterson needed to be needed, especially since the election had brought him so close to government only for entrance to be blocked at the last minute. His audit was a foregone conclusion: his task as the Whig lords defined it was to 'take an account of the public debts, and to represent the miserable condition the nation was brought into'. Harley's brother Edward noticed that attacking Godolphin's work as Treasurer was only the first step in their plan. To ensure he could not retain power, the Junto needed to stop Godolphin resuming an alliance with the Tories. For Edward Harley this was one of the reasons the Whigs began the disastrous process of impeaching Dr Henry Sacheverell, a move that would forever tie Godolphin to Revolution principles and Whig anti-clericalism.[18]

Edward gives a bit too much credit to forethought. The impeachment of Sacheverell was reactionary. The incendiary preacher was invited to give a sermon on 5 November 1709 commemorating the Gunpowder Plot. The date also marked William III's landing at Brixham in 1688, which set off the Revolution that ended with him on the throne. Sacheverell weaved the two events together to insist that the danger to Church and state was not from external foes but from 'false brethren' within England: tepid 'Moderate' politicians unwilling to defend the Church and Dissenters, like Defoe, who actively worked to undermine Anglican supremacy. The sermon challenged the legitimacy of the Revolution and it attacked Godolphin in all but name. Its tone and content placed Sacheverell close to the preacher Defoe aped in *The Shortest Way*. The sermon drove popular prejudices by catering to them. It gave enough biblical cover to justify hatred of religious dissent and push that hatred outwards to those whose politics aligned them with Dissenters. The published version released in the weeks after it was spoken became a bestseller, with one estimate suggesting it clocked close to 250,000 readers.[19]

Sacheverell's popularity demanded a response. The Whigs in government took the lead. After debating tactics, they settled on impeaching Sacheverell for high crimes and misdemeanours, a course that would see him tried before both houses of parliament. As a process, impeachment was drawn out and delayed, which played to Sacheverell's advantage. Mounting the full weight of parliament against the preacher made him into a living martyr, as Defoe suspected it would. In the months after the sermon was published, he counselled ignoring it, reasoning that drawing attention to fringe views would not just legitimate them but would further inflame the public. But when the impeachment was finally brought before parliament in late February 1710 he rallied. He was determined his readers realise what was at stake. On trial was the 'Validity of the Revolution': was it 'legal' and 'just' or, as Sacheverell maintained, 'plain Rebellion'? If Sacheverell were acquitted, it would 'sink' the constitution. Defoe's is a hyperbolic view but it stems from the sound premise that so much of what constitutes Britain – 'Protestant Succession, the Claim of Right, the Queen's Title *de Jure*' – is built on 'resisting Tyranny, and displacing Oppressors'. The Revolution was an act of justified resistance, one that heralded the political order that Defoe defended his entire writing life.[20] The constitution did not sink. Sacheverell was found guilty. His sermon was burnt by the common hangman, and he was barred from preaching for three years. The relative lightness of this punishment suggests that Defoe's strident view did not win out. The Queen was concerned that a harsh sentence would stoke more popular unrest. The votes to convict were tighter than Godolphin hoped and he did not want to lose any more Court Tories in England or Scotland.[21]

The paper battle over the trial showed that arguments defending public institutions and democratic norms were a bad match for the public's anger. Riots broke out across England. Dissenting meeting houses were attacked, with an unguarded animus directed to Presbyterian congregations like the one in which Defoe worshipped. Writers committed to the Revolution Settlement had typically seen 'the people' as their political proving ground. When popular fury rose up against the ideals of the Revolution, it was shattering. To Defoe, this was the first mob that actively rioted against their own liberty. Defoe's first instincts were right. In impeaching Sacheverell, the Whigs (and by imputation the ministry) overplayed their hands. In Edward Harley's phrase, the party of the people lost the very people 'upon whose interests and affections they pretended [claimed] ever since the Revolution … to value themselves … and to whom on all occasions they appealed'. The party of the people was no longer.[22]

During the Sacheverell trial Harley was conspicuously absent. This was partly strategic and partly because he was struck by a violent cold that kept him from Westminster. In the backstairs he was anything but complacent. He gathered that the Junto were moving against Godolphin and Marlborough and would attempt to remove them in order to 'engross' their own power. This presented Harley an opportunity. In previous years he would not have considered an alliance with the Junto. Now, tensions between the Junto and duumvirs, coupled with the Queen's growing desire to break free from the Duchess and Duke of Marlborough, offered a way to complete the ministerial revolution that two years prior had led to his fall.

Marlborough was alert to the moves against him, predicting that the Junto would actively pursue Harley through his confederate in Anne's retinue, Abigail Masham.[23] Masham was indeed Harley's connection and through her he was able to follow the Queen's movements and offer the monarch the kind of counsel that allowed him to re-enter her confidences. By this point Masham had well and truly replaced Sarah, the Duchess of Marlborough, as Anne's favourite. The Queen could no longer suffer Sarah's temper. Sarah could not bring the Queen to yield as she once did, and both took umbrage at the change: Sarah because she would not submit to her diminished status; Anne because of the shame she felt after it dissipated of the hold Sarah once had on her.[24] At Court Sarah saw each action as a slight. Each time the Queen went on a religious retreat, or retired for a moment of contemplation, Sarah thought it was cover for collusion with Abigail. She could not see that the Queen needed quiet. The death of her husband in 1708 had given her depression a darker pall and drained her already broken body. Sarah's behaviour compounded the insult the Queen took when Marlborough pushed to be named Captain-General for life, a request that set in motion a series of disputes over military appointments and control over regiments that pitted the General's tactical domain against the Queen's prerogative. To the Queen, Harley drummed a narrative that was gaining traction more widely: Marlborough wanted the war to continue for his personal gain, to amass wealth and power.[25]

Resentful of how she and her husband had been treated, in early April 1710 Sarah could no longer control her anger. When Anne would give her no answer on the General's position, and retreated into herself during Sarah's interrogation, Sarah cursed 'that God would punish her [the Queen] either in this world or the next'.[26] This was the last time they spoke. Sarah's refusal to apologise confirmed to Anne that she needed to be rid of the Marlboroughs. She also wanted Sunderland gone. Harley worked to convince her that the change she desired would best be achieved if she dismissed Godolphin too.

After two years without contact, Defoe wrote to Harley in July. The prayers the writer offered his erstwhile patron suggest that he saw Harley's return as likely. 'I can Not but hope That Heaven has yet Reserv'd you to be the Restorer of your Country.' Defoe wanted Harley to see that he returned to him before others did. With a mix of hope and faithfulness, Defoe presses Harley to retake the mantle of moderation. As he primes Harley to accept him back, he promises to bring the 'Fixt Intelligence' he has established across Britain into Harley's fold.[27]

Defoe's insistence that Harley pursue moderation speaks less to the writer's worry that Harley may stray from his professed commitment to the middle way and more to how difficult it was to hold the line between the parties. Harley wanted to create a ministry from moderates in both parties. When the Junto acceded to Sunderland's dismissal, he had some encouragement. But the Queen favoured Tories and wanted to be rid of the Junto. She also held the ability to dissolve parliament. As Harley jostled the ministry, this prospect became increasingly probable. Another obstacle was that at first the Queen wanted to keep Godolphin. But this became difficult when he refused to break his connection with the Duchess of Marlborough. Godolphin could not calm talk of his mismanagement either. The war ate money, forcing the increase in taxes and putting pressure on the nation's credit. Godolphin's intransigence on finance and friendship gave Harley the baldest evidence to put it in the Queen's mind that he was challenging her authority. When it came to choose between Harley and Godolphin, the Queen now chose Harley.

On 8 August the Queen sent notice by messenger from the royal stables that Godolphin was to break the white staff that symbolised his

8. Mezzotint of Queen Anne, after Sir Godfrey Kneller (1702).

office. The Queen thought it would be 'easier to us both' if the dismissal happened out of the way. With the note in hand, Godolphin snapped the staff. The end happened so whimperingly fast that he had to shake himself to its reality. He took a moment in his garden. When he re-entered his house the staff was intact. Had he dreamed things? Lashing his mind to reality, he realised that one of his servants had seen the broken rod, assumed it was broken accidentally and silently replaced it. As the trancelike fog dispersed, it set in that Godolphin had lost the office he had worked towards for twenty-five years. The Queen quickly put the Treasury into a commission with Harley serving as Chancellor of the Exchequer. Though run collectively, Harley was now principally responsible for the finances of a united Britain. Defoe saw as much, writing to congratulate Harley on being 'Establish'd Again', not forgetting to note that he always regretted that he had been 'Oblig'd by Circumstances to Continue in The Service of your Enemyes'.[28]

After Godolphin's dismissal the markets suffered a crisis in confidence. The Whig lords did not want to collaborate with Harley, who was pushed by the Queen into selecting ministers of a more High Church Tory cast than he wanted. The only way beyond the impasse of a Tory ministry and Whig Commons was to call for a dissolution of parliament. Harley's hope was that moderate Tories would return, giving him parliamentary ballast to steer things back to the middle. Resistant to such a radical purgative, Anne held off until 21 September. When all other options had closed, she dissolved parliament and set in place an election.

⸸

Defoe's return to Harley brought with it a regular pension. He collected the stipend using the alias Claude Guillot. While it was not enough to stave off his creditors, it finally offered him the acknowledgement of consistent employment. When he called for more sustained instructions, he did so lest 'This Bounty' from the Queen be 'wrong Plac't'. As had been the pattern, Defoe suggested his own mission. Defoe floated the idea that he could embark on another tour like the one of 1705.[29] Harley was not about to let him traverse the country when a far more targeted mission presented. Defoe's indispensable expertise on Scotland meant he could return to Edinburgh during the election to gather intelligence and shape results. His mission involved presenting Harley a comprehensive picture of the Scottish MPs sent down to the Commons. Defoe was also there to offset Presbyterian concerns that the Kirk was threatened by Harley's ministerial tack to the typically anti-tolerationist Tories. Much of this task involved persuading Scots that the Union would remain as the Treaty outlined; that a Tory ministry would not challenge its religious settlement. In order to counter this unease and continued speculation that the Pretender was plotting a return, Defoe immersed himself amongst Scotland's people 'by writing, Printing or Conversation', always working to ensure 'That the Poison of a Factious spirit May Not Spread Among them'. The intelligence gathering and electioneering aspects of his mission required him to maintain and extend his network: 'To Settle and Continue Such Correspondence in Every Part'.

Whether it was the pension, the change in political complexion of the ministry, or the Jacobite plots he encountered when he arrived back in Edinburgh in October, Defoe was newly attentive to his spycraft. He signed his letters Guillot, disguised his handwriting and employed a numerical cypher, replacing the names of key people, groups and locations with numbers. The code is not sophisticated and is easy to crack from the context of each surrounding letter. The precautions reflect Defoe's growing concern that his letters were being intercepted. He no longer trusted John Bell, Harley's agent in Newcastle, bristling against Bell's attempts to deny him his financial dues, and sought new ways to correspond with London.[30]

No doubt thrilled by the cast and equipment of 'true spy', Defoe was brought to reality in the first weeks in Scotland by the election of the sixteen representative peers. The writer's main concern was that amongst those chosen were Jacobites who had been imprisoned for their role in the attempted invasion of 1708. Defoe was completely unaware that Harley supported the chosen list and had even bribed peers to vote for it. His intent was to secure a voting bloc that could counter Whig dominance in the Lords. At first, he wanted to do so by securing the return of moderates. His advisors in Scotland counselled against this as it leaned on the Scottish Whigs and the Squadrone. For Defoe, elevating Scottish Tories (which unbeknownst to him Harley backed) was even more problematic than relying on their English counterparts, as Tories in Scotland are 'a Differing kind of People from Ours of that Denomination, being Universally Jacobite'.[31] This was not entirely true, but the influence of Jacobites in Scotland worried Defoe as he tried to redress the imbalance between securing votes in the short term and protecting the succession in the long.

Any concession to Jacobites was an unacceptable risk, according to Defoe, especially given the persistence of rumours that Queen Anne had arranged the Pretender to succeed her. As the election was carried out, the streets of Edinburgh were flooded with letters, 'industriously spread about . . . full of Cyphers, and *half Sentences*', designed to feed ideas of a plot – to make it seem that the Pretender was on the verge of returning.[32] On this point, Defoe's particular anger was reserved for Mar and Argyll, who had replaced Queensberry as Court managers. Defoe's interpretation of their support for Jacobite candidates vacillated between narrow-sighted expedience and outright treachery. Realising he could not rouse Harley against them, he published a satire, *Atalantis Major*, whose allegory is easier to crack than his cypher. In it, Defoe exposes the utter 'Farce' of electing lords to the parliament of a united kingdom who could not even swear to the monarch of that kingdom.

Defoe knew enough of Harley's alliance with Mar and Argyll to understand that the English minister tacitly backed their approach. To preserve independence and sway the public while maintaining good terms with Harley, Defoe did not merely deny authorship of the satire. He went so far as to claim he had apprehended the 'Vile Ill Natur'd' pamphlet, full of 'Bitter Invective', 'written by Some English man and I have Some Guess at the Man, but dare not be positive' and that he had deployed his agents in Edinburgh publishing houses to suppress the work.

As the election results came in, Harley's turn to the Tories in the hope of a more moderate parliament yielded too well. In England and Wales, it was a Tory landslide. In Scotland there was distinct intraparty shift away from the moderate Court-aligned Tories and towards those who supported Episcopacy – a group that Defoe thought were entirely infiltrated by Jacobitism. In the Lords the Whigs maintained their majority. This was not the result Harley wanted. To hew to the middle path he would have to find ways to suppress the power and influence of the now dominant High Church Tories. For Defoe the results presented a problem in how he saw himself and his service. He now worked for a minister whose backing came from a party that Defoe opposed in his core.

When Defoe returned to London in February 1711, his focus remained on Scotland. His abiding concern was that Harley's policy of backing Jacobites and Episcopalians would cause disaffection amongst the majority Presbyterians. He was right to be concerned. In 1709 Episcopal minister James Greenshields was arrested for conducting services opposite St Giles, a deliberate provocation to Presbyterian control. He was imprisoned and his appeal made it all the way to the House of Lords soon after Defoe returned to the capital. The Lords affirmed Greenshields' right to preach. This decision laid the way for greater toleration of Episcopalianism in Scotland, weakening the protections for Presbyterianism built into the Act of Union. The case exposed the Lords as willing to interfere in the management of Scotland's religious settlement. This was not the only challenge to the Union. In a sobering letter Defoe outlined others. There remained deep 'Uneasyness' in the people of Scotland. There were attacks on presbyteries in the north to which Defoe responded by extending his network further into the Highlands. There were fights over representation in the united parliament. And though notionally open, access to global trade was still gatekept by English companies.[33] With so many of the assurances that carried the Union now falling away, the very compact was vulnerable.

⸸

After the fall of Godolphin, Harley returned to his duties as spymaster. On 8 March 1711 he sat with the members of the cabinet. Because the Queen was not in attendance, it could not be called an official cabinet meeting. The group were instead designated the Lords of the Committee and convened in the Cockpit instead of a royal palace. They were there to examine a French spy, Antoine, Marquis de Guiscard. With hindsight, Defoe condemned Guiscard as 'detestable' and urged readers to condemn him to ignominy without further notice. Guiscard's history, Defoe wrote, was 'not worth enquiring after'. Defoe shielded Guiscard's past because it disrupted the view that the spy only served the French. Had Defoe allowed an investigation, he would have found a man who loved the trappings of secret service. In 1706 Ogilvie informed Harley that Guiscard 'hath no reputation' in Paris and was not worth cultivating as an agent. And yet Guiscard was able to exaggerate his clandestine dealings and access, attracting the patronage of a series of English ministers. Guiscard had served Nottingham during his tenure as Secretary of State. Though Harley had reason to avoid Guiscard, Godolphin and Marlborough continued to employ him. Harley's brother was loath to believe that English ministers 'should intrust a man of so vile a character'. And yet Guiscard's access to France outweighed his moral failings in their calculations, for the spy was awarded a pension by Queen

Anne and met often with her Secretary of War Henry St John. At the same time, he likely served the Dutch as well.

Guiscard carried the paranoia of double dealing. Believing that agents of Louis XIV pursued him, he started carrying a vial of poison in his pocket at all times – ready to kill himself if ever the French King's men caught him. In 1711 he was in the process of shifting allegiance towards his pursuers. Guiscard wanted to become a double agent. The Committee knew as much. The spy's letters arranging a meeting with one of Torcy's agents had been intercepted by Harley's men.

In early March, while carried across St James' Park in his chair, Harley spotted Guiscard walking the Mall. Acting quickly, he arranged orders for the spy to be seized and brought before the Committee. A long wooden table separated the suspect from his interrogators. As Guiscard sat before the Committee, he at first denied any approach to France. When one member lifted his hat to reveal Guiscard's intercepted letters, denial was no longer an option. Guiscard jumped the table pulling a pen knife from his pocket and stabbing Harley in the chest. Harley wore a waistcoat that his sister Abigail had embroidered with gold brocade flowers. Its thickness saved him, cushioning Guiscard's blade so that it broke against Harley's shoulder before it could reach a fatal depth.

Queensberry ran out of the room to alert the messengers and footmen. In Defoe's telling, these officers 'seized upon' Guiscard, injuring him so that he died shortly after arriving in Newgate. The coroner's inquest confirmed that Guiscard 'sustained severe injuries in the struggle' as the footmen attempted to arrest him. Harley's brother saw a conspiracy in the speed of Guiscard's demise. He had heard that Guiscard promised to trade secrets for a pardon. Clearly 'there were some persons very much afraid of his recovery'. Guiscard's 'death in Newgate drew a veil of darkness over the villainy of this man, and those persons that employed him'; to Edward Harley, it prevented the ministry from finding out who had ordered the assassination.[34]

There is scant evidence to suggest that the assassination attempt was coordinated by France or Harley's domestic enemies. If it was, it had the opposite effect than intended. Harley met the chaos with a surprising calmness, one that Edward Harley saw as a sign of his brother's unshakeable faith. St John begrudgingly admired how Harley kept composure while the blood still flowed from his wound. Realising the political boon a failed assassination delivered, St John later asserted that he was Guiscard's true target. Whoever the target, whether Guiscard was part of a secret French plot or merely disgruntled because his pension was in arrears, Harley's bravery in the face of death made him as popular as he ever was. In his office letters piled up from ministers and agents congratulating him on his recovery; at the same time they reported Jacobite manoeuvrings and the role the French might have had in his assassination. In one letter Ker of Kersland warns about how monasteries in Flanders were being used as nodes in the Pretender's intelligence network.

Amidst the letters is one from Defoe that turns away from the competition of European intelligence to Harley and contemplates what his loss might have meant. The writer is moved to quiet fervour when he grasps the extent to which he and the nation as a whole depend on Harley. That God has intervened in such a stark singular manner freights the moment with biblical significance. God chose to save Harley. It must be in part divine acknowledgment of the work he has done, but also a sign that there remains 'Some Great work for you to do, which Must be done; Must be done by you'. Defoe is overcome. He has to cut the letter short because the subject 'is So Moveing, My weakness Betrays it Self'. He cannot gather himself to continue thinking about his patron and the divine project he is yet to complete.[35]

Still recovering from the wound, Harley was made Lord Treasurer and elevated to the peerage as 1st Earl of Oxford and Earl Mortimer on 23 May. For Defoe, the intervention of Providence renewed his sense of Harley as the incarnation of a moderate, popular national interest. On paper he defended Harley from the fringes. Taking the line that it was a French-led assassination attempt, Defoe challenged those who doubted Harley's loyalty. Clearly Harley was a threat to the French King and the Pretender. Why else would they seek to have him killed? This was a potent line and did much to counter the view that Harley's true sympathies had been exposed by his support for Jacobite candidates in Scotland and the fact that he pushed for a peace with France. Defoe did not convince all. There was hope still amongst the Jacobites that Harley was beginning to embrace their cause: a hope that would eventually sap his favour with the Queen. From the other side, Defoe imitated strident Tories in *The Secret History of the October Club*, putting into their mouths a lament that Guiscard was unable to complete his task. To readers this was an unmissable sign that Harley (more in Defoe's wish than fact) held to the moderate line so firmly that Tory extremists saw him as a threat.[36]

In the wake of the failed assassination, Harley reached the height of his popularity and power. For Defoe the two were inextricable. Harley had become 'prime Minister with Applause', as Defoe once advised him. And yet moderation and national interest did not overwhelm the opposition to the extent Defoe had hoped. The threat from the extremes remained. A year later another writer deflected yet another assassination attempt – albeit more directly. On 4 November 1712, the day before the commemoration of the Gunpowder Plot and King William's landing in England, Jonathan Swift came upon a hatbox laid at the entrance of Harley's estate. Noticing a strange thread dangling from its join, Swift cut it. In that moment he disarmed a set of cocked pistols rigged to fire on Harley when he opened the box. Again, the failed attempt on Harley's life only made him more popular. And yet maintaining power still required a delicate negotiation of the extremes. To Defoe's displeasure, Harley continued to cater to the Tory hardliners. Rather than freeing him as Defoe predicted it would, Harley's popularity burdened him. As his power increased, so did the desperation of those arrayed against him. As Premier Minister, Harley was constantly aware that his enemies were willing to take desperate measures to bring him down.

JACOBITE SPIES AND THE SURVEILLANCE STATE

In the autumn of 1712, Queen Anne appointed Hamilton as her ambassador to France. The Duke was eager to go. He had found freedom in Paris during the grand tour of his youth – thrilling to its paintings, its playhouses, its drink and women. He rekindled this passion when Charles II sent him as ambassador extraordinaire to the Court of Louis XIV in 1683. His task was to congratulate the French King on the birth of his grandson. Hamilton stayed on and served Louis for two years. He would have remained had Charles' death not brought the audaciously extended appointment to a definite close.

When Anne selected Hamilton – a known Jacobite, confidante of the French King and thorn in the side of Union – the fear that electrified Westminster and the city Whigs was that Hamilton was chosen for his connections to Versailles and St Germain: the worry was that under the guise of securing peace, Anne had given blessing to the Duke to negotiate with France and the exiled Court to bring the Pretender to Britain to succeed her. Such concern misread Hamilton's recent domestication. He was inducted into the Order of the Garter earlier that year and had been made a peer of Great Britain the year before. He was one of the Queen's Privy Councillors and had called his third son Anne, a much-mocked gesture to both his monarch and mother: the rare instance in this age of an aristocrat who might have preferred a daughter to a son. Far from hoping to be Scotland's king, Hamilton had not returned to his country since 1708. These days he split his time between his English estates and his house in St James's Square. On the morning of 15 November he left his London house, making his way due west to Hyde Park for a duel.

Hamilton's opponent was Charles, 4th Baron Mohun. The two were engaged in a protracted legal dispute over an estate. When they met two days prior at the law courts, flushed dark with drink, Mohun provoked Hamilton into a fist fight. As the men were dragged off each other, Mohun spat forth a challenge. Fight with swords. To the death. Hamilton's pride would not let him refuse.

Hamilton was a good swordsman. He was quick and equally comfortable fighting right- and left-handed. But at fifty-five, his sense of himself as one of the country's more formidable duellists was nostalgic. At thirty-seven, Mohun was younger and his experience with a sword more recent. As the two men and their seconds staked a field next to an oaky grove, it looked like Mohun had the advantage. The fight that ensued betrayed any notion of gentlemanly measure. It was frenzied, brutal and short. It is difficult to discern what happened. The official account is that in the midst of the melee Hamilton took his sword in his left hand and ran it through Mohun's chest. Impaled, Mohun spent his last bit of life slashing wildly at Hamilton's exposed right arm. One blow landed, severing Hamilton's brachial artery. Hamilton instinctively drew his left hand to staunch the bleeding. It did little. The blood pumped through his fingers as he stumbled towards the trees, falling first to his knees and then angling his torso so that, as he slumped, a trunk propped him by the shoulders. Against a Hyde Park oak, Hamilton bled to death.

The accusation quickly circulated that it was not Mohun but his better-abled second, George Macartney, a lieutenant general under Marlborough, who intervened at the final moment to kill Hamilton. Speculation over its action raised questions about the cause of the duel. Was it merely inheritance or was something else at play? Mohun was a client of Marlborough. Hamilton was due to broker a peace in France that Marlborough fundamentally opposed. Though exhausted from the campaign and eager to retire, Marlborough had won a set of victories that left his armies poised to march on Paris. He was unwilling to throw that advantage for an expedient peace. The Queen

9. Duel of Hamilton and Mohun, from *An Excellent Ballad of the Lord Mohun and Duke Hamilton* (1712).

sought a quicker resolution. Harley had secured good terms in a secret deal. Neither wanted to risk the resumption of hostilities, even if it promised a final decisive battle. With the aid of Jonathan Swift, Harley stirred talk of Marlborough's corruption, bringing about an inquiry that ended with Marlborough's dismissal in 1711. The conspiracy theory that gained currency across London was that the same group of disaffected Whigs who had allegedly coordinated the two attempts on Harley's life now managed to snuff the life of a man due to go to France to end the war on Harley's terms. Controversy brought people to the park. Morbid souvenir hunters hacked the blood-soaked bark of the tree that had held Hamilton in his final moments, taking their own relics of the fight.[1]

The Duchess of Hamilton was 'all storme' when she heard about her son's death. It was all just sadly predictable. She felt his loss as another disappointment: one more waste in a wasted life. It was almost as if this last rash, impulsive act weighed the same as all the others. Anne was 'so warm' and her words and deeds 'unfit for malancholy or true grief' that her daughter-in-law worried for the grandchildren in her charge.[2]

†

Hamilton's death was the third in quick succession to strike the major actors in the passage of the Union. Godolphin died exactly two months earlier on 15 September 1712, in the first hours of the morning. Having fought the pain of kidney stones throughout the night, his body at last gave way. In his final years Godolphin's bones and joints were ground down by rheumatism, the disease contorting him into a brittle shell of his once noble self. Though he passed in exile from government, he was given the grudging honour of burial in Westminster Abbey.

Queensberry passed on 6 July 1711. The Scottish Duke suffered a relapsing and remitting course of colorectal problems for much of his adult life. Every time his arse rag came back red, he knew it foretold another period of pain and weakness. In his later years, these periods lengthened and the malnourishment they caused forced the now British peer and Secretary of State for Scotland to withdraw to his house in Piccadilly, where he died. Queensberry's body was repatriated to Scotland to be buried at Durisdeer, near his Drumlanrig estate.[3]

These deaths – both natural and unnatural – marked the beginnings of a generational shift in Anglo-Scottish politics. By 1712, the Queen's health was failing and much to her annoyance, preparations had to be made to smooth the transition to a new dynasty. The old guard would have to fight for their places within it.

⸸

Paterson was left behind with the change. The ruling against him in the controverted election meant that he failed to make what is now a common transition from operative to politician. His support for the Union estranged him from many of his former Scottish allies and supporters. Rather than returning to Scotland, he remained in Westminster for the rest of his life. There he watched the world of ideas. It was with a mixture of vindication and jealousy that he saw many of 'his' plans take hold. While he did not support the actions of the South Sea Company, he saw in it his own plans for buying up national debt and the means for Britain to embark on colonial enterprise in South America. The Union continued and the Bank of England stood firm despite the challenge the South Sea Company posed. Yet most of his time was spent living with his greatest failure – the one scheme to which he could rightly lay proprietary claim. To support his family, he borrowed against his promised compensation from the Equivalent. When it did not materialise, his circumstances were so reduced that he had little option but to continually petition the parliament in which he should have sat. The pain of former achievement and its loss carried him through the last decade of his life. He died in 1719. No record exists of his burial.[4]

Two of the central figures of our story remained at the forefront of politics after 1712. For Defoe, there was a pleasing circularity in his service to Harley. As Lord Treasurer from 1711, Harley was Prime Minister in all but name: the position Defoe urged him to assume in his memorandum on intelligence. Harley's rise came on the back of the constitution-altering achievements of the Act of Settlement and Union with Scotland. As Speaker, Harley had overseen the passage of the former; as Secretary of State, Union commissioner and master of intelligence he drove the latter into being. Yet these changes to Britain and how it was ruled did not usher in their intended era of stability – for the United Kingdom, Harley or even Defoe. Nor did the Union have the effect on Europe Defoe thought it would.

The instability – personal, national and global – meant that Defoe remained a man in many camps. He struggled to reconcile what he owed to each. Part of this struggle was that his return to Harley's service was known – or, at the very least, suspected. Defoe's detractors had good cause to accuse him of betraying his Whig principles in serving Harley's Tory ministry. His inveterate rival, the Whig journalist George Ridpath, tarred him as a 'Tool, who has so far bankrupt his Credit in every Respect', who lacks proper education and was a bad writer, the most '*Verbose*' in all England.[5] Ridpath so angered Defoe that he would eventually call on Harley to suppress Ridpath's works.

Defoe's anger was likely intensified by a realisation that Ridpath's critique had some truth. Defoe's dealings with Harley had been strained since the publication of *Atalantis Major*. When it was revealed in 1711 that Harley had initiated secret talks with French diplomat Nicolas Mesnager and that the two had signed 'preliminaries' towards a peace, Defoe began to doubt the very basis of his service. The secret talks bespoke an intelligence network beyond Defoe's ken. Harley had used another writer, Matthew Prior, to escort Mesnager to England. More worryingly, the clandestine diplomacy raised questions about what else Harley conceded to the French. Was there talk of the Pretender's return? Did Defoe's own drift towards Harley's Tories implicate him in challenging the Protestant succession, the inviolability of which constituted his first article of political faith?

When the preliminaries agreed on with Mesnager were published, Defoe was pushed to defend something he once publicly claimed 'absurd': a peace settlement that allowed the Bourbons to retain Spain. Harley's concession in the name of peace mandated that the thrones of France and Spain remain separate. Defoe was quick to realise that this concession would anger the Whigs and prove a bitter pill for England's Dutch allies. In the end, Harley had to arrange that the peace conference take place in Holland to assure the Dutch that England had not abandoned them. Harley's peace campaign and his increasing reliance on other writers like Prior and Swift left Defoe fearing for his position.

Far from providing the strength of domestic solidity, the Union remained a live issue. Defoe had hoped it would settle and that as it was accepted it would blanket any unease under the stillness of unchanging law. The problem was that as a living compact, the Union could never achieve such stillness. High Church Tories showed themselves willing to intervene in Church affairs. The Episcopal Toleration Act of 1712 and the Patronage Act of the same year violated the protections the Union mandated for Scottish Presbyterianism by respectively allowing Episcopal ministers to preach and giving landowners the right to appoint ministers. The discontent in Scotland was severe enough for Harley to send Defoe north once more to monitor and calm the situation. Defoe was bothered by the infringement of parliament but expressed hope that a body truer to its own principles and the terms of the Union would wind them back.[6]

For much of this time Harley's mind remained fixed on Europe. The new parliament was deeply divided on how to approach his campaign for peace. The Whigs did not want peace at the expense of the Dutch or their other allies and had the capacity to block the passage through the Lords of the Treaty of Utrecht, signed by most of the combatants by mid-1713. To ratify its terms, Harley orchestrated the mass appointment of twelve Tory lords to offset the Whig dominance in the upper house. With their support, Harley could push peace through parliament. Dumfounded by Harley's willingness to skirt proper order, the Whigs turned their animus for Harley's ministry into resisting the Treaty's provisions for new commercial relations with France.

Meanwhile, the promised economic benefits of Union did not materialise. Taxes rose on soap, linen and salt, further burdening a weakened Scotland. The final insult that forced action was the proposed standardised tax on malt that was put before the parliament. A direct violation of article fourteen, the bill that would raise the tax in Scotland united the Scottish parliamentary cohort against it. In June 1713, as it was debated, Seafield rose in the Lords and proposed bringing a bill to dissolve the Treaty of Union. He was supported by a campaign that was spearheaded by Lockhart and the Earl of Mar. Lockhart's hatred of the Union was bone deep. But Mar had been one of the parliamentary managers who worked for its passage. After Queensberry's death he was Secretary of State for Scotland. That he now fought for a debate on dissolution was a troubling sign, one that augured his turn to Jacobitism, and role as rebel leader – marking him, in Defoe's view, 'a Master of Sedition, and a Leader of the Wicked among the People'.[7] The push to repeal gained a threatening level of support. The Scottish lords were joined by anti-Union Tories. The Whigs at first promised votes, if only to weaken Harley and undermine the commerce treaty with France. But they withdrew at the last minute when it looked like the Union might actually be threatened. As it turned out, the first step to dissolving the Union was prevented by a mere four votes. The parliament that was meant to bring the nations into one almost initiated their split after only five years together.[8]

Mar's conversion reflected a broader problem for the Union. After Scotland was yoked to England and its plan for succession, Jacobitism emerged as the most viable place for Scottish nationalists to invest their energy and affection. The movement was strongest in Scotland but it retained its British ambition. As Anne grew weaker, the volatility of the succession plan became more apparent. The Queen resisted efforts to bring the son of the future George I to England as a way of affirming the Hanoverian position. Though Anne's reticence was motivated by a reluctance to confront her mortality, it fed rumours that the Pretender was being prepared to succeed.

The years in exile, the machinations against Union and the aborted invasion of 1708 ensured that Jacobite agents remained in the field: in parliament, at Court, in the courts and residences of Europe, in Scots colleges and Catholic missions. The infrastructure worried Defoe, who spent considerable energy writing against Jacobites in the final year of Anne's reign. In 1713 he published a set of three pamphlets that ironised Jacobite claims on the succession and mocked in similar tone to *The Shortest Way* the putative benefits of having a British King dependent on France.[9] History once again proved cyclical. Defoe's Whig opponents wilfully misread the mockery as genuine Jacobitism. Defoe was prosecuted for seditious libel and returned to Newgate. Harley's intervention this second time was far quicker. Defoe was bailed and pardoned by the Queen. It must have been close to impossible to suppress memories of his former prosecution. With hindsight, this second stint in Newgate was a sign of things to come. Defoe was beset by legal troubles until he died. Accusations of Jacobitism remained a useful point of attack. Though not often levelled at Defoe, they were soon used to strike Harley when he was down.

With peace achieved, the binding force of the Tory party was no longer. Divided on the question of succession, the majority force in parliament splintered. Harley led those who favoured the Hanoverian succession. His former protégé and now rival Henry St John, Viscount Bolingbroke, carried the hopes of those who favoured the Pretender. Harley's relationship with the Queen was strained by the creation of the twelve new lords. Anne protected her prerogative and the upper ranks of her nobility. When Harley asked for a dukedom for his son, she took umbrage and rebuffed him. It was rare that Harley misread someone entirely. But Harley was not as he once was. When his beloved daughter died within months of the Queen's refusal, his grief pushed him further into the depths of drink. No longer the diligent courtier, he was absent from the Queen's sickbed. Anne could not brook the neglect. This was Bolingbroke's opportunity. With Harley away (in spirit if not fact), his rival made his way into the Queen's graces, winning over Abigail Masham as he did. Harley was now cut from the closeness that had been a key source of his power. Bolingbroke and Masham used the Queen's ear to stoke accusations that Harley was disloyal.[10] As he watched his own power slipping, Harley did all he could to shore the succession, forging alliances between Hanoverian Tories and Whigs. Though he outmanoeuvred Bolingbroke in parliament, it was not enough. The Queen had chosen. She dismissed Harley on 27 July 1714.

Anne died less than a week later. Although marred by riots, the accession of George I did not immediately devolve to rebellion. Despite his work in bringing about the Hanoverian succession, the arrival of George I was not good news for Harley personally. The new King still smarted against Harley's pursuit of peace without due consideration of England's allies (Hanover amongst them). He watched with no small vindication as the new Whig majority of his first parliament brought Harley up on impeachment charges for his role in brokering peace. One of the charges was high treason. Harley was condemned to the Tower of London. As he sat in the dismal grey cell that got colder as the months trudged on, the Commons brought a second raft of charges accusing Harley of being a Jacobite. Defoe defended him in writing by taking the line that Harley was not a Jacobite but had only intrigued with them in order to undermine their threat. As spymaster, Harley did not harbour a hidden cause but served the British public. In private letters Defoe fathomed the depths of Harley's politics. Though he had cause for doubt, he ultimately concluded that Harley was for the Hanoverian succession. For this reason, he once again felt secure in the trust he gave his patron.[11] Harley's actual trial was delayed ceaselessly. By the time Harley managed to press it forward he had been in the Tower for two years. Without sufficient evidence or appetite for the scrutiny of a trial, the Whigs dropped the case.

The accusations against Harley reveal that Jacobitism still had a potent presence. Pushing it underground did little to dull its emotional pull – if anything, secrecy was beguiling. In the Pretender, adherents found an alternative form of nationhood – a different kind and family of rule that many believed truer to Britain and its people. This was especially the case in the Highlands where the Stuarts were still seen both as the innate protectors of clan patrimony and its apotheosis.

Alternative forms of government are most attractive during moments of political disaffection. By 1715, disaffection in Scotland had reached new depths. The belief that Scotland's leaders had been duped or bribed into Union gathered force, setting the conditions for a Jacobite rebellion. In Scotland the Earl of Mar commanded the rebel forces. In what was the most successful Jacobite attack to date, he managed to capture Aberdeen, Inverness and Dundee. A second rising sprung from Northumberland. A small set of English MPs were implicated in its planning. The Jacobite strategy was to seed a series of local risings in an attempt to wear the government down. Their abiding hope was that localised victories would win the people over to their cause, priming them for the imminent arrival of James III and VIII, while also attracting the intervention of France. The government response was attrition: they would defend England as their prime objective, giving Mar's erstwhile ally Argyll, who led their forces in Scotland, just enough support to impede and divert the Jacobite forces there. It was only once the English rising was put down at the Battle of Preston that the British government sent adequate backing north. In Scotland, the last battle occurred at Sheriffmuir. While indecisive, the fates had turned and the massing government forces drained the will of the already chaotic Jacobite army. By the time the Pretender arrived in Scotland, the risings had been largely put down. The Jacobite army scattered as Argyll led the push back into the Highlands.[12]

Defeat of the 1715 rebellion stilled the threat of military action in the short term. Yet Jacobite espionage and intrigue continued, keeping the prospect of a Stuart restoration vivid in the eyes of successive governments. Defoe himself played a small role in the games of espionage and counter-espionage that constitute the Jacobite spy wars. He had attacked a Tory lord on grounds of Jacobitism and in 1715 was yet again tried for seditious libel. In a cosmic echo of Harley's deliverance, the Whig Secretary of State Charles Townshend rescued and recruited him. Townshend tasked Defoe with infiltrating and undermining the Tory press: a mission he carried out for six months before Townshend's fall brought an end to Defoe's employment and steady pension. Without funds, Defoe's work for later Secretaries, including Sunderland and Charles Delafaye, was more piecemeal. The 'Little Piece of Secret Service' he undertook for all three Secretaries involved pretending as 'if I were as before under the Displeasure of the Government, and separated From the Whiggs'. This gave him cover to become a double agent 'Posted among Papists, Jacobites, and Enraged High Torys, a Generation who I Profess My Very Soul abhorrs'.[13] Defoe infiltrated Tory and Crypto-Jacobite newspapers with the intent of denuding them. He worked to take the sting out of their criticism of the government. Without a pension and with a reputation for untrustworthiness, Defoe could not muster the same success as he had for Harley, leading some to question which side he was actually on.[14] It is most likely that he was not complicit but spent; that he simply did not have means either financial or reputational to dismantle networks of Jacobite propaganda. With little to show for it, his time as a double agent petered out by 1718.

⸸

A year after running with the writers of the Jacobite underground, Defoe published *The Life and Strange Surprizing Adventures of Robinson Crusoe*. The book set off a period of remarkable productivity. In just under five years Defoe published the novels for which he is now almost exclusively remembered: *Captain Singleton* (1720), *Moll Flanders* (1722), *Colonel Jack* (1722), *A Journal of the Plague Year* (1722) and *The Fortunate Mistress [Roxana]* (1724). Between 1719 and his death in 1731, Defoe also wrote conduct books and a series of book-length treatises on the supernatural.

There's a common affinity struck between novelists and spies, sustained in part by the many instances of those who practised both arts: Aphra Behn, Somerset Maugham, Graham Greene, John le Carré and Peter Matthiessen – to name a few from those whose secret service has been disclosed. The crossover is unsurprising. Spies and novelists are driven by the same impulse to understand people and grasp their motives. Both need to inhabit the life and world of others to succeed. For Defoe, whose fictions required him to become his narrators, the idea of a cover story assumes new meaning, one that draws the early history of the novel into collusion with espionage.

Defoe was a master impersonator but knew its risks. Despite the fact that it twice landed him in prison, he relished his ability to assume the person and voice of another. His narrators and characters show similar delight. But like their creator, they remain alive to the dangers of exposure. Moll and Roxana take on serial identities in order to survive, to pursue their fortunes – through crime – and to dodge the effects of past choices as they close in around them. As we saw, the *History of the Union* began its life as a cover story. The book that emerged from the initial deception – a cover that gave Defoe access to secret negotiations and records – became one of Defoe's chief contributions to the Union cause. It is uncontroversial to say that Defoe's *History* set the tone for much of the early historiography of the Union. In terms of its prose, John Kerrigan maintains that the *History* 'helped Defoe achieve the style of eyewitness immediacy that would be the hallmark of his novels'. To Kerrigan, the one novel that blends this eyewitness style with a content closely drawn from Defoe's work as an agent in Scotland is *Colonel Jack*, whose narrator turns from petty thievery in London and on the Anglo-Scottish border to become the Jacobite rebel par excellence. The actions of the novel speak to the global reach of Scots post-Union. Jack moves between English colonies in Virginia and the Caribbean, at first dodging his Jacobite past but then freeing himself from it by taking advantage of clemencies designed at once to neutralise Jacobitism and to incorporate Scots into an emergent British Empire.[15]

Defoe's time as a spy infiltrated his thinking in less obvious ways. In his final years, Defoe advanced through fiction and treatise an idiosyncratic cosmology in which the battle for the souls of men is pitted as a kind of spy war. For Defoe, there existed a world of intermediary spirits, who watched over humanity and reported to God. Within the hierarchy of angels were those who then passed God's intelligence to people, though not directly (as the revelation of the Gospels all but eliminated the need for direct intervention). These spirits implanted visions and imparted signs, requiring each person to then interpret them – as any good agent or handler would. Defoe called this 'Converse of Spirits, an intelligence'; Robinson Crusoe called it an 'invisible intelligence'. On the other side were Satan's armies who, though less powerful, manipulated the same converse, implanting 'shameful dreams' and deceptive signs to tempt people to sin.[16] Katherine Ellison makes the case that Defoe's vision for the spirit world contains his justification for the intelligence culture that persisted from the time of the Civil Wars, in which targets were increasingly domestic as well as foreign. Key to this justification is a lurch towards intent and interpretation. Collecting intelligence is itself morally neutral: why it is collected and how it is interpreted determines whether it serves a divine or infernal purpose, as handmaiden to truth or a tool of corruption.

The battle between good spies and evil agents is far less clear when cut from theories on the spirit world and brought low to the facts of Defoe's career. Omniscience is innate to divine surveillance. Serious ethical quandaries arise when one considers whether human governors can rightly aspire to such sight. When Defoe came to reflect on his work, he found a rationale for broad domestic surveillance in the notion of order. He maintained that his intelligence work helped impose stability during a tumultuous period. And for him this order was non-partisan, despite the fact that intelligence was deployed in what we would think of as political campaigns. While the British people might 'Dislike' a particular government or politician, Defoe was convinced that, on the whole, 'they have very few Objections to the general Frame of our Constitution; and would not, if it were put to their Choice, change it for any other'. Inherent to this constitutional stability was the Act of Union and the Protestant succession it helped secure.[17]

In part, this appeal to an overriding national interest helped Defoe justify – to himself and to posterity – the fact that he wrote for ministers and in favour of policies that went against his own bedrock principles. He was particularly sensitive to criticism that he was a mere lacky when he supported Harley after he returned to power in 1710. The view in the press at the time was that Defoe could be bought; that Harley currently owned him.

In response, Defoe wrote a letter to Harley. In tone and content, it is all too apparent that Defoe wanted this letter read as part of Harley's papers – when history and its chroniclers came to assess his legacy – for in it he tells Harley things Harley knew bent the truth. Refuting the charge that their relationship was built on 'Bribery', Defoe thanks Harley for the independence he has allowed him; a freedom that means he can say clear heartedly 'That I am Neither Employ'd, Dictated to, or Rewarded for, or in, what I write by any Person Undr Heaven'. Harley's goodness is such, Defoe tells him (and all later readers), 'That your Lordship Never lay'd The least Injunction on Me, of One kind or Other, To write or Not to write, This, or That, in any Case whatsoever'. Puffing Harley's legacy to a dignity that obscures his effective management of the press, Defoe writes that as Secretary of State, Lord Treasurer and man of virtue, Harley never suborned 'the Service of a Mercenary Conscience'. Of course, Harley knew he employed Defoe. As did Godolphin. Sunderland patronised him too, and later so did Townshend and Delafaye. Even if Harley was less than diligent in what he instructed and forbade, so much of Defoe's service involved trying to discern and meet Harley's expectations of him as a writer. As we have seen, Defoe did carve out some independence, publishing works like *Atalantis Major* that were against Harley's wishes and interests. The fact remains, though, that he wrote for multiple ministries and did a good enough job, especially on Scotland, that he received payment to do so for the better part of two decades.

Self-justification shades into a kind of willed delusion when Defoe makes the case that his writing has always been guided by 'principle, and Reason, agreeable to Conscience, Equity, and The good of my Country'. In his own mind his contribution to the overarching good was borne out in monumental works like the Union which, by securing a Protestant succession, answered the charge that he sold out his long-held commitment to Revolution principles. The debt or after bribe of gratitude 'for that Early Goodness' that Harley showed in securing his release from prison is weighed by the writer against the 'Debt of justice to Truth and Liberty': a moral calculus that allows him to all but convince himself that because he serves the stability and continuity of the nation, he has not prostituted his pen to a single minister or ministry, nor compromised his integrity.

Defoe did tend to overstate his contributions. There is no doubt he thrilled to the role of the agent in ways that managed to inflate it: he played with cyphers and aliases, and took pains to disguise his handwriting. In Scotland at a moment when this glamour shed and he felt most acutely the depredations of Harley's distance, he appealed for support to stay in Edinburgh or permission to leave. As he did, he looked at what he had done. 'I Faithfully Serv'd,' he reminded Harley, 'I baulk't No Cases, I Appear'd in print when Others Dared not to Open Their Mouths, and without boasting I Run as Much Risq of my life, as a Grenadier in storming a Counterscarp.'[18] The nature of secret service and the work of political operatives is such that the basic need for recognition is often subordinated to the good of the cause. Exposing secret manipulations by publicly rewarding those who undertook them undoes the work. Defoe's private vaunting of risk and accomplishments is understandable in this context. He needed Harley to acknowledge his worth if only so that Harley would reengage the writer as his agent.

Defoe's exaggerations have more than a germ of truth to them. Opponents and erstwhile friends in Scotland came to realise the character of his work and the very real risks it entailed. Lockhart cottoned on early to what he saw as Defoe's 'mercenary' meddling in Scotland's business. At the time, Defoe responded with incredulity to this and other charges that he was '*hired* Mercenary *sent down to* Scotland *by the Court,* and *Directed there to write for . . . Pay*' : 'if I have been sent hither as you say, I have been most barbarously treated. I have not yet had one Penny of my Wages . . . nor had I had the good Fortune to have my Brains knock'd out in the *High-Flying* Mobs here'. Even if he was conked out, he could not even hope to be canonised a martyr without a barrage of questions over his role '*What business had he with it* [the Union]? What had he to do there? *Who sent him, and the like?*' There's a telling wink in how Defoe parries his neglect by handlers to a defence that he could not possibly be a secret agent. At the same time, he denies himself credit by asking the questions that would in the end bring credit to him. Sir John Clerk of Penicuik asked these very questions after Union and came thereby to know that Defoe

> was sent to Scotland by the prime minister of England ... on purpose to give a faithful account to him from time to time how every-thing past here. He was therefor a Spy amongst us, but not known to be such, otherways the Mob of Edinburgh had pulled him to pieces.

As his service slowly registered – on those he wrote against and those he lived amongst – Defoe's fears appear entirely valid. He could have been 'de-Witted', dismembered by the crowd if they found out.

The risks of the work are there but what, then, of its effects and significance?[19] There are instances in Defoe's letters where he offers a clearer view of what his work did in the world, even going so far as to acknowledge its shortcomings and his. When he re-entered Harley's service in 1710, he reminded Harley that his expenses were necessary: they allowed him to travel and helped in 'Maintaining Useful Intelligences abroad'. The implication then spelt out is that he could do more with more: he has 'Established a Generall Correspondence, and at Some Charge Maintain'd it, by which I have a Fixt Intelligence (I May Say) all Over Brittain, But Especially in the North'. He is loath to let the network lapse for want of funds. He knows, too, that his own state affects the work, for 'Anxieties and Impatience of Perplext Circumstances lessen the Very Capascity of Service'. The other complaint that surfaces in Defoe's dealings with Harley is that the use of his intelligence is restricted by his lack of access to the statesman. He cannot see the intelligence gained in the field through to its rightful application in Harley's decisions when he is too often kept on the 'Outsides of Things'. This lack of access makes it hard for historians to determine the full effect of the work Defoe and other agents carried out.

Even with these constraints, it is clear that Defoe was adept at using his network to both gather information and shape what people read and thought. He garnered 'Constant Advices' from agents, correspondents and informants, 'persons of Probity and judgement', and in doing so sampled opinion from across the United Kingdom: a process that allowed him to propose and push schemes that in today's political parlance have tested well – that are targeted to gain broadest support. In this way, the network helped bring and keep the Union together. The organic metaphor Defoe used to describe the Union as a body with 'one Politick Heart, thro' which the Blood of the whole united Body circulates' belies the raw and bloody edges of its sutures and joins. If the image holds, it is to point us to the connections Defoe helped maintain across the two kingdoms. He laid in place significant parts of the circulatory system he asks his readers to take as natural.[20]

Defoe knew that the idea of a natural, stable stone-set constitution that he promoted relentlessly needed a system of domestic intelligence – not just to bring it into being but to ensure it lasted. Historians of espionage have largely come to the same conclusion. John Laffin goes so far as to call Defoe the 'father of the British Security Service (now M15)'[21] for his contribution in establishing Britain's domestic intelligence service. This exaggerates Defoe's role to a greater degree than even Defoe attempted. England had secret services before Defoe; Secretaries of State before Harley deployed secret agents to know their own people and to seed and shape news. In a more recent and thoughtful assessment, Christopher Andrews maintains that the 'transformation of the English government in London into a *British* government . . . owed much to a domestic intelligence operation' run by Harley with Defoe as his principal agent. Alan Marshall in his thorough reappraisal of Harley's career comes to the conclusion that despite Harley's knack as a spymaster, he did not live up to his promise, nor fully exploit the intelligence resources at his command. For Marshall, Harley would have done both had he reformed his office to the degree Defoe advocated throughout his service.[22]

What distinguishes Defoe's secret service is the degree to which foreign and domestic intelligence run into one another. Despite living in Scotland for significant periods between 1706 and 1711, Defoe could not help thinking of the nation as apart from his own. Looking back over his network, he has a dual sense of its geography: the intelligence he gathered came in from 'abroad'; it covered 'all over Britain' (really just England and Scotland), and it stretched across 'two kingdoms'. Some of this ambiguity is of course characteristic of an incorporative union. Yet we should not dismiss the fact that in pursuit of incorporation, Defoe and the other English agents brought techniques of infiltration and deception that had typically been the domain of foreign intelligence. They spied on politicians from a nation on the cusp of becoming part of theirs, discerning ways to manipulate them, bribe them and entice them into a shared peoplehood. Their spycraft was on a war footing. Because Scotland was a site for international conflict, their work had recourse to a different ethics. The secret campaign to establish and secure the Union thus had cover to extend forms of surveillance taken from global espionage to Britain's own (and future) citizens.

The intelligence operation captured in *A Spy Amongst Us* marks an important point of origin for the development of the surveillance state. The effects of this intelligence infrastructure have stark implications for Scotland's current state of devolution, as they do for any future independence bid. There is a very real question of how far devolved powers can extend while still subject to intelligence services, the oversight of which lies with London. To what extent is monitoring Scotland and its populace still tacitly justified by a sense of separateness? And can an independence campaign be conducted on equal terms when the dominant power still controls a major source for gathering information – for knowing ordinary people and those in power? Holyrood grasps this. In its 2024 prospectus for independence, *Building a New Scotland*, it lays out the need to 'establish a robust and proportionate security and intelligence body for an independent Scotland', one that would ally with but cast M15 from Scotland's borders.[23]

The completion of the Union on the back of Defoe's extended network was no doubt first amongst the 'several honourable, tho' secret Services' he performed after Harley rescued him from Newgate.[24] But secrecy denied Defoe his dues. His bitterness over his neglect was compounded when he looked back on his time as a spy: while he had worked relentlessly to achieve stability for his nation, he never achieved stability in his own life – and died still hiding from creditors. In his final years, such reflections nicked the patina of national good, and Defoe's qualms about extending domestic surveillance began to surface in unexpected places. In his *Political History of the Devil* (1726), Defoe justifies his investigation of Satan by analogy to the work of spies and spymasters. In both, secrecy is necessary. Statesmen need their operations to be shielded from public view in order 'to preserve the correspondences they keep in the enemy's country, lest they expose their friends to the resentment of the Powers whose councils they betray'. The problem is that this same rationale still obtains when the correspondences are at home. With it, 'ministers of state' have a way to shun all oversight and reject 'all party inquiries'. And so, in Defoe's view, there is no good way to track

> the great sums of money pretended [claimed] to be paid for *secret service*; and whether the secret service was to bribe people to betray things abroad or at home; whether the money was paid to some body or to no body; employ'd to establish correspondences abroad, or to establish families and Amass treasure at home; in a word, whether it was to serve their country or serve themselves it has been the same thing, and the same plea has been their protection.

Self-interest breeds corruption and leads the way to tyranny: a prospect that increases as the work of gathering intelligence turns inwards and faces home. When Defoe first entered Harley's service, he saw extensive surveillance as a way to act for and so gain the love of the people. Twenty-two years later, experience taught him that domestic intelligence carried a power which, if unchecked, threatened the liberal order it helped establish.[25]

ACKNOWLEDGEMENTS

I have long wanted to write about Defoe's time as a spy. But it was only after Nick Seager hired me to work on the edition of Defoe's correspondence that I had the confidence, material and method to embark on this book. Nick's rigour is the ideal to which I aspire and his support underwrites the entire enterprise, as does that of Nicola Parsons (in whose class I first read Defoe seriously) and Paula Backscheider, who shared notes from her magnificent Defoe biography and encouraged my research throughout. Christopher Tilmouth and Phil Connell supervised my graduate work on Defoe. I owe much to their exactingness and good humour. My greater debt is for their efforts to draw me into the collective labours of scholarship – into a community that can only ever be partially acknowledged in a list like this.

Friends and colleagues at the University of Cambridge, Keele University and the University of Melbourne have buoyed me through the long process. Clara Tuite and Deirdre Coleman have been generous and incisive mentors. For the advice and conversations that shaped the book I owe particular thanks to Alex Wong, Ben Fried, Joe Hone, Michelle Quay, Stephanie DeGooyer, Elias Greig, Marianne Bauer, David McInnis, Joe Hughes, Miranda Stanyon, Justin Clemens, Ken Gelder, Tyne Daile Sumner, Jordana Silverstein, Catherine Gascoigne, Liz Shek-Noble, Mark Azzopardi, Bruce Gardiner, Amelia Dale, Debra Aarons and Rachael Weaver.

Sarah Balkin, Devani Singh, James Jiang, Nat Brodie and Kate Crowcroft have been the staunchest of friends and the best people with whom to work my way through this book.

Michael Falk and Michelle Aarons undertook the heroic task of reading and editing the entire manuscript. Alexandra Hankinson, Caitlyn Lehmann and Matthew Kidd provided vital research support. Claire Jarvis aided with the transcriptions and Caitlin Stewart-Field corrected my translations from French.

Fellowships from the Folger Shakespeare Library, the University of Melbourne and the Australian Research Council have supported the bulk of the research. Luke Ingram and the Wylie Agency took a chance on me and have championed my work. For this and so much else, I will always be grateful. Julian Loose, Frazer Martin, Rachael Lonsdale, Charley Chapman and the team at Yale have been patient with a first-time author and have sharpened this book immeasurably.

I gratefully acknowledge the librarians and staff of the British Library, Cambridge University Library, National Records of Scotland, National Library of Scotland (with especial thanks to Ralph McLean), Edinburgh University Library, Nottingham University Library, London Metropolitan Archives and the National Archives.

The Algranati and Schmidt-Evans families were my homes away from home during all research trips. Zoë, Caitlin and Hamish Stewart-Field have made Melbourne my home. My final and most enduring thanks go to my family in New Zealand, the US and Australia. My parents Colin and Rosemary and sister Ruth have been unfailingly supportive. This book would never have happened without the fierce intelligence and love of Francesca Short, whose faith in me is all-sustaining. Jay arrived midway through the writing, blowing the deadline out beyond recognition but filling our lives with fun. I joke that this book is in spite of you, but it really is for you – and for Fran – as is everything I do.

Much of the writing was undertaken on the unceded sovereign lands of the Wurundjeri people of the Kulin Nations, to whose elders I pay my deepest respects.

NOTES

ABBREVIATIONS

Defoe's Writings

Appeal	*An Appeal to Honour and Justice* (1715)
Correspondence	*The Cambridge Edition of the Correspondence of Daniel Defoe*, ed. Nicholas Seager with Marc Mierowsky and Andreas K. E. Mueller (Cambridge UP, 2022)
Novels	*The Novels of Daniel Defoe*, 10 vols, gen. eds P. N. Furbank and W. R. Owens (Routledge, 2007–8)
PEW	*The Political and Economic Writings of Daniel Defoe*, 8 vols, gen. eds P. N. Furbank and W. R. Owens (Routledge, 2016)
RDW	*Religious and Didactic Writings of Daniel Defoe*, 10 vols, gen. eds P. N. Furbank and W. R. Owens (Pickering & Chatto, 2005–6)
Review	*Defoe's Review* (1704–13), 9 vols, ed. John McVeagh (Pickering & Chatto, 2004–11)
SFS	*Satire, Fantasy and Writings on the Supernatural by Daniel Defoe*, 8 vols, gen. eds P. N. Furbank and W. R Owens (Routledge, 2003–4)
TDH	*Writings on Travel, Discovery and History by Daniel Defoe*, 8 vols, gen. eds P. N. Furbank and W. R. Owens (Routledge, 2016)

Others

Add. MS (S)	Additional Manuscripts
Addison, *Letters*	*The Letters of Joseph Addison*, ed. Walter Graham (Oxford UP, 1941)
Backscheider, *Life*	Paula R. Backscheider, *Daniel Defoe: His Life* (Johns Hopkins UP, 1989)

Bath	*Calendar of the Manuscripts of the Marquis of Bath, Preserved at Longleat, Wiltshire*, 3 vols (1904)
BL	British Library, London
Bodl.	Bodleian Library, Oxford
Boyer	Abel Boyer, *The History of the Life and Reign of Queen Anne* (Roberts, 1722)
Burnet	Gilbert Burnet, *Bishop Burnet's History of his Own Time*, 6 vols (Oxford, 1823)
Carstares, *State Papers*	*State-papers and letters addressed to William Carstares*, ed. Joseph McCormick (Edinburgh, 1774)
Clerk	Sir John Clerk of Penicuik, *History of the Union of Scotland and England*, abr., trans. and ed. Douglas Duncan (Edinburgh, 1993)
Cobbett	William Cobbett, *Parliamentary History of England from the Earliest Period to the Year 1803*, 36 vols (1806–20)
CTB	*Calendar of Treasury Books (1897–1962)*
CTP	*Calendar of Treasury Papers (1868–1903)*
Downshire	*Report on the manuscripts of the Marquess of Downshire, preserved at Easthampstead Park, Berks*, 2 vols (1924)
EUL	Edinburgh University Library
Furbank and Owens, *Political Biography*	P. N. Furbank and W. R. Owens, *A Political Biography of Daniel Defoe* (Routledge, 2006)
Hamilton, *Diary*	*The Diary of Sir David Hamilton*, ed. Philip Roberts (Oxford UP, 1975)
HLQ	*Huntington Library Quarterly*
Hooke, *Correspondence*	*Correspondence of Colonel N. Hooke, Agent from the Court of France to the Scottish Jacobites, in the Years 1703–1707*, 2 vols, ed. William Dunn Macray (London, 1870–1)
Hooke, *Secret History*	*The Secret History of Colonel Hooke's Negotiations in Scotland, in Favour of the Pretender . . . Written by Himself* (London, 1760)
Jerviswood, *Correspondence*	*Correspondence of George Baillie of Jerviswood, 1702–1708*, ed. G. E. M. Kynynmound, Earl of Minto (Edinburgh, 1842)
Laing	*Report on the Laing Manuscripts, Preserved in the University of Edinburgh*, 2 vols (1914–25)
Letters Relating to Scotland	*Letters Relating to Scotland in the reign of Queen Anne by James Ogilvy, First Earl of Seafield, and Others*, ed. P. Hume Brown (Edinburgh, 1915)
LMA	London Metropolitan Archives
Lockhart Papers	*Lockhart Papers: Containing Memoirs and Commentaries upon the Affairs of Scotland from 1702 to 1715, by George Lockhart, Esq. of Carnwath*, 2 vols (1817)
Lockhart, *Scotland's Ruine*	George Lockhart of Carnwath, *'Scotland's Ruine': Lockhart of Carnwath's Memoirs of the Union*, ed. Daniel Szechi (Association for Scottish Literary Studies, 1995)
Lords	*The Manuscripts of the House of Lords*, 12 vols (1887–1962)

Lovat, *Genuine Memoirs*	*Genuine Memoirs of the life of Simon Lord Fraser of Lovat* (London, 1746)
Lovat, *Memoirs*	*Memoirs of the Life of Simon Lord Lovat; Written by Himself, in the French Language* (London, 1797)
Luttrell	Narcissus Luttrell, *A Brief Historical Relation of State Affairs from September 1678 to April 1714*, 6 vols (Oxford, 1857)
Macinnes, *Union and Empire*	Allan I. Macinnes, *Union and Empire: The Making of the United Kingdom in 1707* (Cambridge UP, 2007)
Mar and Kellie	*Report on the Manuscripts of the Earl of Mar and Kellie, Preserved at Alloa House* (1904)
MGC	*The Marlborough–Godolphin Correspondence*, 3 vols, ed. Henry L. Snyder (Oxford UP, 1975)
Moore, *Defoe*	J. R. Moore, *Daniel Defoe: Citizen of the Modern World* (Chicago UP, 1958)
NLS	National Library of Scotland
Novak, *Defoe*	Maximillian E. Novak, *Daniel Defoe, Master of Fictions: His Life and Ideas* (Oxford UP, 2001)
NRS	National Records of Scotland
NUL	Nottingham University Library
ODNB	*Oxford Dictionary of National Biography*
Paterson, *Writings*	*The Writings of William Paterson*, 3 vols, ed. Saxe Bannister (London, 1859)
Portland	*The Manuscripts of his Grace the Duke of Portland, Preserved at Welbeck Abbey*, 10 vols (1891–1931)
RES	*The Review of English Studies*
Riley, *The Union*	P. W. J. Riley, *The Union of England and Scotland: A Study in Anglo-Scottish Politics of the Eighteenth Century* (Manchester UP, 1978)
Roxburghe	*The Manuscripts of the Duke of Roxburghe; Sir H. H. Campbell, Bart.; the Earl of Strathmore; and the Countess Dowager of Seafield* (1894)
SHR	*The Scottish Historical Review*
Speck, *Birth of Britain*	W. A. Speck, *The Birth of Britain: A New Nation, 1700–1710* (Wiley-Blackwell, 1994)
TNA	The National Archives, Kew
Vernon–Shrewsbury Letters	*Letters Illustrative of the Reign of William III. From 1696 to 1708. Addressed to the Duke of Shrewsbury, by James Vernon, esq.*, ed. G. P. R. James, 3 vols (London, 1848)
Windsor	*Calendar of the Stuart papers belonging to His Majesty the King: preserved at Windsor Castle*, 7 vols (1902)
Whatley, *Scots and the Union*	Christopher Whatley, *The Scots and the Union* (Edinburgh UP, 2007)

INTRODUCTION

1. Leslie Tomoroy, *The History of the London Water Industry* (Johns Hopkins UP, 2017), 65–98. LMA COL/AC/06/014/002.
2. Pat Rogers, *Grub Street: Studies in a Subculture* (Methuen, 1972), 145–74.
3. *Portland*, iv, 43; Paterson, *Writings*, i, cxi.
4. Paterson's house on Queen Square can be found today at 19 Queen Anne's Gate. *Survey of London: Volume 10, St. Margaret, Westminster, Part I: Queen Anne's Gate Area*, ed. Montagu H Cox ([s.l.], 1926), 116–17.
5. Herries [?], *A Defence of the Scots Abdicating Darien* (1700), 19.
6. This and subsequent quotations in the following paragraphs are from Abel Boyer, *The Political State of Great Britain* (1711), i, 270–2.
7. BL Add. MS 28055, f. 3v; *Portland*, iv, 18, 26, 33–4, 43. Paterson had been recommended as a government writer in 1700 but his dispatches from 1703 mark a new phase in his career (Carstares, *State Papers*, 584–6).
8. Burnet, ii, 246.
9. *Wentworth Papers* (Wyman & Sons, 1883), 132; Boyer, 125.
10. Alexander Cunningham, *The History of Great Britain* (1787), ii, 285–6; *Bath*, i, 227.
11. BL, Add. MS 28055, f. 3.
12. *Portland*, iv, 64.
13. *Portland*, iv, 45.
14. *The Correspondence of Jonathan Swift, D.D*, ed. D. Woolley (Peter Lang, 2001), ii, 124.
15. *Portland*, iv, 43.
16. BL, Add. MS 10403, f. 1v.
17. *PEW*, iii, 122–3.
18. Moore, *Defoe*, 124–5.
19. Defoe, *The Shortest Way with the Dissenters* (1702).
20. There is some evidence that Defoe had made contact with Harley the year before, when his debts had landed him in prison.
21. *Correspondence*, 132, 11–14, 12.
22. Bodl. MS Rawl, 132; cf. BL Add. MS 88618.
23. J. A. Downie, *Robert Harley and the Press: Propaganda and Public Opinion in the Age of Swift and Defoe* (Cambridge UP, 1979), 60.
24. Harley endorsed the letter 28 May.
25. On the Union, see Macinnes, *Union and Empire*, and Whatley, *Scots and the Union*. For biographies of Defoe, see Backscheider, *Life* and Novak, *Defoe*. For biographies of Harley, see Brian W. Hill, *Robert Harley: Speaker, Secretary of State and Premier Minister* (Yale UP, 1988) and Elizabeth Hamilton, *The Backstairs Dragon: A Life of Robert Harley* (Hamish Hamilton, 1969). For Godolphin, see Roy A. Sundstrom, *Sidney Godolphin: Servant of the State* (Delaware UP, 1992). For Harley's management of the press, see Downie, *Robert Harley*.
26. W. Ferguson, 'The Making of the Treaty of Union of 1707', *SHR* (1964): 89–100. Karin Bowie's *Scottish Public Opinion and the Anglo-Scottish Union, 1699–1707* (Boydell, 2007) refutes Ferguson's argument that the Union was a 'political job' by uncovering a sophisticated opposition campaign.

CHAPTER 1

1. Luttrell, v, 300–1.
2. *CTB 1704–5*, xix, 408–9; TNA SP 54/18, f. 365; *PEW*, ii, 89.
3. TNA SP 44/352 ff. 103–4.
4. BL Add. MS 29589, f. 400.
5. *The Observator*, 30 December–2 January 1702.
6. *Review*, 29 April 1710.
7. TNA SP 44/352 ff. 103–5.
8. *The Shortest Way with the Dissenters . . . With its Author's Brief Explication Consider'd* [1703], 22.
9. TNA SP 84/225/65.
10. *PEW*, iii, 119.
11. LMA CLA047/LJ/01/0475, f. 14; Backscheider, *Life*, pp. 103, 557, n. 42.
12. *London Gazette*, 11–14 January 1703.
13. Backscheider, *Life*, 128.
14. *A True Collection of the Writings of the Author of the True Born Englishman* (1703), 220–1, 232.
15. *London Post*, 22–4 May 1703; *The Post Man* 22–5 May 1704; *The Nation*, lxxxvii, no. 2255, 259–60; *The Reformer Reform'd* (London, 1703), 7.
16. *CTP 1702–1707*, lxxxv, 153; TNA SP 44/104 f. 295; TNA T 48/17.
17. *Reformer Reform'd*, 7–8.
18. *Journal of House of Commons* (1803), xiv, 207.
19. Boyer, 47–8.
20. *Correspondence*, 4–6.
21. *Review*, 29 April 1710.
22. J. D. Alsop, 'Defoe, Toland, and The Shortest Way with the Dissenters', *RES*, 43 (1992): 245–7.
23. *Correspondence*, 188.
24. *PEW*, ii, 89.
25. *TDH*, ii, p. 77.
26. TNA SP 44/104 f. 296.
27. *PEW*, iii, 115.
28. *Essay upon Projects*, 294–6 quoted in Peter Earle, *World of Defoe* (Weidenfeld & Nicolson, 1976), 246.
29. *RDW*, v, 43.
30. *Correspondence*, 4.
31. Backscheider, *Life*, 101.
32. *Correspondence*, 4–6, 37.
33. Anthony Babington, *The English Bastille* (Macdonald and Co., 1971), 56–8.
34. Joanna Marschner, 'Baths and Bathing at the Early Georgian Court', *Furniture History* (1995): 23–8; J. Floyer, *An enquiry into the Right Uses and Abuses of the Hot, Cold and Temperate Baths in England* (London, 1697).
35. John Howard, *The State of the Prisons in England and Wales* (1777), 13.
36. Babington, *English Bastille*, 56.
37. Defoe, *Moll Flanders* (1722), ed. G. A. Starr and Linda Bree (Oxford UP, 2011), 228.
38. Defoe, *History of the Press Yard* (1717), 4, 9.

39. Babington, *English Bastille*, 56.
40. Batty Langley, *An Accurate Description of Newgate* (1724).
41. *History of Press Yard*, 31.
42. Backscheider, *Life*, 106–7.
43. *History of Press Yard*, 31
44. *Review*, 17 May 1713.
45. CLRO SF 472, quoted in Backscheider, 'No Defense: Defoe in 1703', *PMLA* (1988): 274–84 (277).
46. *PEW*, ii, 46.
47. J. R. Moore, *Defoe in the Pillory and Other Studies* (Indiana UP, 1939), 16–17.
48. *SFS*, i, 161.
49. Novak, *Defoe*, 190.
50. *A True State of the Difference between Sir George Rook, Knt and William Colepeper*, Esq (1704), 6.
51. Moore, *Defoe*, 133.
52. TNA SP 44/104, ff. 316, 318, 320.
53. TNA SP 34/3, f. 4; BL Add. MS 29589, ff. 28–9.
54. TNA SP 44/104 f. 316.
55. BL Add. MS 29589 f. 46r.
56. *SFS*, iii, 106.
57. *SFS*, i, 239–54.
58. Moore, *Defoe*, fn. 44, p. 371.

CHAPTER 2

1. *Journal of House of Commons* (1803), xiv, 207.
2. BL Add. MS 70284, f. 9.
3. Hooke, 'Memoir on England's Reasons for embarking upon war' (Archives des Affaires Étrangères CP iii, f. 182v).
4. *MGC*, i, 6–7, 22, 23, 28, 147.
5. Bodl. MS Add., A. 191, f. 5.
6. *MGC*, i, 151, 156.
7. *The Letterbooks of John Evelyn*, ed. Douglas Chambers and David Galbraith (Toronto UP, 2014), i, 596–7.
8. *Bath*, i, 72 3.
9. *Portland*, ix, 118.
10. *TDH*, iv, 51, 59.
11. *TDH*, vii, 81, 99.
12. Laura Stewart and Janay Nugent, *Union and Revolution: Scotland and Beyond 1625–1745* (Edinburgh UP, 2020), 67–8.
13. Bodl. Rawlinson, D 132, f. 2r.
14. NRS GD 158/932/9.
15. TNA SP 34/2.
16. *Portland*, iv, 39, 42.
17. Jerviswood, *Correspondence*, 27.
18. W. S. Churchill, *Marlborough: His Life and Times* (George Harrap and Co., 1947), 193–5.
19. BL Add. MS 28055, f. 4.
20. BL Add. MS 29588, f. 55, f. 62.

21. P. W. J. Riley, 'The Formation of the Scottish Ministry of 1703', *SHR* 44.138 (1965), 112–34 (114).
22. Whatley, *Scots and the Union*, 38; K. M. Brown, 'Party politics and Parliament', in *History of the Scottish Parliament*, vol ii: *Parliament and Politics in Scotland 1567–1707*, ed. Keith M. Brown and Alastair J. Mann (Edinburgh UP, 2003), 274, 285.
23. NRS GD 205/34.
24. *Portland*, iv, 64.
25. John Macky, *Memoirs of the Secret Services of John Macky* (London, 1733), 182.
26. Macky, *Memoirs*, 184.
27. BL Add. MS 28055, f. 37r.
28. NLS Drumond MSS, cxvi, f. 38.
29. BL Add. MS 61451, ff. 141–196v.
30. BL Add. MS 28055, f. 39v, f. 38r, f. 5v.
31. *Roxburghe*, 216–17.
32. BL Add. MS 28055. f. 39v.
33. *Roxburghe*, 198.
34. BL Add. MS 28055, f, 44v; *Laing*, ii, 88–9.
35. BL Add. MS 6420, f. 10.
36. *Roxburghe*, 198–9.
37. *Portland*, iv, 64–5.
38. *Spectator*, no. 439, 24 July 1712.
39. *SFS*, iv, 49.
40. *Correspondence*, 19.
41. Epictetus, *Discourses*, trans. W. A. Oldfather (Loeb, 1925), ii, 121–4.
42. Longleat House, Portland MSS Appendix II, fols 166r–167v.
43. *Daily Courant*, no. 445, 20 September 1703.
44. *London Gazette*, 20–3 September 1703.
45. BL Add. MS 61118, f. 60.
46. *Portland*, iv, 65, 68–9.
47. *MGC*, i, 160.
48. *Portland*, iv, 74.
49. BL Add. MS 28055, f. 3r.
50. *Roxburghe*, 199.
51. *Appeal.*
52. BL Add. MS 70021, f. 65v; *Portland*, iv, 75; Backscheider, *Life*, 123; Lowndes' receipt: TNA T 38/737, f. 97.
53. *Heraclitus Ridens*, 6 November 1703.
54. *Correspondence*, 24.
55. Luke 17:11–19; Backscheider, 'Personality and Biblical Allusion in Defoe's Letters', *South Atlantic Review*, 47:1 (1982), 1–20.
56. *Correspondence*, 27.

EXCURSUS

1. Lovat, *Genuine Memoirs*, 5.
2. Lovat, *Memoirs*, 118–19.
3. Daniel Szechi (ed.), *The Dangerous Trade: Spies, Spymasters and The Making of Europe* (Edinburgh UP, 2010), 75–8.

4. Edward Corp, *A Court in Exile* (Cambridge UP, 2004), 76–103.
5. Lovat, *Memoirs*, 122.
6. *The Proceedings of the House of Lords, Concerning the Scottish Conspiracy* (London, 1704), 11; Lovat, *Memoirs*, 122.
7. *Proceedings of the Lords*, 11, 17.
8. Nadine Akkerman, *Invisible Agents: Women and Espionage in Seventeenth-Century Britain* (Oxford UP, 2018).
9. James Macpherson, *Original Papers: Containing the Secret History of Great Britain, from the Restoration to the Accession of the House of Hannover* (1775), i, 666–8.
10. *Proceedings of the Lords*, 71.
11. Lovat, *Memoirs*, 154, 157.
12. Lovat, *Memoirs*, 165.
13. BL Add. MS 6420, f. 13r–v.
14. *A Collection of Original Papers About the Scots Plot* (London, 1704), 2.
15. *Proceedings of the Lords*, 57, 91.
16. Szechi (ed.), *Dangerous Trade*, 76.
17. *Original Papers*, 5–7.
18. BL Add MS 6420, f. 16r, f. 14v.
19. *Portland*, viii, 315.
20. Lovat, *Memoirs*, 171, 176.
21. BL Add. MS 6420, f. 50.
22. Lovat, *Memoirs*, 185
23. Melinda S. Zook, 'Turncoats and Double agents in Restoration and Revolutionary England: The Case of Robert Ferguson, the Plotter', *Eighteenth-Century Studies*, 42.3 (2009): 363–78.
24. Backscheider, 'Daniel Defoe and early modern intelligence', *Journal of Intelligence and National Security*, 11.1 (1996): 1–21 (3).
25. Burnet, ii, 358.
26. Aphra Behn, *Love-Letters Between a Nobleman and His Sister* (London, 1684–7).
27. *Proceedings of the Lords*, 14.
28. *Original Papers*, 648.
29. *Proceedings of the Lords*, 35.
30. *Original Papers*, 3, 9.
31. Richard Chandler, *The History and Proceedings of the House of Commons: Volume 3, 1695–1706* (London, 1742), 278–308.
32. BL Add. MS 61136, f. 19
33. NRS GD 406/1/6937; GD 406/1/7292.
34. Lockhart, *Scotland's Ruine*, 41.
35. *SFS*, i, 341–80.

CHAPTER 3

1. *Portland*, iv, 77.
2. *MGC*, i, 289.
3. *Downshire*, i, 832.
4. *Portland*, iv, 75.
5. John Oldmixon, *History of England during the Reigns of the Royal House of Stuart* (London, 1730–5), ii, 399.

6. *Correspondence*, 37.
7. *London Gazette*, 13–16 December 1703.
8. Defoe, *The Storm* (Penguin, 2005), 8.
9. *Correspondence*, 30, 32.
10. *Review*, i, 'The Preface'.
11. *Review*, 19 February 1704.
12. BL, Add. MS 28055, f. 3.
13. Peter Fraser, *The Intelligence of the Secretaries of State and their Monopoly of Licensed News 1660–1688* (Cambridge UP, 1956).
14. Defoe, *An Essay on the Regulation of the Press* (London, 1704); *To the Honourable, the C——s of England . . . Relating to the Bill for Restraining the Press* (London, 1704); Downie, *Robert Harley*.
15. BL Add. MS 70267, item 41x.
16. *Bath*, i, 59, 61.
17. *Correspondence*, 41, 65–6. As Seager et al. show, while there is no physical sign Harley read it, it is very likely he did (56).
18. *Correspondence*, 58, 64
19. Hobbes, *Leviathan*, ed. Richard Tuck (Cambridge UP, 1996), 177.
20. *Wentworth Papers*, 132.
21. *Portland*, v, 647.
22. TNA 44/146 ff. 33–61; Alan Marshall, 'Robert Harley as Secretary of State and his Intelligence Work: 1702–1708', *History* (2023): 328–52.
23. *Bath*, i, 81.
24. *SFS*, iv, 49.
25. BL Add. MS 29589 B, ff. 459–61; *Portland*, iv, 174.
26. BL Add. MS 70037, f. 298.
27. *Correspondence*, 54, 101.
28. John Ogilby, *Britannia, or, the Kingdom of England and dominion of Wales actually survey'd* (London, 1698), plate 5.
29. *Correspondence*, 97–8.
30. *TDH*, i, 120.
31. *Correspondence*, 199.
32. Pat Rogers, 'Defoe's Distribution Agents and Robert Harley', *English Historical Review*, 121.490 (2006), 146–61; *Correspondence*, 100, 109.
33. Rogers, 'Distribution Agents', 155, 157.
34. *Review*, 16 November 1706.
35. Luttrell, v, 469.
36. *Correspondence*, 101.
37. *Portland*, v, 138.
38. Novak, *Defoe*, 244.
39. *Review*, 7 October 1704, 10 October 1704.
40. *Review*, 4 November 1704.
41. Thomas Pittis, *The Proceedings of Both Houses of Parliament . . . upon the Bill to Prevent Occasional Conformity* (1710), 57.
42. SRO, Cromartie mss GD305 addit./bdl., 38 cited in D. W. Hayton, 'Robert Harley', in *The History of Parliament: The House of Commons, 1690–1715*, 5 vols, ed. Eveline Cruickshanks, Stuart Handley and D. W. Hayton (Cambridge UP, 2002).

CHAPTER 4

1. Charles Johnson, *A General History of the Pyrates* (London, 1726–8), ii, 53.
2. *The Tryal of Captain Thomas Green* (Edinburgh, 1705), sig. q2.
3. NLS Adv. MS 83.7.6, ff. 18–19.
4. *Tryal of Captain Green*, sig. A2; *Correspondence*, 440.
5. *The Horrid Murther Committed by Captain Green and his Crue* (London, 1705); *The Merites of Piracie, or a New Song on Captain Green and his Crue* (London, 1705).
6. *Tryal of Captain Green*, 3, 39.
7. NLS MS 3420, f. 9.
8. *Bath*, i, 66; NLS MS 7121.
9. *Bath*, i, 66.
10. *Portland*, viii, 178–9.
11. *Letters Relating to Scotland*, 27–8.
12. *TDH*, vii, 128–32.
13. *Review*, 26 April 1705.
14. *Review*, 7 December 1708.
15. *Portland*, viii, 179; *TDH*, vii, 131.
16. Ferguson, 'Making of the Treaty of Union', 89–110, (102).
17. Lockhart, *Scotland's Ruine*, 188; NLS MS 3366, ff. 108–9.
18. Karin Bowie, 'Public Opinion, Popular Politics and the Union of 1707', *SHR* 82.214 (2003): 226–60 (231).
19. William Dampier, *A New Voyage Round the World*, ed. Nicholas Thomas (Penguin, 2020), 27, 33.
20. In Dampier's time the Cuna or Guna were referred to as the Tule. The terms are ethnonyms. I have opted for Cuna out of respect for the name they currently embrace.
21. Lionel Wafer, *A New Voyage and Description of the Isthmus of America* (London, 1699), 48, 54, 104.
22. *RDW*, x, 167–8.
23. Mark Horton, '"To Transmit to Posterity the Virtue, Lustre and Glory of their Ancestors": Scottish Pioneers in Darien, Panama', in *Bridging the Early Modern Atlantic World: People, Products, and Practices on the Move*, ed. Caroline A. Williams (Routledge, 2009), 133.
24. NLS Adv. MS 83.7.4, ff. 1–2, 3r, 6r, 4r, 3v.
25. P. W. J. Riley, *King William and the Scottish Politicians* (J. Donald, 1979), 98–9; David Armitage, 'The Intellectual Origins of the Darien Venture', in *A Union for Empire: Political Thought and the British Union of 1707*, ed. John Robertson (Cambridge UP, 1995), 100.
26. *Lords*, iii, 160.
27. Lord Belhaven, 'A Speech in Parliament on the 10th day of January 1701' (Edinburgh, 1701), 8.
28. NRS GD 406/1/6944.
29. Rosalind Carr, 'Women and Darien: Female Participation in a Scottish Attempt at Empire, *c.* 1696–1706', *Women's History Magazine*, 61 (2009): 14–20; BL Add MS 6420, f. 3.
30. Douglas Watt, *The Price of Scotland: Darien, Union and the Wealth of Nations* (Luath Press, 2007), 272–4.

31. NLS MS 83.7.4, f. 12r.
32. BL Add. MS 12437, ff. 22, 2, 53–4.
33. William Ferguson, 'Darien', in *The Oxford Companion to Scottish History*, ed. Michael Lynch (Oxford, 2007).
34. BL MS Harl. 2071, ff. 275r–277v.
35. BL Add. MS 12437, f. 22.
36. *A Poem Upon the Undertaking of the Royal Company of Scotland Trading to Africa and the Indies* (Edinburgh, 1697).
37. NLS Adv. MS 83.7.4, f. 13r.
38. *Lords*, iii, 160.
39. BL *Rycaut Letters*, vol. 5; Lansdowne MS 1153, quoted in Oliver John Finnegan, 'Pirates in the Age of Projects, 1688–1707' (PhD University of Cambridge, 2019).
40. TNA CO 391/10, ff. 138–40, 153.
41. NRS GD 406/1/9078.
42. NLS MS 1914, f. 69.
43. Paterson, *Writings*, i, l–liii.
44. John Hill Burton (ed.), *The Darien Papers* (Edinburgh, 1849), 49.
45. NLS Adv. MS 83.7.5, f. 56r, *Two Discourses Concerning Government* (1698).
46. Armitage, 'Intellectual Origins', 105.
47. Herries, *A Defence*, 39–43; NRS GD 406/1/9062.
48. NLS Adv. MS 83.7.5, f. 35r.
49. NLS Adv. MS 83.7.4, f. 128.
50. *Darien Papers*, 60.
51. NLS Adv. MS 83.7.5, f. 35v.
52. NLS Adv. MS 83.7.4, f. 35v, 128r.
53. *Darien Papers*, 63–4, 216; NLS Adv. MS 83.7.4, f. 128v.
54. Francis Borland, *Memoirs of Darien* (Glasgow, 1715), 7.
55. *Darien Papers*, 65.
56. Paterson, *Writings*, i, lxi.
57. *The History of Caledonia: Or, the Scots Colony in Darien in the West Indies* (London,1699), 16.
58. *Darien Papers*, 74–6.
59. G. P. Insh, *The Company of Scotland Trading to Africa and the Indies* (C. Scribner's Sons, 1932), 135.
60. *Darien Shipping Papers 1696–1707: Papers Relating to the Ships and Voyages of the Company of Scotland Trading to Africa and the Indies 1696–1707*, ed. G. P. Insh (T. & A. Constable, 1924), 66.
61. Paterson, *Writings*, i, lxv; *Darien Papers*, 87.
62. *History of Caledonia*, 33–4, 36–46.
63. Paterson, *Writings*, i, lxi–lxiii.
64. *Darien Shipping Papers*, 105–6.
65. *Darien Papers*, 91.
66. NLS Adv. MS 83.7.4, f. 59.
67. *Lords*, iii, 160.
68. NLS Adv. MS 83.7.5, ff. 59v–r.
69. *Darien Papers*, 173, 144, 165–6.
70. Borland, *Memoirs*, 30.
71. *Darien Papers*, 143–5.

72. *Darien Papers*, 147–55.
73. Borland, *Memoirs*, 30–31, 49.
74. NLS Adv. MS 83.7.5, ff. 67–8.
75. D. J. Patrick, 'People and parliament in Scotland, 1689–1702' (PhD St Andrews, 2002), 238–9.
76. Bowie, *Scottish Public Opinion*, 30–4.
77. W. Douglas Jones, 'The Darien Reaction: National Failure and Popular Politics in Scotland, 1699–1701' (MSc University of Edinburgh, 2001), 29.
78. Carstares, *State Papers*, 539–42, 681–3.
79. NRS GD 406/1/698; Patrick, 'People and parliament', 268–70.
80. Borland, *Memoirs*, 63–7,82–3, 89.
81. NRS GD 406/m9/235/1.
82. Bowie, 'Public Opinion, Popular Politics and the Union of 1707', 229.
83. Patrick, 'People and parliament', 261.
84. Carstares, *State Papers*, 638–9, 584, 631.
85. NRS GD 406/1/4562.
86. NLS Adv. MS 83.7.5, ff. 59v–r.
87. BL Add. MS 12437; *Review*, 5 July 1711.
88. *Portland*, viii, 179.

CHAPTER 5

1. BL Add. MS 61123, f. 142.
2. *MGC*, i, 423.
3. *Review*, 17 April 1705, 25 November 1708.
4. *Correspondence*, 133.
5. *Review*, 13 March 1707.
6. Rogers 'Distribution Agents', 159.
7. *Correspondence*, 145, 147.
8. *The Memorial of the Church of England, Humbly Offer'd to the Consideration of all True Lovers of our Church and Constitution* (1705), 27.
9. Downie, *Robert Harley*, 81; Joseph Hone, *The Paper Chase* (Chatto & Windus, 2020).
10. *Correspondence*, 147, 148.
11. *The Works of John Wilmot Earl of Rochester*, ed. Harold Love (Oxford UP, 1999), 187.
12. *Correspondence*, 185, 164, 165.
13. *Correspondence*, 157.
14. *Review*, 18 April 1706.
15. TNA SP 34/6 f. 105.
16. *Correspondence*, 162.
17. *Review*, 25 August 1705.
18. BL Add. MS 70291, f. 38.
19. *TDH*, i, 259.
20. *Correspondence*, 164–5.
21. TNA SP 34/6 f. 105
22. *Correspondence*, 158, 168, 170, 171.
23. Liverpool Record Office, 920 NOR 1/283; 2/595.
24. *Correspondence*, 184.

25. *Review*, 9 October 1705.
26. *Review*, 10 May 1705, 17 August 1706.
27. *Correspondence*, 196.
28. NRS GD 406/M1/247/1.
29. *Portland*, iv, 153, 159, 181, 183.
30. *A Complete Collection of State Trials* (London, 1812), xiv, 1380.
31. *Portland*, iv, 183, 195, 196, 220, 226.
32. *Portland*, viii, 178.
33. NLS Adv. MS 83.7.5, ff. 72r–73r.
34. *Vernon–Shrewsbury Letters*, ii, 408, 451.
35. *Portland*, iv, 197.
36. NLS Wodrow Letters Quarto, iv, f. 42.
37. *Records of the Parliaments of Scotland to 1707*, ed. K. M. Brown et al. (St Andrews 2003–23), 1705/6/15.
38. NLS MS 3366, ff. 36–8.
39. *Portland*, iv, 210, 228.
40. Carstares, *State Papers*, 719–28.
41. *Portland*, iv, 232.
42. Lockhart, *Scotland's Ruine*, 106.
43. NRS GD 406/1/9745, 406/1/8102, 406/1/7434, 406/1/6798.
44. *Portland*, iv, 171.
45. NRS GD 406/1/7142, 406/1/7144.
46. Macinnes, *Union and Empire*, 274.
47. NRS GD 406/M9/253/1–25, 406/1/5346.
48. *Lockhart Papers*, i, 142–3.
49. *Roxburghe*, 206.
50. *Bath*, i, 67–8.

CHAPTER 6

1. *SFS*, iv, 61.
2. BL Add. MS 70023, f. 327.
3. *Correspondence*, 211, 203–4.
4. *PEW*, iv, 43–4.
5. Backscheider, 'Defoe and the Clerks of Penicuik', *Modern Philology*, 84.4 (1987): 372–81 (372); *PEW*, iv, 10; NLS Wodrow Letters Quarto, iv, f. 74.
6. NRS GD 18/3132/1.
7. Whatley, *Scots and the Union*, 272–3.
8. Backscheider, 'Clerks of Penicuik', 373.
9. *PEW*, iv, 79, 66–9, 86.
10. Backscheider, 'Clerks of Penicuik', 373–5.
11. *Review*, 9 May 1706.
12. BL Add MS 70039, ff. 10–27.
13. Harvard University Houghton bMS Eng 1473.
14. *TDH*, vii, 259.
15. *Correspondence*, 214–15, 222, 225.
16. *Portland*, iv, 330–1.
17. Carstares, *State Papers*, 633–4.
18. *Portland*, viii, 243.

19. Paterson, *An Inquiry Into the Reasonableness and Consequences of an Union with Scotland* (London, 1706).
20. BL Add. MS 6420, ff. 22r–23r.
21. *Mar and Kellie*, 275.
22. Angus McInnes, 'Robert Harley, Secretary of State' (MA University of Wales, 1961), 87.
23. *Portland*, iv, 447.
24. *Portland*, viii, 202–8; BL Add. MS 70225, f. 1.
25. *Portland*, iv, 423.
26. BL Add. MS 70038, f. 131r.
27. *Portland*, viii, 331.
28. BL Add. MS 70038, f. 131r–v.
29. *Portland*, iv, 421.
30. *Portland*, viii, 196–7.
31. BL Add. MS 70023, f. 349; *Portland*, iv, 353, 357, 421.
32. *Portland*, iv, 160–1.
33. BL Add. MS 70250, f. 113.
34. *Bath*, i, 70.
35. NUL PW2 Hy 984r.
36. *Bath*, i, 71.
37. *Portland*, iv, 170, 223.
38. BL Add. MS 70250, ff. 108–11.
39. McInnes, 'Robert Harley, Secretary of State', 87.
40. NUL PW2 Hy 984v.
41. *Portland*, iv, 258–60.
42. *Mar and Kellie*, 275.
43. TNA SP 90/4.
44. NUL PW2 Hy 984v.
45. *Portland*, iv, 276–7; Daniel Szechi, *Britain's Lost Revolution* (Manchester UP, 2017), 77.
46. *Portland*, iv, 260, 299, 258, 298; BL Add. MS 70023, ff. 117–18.
47. *Portland*, iv, 354; *Portland*, viii, 234.
48. *Portland*, iv, 296, 424, 449.
49. *Mar and Kellie*, 311; Edmund Calamy, *An Historical Account of my Own Life* (London, 1830), ii, 44–5.
50. *Portland*, viii, 205.
51. *Mar and Kellie*, 301, 273–9, 292, 311, 314.
52. *Portland*, viii, 248.
53. *Mar and Kellie*, 293, 296.
54. *TDH*, viii, 283.
55. *Mar and Kellie*, 301, 298–9; NRS GD 90/2/172/2.
56. *Correspondence*, 315, 228.
57. *TDH*, vii, 283–4.
58. *Correspondence*, 228; *Mar and Kellie*, 299.
59. *Correspondence*, 229; *TDH*, vii, 285.
60. NRS GD/90/2/172/2/4.
61. *Mar and Kellie*, 300; NRS GD 26/7/124.
62. BL Add. MS 70039, f. 70v.
63. *TDH*, viii, 17.

64. *Mar and Kellie*, 300.
65. *TDH*, vii, 286, 288; *TDH*, viii, 19.
66. *Correspondence*, 252–3; *SFS*, i, 75–6.
67. *Mar and Kellie*, 300.
68. *Portland*, iv, 359–60.
69. *Mar and Kellie*, 302.
70. *SFS*, i, 419.
71. *Correspondence*, 227, 234.
72. D. J. Patrick, 'The Kirk, Parliament and the Union, 1706', *SHR*, 87 (2008): 94–115 (99).
73. Backscheider, 'Defoe and early modern intelligence'.
74. *Portland*, viii, 274.
75. *Correspondence*, 240–1.
76. EUL, Laing MS III, 339; C. E. Burch, 'Defoe and the Edinburgh Society for the Reformation of Manners', *RES*, 16 (1940), 306–12.
77. *Review*, 28 March 1704.
78. NRS GD 90/2/172/8.
79. Defoe's third and fourth essays have a degree of overlap with the work of Penicuik, which shows some collaboration (Backscheider, 'Clerks of Penicuik'); NRS GD 406/1/7077, GD 406/1/4925.
80. George Ridpath, *Considerations upon the Union of the Two Kingdoms* (London, 1706).
81. *TDH*, vii, 270.
82. *Correspondence*, 316, 266.
83. NRS GD 406/1/7077, GD 406/1/ 5192, GD 406/1/5195, GD 406/1/5119, GD 406/1/5116.
84. Paterson, *An Enquiry*, 2, 13, 21.
85. BL Add. MS 70039, f. 5.
86. A. V. Dicey and R. S. Rait, *Thoughts on the Union Between England and Scotland* (Macmillan, 1920), 217; *Review*, 18 March 1707.
87. *Letters relating to Scotland*, 100.
88. Ralph McLean '"Literary Symbols": Language and Style in the 1707 Union Debate', *Scottish Affairs*, 27.1 (2018): 20–6.
89. *TDH*, viii, 32–5.
90. Leith Davis, *Acts of Union* (Stanford UP, 1998), 34.
91. *PEW*, iv, 26, 204.
92. *Correspondence*, 256, 265.
93. *The Scots Answer to a British Vision* (1706); *A Reply to the Scots Answer* (1706).
94. *PEW*, iv, 111.
95. *Correspondence*, 338; Backscheider, 'Defoe and early modern intelligence', 7.
96. *Correspondence* 248–9; *Portland*, viii, 251.
97. *Portland*, iv, 325.
98. *Correspondence*, 249.
99. *Review*, 9 November 1706.
100. *PEW*, iv, 131.
101. *Portland*, iv, 378.
102. *Correspondence*, 272.
103. *Laing*, ii, 136–7.
104. *Correspondence*, 273.

105. P. N. Furbank and W. R. Owens, 'Defoe and the "Tipponyale"', *SHR*, 72 (1993): 86–9; *PEW*, iv, 137, 143.
106. *Mar and Kellie*, 290.
107. *Portland*, viii, 250–1.
108. *Mar and Kellie*, 301.
109. Patrick, 'The Kirk, Parliament and the Union', 97.
110. K. M. Brown, *Kingdom or Province?: Scotland and the Regal Union* (Springer, 1992), 90.
111. NRS GD 406/1/9110, GD 406/1/9747.
112. Bowie, 'Public Opinion, Popular Politics and the Union of 1707', 246.
113. NRS GD 406/1/7127.
114. *PEW*, iv, 97.
115. NLS Wodrow Quarto, iv, f. 81.
116. *Review*, 28 November 1706.
117. *Correspondence*, 262.
118. *Portland*, iv, 348.
119. Lockhart, *Scotland's Ruine*, 135.
120. Clerk, 121.
121. *Correspondence*, 258.

CHAPTER 7

1. *TDH*, vii, 317.
2. *TDH*, iii, 199.
3. *TDH*, vii, 278.
4. *Correspondence*, 258–61.
5. *Review*, 19 December 1706.
6. *TDH*, vii, 297–8.
7. *Correspondence*, 313.
8. Bowie, *Public Opinion*, 146.
9. Ker, *The Memoirs of John Ker* (London, 1727), i, 23.
10. NRS GD 406/1/9734, GD 406/1/5327.
11. *Bath*, i, 60.
12. Marshall, 'Cunningham, Anna (d. 1647)', *ODNB*.
13. Burnet, *A History of His Own Time* (London, 1857), 71.
14. NRS GD 406/1/5170.
15. *The History of the Scottish Parliament*, ed. Brown and Mann (Edinburgh UP, 2012), ii, 51.
16. NRS GD 406/1/9110.
17. Lockhart, *Scotland's Ruine*, 195.
18. *The Works of the Rev. Jonathan Swift* (London, 1801), xviii, 237.
19. Hooke, *Secret History*, 22.
20. NRS GD 406/1/9068.
21. Rosalind Carr, 'Female Correspondence and Early Modern Scottish Political History', *Historical Reflections*, 37.2 (2011): 39–57 (48).
22. NRS GD 406/1/8123, 406/1/5165, GD 406/1/6540.
23. *Bath*, i, 187.
24. *Correspondence*, 244; *Mar and Kellie*, 309; NRS GD 18/6080, 252; Hooke, *Secret History*, 20.

25. Daniel Szechi, 'Playing with Fire: The 4th Duke of Hamilton's Jacobite Politics', *Parliamentary History* (2020): 62–84 (64); *Works of Swift*, xviii, 237; NRS GD 406/1/4873, GD 406/1/7418.
26. NRS GD 406/1/7500, GD 406/1/7064, GD 406/6573.
27. William Ferguson, *Scotland's Relations with England: A Survey to 1707* (Saltire Society, 1994), 189.
28. NRS GD 406/1/6705, GD 406/1/9744, GD 406/1/6705.
29. Carr, 'Female Correspondence', 48.
30. NRS GD 406/1/9744, GD 406/1/9735, GD 406/1/8074; Whatley, *Scots and the Union*, 56.
31. NRS GD 406/1/8074.
32. Hooke *Correspondence*, i, 1–20.
33. *TDH*, viii, 67.
34. *Mar and Kellie*, 325–6.
35. NRS, GD 18/6080.
36. *Correspondence*, 313.
37. NLS Wodrow Quarto xl, ff. 27–8.
38. NRS GD 406/1/9733.
39. *Correspondence*, 283.
40. *TDH*, vii, 324, 327.
41. NRS GD 406/1/ 5383; *Correspondence*, 283.
42. Lockhart, *Scotland's Ruine*, 182–3; Bowie, *Scottish Public Opinion*, 148.
43. *Review*, 19 December 1706; *TDH*, vii, 325–7.
44. *Portland*, iv, 359; *TDH*, vii, 327.
45. Jerviswood, *Correspondence*, 170.
46. *TDH*, vii, 328.
47. *Correspondence*, 285.
48. Lockhart, *Scotland's Ruine*, 183.
49. NRS GD 406/1/5383, *TDH*, vii, 327.
50. Rosalind K. Marshall, *The House of Hamilton in its Anglo-Scottish Setting* (PhD University of Edinburgh, 1970), 265–309.
51. Addison, *Letters*, 67.
52. NRS GD 406/1/ 5383; *Correspondence*, 313.
53. NRS GD 406/1/9735.
54. *Correspondence*, 285.
55. NRS GD 406/1/6581, GD 406/1/9735; *TDH*, vii, 327–9.
56. *Correspondence*, 289, 290.
57. NRS GD 406/1/5353; NLS Wodrow Letters Quarto iv, f. 133.
58. NRS GD 406/1/9737, GD 406/1/9738, GD 406/1/9736.
59. NLS Wodrow Letters Quarto iv, f. 120.
60. NRS GD 406/1/7950, GD 406/1/9738.
61. *TDH*, vii, 334–5.
62. *Correspondence*, 292.
63. Defoe, *A Short Letter to the Glasgow-Men* (Edinburgh, 1706).
64. *Correspondence*, 295.
65. NRS GD 406/1/7119.
66. Lockhart, *Scotland's Ruine*, 41.
67. NRS GD 406/1/7138.
68. Lockhart, *Scotland's Ruine*, 42.

69. NRS GD 406/1/8032.
70. *Mar and Kellie*, 306
71. *Portland*, viii, 254.
72. Andrew Fletcher, *Political Works*, ed. John Robertson (Cambridge UP, 1997), 187.
73. *Mar and Kellie*, 310–11, 323.
74. P. H. Scott, *Andrew Fletcher and the Treaty of Union* (John Donald, 1992), 197.
75. Szechi, 'Playing with Fire', 75.
76. *Portland*, iv, 375–6.
77. NRS GD 406/1/5032.
78. *Portland*, iv, 258, 308; NUL PW2 Hy 98v; *Portland*, iv, 375–6.
79. *PEW*, iv, 177–8.
80. *Addresses against Incorporating Union 1706–7*, ed. Karin Bowie (Boydell, 2018), 1.
81. Bowie, *Scottish Public Opinion*, 118, 126; *Addresses*, 5, 19–20.
82. *Portland*, viii, 267–8.
83. Bowie, *Scottish Public Opinion*, 121.
84. NRS GD 406/1/9744, 406/1/6013.
85. Whatley, *Scots and the Union*, 310.
86. Bowie, *Scottish Public Opinion*, 149.
87. *Mar and Kellie*, 323.
88. *Correspondence*, 266, 241; Carr 'Female Correspondence', 241.
89. *PEW*, iv, 13.
90. *Review*, 26 November 1706, 10 December 1706.
91. *PEW*, iv, 181.
92. William Black, *A Reply to the Authors of the Advantages of Scotland by an Incorporate Union; and of The Fifth Essay, at Removing National Prejudices* (1706), 3, 18.
93. Lockhart, *Scotland's Ruine*, 147.
94. NRS GD 406/1/8073; Lockhart, *Scotland's Ruine*, 184.
95. *Portland*, iv, 382.
96. Bowie, *Scottish Public Opinion*, 153–4.
97. *Scotland's Ruine*, 90, 187; NRS GD 406/1/8030; Bowie, *Scottish Public Opinion*, 153.
98. *Correspondence*, 320–1.
99. *Correspondence*, 322; Lockhart, *Scotland's Ruine*, 186–8.
100. NRS GD 406/1/8568.

CHAPTER 8

1. *Correspondence*, 275, 313.
2. Jeffrey Stephen, *Scottish Presbyterians and the Act of Union* (Edinburgh UP, 2007), 5–6.
3. *Correspondence*, 259–60.
4. *TDH*, iii, 186.
5. Ker, *Memoirs*, i, 12.
6. *Correspondence*, 299–300; *Portland*, viii, 272.
7. Stephen, *Scottish Presbyterians*, 165; NLS Wodrow Letters Quarto, iv, f. 119; *Correspondence*, 283.

8. *Correspondence*, 276; *PEW*, iv, 79, 116, 131.
9. *Correspondence*, 283.
10. Furbank and Owens, 'New Light on John Pierce, Defoe's Agent in Scotland', *Edinburgh Bibliographical Society Transactions*, 6 (1998), 134; Luttrell, v, 433.
11. *Portland*, iv, 164; *The Memorial of the Presbyterians* (1706), sig. A3.
12. *Correspondence*, 283, 310–11, 313–14, 309.
13. *Novels*, i, 233.
14. TNA PROB 11/492/483.
15. Bowie, *Scottish Public Opinion*, 147.
16. *Correspondence*, 310–11, 313; Lockhart, *Scotland's Ruine*, 182.
17. *Review*, 9 January 1707.
18. *Correspondence*, 314, 356.
19. Whatley, *Scots and the Union*, 304.
20. Ker, *Memoirs*, i, 30.
21. *Portland*, iv, 467.
22. Ker, *Memoirs*, 30–6.
23. Stephen, *Scottish Presbyterians*, 160
24. NLS, Wodrow Quarto lxxiii, ff. 280–1.
25. Ker, *Memoirs*, i, vi.
26. *Lockhart Papers*, i, 302.
27. Ker, *Memoirs*, i, 28; *Portland*, iv, 276–7.
28. *Portland*, iv, 447, 276.
29. Allan I. Macinnes, *Clanship, Commerce and the House of Stuart, 1603–1788* (Tuckwell Press, 1996), 188.
30. *TDH*, iii, 254.
31. *Mar and Kellie*, 275–6, 280.
32. Hooke, *Secret History*, 106–7.
33. Szechi (ed.), *Dangerous Trade*, 108.
34. *Mar and Kellie*, 275–6, 285.
35. *Windsor*, vi, 550.
36. Thomas Byrne, 'From Irish Rebel to Bourbon Diplomat: The Life and Career of Nathaniel Hooke', (PhD NUI Maynooth, 2006), 1–105.
37. *Works of Swift*, x, 375.
38. Mémoire donné à Monsieur le Marquis de Torcy le 18 Février, 1703: read in council (A. A. E. CP Angleterre Supp. 3, ff 178r–184v), quoted in full in Byrne, 'From Irish Rebel', 364–72.
39. Byrne 'From Irish Rebel', 285–98; Hooke, *Correspondence*, i, 36–8.
40. Hooke, *Correspondence*, i, 36–8, 194–8, 202–8, 383–6, 393–4, 404, 406.
41. Hooke, *Secret History*, 83–91.
42. Hooke, *Correspondence*, i, 466, 477, ii, 347–8.
43. Hooke, *Correspondence*, ii, 388, 348–9.
44. *Portland*, iv, 464–7.
45. Hooke, *Secret History*, 25.
46. Hooke, *Correspondence*, ii, 351–8.
47. Szechi (ed.), *Dangerous Trade*, 116.
48. Hooke, *Correspondence*, ii, 359, 350, 358.
49. Hooke, *Secret History*, 27–8.
50. Hooke, *Correspondence*, ii, 3 63–4, 372–4, 357, 385.
51. Hooke, *Correspondence*, ii, 383; Hooke, *Secret History*, 60.

52. Hooke, *Secret History*, 22.
53. Hooke, *Correspondence*, ii, 400–9.

CHAPTER 9

1. Paterson, *Writings*, i, 222, 237, 245, 247.
2. *Mar and Kellie*, 354, 361–3.
3. *Correspondence*, 307, 275–6.
4. *TDH*, viii, 135–6.
5. *Bath*, i, 167.
6. *Mar and Kellie*, 361; *Review*, 2 June 1713; *TDH*, viii, 130–2.
7. Macinnes, *Union and Empire*, 303.
8. *Correspondence*, 253, 264–5.
9. *Portland*, Appendix, ii, f. 204.
10. *MGC*, ii, 843.
11. NUL, PW2 Hy 984v–r.
12. Hooke, *Correspondence*, ii, 383; Hooke, *Secret History*, 60.
13. *TDH*, viii, 143, 148–9.
14. *Correspondence*, 338, 362.
15. Macinnes, *Union and Empire*, 321; Scott, *Tales of a Grandfather* (Edinburgh, 1889), 769.
16. *TDH*, viii, 158.
17. *Portland*, viii, 276.
18. BL Add. MS 10403, f. 18r, f. 25r–v, f. 3v.
19. *Mar and Kellie*, 311–2.
20. *Portland*, iv, 428.
21. TNA SP 104/73 f. 69.
22. Macinnes, *Union and Empire*, 321.
23. *TDH*, viii, 158; *Mar and Kellie*, 365.
24. *TDH*, viii, 160–1.
25. Lockhart, *Scotland's Ruine*, 172, 142, 252, 253–6; BL Add MS 34180.
26. *Portland*, v, 114–15.
27. BL Add. MS 34180.
28. Lockhart, *Scotland's Ruine*, 257.
29. Whatley, *Scots and the Union*, 288–9.
30. Lockhart, *Scotland's Ruine*, 259.
31. Scott, *Andrew Fletcher*, 184.
32. Atholl, *ODNB*.
33. *Mar and Kellie*, 312.
34. Riley, *The Union*, 260–8.
35. *Mar and Kellie*, 294, 379.
36. *TDH*, viii, 173; vii, 208–11; BL Add. MS 10403, ff. 20v–21r.
37. NRS GD 406/1/7092.
38. Lockhart, *Scotland's Ruine*, 195–6; NRS GD 18/6080, 326.
39. *Portland*, iv, 347.
40. Lockhart, *Scotland's Ruine*, 196.
41. *Correspondence*, 322.
42. NRS GD 406/1/9107, GD 406/1/7950, GD 406/1/9738.
43. *Correspondence*, 326.

44. NRS GD 406/1/9742, GD 406/1/7855, GD 406/1/6519.
45. *Portland*, iv, 381.
46. *Review*, 29 March 1707; *Correspondence*, 329.
47. *TDH*, viii, 190.
48. *Portland*, viii, 285–6.
49. *Portland*, iv, 397, 400.
50. *Correspondence*, 329, 323.
51. *TDH*, viii, 194.
52. *TDH*, vii, 191.
53. Chandler, *History and Proceedings of Commons*, iv, 53–4.
54. *Portland*, iv, 396.
55. *Bath*, i, 166.
56. *Review*, 29 March 1707; *TDH*, viii, 196.

CHAPTER 10

1. *Portland*, iv, 423.
2. *Bath*, i, 178.
3. *Correspondence*, 409, 331.
4. Black, *A Reply*, 3, 18.
5. *Portland*, iv, 466.
6. *Correspondence*, 375–6.
7. *Bath*, i, 157; *Portland*, iv, 384.
8. *Correspondence*, 342, 361.
9. *Review*, 11 March 1707.
10. *Correspondence*, 362.
11. *TDH*, viii, 237.
12. *Correspondence*, 339; *Mar and Kellie*, 374.
13. *Correspondence*, 356, 373.
14. *Review*, 1 May 1707.
15. *Correspondence*, 375.
16. Surrey History Centre, 371/14/e/34.
17. Defoe, *Observations on the Fifth Article of the Treaty* (1706).
18. *Review*, 3 June 1707.
19. *Correspondence*, 412–13, 354.
20. Defoe, *An Enquiry into the Disposal of the Equivalent* (1706)
21. *TDH*, viii, 153.
22. *Mar and Kellie*, 362; BL Add. MS 70225, ff. 35–8.
23. *Portland*, viii, 303–4, 296.
24. Paterson, *Writings*, preface to vol iii.
25. *Correspondence*, 388.
26. *TDH*, viii, 261.
27. TNA 17/1 f. 108; *Correspondence*, 404.
28. *Correspondence*, 400; *Review*, 10 April 1708; *TDH*, viii, 260; NRS GD 406/1/7892.
29. Lockhart, *Scotland's Ruine*, 209–10; *Correspondence*, 420.
30. *Portland*, iv, 409–10, 456, 401–2.
31. BL Add. MS 70021, f. 138.
32. BL Add. MS 70024, f. 72.

33. *Bath*, i, 167.
34. *Correspondence*, 365, 392, 606, 347, 117, 392; Furbank and Owens, *Political Biography*, 77; Riley, *The Union*, 305; Novak, *Defoe*, 320.
35. *Correspondence*, 364, 382.
36. *Portland*, iv, 421; BL Add. MS 70225, f. 32.
37. *Correspondence*, 356, 380, 397; *Review*, 26 July 1707.
38. *Correspondence*, 397; *Portland*, iv, 449–50; Hooke, *Correspondence*, ii, 257.
39. William Fraser, *The Melvilles* (Edinburgh, 1890), ii, 214; *Roxburghe*, 208.
40. *Correspondence*, 421; *Portland*, iv, 452, 457.
41. *Correspondence*, 421, 417, 424.
42. P. H., *An impartial view of the two late parliaments* (1711), 117.
43. BL Add. MSS 70331-3, memo, 9 September 1707; *Portland*, iv, 74–5.
44. G. V. Bennett, 'Robert Harley, the Godolphin Ministry, and the Bishoprics Crisis of 1707', *English Historical Review* (1967): 726–46.
45. Addison, *Letters*, 83; Hill, *Robert Harley*, 112.
46. *TDH* viii, 315.
47. Addison, *Letters*, 91.
48. *Journal of House of Lords*, vol. 18, 518; *State Trials*, xiv, 1382–5.
49. *Examiner*, 15 March 1710–11.
50. Burnet, *History* (1840), ii, 621, 822.
51. *Portland*, iv 469, 475; NUL PW2 Hy 514.
52. BL Add. MS 61618, f. 26.
53. *Portland*, v, 647.
54. *Bath*, i, 189; *Correspondence*, 392.
55. *Bath*, i, 189–90.
56. William Coxe, *Memoirs of the Duke of Marlborough* (London, 1847), ii, 191.
57. TNA 30/24/21/150; Speck, *Birth of Britain*, 134; W. A. Speck and G. S. Holmes, 'The Fall of Harley in 1708 Reconsidered', *English Historical Review* 80.317 (1965): 673–98 (694–5); *Correspondence of Swift*, i, 74–6.
58. *Appeal*, 14–5; *Correspondence*, 434.
59. *Portland*, iv, 484; *State Trials*, xiv, 1384–5; Boyer, vii, 87; *Portland*, iv, 481.
60. BL Add. MS 61618, f. 30; Burnet, *History* (1840), ii, 822; *State Trials*, xiv, 1378.
61. Boyer, vii, 97; *State Trials*, xiv, 1391; *Portland*, iv, 488, 481.
62. *Portland*, iv, 460–1, 375–6, 438 -9.
63. NUL PW2 Hy 988.
64. *Portland*, iv, 425, 438, 460 465–7.
65. Ker, *Memoirs*, ii, 37, 45–55; Hooke, *Correspondence*, ii, 308–9.
66. *Vernon-Shrewsbury Letters*, iii, 365.
67. *Correspondence*, 421.
68. *Bath*, i, 187–8.
69. *MGC*, iii, 1505.
70. *Portland*, iv, 479.
71. Hooke, *Secret History*, 76.
72. *Lords*, viii, 113; *TDH*, vii, 49.
73. Hooke, *Secret History*, 73–4.
74. *TDH*, iii, 257.
75. NRS GD 406/1/5466.
76. *TDH*, iii, 240; *Portland*, iv, 482.
77. Hooke, *Secret History*, 141; *TDH*, vii, 55.

78. Hooke, *Secret History*, 133–4.
79. *TDH*, vii, 48; *Review*, 27 March 1708.
80. Luttrell, vi, 298; BL Add. MS 28055, f. 414; NRS GD 406/1/7964.
81. *The Jacobites and the Union*, ed. Charles Sanford Terry (Cambridge UP, 1922), 51.
82. *Review*, 27 March 1708, 1 April 1708.
83. *TDH*, vii, 57, 48.

CHAPTER 11

1. *Correspondence*, 443.
2. *Appeal*, 14–15.
3. Samuel Johnson, *The Lives of the Poets*, ed. Roger Lonsdale (Oxford UP, 2006), ii, 985.
4. *Correspondence*, 467; Furbank and Owens, 'Defoe as Secret Agent', *The Scriblerian*, 25 (1993): 145–53.
5. *Review*, 22 June 1708.
6. *Review*, 19 June 1708; *Correspondence*, 458–61; Macinnes, *Union and Empire*, 323; Scottish Privy Council Minute Books NRS PC 4 D/8/7. My thanks to Paula Backscheider for this reference.
7. NRS GD/406/1/ 6543, GD 406/1/7964.
8. BL Add. MS 57861, ff. 100–1; BL Add. MS 61628, f. 132.
9. *Correspondence*, 463, 450–1.
10. *Advice to the Electors of Great Britain* (London, 1708); Henry Snyder, 'Daniel Defoe, the Duchess of Marlborough, and the "Advice to the Electors of Great Britain"', *HLQ*, 29.1 (1965): 53–62.
11. Ker, *Memoirs*, i, 57; J. A. Downie, 'Daniel Defoe and the General Election of 1708 in Scotland', *ECS*, 8.3 (1975): 315–28. (323).
12. *Review*,14 September 1712; *Portland*, viii, 313; *Portland*, iv, 489.
13. NRS GD 406/1/8052, GD 406/1/4592, GD 406/1/8041.
14. Saxe Bannister, *William Paterson: His Life and Trials* (Edinburgh, 1858), 379; *Portland*, iv, 511, 525.
15. *SFS*, iv, pt 1, 191.
16. *Lockhart Papers*, i, 308.
17. NUL PW2 H 985v; *Portland*, iv, 681–2.
18. *Portland*, v, 648–9.
19. Speck, *Birth of Britain*, 165.
20. *Review*, 18 February 1710.
21. *MGC*, iii, 1440; *Portland*, iv, 537.
22. *A Letter from Captain Tom to the Mobb, Now Rais'd for Dr. Sacheverel* (1710), 3; *Portland*, v, 649.
23. *Portland*, iv, 532; BL Add. MSS 70419; BL Add. MSS 61134, f. 227.
24. *Portland*, iv, 531.
25. Harley, *Plain English to all who are honest*, ed. W. A. Speck and J. A. Downie, *Literature and History* (1976): 100–10.
26. Hamilton, *Diary*, 25–8.
27. *Correspondence*, 493, 504.
28. BL Add. MS 61118, ff. 47–8, BL Add. MS 7026, f. 24; Frances Harris, *The General in Winter: The Marlborough-Godolphin Friendship and the Reign of Queen Anne* (Oxford UP, 2017), 311–13; *SFS* iv, 45; *Correspondence*, 499.

29. TNA 48/16 f. 1; *Correspondence*, 521.
30. *Correspondence*, 523–4, 537, 546–7, 551.
31. J. A. Downie, 'Defoe the Spy', *British Society for Eighteenth-Century Studies Newsletter*, 9 (1976): 17–18. *Portland*, iv, 602; *Correspondence*, 541.
32. *Review*, 19 October 1710.
33. *Correspondence*, 561–2, 568–70.
34. *SFS*, iv, 69; *Portland*, iv, 338; v, 654, 668–9; *Bath*, i, 92; Christopher Andrews, *The Secret World* (Allen Lane, 2018), 266–7.
35. *Correspondence*, 597.
36. *A Letter to the Whigs* (1711); *The Secret History of the October Club* (1711).

AFTERWORD

1. *The Examiner's Account of the duel fought by the duke of Hamilton and my Lord Mohun* (Edinburgh, 1712).
2. NRS GD 406/1/7221.
3. BL Sloane 3325, f. 173.
4. Saxe Bannister, *William Paterson: The Merchant Statesman* (London, 1858), 394–5.
5. *The Observator*, 5–11 December 1711, 28 November–1 December 1711.
6. Defoe, *The Present State of the Parties in Great Britain* (London, 1712).
7. *A Trumpet Blown in the North, and Sounded in the Ears of John Eriskine, call'd by the Men of the World, Duke of Mar* (London, 1715), 3.
8. *Roxburghe*, 191.
9. Defoe, *And What if the Pretender Should Come?* (London, 1713); *And What if the Queen Should Die?* (London, 1713).
10. *Portland*, vi, 662–5.
11. Defoe, *Secret History of the White Staff* (1714); *Correspondence*, 818.
12. Daniel Szechi, *1715: The Great Jacobite Rebellion* (Yale UP, 2006), 138–69.
13. *Correspondence*, 833–6.
14. Furbank and Owens, *Political Biography*, 159–71.
15. John Kerrigan, *Archipelagic English* (Oxford UP, 2008), 329, 326–49.
16. *Novels*, iii, 221–73; *SFS*, iv, 30–45; *Essay on the History of Apparitions* (London, 1727), 4.
17. Katherine Ellison, 'Espionage', in *The Oxford Handbook of Daniel Defoe*, ed. Seager and Downie (Oxford UP, 2023), 386; *RDW*, ix, 145.
18. *Correspondence*, 697–700, 416.
19. Lockhart, *Scotland's Ruine*, 147; *Review*, 2 September 1707; John Clerk of Penicuik, *Memoirs, 1676–1755*, ed. John M. Gray (Edinburgh, 1892), 63–4.
20. *Correspondence*, 503, 813, 518, 649; *Review*, 11 March 1707.
21. John Laffin, *Brassey's Book of Espionage* (Michigan UP, 1996), 30n.
22. Andrews, *Secret World*, 265.
23. 'Building a New Scotland: An Independent Scotland's Place in the World', https://www.gov.scot/publications/building-new-scotland-independent-scotlands-place-world/documents.
24. *Appeal* in Furbank and Owens, *Political Biography*, 207.
25. *SFS*, vi, 45–6.

INDEX